Haj to Utopia

When you (I) keep anger
& bitterness in your (my)
heart it blocks your (my)
blessings, your (my) creativity,
your (my) ability to enjoy
life and your (my) ability
to experience God's love.
Forgiving isn't something you
(I) do for other people.
It's something you (I) do
for yourself
(myself).

THE CALIFORNIA WORLD HISTORY LIBRARY

Edited by Edmund Burke III, Kenneth Pomeranz, and Patricia Seed

Haj to Utopia

*How the Ghadar Movement Charted
Global Radicalism and Attempted to
Overthrow the British Empire*

———

Maia Ramnath

UNIVERSITY OF CALIFORNIA PRESS

Berkeley   Los Angeles   London

University of California Press, one of the most distinguished university
presses in the United States, enriches lives around the world by
advancing scholarship in the humanities, social sciences, and natural
sciences. Its activities are supported by the UC Press Foundation and by
philanthropic contributions from individuals and institutions. For more
information, visit www.ucpress.edu.

University of California Press
Berkeley and Los Angeles, California

University of California Press, Ltd.
London, England

Library of Congress Cataloging-in-Publication Data

Ramnath, Maia, 1973–.
   Haj to Utopia : how the Ghadar movement charted global radicalism
and attempted to overthrow the British empire / Maia Ramnath.
     p.   cm. — (The California world history library ; no. 19)
   Includes bibliographical references and index.
   ISBN 978-0-520-26954-5 (cloth : alk. paper) —
   ISBN 978-0-520-26955-2 (pbk. : alk. paper)
   1. Hindustan Gadar Party—History—20th century.   2. India—
Politics and government—20th century.   3. India—History—Autonomy
and independence movements.   4. Nationalism—History—20th
century.   5. Social movements—History—20th century.   6. Political
activists—History—20th century.   7. Social reformers—History—20th
century.   8. Revolutionaries—History—20th century.   9. World
politics—1900–1918.   10. World politics—1919–1932.   I. Title.
DS480.4.R37   2011
320.540954—dc22   2010052331

Manufactured in the United States of America

20 19 18 17 16 15 14 13 12 11
10 9 8 7 6 5 4 3 2 1

In keeping with its commitment to support environmentally responsible
and sustainable printing practices, UC Press has printed this book on
Cascades Enviro 100, a 100% post consumer waste, recycled, de-inked
fiber. FSC recycled certified and processed chlorine free. It is acid free,
Ecologo certified, and manufactured by BioGas energy.

The publisher gratefully acknowledges the generous support of the Valerie Barth and Peter Booth Wiley Endowment Fund in History of the University of California Press Foundation.

CONTENTS

MAPS

ACKNOWLEDGMENTS

Of the many people who contributed to this writing, thanks are due first to Terry Burke, Dilip Basu, Gene Irschick, Radhika Mongia, and Barbara Epstein, all advisors and mentors at the University of California, Santa Cruz and Berkeley, for equipping my sense of context and helping me to make so many connections, while also granting me your confidence and trust to go in unorthodox directions. (Barbara, you continued to insist that you knew nothing about my material, while I continued to insist that it was your way of thinking about *any* material that I found of such great value when applied to mine.) Thank you also to the following:

The ACLS/Mellon Foundation and the Draper Program in Interdisciplinary Humanities and Social Thought at NYU for making possible the conditions of work and life necessary for intensive writing and thinking and to the many relatives, friends, comrades, and acquaintances I encountered during the many years over which this project developed, for providing me with hospitality, support, political and intellectual stimulus.

The helpful and knowledgeable staffs of the Bancroft Library's South and Southeast Asia collections, the Center for Contemporary History at JNU, the National Archive in Delhi, the Nehru Memorial Museum and Library, and the British Library.

John Mock and all the wonderful teachers at the AIIS Urdu Language Program in Lucknow, especially Ahtesham Ahmad Khan for equipping me not just to read standard Urdu and Hindi but to decipher the Urdu scrawled in terrible handwriting jammed on scruffy 90-year-old clandestine newspapers.

Harjit Singh Gill and Vijay Prashad for their generosity in sharing documents and for sharing my delight in these documents.

Harish Puri and Chaman Lal for enlightened and enlightening scholarship guided by political integrity, and likewise for their kindness to me.

Ben Zachariah, Franziska Roy, Michele Louro, Ali Raza, and Carolien Stolte for stimulating and very enjoyable cross-fertilization and for making me feel like part of a "transnational turn" rather than a marginal explorer wandering alone on the beach with a metal detector and my convictions—although that would be ok too.

Kevin, Anjuli, Allie, Valerie, and Monet for keeping me sane and grounded by getting me off the ground while I completed the foundation—you witnessed the whole thing and I promised to say so!

Above all, my humble gratitude to those of whom I write: The makers of Ghadar, for their undying inspiration and example. May we who come after prove worthy in keeping the flame lit—not only by remembering what they did but by continuing to contribute to the struggles for freedom and justice that they would be supporting if they were here today.

ABBREVIATIONS

AA   Auswertiges Amt (German Foreign Office)
BIC   Berlin India Committee
CCP   Chinese Communist Party
CID   Criminal Investigation Department
CPGB   Communist Party of Great Britain
CPI   Communist Party of India
CPUSA   Communist Party USA
CUP   Committee of Union and Progress
DCI   Director of Criminal Intelligence
FFI   Friends of Freedom for India
GMD   Guomindang
HGP   Hindustan Ghadar Party
HRA   Hindustan Republican Association
HSRA   Hindustan Socialist Republican Association
INC   Indian National Congress
INP   Indian National Party
IOR   India Office Records, British Library
IRB   Irish Republican Brotherhood
IWW   Industrial Workers of the World
KDP   Kommunistische Partei Deutschlands
NAI   National Archives of India
NARA   United States National Archives and Records Administration
NBS   Naujavan Bharat Sabha
NMML   Nehru Memorial Museum and Library

NWFP   North-West Frontier Province
PCHA   Pacific Coast Hindi Association
PGI   Provisional Government of India
PLM`   Partido Liberal Mexicano
SANA   South Asians in North America Collection
UP   United Provinces
WPP   Worker Peasant Party

Introduction

History is the haj to utopia.
KIM STANLEY ROBINSON,
RED MARS

A week after Britain declared war on Germany on 4 August 1914, a clarion call appeared in the *Ghadar,* an ardently revolutionary newspaper emanating from San Francisco to reach a readership of overseas Indians in East Asia, North and South America, Mesopotamia, and East Africa: "O Warriors! The opportunity you have been looking for has arrived." The prodigal children of Hindustan were summoned to return home and fight, for the battle of liberation was at hand.

The message of the paper's *Ailan-e-Jang* (Declaration of War) was stirring and simple:

Arise, brave ones! Quickly . . . We want all brave and self-sacrificing warriors who can raise revolt . . .

Salary: death
Reward: martyrdom
Pension: freedom
Field of battle: Hindustan.[1]

From the expatriate intellectual circles in London, Paris, Berlin, and San Francisco to Gandhi's early career in South Africa to the passage of subcontinental natives throughout the realms mapped out by the Pan-Islamic Khilafat or the Communist International, much of the power of the independence struggle was incubated outside the territory of British India. Any dramatic events visible upon the lighted proscenium of the subcontinent were profoundly affected by a multitude of actors busy in the shadows offstage, including students, soldiers, pilgrims, traders, and laborers originating from a variety of distinct regional, linguistic, class, religious, and political backgrounds. And no small portion of this power was routed, sooner or later, along the channels of a circulatory system with its heart in California, headquarters for the diasporic Ghadar movement. Its name, it declared, was its work: the word meant "mutiny" or "revolt."

As restrictions tightened on what activities counted as legal inside British India, prewar anticolonial activists in the throes of the Swadeshi movement in Bengal and the Canal colony unrest in Punjab had either to go underground or to go abroad, where they might "function in an atmosphere of greater liberty."[2] Har Dayal, later one of the Ghadar movement's key intellectual shapers, wrote from Paris in the March 1910 Bande Mataram: "We must . . . try to strengthen all groups of workers outside India. The centre of gravity of political work has been shifted from Calcutta, Poona, and Lahore to Paris, Geneva, Berlin, London, and New York."[3] Indeed, these foreign bases became increasingly important as staging grounds and logistical support points as "revolutionary movements at home and abroad gained momentum and world events evolved in their favour."[4] The irresistible opportunity arose not only because Britain was at war, leaving its precious colony vulnerable and depleted of troops, but also because its archenemy, Germany, was offering support to those with their own interest in undermining the strength of the empire, such as the Indian and Irish national revolutionists and pro-Ottoman Pan-Islamists.[5] It was largely through the German connection that the movement impinged upon the United States' historical record, as the Ghadarites were put on sensational trial in San Francisco for conspiracy, sedition, and espionage during World War I, almost three years after their most spectacular thwarted attempt at mutiny in February 1915.

By the summer of 1915, when the Lieutenant General of Punjab Sir Michael O'Dwyer announced that the movement inside India had been crushed, the Ghadarites and their larger network had lost a major battle, but not a war. Revolutionary activities, sporadic fighting, and invasion plans continued to unfold beyond the northeastern and northwestern frontiers, while those jailed carried on the struggle through hunger strikes and other forms of resistance.[6] Some veterans reemerged in time to take part in the next generation of militance, which they themselves had inspired, in the late 1920s and early 1930s. In this way the Ghadar movement served as a missing link, a source of hidden continuity between the Bengali "anarchist" conspiracies, "national revolutionary terrorism" and Punjabi agitations of the early twentieth century; and the radical Left and revolutionist movements of the 1920s. Far more than an abstract inspiration, however, Ghadar's printed materials and personnel served quite concretely as connective tissue or switching circuit, capable of linking various elements among the Indian radicals abroad, linking Indian radicals to other networks, and linking pre- to postwar revolutionary movements inside the country. In fact it could be hazarded that the movement's wider network overlapped at some point, at no more than a degree of separation, with every radical tendency of its time. Of course this is a large claim, and so requires some careful qualification; we must distinguish relationality from identicality, while recognizing both where appropriate.

Why was Ghadar able to serve this function? One factor was its geographical reach. Another was the unique experience of its founding members, located as they were at a conjuncture of contexts enabling them powerfully to articulate American class and race relations to the economics and geopolitics of empire, by linking the grievances of discrimination against a low-wage immigrant labor force to the colonized status of their home country. Furthermore, amid the ambient dynamism of prewar social ferment, they managed to forge an eclectic ideological synthesis that in turn created possible points of contact with a variety of potential partners. Thus, to fully unravel the story of the movement we must examine its complex interfaces with other international radical networks in order to reveal at what nodes, through which actors, and based on which common threads of ideological principles, methods and tactics, instrumental goals, or political aspirations the radical networks were woven together; or, to put it another way, to reveal which molecular particles in this incendiary chemistry were being shared or exchanged at each covalent bonding site.

GHADAR AND ITS CORE PRINCIPLES

Ghadar is most often portrayed as a nationalist movement, pure and simple. Its members were indubitably patriotic, and their goal of a homecoming to liberate territory from foreign occupation is easily intelligible to a nationalist logic. Yet in both geographical and ideological terms they overspilled the purview of mainstream nationalism. Their indictment of tyranny and oppression was on principle globally applicable, even while generated by a historically specific situation and inflected in culturally specific terms; moreover, they increasingly envisioned a comprehensive social and economic restructuring for postcolonial India rather than a mere handover of the existing governmental institutions.

Ghadar is also often identified as a Sikh movement, exclusively and by definition, with the *Komagata Maru* incident triggering a burst of heroic activity to redeem the community from the lingering shame of loyalism in 1857. The *Komagata Maru* was a ship bearing several hundred South Asian immigrants to Vancouver in the summer of 1914. Conceived by its organizer, Gurdit Singh, as a deliberate challenge to new immigration restrictions, the voyage proved a catalyst for radicalization on both sides of the Pacific after the passengers were refused entry to Canada. The voyage culminated in a violent standoff in the harbor before the ship turned back to sea, and in a shoot-out on arrival in Calcutta in which more than twenty passengers were killed. This narrative reflected the tensions present within the coalition out of which the original movement itself was formed, by rejecting the original non-Sikh elements as no more than a superficial accretion of blowhard intellectuals speechifying about side issues, while the movement's true heart was to be found among the salt-of-the-earth soldier-farmer-poets who went off to get things done. And without doubt these men were at the heart of the movement; particularly in the second phase, during the 1920s, the movement could be thoroughly identified with this community.

But the uniqueness of Ghadar's radicalism was born of its combinations: of contexts, populations, issues, frames, scales. There was no hermetic seal between the Bengalis and Punjabis, the students and laborers; between activities initiated in California, or elsewhere in the Indian political network abroad; between schemes underwritten only by subscription among the farmers, or aided by German funds. None of its components in isolation could have produced the same phenomenon. Furthermore, to portray Ghadar as a Sikh organization by design would be to disregard its members' own expansive universalist principles. Their minds were not narrow, and I believe that they themselves would have wanted to be defined not by ascriptive ethno-religious identity but by their ideological affinities and commitments. In this sense we could consider the Kirti Communists (regional rivals to the M. N. Roy-dominated Communist Party of India infrastructure), rather than the Akali Dal (aimed at regaining control of Sikh holy places, and later associated with the Sikh separatist movement), as better representing the true spirit and intention of the Ghadar movement among the next generation of Punjabi radical movements, although its returned veterans moved into both formations. Indeed, the Ghadar veterans were credited with injecting a more radical social justice and anti-imperial orientation into the Akali movement, which otherwise pointed the way toward a narrower Sikh nationalism.

Any attempt to validate or disqualify an activity as a Ghadarite enterprise based on whether it was conceived, authorized, and directed by a central guiding committee in California is to misrepresent the formality of its party structure. The reality was far more decentralized, as autonomous branches sprang up in various places among those who received the *Ghadar,* without any direct coordination regarding their activities or decisions. Any influence attributable to a core group stemmed from the stirring content of the published materials flowing from the San Francisco fountainhead, and the inspiration provided by the Ghadarites' manifest willingness to act upon these ideals.

Similarly, when I argue that the movement functioned to provide connecting links and switching points to other related anticolonial movements, I do not mean that an official unified party line had necessarily endorsed or established formal links with any of them, but that numerous individuals wore multiple hats without conflict. Many activists who had been associated with California Ghadar, and were closely tied to its Yugantar Ashram headquarters in San Francisco, also participated in or supported other formations. There were Ghadarites or

Ghadar supporters active in networks of revolutionary (Hindu) nationalism (Taraknath Das, Har Dayal), Marxism (Rattan Singh, Santokh Singh), Pan-Islamism (Muhammad Barakatullah, Obeidullah Sindhi), and various combinations thereof. Thus tracking relationships and connections is less a question of "Ghadar" than of Ghadarites. So we might speak of a party, referring to a distinct organization of particular people at a certain place and time; and a movement, referring to an idea, a sensibility and a set of ideological commitments that took wing—or rather, took ship—exuberantly outrunning their originators' control.

Both ideologically and tactically, the Indian revolutionaries drew from a variety of sources, combining them without concern for the constraints of any existing orthodoxy; this very richness of ingredients, of facets, of splice-able threads, is what provided so many different opportunities for collaboration. "In the literature of unrest," commented Valentine Chirol, then foreign bureau chief of the (London) *Times* and inveterate demonizer of revolutionists, "one frequently comes across the strangest juxtaposition of names, Hindu deities, and Cromwell and Washington, and celebrated anarchists all being invoked in the same breath."[7] Yet I do not think the links were casual or contingent, and though many observers and historians have tended to dismiss Ghadar's political orientation as an untheorized hodgepodge, I believe we can perceive within Ghadarite words and deeds an eclectic and evolving, yet consistent radical program. A. C. Bose sums up a range of influences, as well as a range of target audiences: "Just as their sources of inspiration ranged from Rana Pratap and Victor Emanuel II to Sivaji and Garibaldi, and from Mazzini and Guru Govind Singh to the daring terrorists among the Carbonnari [sic], the Nihilists and the Fenians, their appeals for co-operation too were directed at the educated youth of their country and the near-illiterate soldiers as well as at conservative businessmen and the reactionary Indian princes."[8] Indeed, the Ghadar propagandists were far from insensitive to the knack of tailoring material to audience.

Elsewhere Bose quotes a Bengal official's observation that in their practices the "Indian revolutionists imitate the Irish Fenians and the Russian anarchists. Their literature is replete with references to both. Tilak took his 'no rent' campaign from Ireland, and the Bengalees learnt the utility of boycott from Irish history. Kanai Dutt was compared to Patrick O'Donnell, who killed James Cary. Political dacoity to collect money they have learnt from the Russians."[9] Of course, these were not instances of slavish imitation but of active selection, adaptation, and application, or the recognition of analogies. Elements picked up as "influences" or "borrowings" were those with which the borrowers already felt resonance, or which they deemed most relevant to their situation. For example, egalitarianism was a Sikh value long before contact with American democratic discourse—hence the receptive recognition of that particular element rather than another of many available varieties of Western political philosophy.

Moreover, their encounter with an ideal in the founding values of French and American political liberalism, combined with disgust at the distance between this ideal and the reality they encountered, was an important impetus of the emergent Ghadarite thinking, which gravitated toward the politically libertarian aspects rather than the classical economic elements of Enlightenment thinking as it invoked the touchstones of freedom and democracy. This was especially true of texts intended for potential sympathizers among American audiences:[10] Ghadar editor Ram Chandra wrote to the *Boston Daily Advertiser* in October 1916, in response to accusations of a conspiracy "to stir up trouble against British rule in India" through the publication of seditious literature and fomentation of an uprising. Ram Chandra met these accusations with aplomb, saying: "We very cheerfully admit all this, but we wish to emphasize the fact that all we are doing is to preach Liberty, Equality and Fraternity, the birthright of every human being, and to awaken the world to a realization of the enslaved condition of India, where these great principles are denied to all."[11]

Another audience to whom Ghadarites soon began making "passionate appeals" was "the labour unions of the world."[12] These appeals elaborated on the familiar economic drain theory and exhorted the people of the world to make common cause against systems of imperialism.[13] Such a blending of political libertarianism and economic socialism, along with a persistent tendency toward romantic revolutionism, and within their specific context a marked antigovernment bent, is why one may argue that the Ghadar movement's alleged incoherence is actually quite legible through a logic of anarchism—which thereby provides a somewhat ironic bridge between rival nationalist and Communist readings of the Ghadar story. In short, not only did Ghadar manage to join the impulses toward class struggle and civil rights with anticolonialism, it also managed to combine commitments to both liberty and equality. Initially drawing sustenance from both utopian socialism and libertarian thought, their critique of capitalism and of liberalism's racial double standard gained increasingly systematic articulation in the course of the war and the world political shifts in its aftermath.

As to the blending of tactical models, since this was a definitively action-oriented movement, the method was no less important than the motive. This required balancing instrumentality with integrity, strategic with idealistic thinking. Ghadar is often positioned as a transitional phase between two modes of revolutionary struggle, namely, the conspiratorial secret society model and the mass organization model, which is also to say the voluntarist and structuralist theories of precipitating change. However, Ghadar's should be seen not just as a temporary or intermediate half measure, but as a relatively stable mode distinct from other more unequivocal tendencies (in both directions) during both the prewar and the interwar periods.[14]

To sum up a distinct ideological and tactical profile, an internal logic and a common denominator of identifiable core values and approaches that remained consistent across periods, contexts, and idioms, a proper Ghadarite was

anticolonialist (which should go without saying);

passionately patriotic;

internationalist, pledging figurative kinship and active solidarity wherever people struggled against tyranny and oppression anywhere in the world;

secularist, emphatically opposed to communalism and the politicization of institutional religion, although not necessarily atheist or irreligious;

modernist, critical of tradition's weight of fatalism and "slave mentality";

radically democratic, and egalitarian in the face of class and caste differences;

republican, favoring a decentralized federation of Indian states;

anticapitalist (some by implicit moral terms, others, especially after 1920, by explicit Marxian analysis);

militantly revolutionist, opposed to constitutional methods or any compromise with the existing system;

in temperament audacious, dedicated, courageous unto death; in aesthetic romantically capable of gestures such as declaiming a bold slogan, witticism, or verse of farewell poetry at the foot of the gallows (the exemplary Ghadarite in this sense was the prototypical figure of Kartar Singh Sarabha, executed at the age of nineteen or twenty for his role in the attempted uprising of 1915, on whom Bhagat Singh later consciously modeled himself).

As for the Ghadarite goal, it grew increasingly sharper of outline and ambitious of scope over the years: from dignity and respect as Hindustanis at home and abroad

to a free Hindustan

to a free Hindustan, along with a free Ireland, Egypt, and China,

to a free Indian democratic-republican federation, plus a free Ireland, Egypt, and China,

to a free Indian democratic-republican socialist federation, plus a free Ireland, Egypt, and China,

to a free Indian democratic-republican socialist federation, and an end to all forms of economic or imperial slavery anywhere in the world.

The juxtaposition that was so incomprehensible to Chirol, who deemed it clear evidence of the muddleheaded irrationality of the insurgents, is exactly what I want to explore here, by seeking to understand the logic by which the insurgents selected, combined, adapted, and applied tactical and ideological content into a form that continued to develop, dynamically and yet consistently, throughout the trajectory of the revolutionaries abroad.

TRANSPOSITIONS

Beyond Nationalism

Ghadar's definitive early theorist and propagandist, Har Dayal, in an October 1912 Nation Day speech to Indian students and select faculty at the University of California, declared himself an internationalist who did not believe in "narrow views of nationalism." Perennial "seditionist" Taraknath Das, speaking at the same event on the "scope and aim of Indian nationalism," pledged that beyond autonomy from Britain, Young India must "demand a revolution in social ideals so that humanity and liberty would be valued above property, special privilege would not overshadow equal opportunity, and women would not be kept under subjection."[15]

The research that has culminated in this book began in an attempt to escape the reductive equation of anticolonialism with nationalism. Given numerous reservations about that project, both analytical and political, I hoped to identify precedents for ways of conceiving anticolonialism that transcended or critiqued it, and that were capable of proposing alternative visions of a liberated society that neither mirrored the logic of imperialism (and Orientalism) nor replicated the extractive and disciplinary institutions of the modern state while merely replacing foreign with local control. On the other hand, the historical salience and emotional power of a national liberation struggle in undertaking the work of decolonization is impossible to deny. Yet as the revolutionaries of Kirti and the Hindustan Socialist Republican Army well knew, truly liberatory struggle is not only *against* that which restricts freedom, but also *for* that which facilitates or produces freedom. The ejection of foreign rule is one thing, and the implementation of a postindependence socioeconomic and political order based on maximizing substantive liberty, equality, and solidarity quite another. What does the independent society actually look like?

A comprehensive radical critique of colonial rule entailed more than an analysis of the foreignness of the regime; it also required a response to the regime's very structure and character. Colonization imposed complex processes of rationalization, bureaucratization, and technical-industrial development, as well as insertion into the unprecedented expansion of global capitalism.[16]

Regardless of what alternate forms of modernity would have emerged in the absence of European intervention, that intervention did produce a situation in which the material conditions, social destabilizations, and economic transformations associated with the modernization process were perceived as corollaries of colonization. By contextualizing the revolutionary movement abroad relative to the shifts, trends, and currents of international radicalism over the first few decades of the twentieth century, we may see the configuration of factions within the Indian independence struggle mirroring the spectrum of possible responses to these conditions manifest within Western movements of opposition and critical resistance, including varieties of accommodation, incorporation, synthesis, transcendence, resistance, and rejection.

Three Anticolonial Discourses

In my exploration of ways of conceptualizing anticolonial struggle that transcended nationalism during this globally turbulent period (1905–1930), two major antisystemic movements stood out as transnational vehicles for opposition to Western imperialism and critique of modern capitalist society, both of which were available in various forms to Indian radicals: Socialism and Pan-Islamism. Yet any attempt to define either of these complex, multifold terms is fraught with as many contradictions and counterexamples as in the case of nationalism.

If we approach the three "isms" not as ideological monoliths but as heteroglossic discourses,[17] we can recognize an analogous range of positions within each of them on the debates then in progress over how to respond to the confrontation with modernity—whether by espousing Enlightenment rationalism or by embracing its various antitheses, whether defined as spiritual, mystical, nihilist, millenarian, or romanticist.

Rationalism forms an important axis in the intellectual history of revolution, cutting across leftist, nationalist, and religious responses. While this epistemological axis does not replace those based in material economic or political structures, it is nevertheless necessary to take account of modes of resistance that cannot be "legitimated by a post-enlightenment rationalist frame,"[18] and furthermore to acknowledge that such modes cannot be wholly identified with religious movements; rather, mystical/romantic or antiliberal modalities occur within all three discourses alongside those modalities legible to a rationalist, material interest–based analysis, whether of the liberal or socialist orientation. I suspect that in actuality both modalities may almost always be operating at once, and that it is simply a matter of relative proportion in each case. Ghadar and its analogues certainly contained elements of both.

In such a way (e.g., by positing nationalist, leftist, and Islamist modalities) each as a discourse or flexible idiom in which various ideological statements could be made, and a range of political and philosophical positions taken, rather than a unified ideology itself—the interaction of the three movements during this period could be reframed as a transposition of analogous ideas, goals, and aspirations among them. The Ghadarite network, through its various alliances and alignments, was capable of engaging with those who were making compatible utterances—that is, statements of militant anti-imperialism, economic egalitarianism, and social emancipation—in any of these three languages.

The Limits of Translatability

In order to recognize functionally comparable statements within separate "semantic fields," a practical theorist must look underneath form for content, within idiom for intent, behind problematic for thematic.[19] More directly, an organizer must ask whether alliances and coalitions are all necessarily provisional, based only on a negative term; whether a shared opposition is their common immediate goal. But is this enough? How much compatibility is necessary between the positive terms of multiple alternative visions to enable their adherents to work together beyond resistance? Which differences are semantic and superficial, and which are substantive and prohibitive?

Some of the confusion in defining an "ism" arises from equating a discourse in its totality only with the most dominant or authoritative statement it has been used to make (or with one's preferred interpretation, dominant or not). The same tendency is also behind many orthodox exponents' refusal to admit any possibility of rapprochement or compatibility with other discourses, or even with dissenters claiming to be part of their own. If X and Y may be defined as X and Y only in their most purified and homogenized form, then indeed there is no common ground, no possible overlap; the meanings of X and Y are polarized. But more often than not, I would guess, the strands that can most successfully interweave across categoric boundaries are likely to be the heterodox or counterdominant ones on both sides, the threads straggling from the fringes beyond the reach of doctrinal enforcement, though still recognizably part of the fabric.[20]

A caveat, however: I am not therefore suggesting that all discourses were interchangeable, or even that the parameters of each spectrum were isomorphic. The threads they shared were nevertheless woven into fabrics of different shades and patterns. Moreover, every language imposes its own limitations and tendencies regarding what it is equipped to express most directly in its available vocabulary or repertory of concepts, and what requires more complex circumlocutions. And while each language is versatile, there may be points at which it becomes expedient to borrow words or even switch to another tongue better suited to the concept or construction one is trying to express.

Nevertheless, if the emphasis is on connections and alliances, the interface between different ideological networks, and the points of translatability between their idioms, then we might ask not what a nationalist says and does, but what is being said in the idiom and done according to the logic of nationalism; not what a socialist or Pan-Islamist stipulates, but what kind of socialism and what kind of Pan-Islamism are operative. In that regard, the question then became with what kind of nationalists, leftists and Islamists, in what contexts, and at what points of each network, via interfaces based on which shared traits or common elements, were the Ghadarites engaged in meaningful interactions; and how, precisely, were these Indian anticolonialists situated in the context of the international radicalism of the time.

Praxis

Finally, notwithstanding all this talk of ideology and discourse, this work is not intended to be an abstract philosophical exercise. Rather, my approach to intellectual history is much like that described by Israel Gershoni and James Jankowski in the preface to their 1986 book on Egyptian nationalism. Combining the "internal" and "external" approaches, the authors explain: "This work proceeds on the basis of several assumptions about historical inquiry. Perhaps the most basic of these is that there are crucial interrelationships between the intellectual life of a society and its political development. An adequate understanding... demands that attention be given to the complex connections between ideas of the world and behavior in the world."[21] Like theirs in this way, my work here is concerned with praxis; that is, not with theory in isolation, but with the way that ideas are generated within historical context and play a substantive role in bringing about historical change.

Moreover, this work is a narrative about people who felt the same way. The Ghadarites were pragmatists, not dogmatists; activists above all, not systematic armchair theorists. Above all, as Rattan Singh recalled, "Every step taken by the Ghadr Party... has been practical and has meant action. Its resolutions have never remained on paper; they have always been put into action."[22] Indeed, radicalism itself resides as much in the commitment to acting on ideals, making them effective in reality, and translating them into social form, as it does in the actual content of the ideas. In selecting their allies, the Ghadarites allotted more weight to shared goals and common sensibilities (notably their appreciation for fierce and total commitment to one's objectives) than to niceties of doctrine. Yet neither were they ideologically vacant. Far more than an inchoate burst of quickly dispersed revolutionary energy, they created an important missing link in the genealogy of South Asian radicalism, as well as a bridge between contemporaneous radical movements. Therein lies not the least of their contributions to history.

Overview

Chapter 1 concerns the birth of the Ghadar movement on the Pacific coast in 1913, its activities in California, and the content and spread of its propaganda, culminating in its homeward journey of intended liberation launched at the outbreak of World War I. Although the attempted uprising of February 1915 was crushed by means of the First Lahore Conspiracy trials, the ideas it had reimported lingered significantly: when the would-be freedom fighters of 1914–1915 set out upon their return to India "to inform their kinsmen of the unequal treatment that was meted out to them" overseas, they did so by "preach[ing] the doctrines of revolution that they had learned from the Ghadr and the crude socialism that they had picked up in the towns of western Canada and the United States."[23] Crucially, the radicalization of South Asians in North America in the early twentieth century was defined by labor relations as refracted by race, which facilitated their affinity with the IWW's American form of syndicalism, as shown in chapter 2.

Chapters 3 and 4 together mark a turning point in the narrative, in which the nationalist aspect comes to the fore. Here I focus on the period of strategic anti-British partnerships in the context of World War I, through which a number of elaborate covert operations were carried out with German/Ottoman patronage, in contrast to the 1915 outbreak that the California Ghadarites had initiated autonomously. Nationalism also mediated the collaborations among Indian, Irish, and Egyptian revolutionists active in Europe and North America, and the analogies in sensibility and situation that they recognized among themselves. This period was shut down with another legal case in 1918, the sensational Hindu-German Conspiracy trial in San Francisco.

But the Ghadar Party appeared in a second distinct incarnation, this time Communist in the more orthodox Marxist-Leninist sense, in contrast to its prewar leanings toward the less systematic (though perhaps more holistic) utopian socialism associated with Har Dayal. This is the matter of chapter 5. Following the exhilarating success of the Bolshevik revolution, and given the Comintern's strategic commitment to supporting Asian national liberation struggles, Ghadarites turned to Moscow as their new self-described mecca for political training, theoretical guidance, and moral and material support. During the 1920s, Ghadar sent batches of trainees to Moscow while establishing new organs and organizing centers in China and Punjab.[24] At the same time it helped seed the growth of civil rights and antideportation campaigns in the United States through the Friends of Freedom for India (FFI). In India meanwhile it helped seed the growth of the next generation of militant anticolonial struggle through Bhagat Singh, the Kirti group, the Naujavan Bharat Sabha, and the Hindustan Socialist Republican Army.

In the final two chapters I back up in time to pick up the parallel thread of Pan-Islamism, which had been continuously intertwined with Ghadar's activities starting from the latter's prewar overtures to Muslim soldiers identified as potential mutineers in the British Indian army. The interaction became even more significant through the German/Ottoman-backed schemes in west and central Asia during the war, reflecting the goals and preoccupations of this alliance. After the war, when Moscow displaced Berlin as center of patronage, this pattern of relationships did not change. It culminated in a rapprochement with the Khilafat movement of the early 1920s and its subset, the Hijrat movement. Theoretical links were elaborated by Obeidullah Sindhi and Mohammed Barakatullah, both of whom had complex Ghadar ties.

A Word for the Journey

Har Dayal commented in the *Bande Mataram* in 1910: "Exile has its privileges. It is the price paid for the right of preaching the truth as it appears to us. We do not deal in political casuistry mingled with erroneous philosophy. . . . We may pay homage only to our conscience and defy all the governments of the world to make us deviate a hair's breadth from the path of Duty and Righteousness."[25]

The Revolutionary Movement Abroad was a phenomenon of travelers; it could not have occurred otherwise. As perspectives opened out for economic migrants encountering new contexts, and as political trajectories became literal journeys of enforced exile and clandestine organizing, the leading edge of radicalism passed literally and figuratively beyond the bounds of the territorial nation-state. Yet in all these journeys, whether the world traveler's face was set toward a home as a free Indian citizen or a free American or Soviet one, the destination was always a dream of utopia.

Kim Stanley Robinson has one of the transplanetary nomads in his speculative Mars trilogy declare that "history is the haj to utopia."[26] In simplest terms, Robinson's book is about the colonization and terraforming of Mars. But more deeply, it is about the process of designing a society, initially far beyond the reach of the old earth's interstate relations and corporate economics, though these interests of course are pulled closer as breakthroughs in transport and communications occur, and as the immigrant population increases. Nevertheless, as the new society develops, the Martians have an unprecedented opportunity to define new categories of identity within social units based rather in affinity and ideology than in ethnic or national affiliation; and to negotiate a framework of principles for accommodating difference, by which the autonomy of communities who use different social blueprints can be maintained within a larger federation, in which ecological survival rather than political power forms the baseline for collective control. Aside from the anachronistic ecological aspect, this seems to me quite applicable to the vision of a Ghadarite India.

Lamin Sanneh has described the functions of ritual pilgrimage in spatially marking off an identity, purified and confirmed by certain practices carried out along the way and especially on reaching the destination—where, upon arrival, the traveler experiences the intensity of a sense of identification with a transnational community or "brotherhood" of spiritual kindred, resulting in a recommitment to an ideological program.[27] I am certainly not suggesting that the future Ghadarites set sail for America with any such conscious sense of ritual significance. Their journey began not as an intentional pilgrimage but a prag-

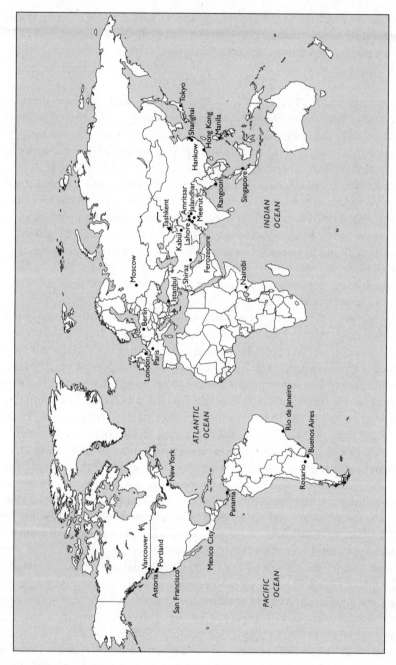

MAP 1. Ghadar's global range

matic journey of economic or educational opportunity. However, I suspect that they would recognize the effect that Sanneh describes. And the revolutionaries did begin to speak in the language of pilgrimage. For the Ghadarites "Moscow became Mecca." Meanwhile, *hajis* bound for the real Mecca and *muhajirin* bound for the heart of the caliphate at Istanbul became literal fellow travelers. There was a mission to be fulfilled across the sea, and if they could not make it to the other shore, they were ready to immolate themselves so that others could. They spoke of an altar, and a sacrifice; they spoke of moths to the flame. But the Swadeshi activists' Bharat Mata had been replaced as deity on the blood-spattered dais by *inqilab* (revolution) or *azadi* (freedom).

And after the revolution, upon reaching the odyssey's end, would they dwell within the kingdom of god, the dictatorship of the proletariat, or the federated United States of India? For those who preached liberty, equality, and fraternity, would it make a difference whether their foundational logic and social ethic had been derived from transcendent or divine sources, natural law, or human reason? Would it matter by what map or method they had traced their path? Around what polestar they had oriented their voyage? Whether they had been steered by God's plan, a Hegelian world spirit, a Marxian structural dialectic, or their own fiery wills?

1

"The Air of Freedom"

Ghadar in America

IMMIGRANTS

There had been a smattering of Indian sailors in New England ports since the late eighteenth century, and the odd celebrity religious philosopher since the late nineteenth, starting with Vivekananda's star turn at the Chicago World's Fair in 1892, which garnered a cult following of theosophists and countercultural practitioners among a northeastern elite. Meanwhile, the flow of indentured labor to the Caribbean islands and the north coast of South America began in the 1830s, to fill the vacuum left by the abolition of the slave trade.[1] But the first South Asian immigrant population of significant size in mainland North America were the Punjabi Sikhs who began arriving on the West Coast around 1903.[2]

The leap from tens to thousands arriving per year was rather abrupt.[3] Even so, according to an official count, only 6,656 South Asians entered the United States (legally) between 1899 and 1913. Hundreds more waited in Shanghai, Hong Kong, Manila, and other East Asian ports for trans-Pacific passage, hoping for a little help from friends who had already made the crossing. By the eve of the war in 1914 there was an estimated total of 10,000 South Asians in North America.[4]

Most of the Punjabi laborers came from relatively prosperous families of small independent landholders, overwhelmingly concentrated in the Doab region. About half of them were veterans of the British army or military police. After their service, having seen a bit of the world, many of these men of cosmopolitan experience if little formal education now had a taste for further adventures rather than settling back down in the sleepy villages of their birth. Lured by the opportunity to make some good money, and offered incentives by steamship

17

companies looking to fill in their dwindling manifests of Chinese working-class passengers (the Chinese Exclusion Act had been signed into U.S. law in 1882), the Punjabis came to work in lumber mills or laying railroads, a few in canneries or construction. But overwhelmingly they filtered into the migratory agricultural labor force. Disciplined and adaptable, they were much in demand, claimed the Immigration Department's official translator Dady Burjor, to the point where big landowners from the Sacramento Valley sometimes went directly to Angel Island to hire new arrivals. (The noncombatants who came directly from the village, usually as a result of a collective economic decision by an extended family, were in Dady Burjor's opinion a lesser quality of crude yokel.)[5]

This positive desire to emigrate was compounded by straitened economic circumstances brought about by colonial agricultural policies at home. The 1901 Alienation of Land Act, by restricting the transfer of land from traditionally landowning groups, had been designed to prevent the loss of rural control to urban (usually Hindu) moneylenders. But it also had the effect of institutionalizing existing inequities of access for some Sikh and low-caste populations. Then the 1906 Colonization Bill and Bari Doab canal scheme led to a sharp rise in water rates and micromanagement of its use, which aimed at maximizing the region's rich agricultural output for the British commodity market, thereby rerouting it away from local control and subsistence needs.

This had sparked a wave of agitation in 1907, led by the brothers Ajit Singh and Kishan Singh, future Ghadar collaborators and the respective uncle and father of Bhagat Singh. Notably during the course of the unrest, Ajit Singh had spoken not just for reform of the offending legislation but for the unequivocal expulsion of the British from India, by violent means if necessary. He also founded the Indian Patriots' Association, the Bharat Mata Society, and a newspaper, the *Peshwa*. For his activities he was sent to jail in Mandalay until 1909, when he decamped to Persia along with his *Peshwa* collaborator Sufi Amba Parishad. Here they set up a revolutionary center from which they facilitated contacts among revolutionaries throughout Europe and North America for many years. By 1914 Ajit Singh was living in Paris, under the faux Persian identity of Hassan Khan, and supporting himself by giving English lessons. His travels during the war later took him as far as Brazil and Argentina. As fate would have it, he died literally on the eve of independence, 15 August 1947.[6]

But the general Punjabi population was not yet connecting their grievances to a larger, secular and/or national context. Much of the political consciousness-raising at that time was occurring rather through the religiously defined Arya Samaj and Sikh Sabha, while the British army remained a strong focus of collective identity and allegiance.[7] In theory these veterans had the right to settle in Canada as subjects of the dominion, taking pride in the community's sterling record of military service to the empire and the status it supposedly conferred. In practice they encountered worsening racism, both popular and legislative. Why such antipathy? After all, notes Harish Puri, the Indian threat could not have been simply about racial purity, since there were far more Chinese and Japanese entrants at the time. But politically the Indians were a special case, bearing on the delicate stability of colonial rule. Among the fears of the Secretary of State for India about what might happen if emigration to Canada were allowed to continue were the following:

i. That the terms of close familiarity which competition with white labour brings about do not make for British prestige; and it is by prestige alone that India is held not by force;

ii. that there is a socialist propaganda in Vancouver, and the consequent danger of the East Indians being imbued with socialist doctrines;

iii. labour rivalry is sure to result in occasional outbreaks of feelings on the part of the whites and any dissatisfaction at unfair treatment of Indians in Vancouver is certain to be exploited for the purpose of agitation in India; (and)

iv. East Indian affairs are sometimes made use of by unscrupulous partisans to serve the cause of their political party.[8]

On none of these points was he necessarily wrong, as time would show.

In the same vein Brigadier General E. J. Swayne warned in a confidential memorandum that Indians who came as free laborers to Canada were "politically inexpedient" due to the risk that "these men [might] go back to India and preach ideas of emancipation which would upset the machinery of law and order."[9] The fresh air of freedom, it seemed, was a dangerous gas.

Ghadar narratives (both contemporary and retrospective) repeated the notion that in America the "settlers" now breathed the air of modernity, freedom, and equality. And yet a gap remained between this stated American ideal and their own American experience. Once they reached California, they could obtain a daily wage of up to $2–$3 for harvesting asparagus, celery, potatoes, beans, lemons, and oranges.[10] It is interesting that chroniclers of the community seem to find a source of pride in some of the very factors used as pretexts for racial discrimination against them: the white laborers were jealous and resentful of the immigrants' strength, endurance, industriousness, and ability to live with such astounding frugality. To help in doing so Indian laborers developed mutual support networks for living and work situations, often rooming, cooking, and eating collectively, and forming work teams represented by an Anglophone spokesman with the task of procuring work and negotiating terms, or dealing with lawyers as necessary. Some teams even divided their wages equally at the end of the week.[11] The young network of *gurdwaras* (Sikh temples serving as community centers) also served as a important sites of mobilization, resistance, and solidarity, furthering a tradition of Sikh *granthis* as community leaders, representatives, intermediaries, and mobilizers around the Pacific Rim.

For example, one of the most important political spokesmen for the British Columbia Sikhs prior to the formation of the Pacific Coast Hindi Association was Teja Singh, a respected preacher who had been studying at Columbia University when he received an invitation in 1908 to represent his community on the West Coast. Although more a scholar and cleric than a rabble-rouser, he began addressing meetings in the *gurdwaras* to mobilize defense against the threat of deportation, all the while framing his actions as a sacred mission guided by Guru Nanak, and phrasing his speeches in the idiom of spirituality.

But although the *gurdwaras* did remain convenient organizing bases for Ghadarite activities, offering an ideal infrastructure for communicating and assembling people, their original mission was oriented toward defensive self-purification in line with the work of the Sikh Sabha in Punjab, preserving community identity against the danger of its erosion in a foreign country. These efforts, carried out though the leaders of the Khalsa Diwan Society, were concerned with counteracting deviations in orthodox dress and food habits among the Sikh laborers through evangelization and the foundation of new *gurdwaras* (and if necessary the boycott and ostracism of apostates).[12] However, Puri attributes this attitude, as well as the attachment to martial-caste loyalism to Britain, to elites among the immigrants. The Ghadar Party, when it emerged, represented quite a different stance.

Meanwhile, Indian students began trickling into the United States around 1906 seeking technical training or degrees in fields emblematic of modernity, such as engineering and chemistry; or if they had followed Har Dayal's recommendations, economics and sociology. Many had first tried Japan only to find that the Anglo-Japanese agreement prevented their access to the specific types of training they sought. The majority of students were Bengali, and their most immediate context of political radicalization had been the Swadeshi movement and the connected revolutionist centers in London and Paris.

In 1912, Jawala Singh, a prosperous potato farmer and agricultural entrepreneur near Stockton, approached Har Dayal with a proposal to endow a scholarship with the goal of bringing students from all over India to study in the United States, preferably at the University of California, where most were enrolled.[13] Along with important future Ghadarites Wasakha Singh and Santokh Singh (whom Behari Lal described as "exceptionally patriotic and pious men"),[14] he had formed a society in 1912 whose members pledged "one hundred per cent dedication" to their country's liberation. The first competition for the Guru Gobind Singh scholarships was to be judged by a selection committee consisting of Har Dayal, Teja Singh, Taraknath Das, and Arthur Pope, a sympathetic philosophy professor of the University of California. The scholarship was supposed to cover tuition, textbooks, lab fees, room and board, second-class return passage to India, and a $50 monthly stipend. Eligibility was in theory to be unrestricted by caste, religion, race, or gender. Out of six hundred applicants, six were selected for the 1912–13 academic year, including Gobind Behari Lal.[15] But by the time they arrived, Jawala Singh's harvest had proven significantly less lucrative than expected due to a drop in potato prices that year, and the promised funds were not forthcoming. The scholarship winners decided to stay and enroll anyway, using their own resources.

Together the six scholars rented a house near the campus. Among the six, Nand Singh was the designated mediator to the scholarship committee, ensuring their material needs were supplied. They took turns cooking "Indian food of a very simple kind, rice, dal, milk, vegetable or meat" and also got a small weekly allowance for pocket money. By the end of 1912, however, the funds dried up completely. The notion of "self-supporting," said Behari Lal, was "a peculiar American system" quite new to them.[16] Now, like the rest of the students, they earned their living by working in the mornings or afternoons, or during holidays, waiting tables in boardinghouses, washing dishes in restaurants, selling newspapers, or even working in canneries. During the summers, they often worked in "the fields and orchards where, almost always in the company of Indian farm workers—Sikhs, Moslems, Hindus, Pathans—they picked fruit from the trees or planted celeray [sic] or potatoes or did some thing or other."[17] On a 25¢ to 30¢ hourly wage, or by selling Indian handicrafts such as shawls (was it assumed they would bring the stock of goods with them?), one could live comfortably for a year on $250 and like a king for $350.[18]

In 1911, Calcutta's English-language magazine *Modern Review* printed a series of articles offering advice to Indian students on how to deal with arrival and life in America, such as how to find housing and employment. One should bring identification papers from a sponsoring organization and then get a recommendation letter from the American consul general in Seattle. (Students also were advised to just say no if the immigration inspector asked if they believed in polygamy. Such a traditional form of Oriental deviance was certainly no less controversial than the very modern Western practice of free love, advocacy of which was to get Har Dayal into trouble the following year.) Someone would then meet and escort them to G. D. Kumar's new India House. From there they could write to Berkeley, and someone else would come up to meet them. The recommended course was to arrive in the spring, work over the summer, and enroll in the fall, either at the university straightaway or at a free Berkeley high school for a year first.

Har Dayal also published a series of articles in *Modern Review,* praising the United States as the ideal place in all the world "from which a solitary wandering Hindu can send a message of hope and encouragement to his countrymen." As the future-oriented nation par excellence, the United States was the perfect foil for India, whose ancient culture it was thus eager to embrace. Indeed, such a rap-prochement would be mutually beneficial: Vedantic philosophy would do wonders for the superficial, "restless, noisy," "overfed, self-complacent" Americans, while modernity would stimulate and inspire the Indians mired in tradition, stunted by colonial chains, and hampered by current repression. He thought the social and political climate of the United States would be very salubrious for Indian stu-dents, virtually "an ethical sanitarium." Here they could openly explore "the value of unity, the lessons to be learned from Japan, the importance of industrial progress, the greatness of the American people, the blessings of democracy, the honourableness of manual labour, the meanness of Theodore Roosevelt and the necessity for education, liberal and technical, for the uplifting of the people of India." As they were in Har Dayal's opinion "endowed with energy and brains but little money," they would benefit in practical terms not only from technical training but from the moral effects of supporting themselves for the first time through manual labor, thereby "learning self-reliance and resourcefulness of mind."[19]

In a similar vein Harnam Singh Chima published "Why India Sends Students to America" in 1907. He asserted that the real purpose for him and his fellow students was "that we may deserve the title educated in the fullest and practical sense of the word. We came here to imbibe free thoughts from free people and teach the same when we go back to our country and to get rid of the tyranny of the rule of the universal oppressor (the British)."[20]

No less than the workers, the students experienced racism. Boardinghouses and restaurants often declined to serve them, and they were ineligible for mem-bership in most campus clubs. This, along with the need for them to do menial labor, may to some degree have neutralized the class privilege they had enjoyed in India. In any case the Ghadarites and their immediate predecessors deliber-ately fostered secularism, tolerance, and fraternization across religious and caste lines. Of course it would be disingenuous to suggest that all differences of class, caste, religion, and regional origin were erased in the New World. However, it does seem that these differences faded into lower relief in comparison to their mutual interests and experiences in the North American context. Even if these and other differences were not completely erased—only temporarily deempha-sized to reemerge later—by 1912 the Ghadar community's two main ingredients were present. The movement's "outstanding characteristic," in participant Gobind Behari Lal's opinion, was the "combination of university-bred scholar and the cultural leader and of the pre-educated Indians, workers, farmers and small shopkeepers etc. of the Pacific Coast."[21] But the ensuing emphasis on edu-cation for workers and manual labor for students closed the distance between them and encouraged the merging of each group's concerns with those of the other—a volatile fusion that illuminated and ignited both of them.

Neither students nor laborers as a group were overwhelmingly political upon arrival, as the majority were focused on their own personal advancement. The farmers had come seeking prosperity, the students professional success. However, an important minority had come with other ideas in mind. A professor complained: "[The students] are generally revolutionaries, or if not such when they come, are soon taken in hand by their fellows and converted," after which, "having come under the influence of the socialistic and revolutionary ideas they regarded it as their mission in life to work for the subversion of the British rule in India."[22] A California Immigration officer observed in 1914 that "most of the Indian students residing there are infected with seditious ideas," so thoroughly that "even Sikhs of the labouring class have not escaped their pernicious influence."[23] But who radicalized whom?

In *Modern Review* Har Dayal said, of the peasants as much as the students, that America had "lifted [them] to a higher level of thought and action. The great flag of the greatest democratic state in the world's history, burns up all cowardice, servility, pessimism and indifference, as fire consumes the dross and leaves pure gold behind."[24] Of course this exposure to liberal discourses and rising expectations advertised by the land of opportunity, *combined* with systematic exclusion from access to the same, is what fired their ire, not merely the imbibing of some magically liberating influence inherent in the American atmosphere.

Between 1907 and 1910, white American anxiety and hostility increased apace as the number of Indians grew, although opinion was far from unified during this period of dramatic social and cultural flux. Moreover, class positioning on both sides conditioned American responses to Indian newcomers, causing Indians to be read as exotically tantalizing Orientals if they came from educated elite backgrounds, and as threatening dark-complected aliens if they came as low-wage workers. According to Rattan Singh's account, the Sikh "pioneers" did fairly well in prosperous periods, but an economic downturn in the United States in 1907 led to tensions with white workers. Joan Jensen attributes this to a predictable pattern: whenever the economy put pressure on low-income white laborers, anti-Asian hysteria rose in direct proportion, as the incoming workers, who were ready to accept even lower wages, were seen as competition. Just as the West Coast's Asiatic Expulsion League had thought things were under control with the Chinese and Japanese, now here came the latest manifestation of the "Yellow Peril," this time in the form of a "tide of turbans."[25] Organized labor accused Sikhs of being in league with the bosses who colluded with the steamship companies in recruiting Asian laborers. Often even Socialists judged Asian workers backwards and unorganizable, a drag on the progress of more advanced and "modern" white labor.[26]

Indian laborers were used as strikebreakers in Tacoma.[27] An escalating series of hostile incidents followed, beginning with the August 1907 riot in Bellingham, Washington, that literally drove the Indians out of town, in an act premeditated to be the grand finale of a Labor Day parade, and followed by other acts of vandalism and vigilantism in California and Oregon. In March 1910, "white hoodlums" in St. John, Oregon, apparently with the collusion of the police, attacked the quarters of Indian workers, who beat them back with sticks and clubs.[28]

The views of the West Coast anti-Asian groups and certain sectors of the white labor movement notwithstanding, the American public as a whole was not ill disposed to the Indians; Americans identified with the rhetoric of an anti-British independence struggle and tended to sympathize with refugees from foreign tyranny. But as American power on the world stage, along with the United States' imperial ambitions, waxed around the turn of the nineteenth to twentieth century, the balance of social attitudes toward the rest of the world and its émigrés was shifting. President Theodore Roosevelt, recent recipient of congratulations and approval from Rudyard Kipling on his successful conquest of Cuba and the Philippines, along with a copy of Kipling's poem "White Man's Burden," affirmed his appreciation for the British Raj's effectiveness as "the most colossal example history affords of a successful administration by men of European blood of a thickly populated region on another continent . . . one of the most admirable achievements of the white race during the last two centuries."[29] Still, the Indians continued to find support among progressive leftists and left-liberals, civil libertarians, pacifists, and anti-imperialists, who opposed World War I, and of course Orientalist intellectuals and theosophists.

Meanwhile policymakers proposed increasingly sly ways to keep Indians out without explicitly banning them. For example, the United States might make an agreement with the British requiring Indians to carry passports, and then refuse passports to laborers.[30] Or the United States might persuade shipping lines to discontinue service for Asians or to refuse to sell tickets to Indian laborers, thereby in effect privatizing or contracting out enforcement of an exclusion policy.[31] A 1910 Immigration Commission report recommended congressional exclusion and a gentlemen's agreement with Britain to stem the flow of East Indians, as they were by now "universally regarded as the least desirable race of immigrants thus far admitted to the United States";[32] also, the report suggested, requiring a literacy test might help curtail East Indian immigration.

In 1912, the Root amendment to the pending Dillingham immigration bill called for the deportation of "any alien who shall take advantage of his residence in the United States to conspire with others for the violent overthrow of a foreign government recognized by the United States." It was defeated. In 1913 the Alien Land Law was passed, in part to prevent Japanese or Sikh agricultural workers from accumulating their own profitable land base in California's Central Valley, a process already underway. At the same time another bill was debated though not passed, restricting not entrance, but eligibility for citizenship. Of course, restricting immigrants from entering and disqualifying them from citizenship were two different tasks. It was not until 1917 that the Asiatic Barred Zone was declared, drastically restricting entry for anyone originating within a geographically (if not politically) arbitrary latitude and longitude that covered most of China, part of Russia, part of Polynesia, and all of India, Burma, Siam, the Malay States, Arabia, Afghanistan, and the Indian Ocean islands.

ACTIVISTS

As early as 1907, officials in Punjab noted the circulation of "seditious pamphlets" addressed to soldiers in the local army garrisons "pointing out to them how easy it would be to throw off British rule. . . . The circular emanated from some Natives of India now in the United States."[33] As North America grew as an organizing center, revolutionaries abroad in Europe, such as Har Dayal, Ajit Singh, and Bhai Parmanand, increasingly started looking west in hopes of advancing their work. Once there, the necessary tasks would be to carry out anti-British "sedition" and to protect the community from North American racism. The two imperatives were complementary: in the organizers' calculations, the latter was precisely what might prime a potential mass movement to develop its consciousness of the former. In other words, the rage fueled by discrimination might be channeled toward anticolonial struggle. Still, this conjunction of Indian independence and American civil rights could also lead to conflicts in priority. The difference in *primary* aspirations for status as American citizens versus status as free Indian citizens was eventually reflected in a divergence of interest between moderate permanent settlers and radical temporary sojourners, though this may ultimately be a circular argument, given that it was the radicals who left to go fight in the mutiny, leaving the moderates behind. But it was only between 1912 and 1918 that the Indian frame came to override the American one with such urgency, and that the narrative arc of national liberation came to blot out that of immigrant arrival and success. Before the Ghadar movement coalesced, while organizers did habitually speak against British rule, in the immediate sense they prioritized worker education and the social welfare of the immigrant community. A few examples of the organizers follow.

Ram Nath Puri

Ram Nath Puri was a bank clerk in Lahore when he first drew the attention of the British authorities for a few "objectionable pamphlets" and a "seditious cartoon" he had published in 1905.[34] In 1906 he left for America. There he worked first as a hospital watchman and then as an interpreter for the Sikh laborers who were then beginning to arrive in larger numbers. It was also reported that he "employed his talents in cheating them at every opportunity" and was "regarded by the Indians as a swindler and by Americans as a loafer." He enrolled in a mining college, and later worked in the fields picking fruit, as a "waiter in the house of an American lady," and as an unsuccessful entrepreneur. Both his Eastern Employment Agency and his Indo-American General Trading Company failed.

But Puri also started a Hindustan Association and a dormitory called the Magnolia Street Union, which provided Punjabi laborers with room and board for 10¢ a night.[35] He also published a short-lived Urdu paper called the *Circular-i-Azadi* (Circular of Freedom), which appeared in June, July, and August 1907 in San Francisco and Oakland. One of the first significant pieces of anticolonial propaganda literature circulated on the West Coast, it was prohibited from shipment to India due to its "seditious" content. According to the report of the director of criminal intelligence for January 1908, its "object . . . is to organise an Indian national party among the Indians who go to America for employment. . . . It seems to owe its existence to the collision which has occurred between the white and coloured labour at Vancouver and at places in California, the state of Washington and elsewhere in the west of America."[36]

Puri's paper was allegedly connected to an "Indian Association" based in San Francisco, and with branches in Astoria and Vancouver, the purpose of which was "to impart instructions to Indians on national lines, to teach gunfiring, Japanese exercises, and the use of spear, sword and other weapons in self-defence, and to foster American sympathy with India."[37] Although copies of the original paper are now impossible to find, the Director of Criminal Intelligence (DCI) reports inform us that the August issue included an article advocating a boycott of government service; and that both the July and the August issues contained extracts from the anti-British *Gaelic American* (of which we have not heard the last) and from other Indian newspapers—presumably the *Bande Mataram* and *Indian Sociologist,* since they shared material with the *Gaelic American.*

Puri acquired a modest bit of land in Oakland around 1910 and considered settling in the United States, since he was still afraid to return to India. But he apparently changed his mind, reaching Tokyo in time to make a "very objectionable" (which presumably meant militantly seditious) speech at a farewell dinner for Muhammed Barakatullah, who was leaving his teaching post there in summer 1910. Puri then "turned up unexpectedly" in Bijnor (his hometown) in 1911 and advised the youth at the Arya Samaj *gurukul* (religious school) there that they should "go to America where they would learn how a man could achieve liberty." The report is silent as to what happened to him later, whether he stayed in Bijnor, and whether he reconnected with the Ghadarites when they returned in 1914–15.

Guru Dutt Kumar

Guru Dutt Kumar arrived in British Columbia around 1907 and opened a grocery store in Victoria.[38] Born in the North-West Frontier Province (NWFP), he was exposed to the revolutionary movement in Calcutta, where he had studied at the National College, briefly taught Urdu and Hindi, and apprenticed at a photographer's studio. In Calcutta he also met Taraknath Das, who assisted him in coming to North America, along with Harnam Singh Sahri, a veteran of the Fourth Cavalry.[39]

In 1909 Kumar became the secretary of a new Hindustan Association in Vancouver—the same association linked to Puri's Circular of Freedom. Its ultimate goal was "complete self-government" for the "Hindustani Nation," which for him would entail not only the elimination of foreign exploitation but the promotion of domestic education, industry, trade, and agriculture.[40] The organization boasted some 250 members and ministered most to "students and educated men." F. C. Isemonger and James Slattery's official report claimed that it functioned chiefly to entice Indian students to America, where they could be "instructed in nationalist, revolutionary, and even anarchical doctrines."[41] Initially working closely with the Khalsa Diwan Society, Kumar emphasized social reform, moral uplift, teetotaling, and caste and religious harmony. While agitating against entry bans on new immigrants, including families attempting to join their loved ones who were already there, an anticolonial strain was becoming increasingly overt.[42]

Kumar and his colleagues also opened the Swadesh Sevak Home in Vancouver, modeled on Krishnavarma's London India House. It offered a school for immigrants' children (although with families barred from entry, surely there could not have been many of them) and evening English classes for the immigrants themselves. Its corresponding organ was the *Swadesh Sevak*, started in 1910 as the Gurmukhi counterpart to Taraknath Das's *Free Hindustan*. Both papers reprinted articles from the *Bande Mataram* and *Indian Sociologist,* which were published by their radical movement counterparts in Europe, and advocated mutiny among the Sikh troops in the British Indian army. The paper was put on the list of "objectionable" literature prohibited from entering India under the Sea Customs Act, as of March 1911.[43]

Meanwhile, Kumar, Sahri, and others took up the practice of visiting groups of Indian laborers at their workplaces to talk with them about "social and political problems."[44] In addition to circulating the paper, they held meetings and raised funds for combating the entry ban or reversing the arrests of confederates who had been threatened with deportation.[45] Upon his arrest in October 1910, Kumar was found to be in contact with Das, and "in possession of the addresses of a number of Hindu [i.e., Indian] agitators in America, Africa, Switzerland,

Egypt and France, and also had some notes on the manufacture of nitro-glycerine." The deportation case was decided in his favor, and he stayed on to become "a leader in the agitation against the immigration laws."[46]

Kumar and Sahri also focused (secretly) on recruiting new immigrants as potential anti-British revolutionaries, offering training in the procurement and use of arms and explosives. An association requiring an oath of secrecy for membership was formed in 1911, whose aim was "to establish liberty, equality and fraternity of the Hindustani nation in their relation with the rest of the nations of the world."[47]

The arrests on the pretext of illegal entry were symptoms of the suspicion and surveillance under which the British and Canadian authorities kept the Hindustan Association. In May 1911 the *Vancouver Daily Province* printed a story claiming that the "Vancouver Hindus" had sent thousands of dollars to "plotters in India" for the purchase of rifles. Kumar wrote scathingly to the editor, refuting the headline as slander, but nevertheless closed down the association soon afterward, along with the paper and the house, and left the country to join Taraknath Das in Seattle.[48]

Taraknath Das

Taraknath Das had been recruited to the original Bengali Anusilan Samiti in 1903 and helped to form its Dacca branch in 1905.[49] The following year he took the familiar route through Japan to New York at age twenty-three. After earning a college degree in Seattle, he went to work as an interpreter in the U.S. immigration office in Vancouver. But he was fired in 1908 for his obtrusive habit of exhibiting scathing anti-British opinions.

In April, just before Das's dismissal, the first issue of his eight-page English-language journal *Free Hindustan* had appeared. After two months he relocated printing to Seattle, where the Socialist paper *Western Clarion* provided the use of its press,[50] and then to New York, aided by the press and the comradeship of George Freeman, editor of the Irish-American Fenian Brotherhood's organ *Gaelic American*. In fact, the DCI noted in July 1908 that the first two issues of *Free Hindustan* had arrived enclosed inside a copy of the latter, even before the partnership officially began in August. The new paper was "similar in size and character to the *Indian Sociologist*," and Das, its editor, also happened to be the treasurer of the Vancouver Indian Association. "The subject to which most attention is directed in these two numbers," noted Sir Charles Cleveland, Director of Criminal Intelligence, "is naturally the immigration question and, in addition, the impoverishment of India by England, and a few other grievances are discussed with considerable bitterness."[51]

Like the *Indian Sociologist,* whose tone it echoed, *Free Hindustan* took its masthead motto from Herbert Spencer: "Resistance to Tyranny is Obedience to

God." The paper's claimed purpose was "political education of the masses for revolution." A 1910 issue "advised political work among the Sikh soldiers for an 'organised uprising'";[52] it noted that "considerable numbers [of Sikhs] were settled in Canada and the Western States, and . . . were already much irritated by the Canadian immigration restrictions."[53] The first issue contained an account of a mass meeting of Vancouver Indians outraged by such measures and protesting the threat of deportation. The meeting had sent a cablegram to the Secretary of State for India, Lord Morley, expressing as much. The paper also contained articles accusing Britain's "murderous commercial policy" of wreaking catastrophic famine in India, and compared its "Measures of Oppression" to those of czarist Russia—a comparison the Swadeshi radicals had also made.

In 1908, Das entered a prestigious military school in Norwich, Vermont, but was forbidden to enroll in advanced coursework or to join the Vermont National Guard as most alumni did. Aside from his foreign nationality, his political history also worked against him. Despite his popularity among the students and his "great interest in everything pertaining to military matters," he refused yet again to tone down the hostility to Britain that he had been warned against expressing "on all occasions, appropriate and otherwise."[54] He moved on instead to earn advanced degrees in political science at the Universities of Washington and California, during which period a British Foreign Office Memorandum on Indian revolutionaries abroad identified him as a West Coast "ringleader."[55] (Given his skill in negotiating mainstream American society, he had become something of an advocate and representative of the Indian community.)

In 1910 he helped set up the United India House in Seattle, where he and other Bengali students lectured to gatherings of around twenty-five laborers every Saturday.[56] Das gave frequent lectures to the "students and settlers" on the Pacific coast, mainly on the theme of the economic exploitation of India. In addition to such efforts at public education, Das modeled some of his secret society methods of organization on the Bengali groups, with whom he remained in contact. They were kind enough to pass on their notorious bomb manual, which Das later shared with his San Francisco counterparts when invited down to address a meeting in 1914.[57]

This activity must have eluded the knowledge of the immigration and naturalization authorities, who permitted him to attain U.S. citizenship in 1914. In the 1920s he married a white American woman named Mary Keatinge Morse, a noted women's suffragist and founding member of the NAACP. He later became a professor of political science at Columbia University, and remained prominent in Indian politics in North America until his death in 1958, though his path would diverge from the Ghadarite lineage as he turned toward a more conservative form of nationalism and fell out with the leaders of the reborn Ghadar Party in the early 1920s.

Pandurang Khankhoje

While Kumar and Das were most associated with Vancouver and Seattle, Pandurang Khankhoje could claim much credit for starting up the Indian Independence League in Portland and Astoria, which formed the seed of the Ghadar Party.[58] Khankhoje's inspiration was Tilak, who had first encouraged the young man to seek military training outside of India. Like many others, he too had first tried Japan, but found that the Anglo-Japanese Alliance forbade his study of the "modern methods of warfare" there. He proceeded to California in 1905 and enrolled first in agricultural science at the University of California and then in 1908 at the Tamalpais Military Academy. He hoped to continue his training at West Point but was rebuffed as a non-U.S. citizen; his application for citizenship was also turned down. Nevertheless, he had already learned enough to drastically readjust his thinking on the possibilities of Indian military resistance, as he realized that modern weaponry and chemicals based in advanced technology were not within feasible reach of most Indians, although, says Emily Brown, "he did find the books on discipline, quick action, and secrecy to be of some value."[59]

Early on, he had tried to use his school holidays not only to work—building roads, lumbering, and picking hops, grapes, and strawberries—but to talk with the laborers alongside him about the evils of British rule and encourage them to join the Indian Independence League. As of yet these efforts proved premature, but not for long. After graduation he drifted for a time, looking for work. In Portland he made the significant acquaintance of Pandit Kanshiram, an "old revolutionary and disciple of Sufi Amba Prasad." Kanshiram was now a prosperous lumber-mill owner who often provided financial support to both students and workers. Khankhoje proposed that they start a new Indian Independence League in Portland, "similar to the ones we had in Japan and San Francisco." He recalled: "The sight of so many Indians in one place had inspired me. I had to find some way to organize a movement with the Indian workers in America and spread the word right up to India."[60]

But Kanshiram had reservations, based largely on the persistent mistrust of the workers for the educated youngsters, whom they felt liable to deceive, cheat, or condescend to them. But Khankhoje worked hard to dispel this perception, with Kanshiram's help, gradually earning trust through his integrity and good faith as he made himself "indispensable" when translation, medicine buying, or letter writing was needed. Finally the establishment was successful; though Sohan Singh Bhakna proved a tough nut to crack, as one of the most vocal in reluctance to trust a *babu*. Bhakna worked at the timber factory in Astoria while also serving as the local *granthi* and striving to represent the rights of Indian workers on both sides of the border. As a gesture of good faith Khankhoje proposed Bhakna as founding president, and Kanshiram as treasurer, of what workers would call the Azad-e-Hind (Freedom of India) Party.

As Kanshiram recognized the need to delegate, he assigned Khankhoje to local leadership of the Astoria branch. A Punjabi-owned lumber mill there welcomed him with open arms, thanks to his letters of introduction from Kanshiram and Bhakna, who had now come around to be a staunch ally. Astoria then became the hub of the North American movement and the birthplace of what would become the Ghadar Party. There were also branches of the movement now in Sacramento, San Francisco, and Portland.[61]

Once things seemed to be running smoothly, Khankhoje returned to his studies at the Agricultural College in Corvallis, and later Washington State College, still nursing his dream of "training an army of farmer revolutionaries" and torn as he would be for much of his life between, quite literally, the sword and the plowshare.[62] This conflict is a recurring theme in his biography; as his daughter puts it, "He was now simultaneously engaged in two fields: agriculture and revolution."[63] It was in agriculture that his life's work would be celebrated. Diego Rivera immortalized Khankhoje in a mural for his contribution to the nourishment of the Mexican people through development of special strains of maize, and the Mukta Gram project that he established decades later in independent India, as a model for village self-sufficiency in food production and cottage industries, was inspired by his visit to Booker T. Washington's Tuskegee Institute around 1912. For the moment, however, he used all his spare moments outside of soil and crop genetics research conducting military trainings and touring the region with his old roommate and longtime comrade Bishan Das Kochar, armed with lectures, magic lantern slides, and a cutting-edge cinematograph machine, raising funds and awareness.[64]

Vishnu Ganesh Pingle

Another important figure in this circle was Vishnu Ganesh Pingle, at the time an engineering student at the University of Oregon. He also studied for a time at Berkeley, despite having been initially refused entry; this had, as usual, stimulated further agitations against the immigration laws. After meeting Khankhoje, a like-minded fellow Maharashtrian, Pingle began to neglect his studies and became preoccupied with the prospect of building a revolutionary army. He eventually took on leadership roles in the Portland and Astoria organizations, but his primary interest was Indian national liberation rather than American immigration woes, though the two matters were always linked. Thus, as the Portland group got more enmeshed in legal immigration issues on behalf of both Canada and United States entrants, Pingle was drawn back down to the Ghadarite stronghold of the San Francisco Bay Area, where the concern for national liberation was ascendant.

The Pacific Coast Hindi Association (PCHA)

Thanks to the work of these early activists, the building blocks of the movement were all in place by 1913. At that time, leading organizers, supported by those farmers and agricultural workers whose discontentment was acute, started looking for someone who could consolidate the existing nodes of activity, unite the students and the workers, channel the pervasive and building unrest, and beef up the political content of cultural and social reform projects. This person turned out to be Har Dayal.

Accounts vary as to who actually suggested that Har Dayal take the helm of a unified organization of the West Coast Indian community.[65] It may have been Thakur Das, who had been active for some years in Iran under the name of Ghulam Hussain, working with Ajit Singh—himself an initial suggestion for California leadership—and Sufi Amba Prasad. Hussain/Das had then worked among Cama and Rana's Paris circle until they sent him to Portland in 1912 as "a skilled agitator . . . with a specific mission to stir up disaffection among the Sikhs."[66] Initially Har Dayal asked if this mission could wait; his schedule was booked with activities in San Francisco progressive circles, including projects such as his Radical Club, the utopian Fraternity of the Red Flag, and the IWW branch secretaryship.[67] All this was soon to change, however.

There had already been a series of meetings in the Pacific Northwest throughout the spring of 1913 (the largest attended by 120 workers) by the time Har Dayal arrived for the fateful gathering in Astoria in early June.[68] Also present were Hussain/Das, Sohan Singh Bhakna, Ram Chandra, Kanshi Ram, and Nawab Khan. "Two electric tram cars and two motor cars are said to have been hired for the occasion," reported Isemonger and Slattery, "and the cars were decorated with placards bearing the words 'India' and 'Freedom.' Har Dayal was hailed with the words 'Bande Mataram,' but declined to be garlanded."[69]

Reconfirming the leadership of Khankhoje's group, Sohan Singh Bhakna was elected president and Kanshiram treasurer.[70] Har Dayal was named secretary. Now all the main components of the organizational infrastructure were in place, under the new name of the Pacific Coast Hindi Association (PCHA). In addition to a committee for collecting funds and a fifteen-member working committee (soon swelling to twenty-four) of annually elected representatives of local branches, there would be a general association comprising representatives from all the local communities up and down the coast, including both students and workers. The group then selected San Francisco as the publishing and propaganda hub because that was where Har Dayal's influence was strongest.[71]

Nawab Khan provided a lengthy transcription of Har Dayal's speech: "You have come to America and seen with your own eyes the prosperity of this country. What is the cause of this prosperity? Why nothing more than this, that

America is ruled by its own people. In India, on the other hand, the people have no voice in the administration of the country." Deploring the situation in which a rich agricultural land was wracked by famine as its crops were exported, he urged his audience: "Desist . . . from your petty religious dissensions and turn your thoughts toward the salvation of your country. What you earn, earn for your country. What work you do, do it for your country. . . . Collect money and get the youth educated in America in order that they may become equipped to serve. . . . Prepare now to sacrifice yourselves."[72] He then rhetorically reframed their immigrant status as an explicit function of Indian liberation. It was useless to keep struggling for American civil rights without the backing of an independent government, he said, arguing that "as long as the Indians remained in subjection to the British they would not be treated as equals by Americans or any other nation."[73]

Ghadar was the fruit of a very particular synthesis: of populations, of issues, of contextual frames, and of ideological elements. It is precisely the richness of this combination that enabled it to play the role of missing link in the genealogy of Indian radicalism, and of medium of translation among coexisting movement discourses. Still, to a degree unprecedented within the revolutionary movement abroad, Ghadar was overwhelmingly a workers' movement, in which, moreover, the line between workers and intellectuals had become rather smudged. The impact of racial discrimination and its crucial intersection with class cannot be underestimated as a catalyst for the radicalization of South Asians in North America. Yet only when this frame was overlaid on the geopolitical reality of India's colonized status would American discontent transmute into Indian mutiny.

2
___

Our Name Is Our Work

The Syndicalist Ghadar

RADICALS

Almost immediately the Ghadar propaganda tours hit the fields. Kartar Singh Sarabha was particularly inspired in generating publicity, said Behari Lal, arranging meetings such as the one in Yolo that he describes here: "A good number" of farm workers gathered around, sitting on the ground around him and his kinsman. "They sat quietly and I said a few things. Then Har Dayal talked about the position of the Indian people in India and abroad, the need of independence." Unresponsive silence met his finish. But after a few minutes, "one or two men came forward awkwardly, saluted Har Dayal with reverence and placed a few dollar bills before him, as they used to do when offering their contributions in a temple."[1] Within a half an hour, they had collected a few hundred dollars in cash and checks. Har Dayal refused to take the money himself, insisting instead that it should be entrusted to a fully transparent and accountable committee. This went over brilliantly, setting him apart from "the other Babus," whom Sohan Singh Bhakna had accused of cheating his constituency of hard-earned money under the guise of doing patriotic work.

An informant known as C later described the whirlwind West Coast "missionary tour" to his British handlers as follows:

Ram Chandra, Gobind Behari Lal, and others go out to the ranches, where poor labourers are working, on Saturdays and Sundays; they preach revolution to them until these poor and illiterate people think they must drive the English out of India or kill them. It becomes a fixed idea with them. The revolutionary songs which they sing have been committed to memory, and they sing them with great fervour. They do not know the meaning of what they are singing [!], but they almost treat it as a religion. Ram Chandra and the others who visit the ranches tell these people that the British are ruining them, and keeping them poor. The great danger lies among these poor people in America. The ordinary educated man soon commits himself and is arrested, but the labourer merely goes back to India and commences to sing these revolutionary songs in his native village, and in this way spreads the movement in India.[2]

The British ambassador to the United States, Sir Cecil Spring-Rice, commented after the mutiny attempt: "The truth of these statements is abundantly illustrated by the long list of returned emigrants of the coolie class which figures in India judgments."[3] Aside from the astounding level of contempt with which Spring-Rice assumed that the Indian laborers, being poor and illiterate, could have had no understanding of the very matter that so inflamed them—as if their very enthusiasm was proof of naïveté, rather than conviction!—and that any catalyzing or leadership roles would have had to come from the educated elite, nevertheless he was plainly identifying the Ghadar mobilization as a class-based mass movement of racialized, low-wage migrant laborers—in a word, "coolies."

The Ghadar Party

Building on the summer of touring, a November meeting in San Francisco consolidated and extended the PCHA infrastructure set forth in Astoria six months before. This time two new vice presidents, and two more organizing secretaries were elected, plus three coordinators—Kartar Singh Sarabha, Harnam Singh Tundilat, and Jagat Ram—assigned to "secret and political work."[4] Bhai Parmanand made a proposal to institute scholarships, according to the logic that a free India once attained would require educated people. Har Dayal agreed, but some of the workers took offense. Bhakna and Tundilat made an alternate suggestion to prioritize "direct and effective" propaganda to the ripe constituency of Jat yeoman in their own language.[5] This would be the *Ghadar*.

In his autobiography Bhakna identified the opening of the Yugantar Ashram in San Francisco and the activities based there as the real start of what can really be called the Ghadar movement.[6] But the claim to the name was and is still contested: who were the real Ghadarites? Har Dayal's use of the word in the first issue of the paper referred expansively to all of India's patriotic revolutionaries to date, encompassing all the Bengalis, all the Punjabis, and the activists in the London and Paris circles.[7] Yet at the same time he was stressing the need to form a party in the more specific sense: this would be comprised of the dedicated inner core of students and organic intellectuals who lived and worked at the Yugantar Ashram and put out the paper. It is perceptible from the account of Darisi Chenchiah, one of the Berkeley students, that class snobbery may have been difficult to eradicate completely, despite the Ashram's egalitarian ideals. At the time, he and the other students saw themselves, despite the presence of such crucial planners as Sarabha and Tundilat, as the real brains of the operation, while portraying the equally committed Sikh workers largely as the muscle and the moneybags.

Meanwhile the PCHA officers and members of the Working Committee, consisting mostly of farmworkers along with a few big contractors or independent farmers, also considered themselves to be the true Ghadar Party. Both nuclei were making decisions and doing work on the ground, thereby leaving the door open from the start for a parallel leadership situation, and thus for confusion and potential conflict. For example, when Har Dayal left, some seemed to be under the impression that Santokh Singh was his designated successor, and others that Ram Chandra was. This may have reflected a tension between Hindu/intellectual- and Sikh/worker-dominated sectors, and historical narratives. However, setting these two groups up as polarities misses the point that the movement emerged, and could only have emerged as it did, from the synthesis between the two.

The Yugantar Ashram

As usual, Kartar Singh illustrated the ideal: folklorist Ved Prakash Vatuk described the youthful chemistry student at Berkeley, fresh off the boat in 1913, as being "at ease in the company of peasants as well as among intellectuals," and embodying the link between them. He worked as hard in the fields as at his engineering and aviation studies, or as at the *Ghadar* office, where he wrote articles and poems as well as running the printing press.

In the introductory *Ghadar*, Har Dayal declared of the new party headquarters: "This is not an Ashram but a fort from which a Cannonade on the English raj will be started."[8] It also offered a kind of home to many who were far from theirs, which, according to Gobind Behari Lal, "a great many laborers and Hindus migratory in the United States and in Canada . . . generally use . . . as an address so that they can get their mail."[9]

As Har Dayal conceived it, at the nucleus of the movement would be a disciplined, secretive, and exclusive group based at the Ashram and structured similarly to London's Abhinava Bharat, which had drawn its recruits from the larger and more public-faced Free India Society. He also drew upon some of the rules used by the secret societies of Calcutta and London. To join, an activist had to be recommended by two members of the *Ghadar* staff; to be taken into confidence on important decisions he had to have worked at the Ashram for six months. Telling secrets or misappropriating funds could get him killed. Insiders used cipher codes for exchanging messages, and only the secretary or editor was authorized to open the mail. Cellular propagation was encouraged: "Let us form a secret society of those who prefer death and make the foundation firm by opening branches elsewhere."[10] Within a few months, membership had swelled to five thousand, with seventy-two North American branches, including Berkeley, Portland, Astoria, St. John, Sacramento, Stockton, and Bridal Veil.[11] Among them organization was relatively informal, sans official hierarchy but with active leaders selected by consultation among core participants. Division of labor, too, seemed to emerge more or less spontaneously.[12]

Though not their only activity, the most time-consuming and resource-intensive must have been the newspaper. And if there is anything available to us by which to anchor the identity and principles of a sprawling and slippery formation, it is the body of publications produced by the Hindustan Ghadar Press. Soon after the Astoria meeting, Kartar Singh, Harnam Singh, and others entered into discussion with Har Dayal as to what sort of paper they should produce. He "insisted on a straight fighting newspaper—which will be carrying forward the revolutionary nationalist work which had been started in London, Paris, Calcutta, other Indian cities, but had been almost entirely suppressed by the British."[13]

The first number was dated 1 November 1913. It came out in an Urdu print run of six thousand, with a comparable Gurmukhi edition starting a month later, and a smaller Gujarati edition in May 1914.[14] Behari Lal said that in accordance with the custom of Indian nationalist journalism of the time, only Har Dayal's name appeared as editor-publisher, for security reasons. As in India, "when the authorities eventually put him away in jail, another stepped forward—just ONE MORE. . . . The succession was to be maintained . . . one by one."[15] Nevertheless, Har Dayal was adamant that "no man was ever to usurp all power, all responsibility," and that although "the Editor was to be at the front, facing the public, and the opponents, . . . he must deal on terms of democratic, constitutional equality with the men of the Council."[16]

The writing, translating, lettering, and printing were a true collective effort. About twenty-five volunteers lived and worked full-time at the Ashram in exchange for food, clothing, and "two dollars a month pocket money,"[17] while everybody else available on the premises chipped in. According to Vatuk (who may be harboring a romantic bias, though since the core Ghadar workers were themselves consumed with this kind of idealism, maybe it isn't inappropriate), "People lived there in a democratic way in a life style based on equality and devoid of any casteism, racism, religious bigotry and sectarianism of any kind. All who lived there were just Indian. They cooked, ate, and lived together like a family. They were the followers of one path."[18] This is quite a telling statement; however, rather than limiting the significance of the observation that they were all "just Indian" to nationalism per se, I find the inference of egalitarian participatory democracy equally suggestive. Moreover, this prefigurative practice implies that they were more clearly conscious of what their desired postrevolutionary society should look like than the Ghadar movement is often given credit for.

Important staffers among this utopian family included Ram Chandra, Amar Singh,[19] Kartar Singh, Munshi Ram, and Hari Singh Usman.[20] Godha Ram Channon was the chief Urdu calligrapher, among other tasks. Behari Lal described his good friend as a quiet man who never pushed himself forward but "served with devotion" throughout the editorial regimes of both Har Dayal and Ram Chandra, and on into the 1920s incarnation. Behari Lal himself was kept busy as main liaison to the Anglophone world, in charge of maintaining contacts with the network of Bay Area intellectuals who regarded him as "Har Dayal's younger brother . . . a Horatio to that Hamlet." For their benefit he wrote pieces in English in addition to those he was contributing to the *Ghadar* almost daily. It became "a matter of principle" for him to write Urdu and Hindi articles on history and natural and social science, passing on the content of his own postgraduate studies at the University of California to those who would otherwise have no access to such information. To that end, he said: "I gave my books to the growing Gadar Office library. Now and then I would discuss for hours some new scientific or historical or ethical concepts with the boys."[21]

The Ghadar

The paper's purpose, in a nutshell, was stated in the first issue: "It conveys the message of a rebellion to the nation once a week. It is brave, outspoken, unbridled, soft footed and given to the use of strong language. It is lightning, a storm and a flame of fire. . . . We are the harbinger of freedom." It was also, according to the masthead, the "Enemy of the British Race."[22] The lead article, "Our Name and Our Work," declared the two to be identical: in a word, mutiny. A rising would be inevitable within perhaps a decade, and in the meantime all must prepare for it.

The paper's task, the editor continued, would be to nurture the mental and spiritual growth necessary to future mutineers, offering the right type of nourishment and edification to "purg[e] the soul of avarice, greed, pride, fear and ignorance" while exhorting young men to embrace the ideals of sacrifice, revenge, and unity in taking action. Recalling the stages of "Hardayalism," this was the first stage of moral preparation. But stage two was coming soon, at which "rifle and blood will be used for pen and ink."[23] (Yet at the same time, the editor noted, in the pages of the *Ghadar* "the pen has done the work of a cannon, shaken the foundation of the tyrannous government.")[24] In accordance with Sohan Singh Bhakna's earlier advice, Har Dayal extolled the value of vernacular materials in movement building among the people and (although the label fit much of the staff) accused English-educated Indians of selfish hypocrisy: "No movement can grow strong till books, pamphlets and newspapers written in easy vernacular are brought out. No great work has ever been accomplished with the aid of a foreign tongue."[25]

Har Dayal's introductory editorial stressed the need for an accurate understanding of politics and the science of political economy. Indian youth should be sent to military schools or to "schools of other nations to learn how to govern" and to root out spies and traitors, all in order to hasten the coming mutiny. He made sure to associate the present movement in the minds of readers, allies and foes, with all the revolutionists that had come before, in 1857 and 1905, and in a subsequent issue yet again compared the work of the Bengali militants to the Russians who had been enforcing justice against "bad officers" since 1881. He invoked the names of Ajit Singh, Lajpat Rai, Tilak, Hemchandra Das Kanungo, Aurobindo, Sufi Amba Parishad, Krishnavarma, and Cama, of whose august company now "a band of the same army has arrived in America." California offered to them "a second free Punjab where they can talk openly to their brothers."[26] Har Dayal seamlessly and cumulatively melded the casts of both revolutionary streams.[27]

A typical weekly issue might contain accounts of past and present revolutionary actions, often featuring appeals or references to the other nationalist groups within the British Empire, namely, those in Ireland and Egypt; or other groups recently and currently involved in struggles against autocratic or imperial rule, such as those in Russia, China, and Mexico. One might also find biographical sketches of independence fighters of India, Ireland, Italy, Poland, or even colonial America, such as that renowned anti-British guerrilla fighter George Washington. Other edifying historical examples ranged from episodes of the French Revolution to services rendered by the likes of William Tell or Lafayette against foreign domination and for the principle of freedom, to even the unification of Germany.[28] There was a special edition of *Rusi Bagion ke Dastaanen* (Stories of Russian Revolutionaries),[29] praising the faithful toils, daring exploits, stirring statements, abscondments from oppressive marriages, prison stints, prison breaks, and martyrdoms of radicals such as Vera Figner, Leo Deutsch, and Vera Zasulich.

There was much praise of the Bengali movement for keeping the government in a state of anxiety, and of course frequent invocation of the Mutiny of 1857 ("the old Gadar"), including serialized installments from Vinayak Damodar Savarkar's book on the Mutiny of 1857. Following the practice of the London India House group, these were read out at public meetings, and a special anniversary issue came out annually on 10 May, featuring the Rani of Jhansi's image on the cover.[30] Special issues commemorating such landmarks as 1857 or the Hardinge bomb of 1912 were printed on red or yellow paper, making visual the text's exhortations to don the saffron of the patriot, martyr, and warrior.[31]

The *Ghadar* also printed meeting notices and accounts of proceedings, such as an important gathering described in the 6 January 1914 issue, held in Sacramento on 31 December 1913. Here, according to quite another sort of description, courtesy of the ubiquitous intelligence agents, "poems were read and violent seditious speeches delivered, the point of which was emphasized by lantern slides. Portraits of famous seditionists and murderers and revolutionary mottoes were displayed on the screen."[32] The now-familiar gallery included Mazzini, William Tell, Lenin, and Sun Yat-sen; 1857 heroes Nanasahib Peshwa, Tatya Tope, and Lakshmi Bai; and Swadeshi-era revolutionists Khudiram Bose, Kanailal Dutta, and the Maharashtrian Chapekar.[33] This pantheon was always expanding: there was a notice in the 13 December 1916 issue kindly requesting "from 1857 to date, photos of all the martyrs . . . from those brethren having them," and noting: "Some of the Punjab martyrs' photos have reached the Gadar. Photos of the Bengal and Madras martyrs are wanting." The Ghadar office planned to reproduce and distribute thousands of copies and asked: "Those brethren who wish to hang them in their houses, will please let the Gadar know by postcard. This is most necessary."[34] After an announcement that Har Dayal and Ram Chandra were to preach in upcoming issues on the nature of patriotism,[35] Kartar Singh led them all in song: the chorus was, more or less, "Come, let's go, join us in the battle for freedom."

Then there were news articles on current and relevant legal, political, or economic matters, especially regarding immigration or nationalism. Updates were requested from all towns, villages, districts, and departments, on recent dacoities and political killings, as well as on any acts of British government tyranny or police abuses.[36] One much-circulated item was titled "Angrezi Raj ka Kacha Chittha" (Balance Sheet of British Rule),[37] which, with "Ankon ki Gawahi" (Evidence of Statistics),[38] collated damning numbers that more or less echoed Dadabhai Naoroji's economic drain theory: how much money was removed by British taxation, how much was spent on the army, how much on education, how much grain produced, how many lost to famine or treatable disease, and so forth. In this, in Behari Lal's words, "For the first time the readers received the kind of information which they had never before been given—a revelation that shook them to their very depths";[39] and at the same time they were provided a stock of facts and figures in which to frame grievances credibly to those who might previously have dismissed them. Among the damning legacies of colonial rule were the following: land tax over 65 percent of net produce; army expenditure (29.5 crore) over four times the amount dedicated to the education of 240 million people; 20 million dead of famine in the last ten years; 8 million dead of plague in the last thirty years, and rising; intercommunal strife instigated; arts and crafts industries destroyed; money and lives sacrificed to the conquest of China, Afghanistan, Burma, Egypt, and Persia.[40]

The Ghadar Press also put out various individual pamphlets and leaflets both in English and in Indian languages. Some of these reprinted previous articles, such as "Zulm! Zulm! Gore Shahi Zulm!" (Tyranny! Tyranny! The Tyranny of White Rule),[41] which was first printed on the occasion of Bhagwan Singh's deportation in 1913; William Jennings Bryan's scathing indictment entitled "British Rule in India";[42] and Har Dayal's "Nayen Zamane ke Nayen Adarsh" (New Ideals for a New Age), which decried benighted social and religious causes that distracted from the struggle for freedom and equality,[43] "Social Conquest of the Hindu Race," which pointed toward what we now might call hegemony as well as domination, and "Barabari da Arth" (The Meaning of Equality).[44]

Overall the movement revealed in the Yugantar Ashram publications with a romanticist emotional intensity was militant, insurrectionist, patriotic, internationalist, modernist, secularist and antisectarian, and egalitarian, favoring politically federated democratic-republicanism, while leaning ever more toward socialist redistributive economics—two factors that can be seen as the strongest expressions of their two beloved guiding principles, liberty and equality. But at this point tyranny and exploitation were still being framed in primarily moral terms, awaiting a more scientific restatement in the 1920s.

The Ghadar Press also produced a different and very popular (and populist) literary corpus: a series of poetry collections called *Ghadar-di-Gunj* (Echoes of Revolt).[45] The first edition came out in booklet form in April 1914. Unlike the editorials, essays, and reportage that appeared in the weekly, the poetry was primarily the work of the farm laborers. These Punjabi couplets were equally explicit in their indictments of British rule and their exhortations to prepare rebellion (and explanations of how to do it) and plainly well aware of the implications of colonial economics.[46]

It may seem remarkable, commented Vatuk, that a print medium should become the glue and fuel of a massive movement of which only a small minority of the initial membership was literate. This was possible because of a thriving oral culture in which it could be read aloud and shared, and the songs and poems of *Ghadar-di-Gunj* were memorized and sung at gatherings.[47] Inder Singh, *granthi* at the Stockton *gurdwara,* formerly of Hong Kong, even "learnt by heart most of the poems . . . and prepared a cypher system into which he transcribed [them]."[48]

Darisi Chenchiah recalled that as "intellectuals arose" from among "the Punjabee labourers," they began to contribute articles and poems to the newspaper and to address public meetings. "They were sincere and brave," though until quite recently "ignorant and illiterate." But now they had "suddenly become politically conscious, highly patriotic and intensely revolutionary. As a result, the Ghadar movement passed rapidly into the hands of these masses."[49] As a leader Har Dayal evinced great confidence in their potential as revolutionary fighters; this may be why they liked him as well. Moreover, while he may have been a professional intellectual, he was a Punjabi nonetheless. Har Dayal happily supported and encouraged their vernacular contributions, Chenchiah continued, even when they contained mistakes or "abusive words," precisely because they were—to use an anachronistic term—organic.

Some translated excerpts courtesy of Gerald Barrier powerfully express the themes of sectarian and ethnic unity, courage and sacrifice, and redemption through taking responsibility for the plight of the country, all the while exhibiting a global perspective and a social vision linking personal and collective transformation. While addressed to the lionhearted Singhs, these poems also showed broad awareness of issues and allusions relevant to Hindus and Muslims.[50]

The very first poem of the first collection set the tone:

> The world calls us coolie.
> Why doesn't our flag fly anywhere?
> . . . .
> How shall we survive, are we slaves forever?
> Why aren't we involved in politics?
> . . . .
> From the beginning we have been yoked to thralldom.
> Why don't we even dream of freedom?
> Only a handful of oppressors have taken our fields.
> Why has no Indian cultivator risen and protected his land?
> Our children cry out for want of education.
> Why don't we open science colleges?[51]

Poem 6 called for unity as the veterans of foreign battles turned their attention homeward:

> Why do you sit silent in your own country
> You who make so much noise in foreign lands?
> Noise outside of India is of little avail.
> Pay attention to activities within India.
> . . . .
> You are quarreling and Hindu-Muslim conflict is prevalent.
> The jewel of India is rotting in the earth
> Because you are fighting over the Vedas and the Koran. [Does this imply
>   Sikhs were above sectional strife?]
> Go and speak with soldiers.
> Ask them why they are asleep, men who once held swords.
> Muslims, Pathans, Dogras and Sikh heroes should join together.
> The power of the oppressors is nothing if we unitedly attack him.
> Indians have been the victors in the battlefields
> of Burma, Egypt, China and the Sudan.[52]

Poem 8 interpreted faith as a call for social justice and reproachfully invoked the Sikhs' historical role in the first mutiny:

> The Gurus founded this Path for the welfare of others.
> Otherwise what was the need?
> Open your eyes and look at the world. . . .
> People say the Singhs are cruel and insensitive.

Why did they turn the tide during the Delhi Mutiny?
The country would have enjoyed freedom.
How and why did they commit this blunder?[53]

Poem 11, after touching on the same themes of Sikh history, martyrdom, and sacrifice, called on the Singhs to avenge Bhagwan Singh, put in a cage; to think of Ajit Singh, Cama, and Krishnavarma in France; of Gandhi (is this the first mention of him?) rotting in jail for the injustice of Africa; and of Muhammed Barakatullah in Japan, for "he has complete faith in god alone."[54]

Song 17 was a striking reflection juxtaposing tactical guidelines with the ethical, psychological growth of the revolutionary needed in the process of creating a new society:

We have tired of just observing; let us work out a program for doing something.
We should make cowards lions before acting; convert men who have said "sir, sir" for ages.
We should be cautious lest on a rapid ascent we fall down.
We should first memorize the alphabet, then learn mathematics.
We should first handle fire and pistols. Then we will not be afraid of guns and rifles.
We should develop brotherly love so that we cannot be divided.
The enemy is initially the traitor within;
We shall deal with the whites after we teach the unfaithful a lesson. . . .
If they are willing to be treated like gentlemen, we shall plead with them.
If they do not come to terms through dialogue, then we must consider other ways to make them understand. . . .
You must meet the traitors in the way they deserve, with full force.
In this way you should unite and form a branch of the Ghadar party.
Then we shall send some brave persons to India. . . .
They will organize secret societies.
Some branches should be left in foreign lands, branches with deep roots.
We can then commit dacoities on the government
And in this way awaken the Punjab and the whole country.
At some places we should use guerrilla warfare and adopt the methods that best suit us.[55]

This was the source of the movement's global influence, cementing its stature as a broad movement rather than as a localized party. As it spread abroad, the global "branches" functioned in an autonomous and self-organized way, not subject to the central authority or direct guidance of San Francisco. But the paper that issued forth from that source was nevertheless a tangible guide and inspiration. The Ghadarite ideas "spread like wildfire in foreign countries where there are Indians," said Chenchiah. "Even the individualist terrorist movement in Bengal paled into insignificance in the face of this mighty mass movement in the estimation of the British Rulers."

One might map the diaspora by the *Ghadar*'s path: by June 1914 Yugantar Ashram publications had been spotted in Egypt, South Africa, Fiji, Canada, British East Africa, and British Guiana. Ghadar organizers were reported to be active on the ground in the Philippines, Hong Kong, Thailand, Burma, the Dutch East Indies, Mexico, Panama, and Brazil.[56] In January 1915 the paper was intercepted in Trinidad, Sudan, and Aden; in March, Morocco, Manila, Siam, and Java; in April, Madagascar and Reunion; June, Canton; and July, Johannesburg and Nairobi, Fiji, and Australia. To this list F. C. Isemonger and James Slattery added Japan, Shanghai, Hankow, Tientsin, Singapore, the Malay States, Trinidad, and Honduras. It reached, "in fact, to every place where Indians were known to be residing," and was often re-posted from these places to India.[57]

The first copies arrived in India on 7 December 1913. Despite instant proscription and heightened interception efforts through the Sea Customs Act, hundreds of copies trickled into the country in the next few months via Shanghai, Hong Kong, and Bombay. Often the shipments were divided into small parts and "contained in ordinary envelopes, addressed by hand and having the appearance of private letters." Some contained personal messages on "small slips of paper instructing the recipients to read the paper to others or to pass it on."[58]

The writer of one such letter began by exhorting fellow Sikhs not to stand for the whites' expropriation of the Golden Temple and Khalsa College back home—a foreshadowing for the returned Ghadarites who flowed into and radicalized the Babar Akali mobilizations in the 1920s. He then proceeded to convey his New World perspective: "Now I will write about this country and what we see with our own eyes. The country belonged formerly to the Canadians but the English conquered it four hundred years ago. The original inhabitants now are not allowed to walk in the streets and they go about the country like wandering tribes. They do not possess an inch of land but subsist by fishing on the sea. In our country there is no sea. What shall we do?"[59]

It is quite striking that he draws an implicit analogy between the plight of indigenous Canadians and his own Punjabi people, who nevertheless from one sentence to the next seem to have grown less landlocked: "This pride in the Feringhis will uproot us and throw us into salt sea water, and no trace of the name Bharat will be left"; then, "Sikhs, Hindus and Muhammadans all will be treated alike. Brother, the means of salvation is this. Educate all your children, boys and girls. Hindus, Muhammadans and Sikhs must cultivate love among themselves and then the work will gradually be accomplished. Read to all what I have written and also the paper I am sending. The paper may be read by anybody, but do not give the letter to anyone. Burn it after you have gone through it yourself and read it to others. The paper may be read by anyone; there is nothing to fear on that account as the paper is printed in America and the English cannot stop it."[60]

Another letter, this time sans newspaper, was written from a Sikh in California to a soldier in the Eighty-second Punjabis at Nowshera: "At first there were about ten thousand of our countrymen here but now only about six thousand remain. The English no longer require us and have stopped our migration here. These badmashes have plundered us and we shall not escape disgrace unless we get out of their hands. . . . All Indians living in America and Canada are prepared to kill and die. No one wishes to see these evil Englishmen. . . . It is written that it is far better for the community which loses its sacred places to die. . . . The only remedy against these tyrants is that the troops should mutiny." The writer then repeats some of the facts contained in *Balance Sheet of British Rule* concerning economic drain and plague. As with the first letter, the writer's concern for the control of Sikh sacred places by foreigners points the way toward the Akali Dal.

The writer concludes: "All these facts which I have written have been copied from a paper called Ghadr, which is printed in America. I intended to send you the paper in original, but as its entry into India is prohibited I have written these few things in this letter. . . . You should write to me what is going on in India at the present time. . . . Do not let the white men know what I have written. Remember, lest you get into trouble; but understand and inform your friends."[61]

It is easy to forget in the homosocial environment of work, study, and political organizing abroad, that some of these men still had wives and children in India—the restriction on whose immigration to North America had been a sharp goad to early discontent. Among the intercepted messages was one from a husband to a valiant wife: "Times are hard, very hard; there is no certainty of life. Here I hope the war with Englishmen is beginning and that in a short time there will be a great mutiny. The tyrants are ruling over us. We are justified in killing. We shall see the sword and gun in our hands and pressing forward we shall kill and die. . . . We shall meet if we survive. Is there any disturbance about the Government in India? Write about this. Receive *Fateh* like a brave woman. Pain comes first, but is followed by comfort. Do not despair, for the days of your comfort are drawing near."[62]

The Action Committee

Next to the propaganda corps helmed by Har Dayal, the second-most important committee among the Yugantar Ashram inner circle was focused on militant action and directed by Pandurang Khankhoje, in collaboration with Vishnu Ganesh Pingle and Harnam Singh Tundilat.[63] While Har Dayal's *pracharak* (propaganda) project depended by definition on broadcasting its message as loud and far as possible, the *praharak* (action) branch depended upon secrecy. Khankhoje was adamant on this point, wary of the danger of infiltration from British intelligence, and not without good reason, as it happened. So although he recalled in his memoir that there was no lack of "young freedom lovers" willing to "fight and die for the revolution," he still maintained strict screening procedures. Even once enrolled, the workers often did not know what was going on beyond their own tasks. (Sadly, it would seem that as the mutiny preparations got under way, not everyone was up to Khankhoje's disciplined security standards.)

The action committee derived a great deal of tactical inspiration not only from the previous Indian extremists but from Sun Yat-sen's republican nationalists, who had recently effected a successful Chinese revolution from abroad in 1911, just as the Indians wanted to do. This had even included an "assault force" of Chinese militants launched from San Francisco.[64] Har Dayal had already been in communication with Sun when he was in Hawaii, and Sun's son, as it happened, was a contemporary of Chenchiah's at the University of California. Chenchiah met with his classmate's illustrious parent in Tokyo in 1912; Dr. Sun encouraged the Ghadarites' enterprise of overthrowing British rule and offered them the benefits of his party's experience. Though the leader of the San Francisco expedition, renegade American Homer Lea, had recently died, Emily Brown speculates that some of his veterans or confederates may have been available in San Francisco to speak with Khankhoje and his Ghadar action squad.[65] Khankhoje had been in the habit of visiting Chinatown during his period at Tamalpais, with a Chinese classmate who was one of Sun's veterans. There, says Savitri Sawhney, "he had many discussions with the Chinese about India's independence and his own aspirations. . . . The idea that Chinese and Indians could join in their quest for freedom and help each other fulfill their mutual goals was never far from his mind. He had developed a tremendous rapport with the Chinese whom he admired for their tenacity and grit. Some years later, after the inception of the Ghadar, this was to translate into a more meaningful exchange of ideas." Sawhney comments further: "It was only natural that the cadets in the academy—particularly the Chinese, the Mexicans and the Irish—with insurrection on their minds would meet and discuss problems common to their countries." Khankhoje also drew inspiration from the Mexican revolutionaries, who were never far from his awareness; he had friends among the Zapatista patriots who joined the Yaqui rebellion in southern California, and hoped they might help train the (Asian) Indians in "practical warfare."[66]

The plan the Chinese recommended was to start by cutting communications and telegraph lines, disrupting railways, and then destroying police outposts and military camps. When all of that was under way, they should proceed to establish revolutionary bases in the jungles, hills, valleys, and border regions, from which to harass British administrative and military functioning. They should get weapons and ammunition by raiding armories and military encampments; they couldn't buy them. This, recalled Khankhoje, was exactly how they began to mobilize. (It seems the basic blueprint of guerrilla insurrection has remained unchanged for a hundred years!)[67] But once in motion, events quickly got away from such a neat, efficient plan.

Har Dayal's arrest came only a few months after the launch of the paper, on 25 March 1914. He fled the country not long afterward. Although he continued sending incendiary articles back for publication—notably, "Do Cheezon ke zarurat hai . . . Ghadar aur banduqen" (Two Things Are Necessary: Ghadar and Guns) and "O Soldiers of the Ghadr! O Stars of the Eyes of India!" (which appeared 14 July 1914)—and played a role in the Berlin India Committee's work in Europe and the Ottoman realm, this was the end of his functional involvement in the North American organization. Yet belying the notion that the movement's radicalism went no deeper than Har Dayal's idiosyncrasies, Isemonger and Slattery took note that far from dampening the Yugantar Ashram's work, his departure actually seemed to give "fresh incentive to the revolutionary movement."[68] The "Big Three" triumvirate of Ram Chandra, Bhagwan Singh, and Mohammed Barakatullah stepped into the momentary leadership gap, taking on the duties of the endless round of motivational tours, editing the paper, and handling finances and ashram affairs. One matter that shortly required their urgent attention was the *Komagata Maru*.

The *Komagata Maru* Incident

The *Komagata Maru* incident is one of the most amply documented episodes in the history of South Asian immigration to North America.[69] The facts in brief are these: in May 1908 the government of India had discreetly authorized the Canadian government to take the necessary steps to defend the whiteness of its shores without being too obvious in "express discrimination against British Indians."[70] The governor-general announced the continuous journey stipulation (that only those who had sailed directly from their port of departure would be allowed to enter, which disqualified every voyage originating in India) and a prohibitive entry fee of $200 a head. British authorities (including then viceroy Lord Minto) expressed their appreciation for the subtle elegance of this solution, keeping out Indians without needing to be clumsily direct in acknowledging the awkward two-tiered status of the dominions separating the white-settler colonies of Canada and Australia from His Majesty's Asian and African possessions.

In April 1914, Gurdit Singh, a prosperous Singapore-based labor-transport contractor, chartered a ship to take a load of passengers to Canada from among the hundreds of his compatriots then awaiting passage in Hong Kong and other East Asian ports. Besides being a deliberate challenge to the statutes, it was also an act of altruistic self-interest, serving the community while also benefiting his own future shipping interest. After stops in Shanghai, Kobe, and Yokohama, the total manifest included 376 passengers, the majority adult male Sikhs, except for twenty-one Muslims.

When they reached Vancouver on 23 May 1914, however, they were refused entry. As they waited at anchor for weeks, provisions on the ship ran low and tempers ran high. A shore committee was formed consisting of Balwant Singh, Husain Rahim, and Sohan Lal Pathak; a support meeting in Vancouver in July was attended by "some 400 Indians and 150 white men. The latter were mainly socialists."[71] This was attributed to the fact that Husain Rahim, then editor of the *Hindustani*,[72] was also the secretary of the local Socialist organization, one of whose more "rabid" members now "advised the Indians to return to India, raise the standard of revolution and become masters of their own country."[73]

Despite the efforts of the shore committee, the climax of the standoff was an attempt to forcibly transfer the passengers to another liner to be sent back. While a militia guarded the food stores on the wharf, which were to be loaded onto the new ship, a tugboat approached, bearing 120 police along with the chief and four inspectors, plus forty special immigration officials. Among them was the hated William C. Hopkinson, at whom the defenders of the ship were aiming particular wrath. The *Komagata Maru* passengers took over their ship and beat off the approaching vessel, outmatching its grappling hooks and water hose by throwing coal, bricks, scrap metal, and concrete. They had armed themselves with stoking irons, axes, swords, lathis, clubs, and even some spears handmade on shipboard. (We are reminded that many of them were, after all, "battle-seasoned veterans" of the British army.)[74] The wounded tug and three picketboats patrolled the harbor around them until a Canadian naval cruiser (one half of the national fleet at the time) came to support them, with orders to seize the ship. This time the furious passengers threatened to hold immigration official Malcolm Reid hostage until food and water were supplied to them for the return journey by the same vessel on which they had come. Eventually the Minister of Agriculture from Ottawa managed to talk them down to a tense compromise, agreeing that if the Indians relinquished control of the ship to its Japanese captain they might return across the Pacific in peace with full provisions.

On 23 July 1914, two months after arriving, they were escorted from the harbor by a cordon of navy vessels and an armed battle cruiser.[75] But Hopkinson, bespoke spy for the West Coast "Hindus," had been warning authorities that the *Komagata Maru* passengers' stiff resistance was being instigated by "a conspiracy headed by educated Indians living in the U.S." This was something of an exaggeration, although it wasn't untrue that the Ghadarites had approached the *Komagata Maru* passengers, spotting a ripe opportunity for propagandizing among their primary demographic. Bhagwan Singh, Barakatullah, and Balwant Singh had been making speeches and distributing literature on the ship in its East Asian ports of call on the outward voyage.

Angry and frustrated, the travelers docked at Budge Budge near Calcutta in late September only to be met on shore by police who tried to herd them onto a train to Punjab, subject to the new Ingress of India Ordinance passed on 5 September. The law allowed potential subversives entering during wartime to be immediately arrested and detained without trial. (Yes, as the ship steamed across the Pacific, there had been a shooting in Sarajevo.) Ironically, many of them hadn't even wanted to come to India at all, preferring to return to Japan and coastal China, where they had been before the voyage, but none of their previous embarkation points would let them land. Now, refusing to board the train, the majority of the Sikh passengers marched en masse toward Calcutta. The panicked police then foolishly escalated the situation into another standoff and shoot-out in which eighteen passengers were killed, twenty-eight fled, and most of the others were arrested, all of which simply increased the appeal of the Ghadar Party still more.[76]

Meanwhile, news of the *Komagata Maru*'s fate lit a fuse for the already-primed West Coast community, speeding the escalation of demands for armed action to avenge such a grievous insult. Sohan Singh Bhakna caught up with the ship at Yokohama with a delivery of two hundred pistols and several hundred cartridges, before continuing on to India with another group from Shanghai. The first Ghadarite *jatha* (squad) reached Calcutta from Shanghai not long after. To the consternation of officials, many of the Sikhs apprehended at Budge Budge were found to be armed with American-made revolvers.[77] (On one of the propaganda stops Bhagwan Singh had reportedly sold a pistol to Gurdit Singh, and it was suspected that there had been an attempt to smuggle arms aboard at Vancouver as well.)

Meanwhile Bhagwan Singh, Muhammed Barakatullah, and Ram Chandra addressed public meetings along the length of California, holding mass meetings in Sacramento, Fresno, Stockton, Portland, and all the smaller towns where there were Indian communities, at which they collected funds and gathered recruits, who then converged on San Francisco to board ships. The *Ghadar* reported on the massive Fresno and Sacramento meetings of 9 and 11 August, informing readers of the war, telling them to be on alert for the mutiny, and to make haste for India if they wanted to fight in a rising that would join with all the "enemies of the Empire" to overthrow the existing government and found a republic.[78]

Ram Chandra exhorted those gathered in Fresno: "The ghosts of our ancestors are branding us as a shameless progeny. They . . . will never know rest until we cut down every Englishman. Our Motherland is summoning us to come and free her from the clutches of these tyrants. If you claim to be sons of India deposit your belongings with the Yugantar Ashram and be ready to board the ship for India. Let each of my countrymen, who is prepared to undertake the work, come to the hotel and give me his name."[79] Between five and six thousand men were counted present, in addition to some new recruits who had accompanied Amar Singh from Oregon, and between $5000 and $6000 was collected for weapons and ship passage.[80] Moreover, at all the gatherings "the speakers declared that India had received assurances from Germany that if they would revolt against England help would be received from the Germans," and that although such a revolt was inevitable in time, "to strike now would mean victory for India." The conspirators had not fully mastered the art of secrecy, it appears.

This article also hinted at how a mobilization of agricultural workers necessarily followed the rhythms of the harvest. Lecturers were fanning out from San Francisco "to different sections of the state where Hindus are employed in the fruit, and mass meetings are being held," but "it is probable that no more meetings will be held in Fresno. The grape picking is almost finished and the Hindus in a few days will start to move. The next meetings will likely be held in Stockton and Sacramento."[81]

MUTINEERS

After the declaration of war, things started moving very quickly. Kartar Singh set out almost immediately, at the beginning of August.[82] Between sixty and eighty eager mutineers followed him on the SS Korea at the end of the month.[83] Small autonomous jathas, or squads, of four or five began organizing themselves at mills and ranches, pooling money to book passage.[84] The Stockton Khalsa Diwan was receiving numerous requests to handle the sale of land owned by Sikh immigrants to finance their return—thereby literally sacrificing an American territorial future for an Indian one.[85]

Chenchiah recalled in his memoir that upon the outbreak of the war Berkeley radical Jatindra Nath Lahiri had proposed, and Kartar Singh and Chenchiah concurred, that while the Punjabis should depart immediately, the students had more learning and preparation to do. Presumably the Punjabis had already received sufficient military training during their army stints. Since military training was impossible at the university, they decided to seek out other schools, some quite remote. Chenchiah was one such; when he returned a year later in 1915 to await orders, he said, he was taken aback "to find myself in the midst of strangers in the headquarters."[86] His old comrades had gone into battle.

The Big Three saw the travelers off with hortatory farewells, along now-familiar lines: "Your duty is clear. Go to India and stir up rebellion in every corner of the country. Rob the wealthy and show mercy to the poor. In this way you will win universal sympathy. Arms will be provided for you on your arrival in India. Failing this you must ransack the police stations for rifles. Obey without hesitation the commands of your leaders."[87] At each port of call they paused to gather recruits and contact soldiers.[88] At Yokohama they picked up extra weapons, and at Kobe they met another shipload of rebels coming from Vancouver. At Manila they were met by Hafiz Abdulla, president of the local Ghadar branch; Nawab Khan and Jagat Ram then addressed a meeting on the beach, at which "a quantity of seditious literature was also distributed."[89] By the time they reached Hong Kong their numbers had swelled to three hundred. But there a telegram arrived from Nidhan Singh, who had left the *Korea* at Nagasaki and gone on ahead to Shanghai. He warned them that they would be searched on arrival in Hong Kong for weapons, ammunition, and seditious literature, so the leaders collected all such incriminating material and threw it overboard. They were also informed that no ship would be allowed to land with more than two hundred Indians on board, so they divided themselves up. Two hundred transferred to the *Tosa Maru,* the bulk of whom were interned on arrival in Calcutta on 29 October.[90] Indeed, the Sedition Committee Report deemed the *Tosa Maru* group "the most dangerous" of the shiploads, as it "contained malcontents who had divided themselves into sections each of which was to work under a leader in a particular area of the Punjab," had the mass internment not "disorganized these elaborate arrangements."[91] After that they soon learned to travel in less conspicuous handfuls to avoid this problem. The *jathas* arrived throughout the fall and winter, often choosing Japanese vessels in order to avoid British shipping lanes; once ashore they proceeded individually to Punjab to regroup at a set date.[92] For inconspicuous travel, one returnee also noted that he had "exchanged my small turban for a large one to avoid being detected as a returned emigrant."[93]

From that fall to the spring of 1915, 579 "brave ones" embarked from North America, and 470 from East Asia.[94] During the first two years of the war, Rattan Singh estimated that 8,000 of his fellow Ghadarites made the return voyage, about two-thirds of the total overseas membership.[95] The government knew not yet how to gauge the new arrivals' "relative inherent capacity for mischief," but it did know that there was a hostile organization in America, and that the "abnormal number" of emigrants returning after absences of some years had risen enough to attract uneasy attention.[96] Further investigation hinted that scant few of the Indians in North America seemed to have "escaped contamination" from the "taint" of Ghadar ideas. Therefore, police authorities warned, "prima facie every Indian returning from America or Canada, whether labourer, artisan or student, must be regarded with the greatest suspicion as a probable active revolutionary, or at any rate a sympathiser with the revolutionary party."[97] The disease was just as epidemic in Hong Kong and Manila, where Bhagwan Singh had returned from California to rouse and recruit, while others went to rouse the Malay States, Singapore, and Burma. Therefore "those returning from the Far East, other than Government servants and other persons vouched for by the Hong Kong and Shanghai authorities, must be regarded in the same light."[98]

Many arrivals were promptly interned or confined to their villages on security.[99] But for those who did reach their destinations undetected, the next step was to divide up into what Rattan Singh called "guerrilla bands" of four to five people, and then into gangs of around sixteen, under different leaders, concealing themselves throughout the country until the moment came to unite for a campaign. The decentralization was intended to reduce the chances of movement decapitation should any one leader and his party be captured.[100] Unfortunately, scattered arrests, some leading to confessions, discombobulated the organization from the start. Moreover, there were no systematic communication channels between the groups nor any structure in place to receive new arrivals.[101] A few early dates proposed for an uprising passed without event: a general mutiny to be sparked by an attack on the Mian Meer arsenal on 15 November, with some soldiers assisting; a declaration of rebellion to follow a mutiny in the Lahore cantonment on 26 November; a rebellion to follow an attack on the Ferozepur magazine soon after. By December the efforts at rebellion appeared quiescent. In the meantime the gangs gave up waiting for vague and conflicting instructions from Lahore, where Bhai Parmanand had established a base intended for political and press work, and instead "wandered about from village to village," having taken the initiative "to meet other returned emigrants, organise gatherings and look for likely places to commit dacoities" for arms or funds, to "preach sedition" and "corrupt the Indian troops," or to pursue secret contacts.[102]

Some looked beyond the imperative of resistance to take positive steps toward a postrevolutionary vision. A student in Ludhiana named Dalip Singh, who became an ardent Ghadar supporter after being "led astray by the anti-British and socialistic conversation of Nidhan Singh, Parmanand and others," related:

> Every time I met these men, I questioned them as to how they could overthrow such a powerful Government; and their reply was that the mainstays of the Government were their own brethren. . . . The Government was much preoccupied by the European war, and the number of British soldiers in India was very small. Hence we should soon be able to turn them out and form our own Parliament. In each village we should appoint representatives and decide cases in "Parliament." This would be a success as villagers knew best what was happening in their neighbourhood.[103]

Between 1913 and 1915, Balwant Singh, who hoped to win "converts" in the vicinity of his home village of Sangwal by reading to them the *Ghadar* newspaper that he received under multiple false addresses, created a village society that ran a school, a veterinary hospital, a library, and an on-the-ground criminal court—in effect, an autonomous community.[104] Piara Singh and some of his fellows established a school in Namana village with the aim of "educating their fellow countrymen and inspiring in them ideas of freedom and of their political rights," a goal they had discussed while in Canada.[105] By 1915 the school had a *gurdwara* above and a schoolroom below and served as a meeting place for the revolutionaries. Overall, noted the comprehensive 1918 Sedition Committee Report, the returning rebels had been "indoctrinated with ... ideas of equality and democracy in America and led to believe by Har Dayal ... that India can be made into a Utopia in which all will be equal, and plague and famine cease to exist by the simple expedient of driving out the British."[106]

Progress toward that goal resumed once the returnees started to establish better contact with the Bengali Yugantar group, an important sector of the national-revolutionist Swadeshi movement. The conduit was the branch based in Varanasi, led by Rash Behari Bose and Sachindranath Sanyal; the latter became one of the most important liaisons between the Bengali revolutionary network and the returned Punjabi militants. Upon first meeting with Ghadarites Kartar Singh, Amar Singh, Pirthi Singh, and Ram Saran Das, Sanyal inquired about the conspirators' arrangements, numbers, and needs: they had ample personnel but were lacking in money, arms, and capable, well-coordinated leadership. Sanyal left them a revolver and some cartridges, plus instructions on how to contact him for another meeting. But the arrest of Pirthi Singh, who had the information, forestalled this.

A month later Pingle, one of the architects of the Ghadar action wing back in California and Oregon, arrived as the next emissary tasked with making "definite arrangements for cooperation" between the Bengalis and the returned Punjabis, and building upon Sanyal's initial contact. A Maharashtrian, he had returned to India in November 1914 with some Sikh Ghadarites but then joined with Rash Behari Bose's "Bengal anarchist" circle and continued working to facilitate communication and organizational collaboration between the two groups.[107] Sanyal and Pingle then went through a round of secret meetings with revolutionaries throughout North India until Sanyal went to direct the eastern centers.[108]

Early in the year a tactical headquarters for the Ghadar activities was set up in Amritsar, coordinated by Mula Singh. To the empire's secret eyes, Bose's arrival in Amritsar opened up a period of "the most concerted and the most dangerous activity since the birth of the movement."[109] When Mula Singh met with Pingle and Sanyal in the Amritsar bazaar, accompanying them to a headquarters above a sympathizer's *dharmsala* to confer, "Pingle told him that he could obtain four or five pistols, but needed money to bring a Bengali friend of his who knew how to manufacture bombs like that thrown at the Viceroy (Lord Hardinge) on his ceremonial entrance to Delhi two years before. Mula Singh asked if the friend was the man who had thrown it, but he was met with a smile and told that it was not necessary for him to know that."[110]

Soon afterward, the headquarters moved from Amritsar to two secluded houses in Lahore to avoid police attention. Bose himself, when he arrived in Lahore after informing his comrades in Varanasi that he was going to "fix dates in consultation with the Sikhs," then laid claim to the role of directing "all departments of revolutionary work."[111] Bose's claims aside, these departments included (a) the seduction of troops, (b) the massacre of loyal subjects and officials, (c) the setting up of a revolutionary flag, (d) the breaking of jails, (e) the looting of treasuries, (f) the seduction of youths, (g) the propagation of seditious literature, (h) union with foreign enemies, (i) the commission of dacoities, (j) the procuring of arms, (k) the manufacture of bombs, (l) the foundation of secret societies, (m) the looting of police stations, (n) the destruction of railways and telegraphs, and (o) the seduction of villagers.[112] The latter were to be encouraged toward actions of resistance, starting with the refusal to pay revenue, and eventually leading toward more confrontational tactics.[113] (If we were to rephrase this agenda, replacing "seduction of" with "outreach to"; "massacre of [loyalists]" with "assassination of [loyalists]"; and "seditious" with "revolutionary," I doubt any Ghadarite would have denied it.)

The planning committee in Berlin had given returnees to understand that they would be supplied with weapons upon arrival, but the promised German shipments went awry.[114] The returnees smuggled in a few guns and cartridges themselves, having taken them aboard in small quantities in Japanese or Chinese ports, and sometimes hiding such weapons acquired en route under false bottoms of packing cases or in hollow table legs. But this would not be enough; raids on armories, magazines, and police posts would be necessary to build up their arsenal.[115] Resourceful rebels armed themselves in the meantime with cavalry swords or bamboo staves topped with removable axe-blades.[116]

Besides weapons, the other pressing need was money. Throughout October and November, debates occurred on whether and where to loot treasuries. Although some leaders felt that this would simply invite unwanted attention and needlessly risk premature arrest, nevertheless they undertook a modest series of fundraising dacoities.[117] The Bengalis collected 59,410 rupees in their home territory, while the Punjabis carried out up to fifteen attacks on villages, treasuries, and train stations, in one case leveraging a mandatory contribution of 22,000 rupees from "a pro-British rich man" whom they induced to do his duty and "replenish the national treasury."[118]

Some were punctilious in their intention to choose targets in accordance with wealth and sympathies, and in their adherence to chivalry in action. One anecdote, for example, portrayed Kartar Singh taking pity on a widow whose house they were robbing, and leaving her with sufficient funds to get her daughter married honorably. In total, between mid-October 1914 and January 1915, "no fewer than 33 serious crimes, including five murders and several raids by large and well-armed gangs, were definitely traced by the Government of India to the 'Ghadar incitement.'"[119]

A fascination with explosives had not abated since the Swadeshi days, and now the returnees from abroad were seeking out a mysterious "Bengali expert."[120] Ram Saran Das recommended blowing up all the railway bridges in Punjab to forestall troop movements once the rising was initiated. "Hundred pound bombs would do the work," he supposed, "unless the Bengali whom Sanyal had gone to fetch preferred the use of dynamite."[121] Not that the returnees lacked their own expertise, having trained with the same manual as their domestic counterparts had. Mathra Singh, bombing coordinator for the returning Ghadarites, had recently produced some successful samples from easily obtained ingredients. He had been part of a team that also included Amar Singh and Harnam Singh Tundilat, to undertake experiments at a remote workshop at Jawala Singh's ranch in California, based on a copy of the bomb manual compiled by the Swadeshi activist Hemchandra Das in Paris under the tutelage of Russian Revolutionary Socialist exiles and delivered to California by Taraknath Das. (In the process an accident led to the loss of Harnam Singh's hand.) Amar Singh, who was experimenting with electrical ignitions, suggested an iron foundry in Lahore where casings could be made. When the foundry proprietor's growing suspicions led them to cancel the order, they made use of some brass ink pots they found in the Amritsar bazaar.[122]

But even explosives would be useless without the most important component of all: popular support. Soon after the shift to Lahore—which had for the moment overtaken San Francisco as functional operating center, once most of the leaders had crossed over—they had purchased six duplicators to churn out revolutionary leaflets in Urdu, Gurmukhi, and Hindi.[123] Printing and distributing materials from inside India could circumvent the increasing hazards of smuggling them in past the customs inspectors; lately some travelers had taken to simply learning texts by heart and importing them that way. Moreover, since their arrival the returnees had been addressing gatherings at fairs and festivals in Sikh holy places, urging people to rise in rebellion against their British rulers.

While Harnam Singh Tundilat tramped from village to village bearing the message of revolt, Kartar Singh racked up hundreds of miles on his bicycle, making the rounds of the cantonments to talk with soldiers.[124] Above all, the envisioned rising depended upon the mutiny of troops; without this element, the agitators must remain ineffectual. With the empire's military strength concentrated elsewhere, the Indian posts were being refilled with relatively raw and inexperienced "territorials." As for the Indian soldiers, the Ghadarites felt deep kinship with them, so why not rally them? They were family, friends, and fellow villagers, and they held all the weapons. Their eyes only needed to be opened. Although most were content to spread literature and persuasion among the cantonments, a few, including Balwant Singh, even enlisted in order to better implant the desire for mutiny from within. "Already the army was seething with discontent," said

Rattan Singh. "Soldiers hated the idea of going abroad, to Mesopotamia, to France, to strange lands to die at the bidding of the British Government."[125]

During January and February of 1915, Ghadar emissaries reached most of the cantonments in northern India. Kartar Singh, Randhir Singh, and Nidhan Singh focused on Ferozepore, while Harnam Singh and Pyara Singh traveled to the frontier cantonments; Nidhan Singh and others to Jhelum, Rawalpindi, and Hoti Mardan; and Mathra Singh and Amar Singh to "stir up the Afridis on the frontier."[126] The emissaries were equipped with tricolor flags (yellow for Sikhs, red for Hindus, blue for Muslims) and tools such as files, safety pliers, and wire cutters thought to be for use on telegraph or electric lines.[127] Their most successful "seductions" were among the Twenty-third Cavalry at Lahore Cantonment and the sepoys of the Twenty-sixth Punjabis at Ferozepore, whose "infect[ion] with sedition" while stationed in Hong Kong had already led to their redeployment back to India. But the Ghadarites also found receptive ears among the 128th Pioneers, the Twelfth Cavalry regimental lines at Meerut, and a few others.

In late October 1914 a reservist *sowar* (cavalryman) brought news to the Twenty-third that a sizable group of returned emigrants armed with guns, pistols, and bombs was planning to capture the fort at Lahore and was hoping for regimental support in this enterprise. Several *sowars* and officers were sympathetic, although reticent about unleashing mutiny prematurely. They wanted to be sure the rising was actually under way before risking it. But if a solid six to seven hundred emigrants were in place to attack the cavalry lines, they allowed, that might be a sufficient signal for the mutinous troops to kill their officers, commandeer the rifle racks and magazine, and deal with any unconvinced comrades-in-arms.

The "disaffected" cavalry regiment (stirred by two freshly enlisted returnees among their ranks) then kept faithfully in touch through Prem Singh and Hira Singh throughout the intervening lull, awaiting their moment for months.[128] Even so a few restive soldiers decided they couldn't wait any longer and left to "do some mischief to the Government" by cutting telegraph lines and breaking railroad insulators.[129] Meanwhile, several Ghadarites had met some of the men of the Twenty-sixth Punjabis at the Ferozepore depot, encouraged them to take part in the rising, and arranged bomb-making instruction for them. Kartar Singh reported back to the Amritsar headquarters early in 1915 that the Ferozepore troops were ready.

On 12 February, Rash Behari Bose announced the date for the rising as the 21st, only a week and a half away. Emissaries fanned out to the cantonments and military installations to confirm their readiness and pin down the plan. Lahore and Ferozepore would serve as flint and tinder to the rest, which they hoped would then explode like a string of firecrackers spanning northern India from Lahore to Dacca. They would have to move fast, as there was a rumor that the Twenty-third Cavalry was soon to be transferred out to the front. Indeed, some regiments were already gone. When Kartar Singh brought the news to Randhir

Singh, a priest serving the garrison at Ferozepore, he found the latter leading a prayer meeting in honor of some Indian soldiers stationed in France.[130]

Meanwhile, there were still flags, uniforms, emblems, and declarations of war to be prepared, recalled Rattan Singh,[131] corroborating the Sedition Committee Report's list of last minute tasks: "Bombs were prepared; arms were got together; flags were made ready; a declaration of war was drawn up; instruments were collected for destroying railways and telegraph wires." When the latter were cut, the last message they sent would be the signal for the uprising.[132]

The plan was carefully laid: at Lahore, a small group of returnees would gather by the railway line. A guide from the cantonment would lead a half dozen of them to infiltrate the barracks emptied during roll call and collect the swords abandoned there, while another guide escorted a second squad to the reservists' quarter guard to seize rifles and ammunition. At this point the cavalrymen would unleash the "massacre of the Europeans and British Artillery"[133] in pursuit of the maxim "Maro firangi ko!" (Kill the westerners!).[134]

At Ferozepore, eight "disaffected" sepoys of the Twenty-sixth Punjabis were tapped as guides for teams of returned Ghadarites in attacks on several depots, the magazine, the arsenal, and the regimental lines. Amid the roar of the rampaging troops, the rebels would then mob the army camps, release political prisoners, secure all stores of arms and ammunition, and fortify all local cells sufficiently to hold out for a full year (in the process of which they too must *maro firangi ko* as much as they could). Randhir Singh set forth the plan to his flock after a prayer meeting and received a positive response.[135]

However, they were betrayed by an informer in their midst. Raw Punjab Criminal Investigation Department police recruit Kirpal Singh was Balwant Singh's cousin, whom Nidhan Singh had also known and vouched for in Shanghai. With such credentials all had trusted him, and he had won his way with (in retrospect) disturbing swiftness into the confidence of Bose and the inner circle. As soon as Kirpal Singh learned the proposed date of the uprising he informed the authorities, revealing to them the details of ongoing subversive activities. In the meantime he wired the Amritsar police to notify them of a large gathering of the chief conspirators in Lahore. Luckily he lacked contacts among the Lahore police, who would have gotten there faster, and so the mutineers slipped the noose this time. Kirpal Singh then carried on as if he were a committed revolutionary, helping with final preparations among the Twenty-third Cavalry and also among the villagers of Dadher near Amritsar, some of whom had been assigned to loot the local police station, seize its arms, and march to Lahore. In actuality he was arranging to have them ambushed.[136]

But Kirpal Singh had started to provoke suspicion through some indiscretions in asking questions, and even more after being sighted at the railway platform in Amritsar (waiting for the police) when he was supposed to be at Lahore with the Twenty-third. Realizing there had been a leak, the organizing committee pushed the date of the rising up a couple of days to 19 February. When the informer returned to Lahore on the morning of the 19th, he found the gears already in motion. He nevertheless managed to get an emergency alert to his contact, K. B. Liaquat Hayat Khan, deputy inspector of police in Amritsar: "It's happening tonight."

At his signal, the police rushed the movement headquarters in Lahore and captured seven key organizers. Three more were apprehended, returning unawares to the house. The police also seized three finished bombs and sundry other materiel, flags, and incriminating papers. A coded warning was then radioed to the cantonments in plenty of time for military authorities to take preventive actions, which even Michael O'Dwyer admitted were "in some cases perhaps excessive."[137] Indian guards were replaced with English ones, and all absent personnel were recalled to bases, at which troop levels were already the lowest in years. "Truckloads of white soldiers pour[ed] in" as British troops patrolled Lahore, Delhi, Ambala, and Ferozepore, rounding up as many of the rebel leaders as they could find.[138]

In Shaukat Usmani's pithy assessment, "Alas!"[139] The rest crumbled. At 7:00 p.m. when the entire regiment at the Lahore Cantonment was abruptly ordered to fall in, mutiny coordinator Lance Daffadar Lachman Singh of the Twenty-third Cavalry knew something was wrong. He sent Balwant Singh with an urgent warning to the other returnees: stay away, and tell the others immediately![140] Meanwhile in Ferozepore the eight guides had already been discharged for seditious conduct. But rather than departing to their homes they stayed nearby, in contact with Kartar Singh. Around 9:00 p.m. he met fifty or sixty rebels who had arrived by train, and led them to the nearby rifle range to rendezvous with the guides. Along the way they managed to trick a patrol of territorials, called up for duty in response to the mutiny alert, into thinking they were just "an ordinary singing party," since luckily one rebel had brought along a harmonium—"whether to accompany the singing of hymns or war songs is not known."[141] But the discharged sepoys did not appear; the revolutionaries waited until dawn and then dispersed. It turned out that the soldier whose task it had been to fetch his fellows was taken into custody before he could do so, and was held all night long for disobeying the order not to return.

Still loath to give up, about fifteen Ghadarites, including Harnam Singh and Balwant Singh, then took the train to Doraha bridge, intending to blow it up and attack the military guard there. But the guard was too strong to approach. They buried the bombs for safekeeping and planned to return later, but they never made it back. The bombs were eventually recovered by the police and were quite big enough, it was judged, to have done some serious damage.[142]

Sanyal, waiting in vain with his people on the parade ground at Varanasi for the go signal that never came, still had not heard the catastrophic news, until the evening papers came out, and he read, with horror and disbelief, what had happened.[143] Back at the raided headquarters, Kartar Singh found Rash Behari Bose in a stupor of despair. Bose then fled to Japan, where he lived for the rest of his life. But the younger militant refused to give up until he was captured, along with Tundilat and ex-*sowar* Jagat Singh, still trying to subvert Jagat Singh's old regiment, the Twenty-second Cavalry. "As might be expected of three such firebrands," said Isemonger and Slattery, they continued to "harangue the bystanders" even as they were arrested.[144] Pingle hadn't given up either; after fleeing Lahore he tried to carry through the planned rising at Meerut anyway, only to be caught there in March amid the lines of the Twelfth Cavalry, carrying, in O'Dwyer's words, "a collection of bombs"—(actually a box of ten)—"sufficient to blow up a regiment."[145] Both Pingle and Jagat Singh were sentenced to death in the First Lahore Conspiracy Case.

Over the next days and weeks, the Lahore police swept up other conspirators, absconders, and incriminating materials, a process greatly expedited as Nawab Khan, Amar Singh, and Mula Singh turned approver, revealing detailed information on actions, methods, names of participants, homes, and meeting places. It was on their testimony that the conspiracy case largely rested. Contemporary documents revealed the magnitude of the colonial government's panic, retroactively downplayed, at the closeness of their brush with disaster as bit by bit further details of the events came to light.

Clashes continued sporadically throughout the spring and summer of 1915 as those who had not yet been arrested "continued their revolutionary activities, spreading propaganda on the university campuses and in the military cantonments."[146] For example, even after the failed rising a couple of the Ghadarites had been teaching the indomitable *sowars* of the Twenty-third Cavalry to make bombs and dynamite according to Mathra Singh's recipes. They hoped in the future to seize opportunities such as large gatherings of officers and also plotted the death of the traitor Kirpal Singh. The accidental explosion of one of these bombs in their quarters led to the revelation of their participation in the February attempt. Eighteen *sowars* were court-martialed and sentenced to death. Twelve were executed forthwith, and the rest sent to the Western Front to die a slower death. According to O'Dwyer, the rest of the regiment had already left India, because "in time of war it was not thought advisable by the military authorities to have a court-martial which would make public mutinous preparations."[147] Meanwhile, soldiers Puran Singh and Wasawa Singh had thought to get in touch with Hira Singh, a man "of strong revolutionary views" with a following in a nearby village who was working to convert other villages to the cause. He was also thought to be in touch with "a

Beloch chief" boasting forty thousand followers and plentiful arms and ammunition, ready to join the rising upon receipt of a telegram bearing the coded signal "white wool." After their regiment received its active service orders in late April or early May, the conspirators packed two bombs in Puran Singh's luggage in case of opportunities to use them en route. One exploded on 13 May, injuring five people. The second was thrown down a well. But these actions remained fragmentary and failed to generate the cumulative synergy necessary for a large-scale rising. The republic would not yet be proclaimed.

AFTERMATHS

The rebels were tried under the Defense of India Act in a series of twelve special tribunals with no possibility of appeal. The main trial lasted from April to September 1915, followed by four supplementary cases, and several subsidiary cases between July 1915 and September 1918.[148] Of the 64 accused in the initial case, the results were 2 discharged, 4 acquitted, 24 sentenced to death, 27 to transportation for life, and 6 to lesser prison terms; commuted to a total of 7 executions, 34 life sentences, and 16 shorter terms.[149] In total 175 people were tried, resulting in 136 convictions, including 42 death sentences, though about half of these were commuted to transportation for life.[150]

Official postmortems continually cited Ghadar's fatal disconnection from the sentiments of the countryside, whose denizens, authorities liked to claim (just as Ghadarites liked to deny), were generally "loyal and contented,"[151] sure in a crunch to "rall[y] stoutly on the side of law and order."[152] And yet it may stand as a testament to the Ghadarites' persuasiveness, that 121 of 231 defendants tried in all of the conspiracy cases in Punjab were local residents rather than returned emigrants.[153] When the returnees of 1914–15 set out "to inform their kinsmen of the unequal treatment that was meted out to them" overseas, they did so by "preach[ing] the doctrines of revolution that they had learned from the Ghadr and the *crude socialism that they had picked up in the towns of western Canada and the United States.*"[154] Once the Ghadar community consciousness was dominated by a mass of workers, rather than by an elite intellectual secret-society network, a leftward evolution seems logical enough.

Before leaving on their doomed campaign, the party hard core in California had had the foresight to elect "a new collective to carry on the work" in their absence, with an executive committee consisting of Bhagwan Singh as president, Santokh Singh as general secretary, Ram Chandra as manager of the paper, and Gobind Behari Lal as editor, plus ten other Yugantar Ashram staffers.[155] Yet there were intimations of increasing disunity and ugly factional strife. Ram Chandra had taken over editorship of the *Ghadar* after Har Dayal's departure in April 1914, and officially changed its name to *Hindustan Ghadar* in a deliberate move to deflect the persistent taint of anarchism linked to the name of Har Dayal. (Restricting revolt to Hindustan signaled that they had a specific grievance against British rule in India but posed no threat in principle to regimes elsewhere.) As the war gathered momentum key figures scattered to various tasks: Barakatullah to Berlin, and Bhagwan Singh to Manila, Tokyo, and Panama.[156] With his two cohorts gone, Ram Chandra was the dominant figure in San Francisco. It appeared to the informer identified in reports as C that Ram Chandra had taken over from Har Dayal and now reigned "supreme," exercising "autocratic control" of the Yugantar Ashram, assisted in the work by "a few Indians of the educated middle class, such as Gobind Behari Lal," plus "a large number of Indians of the lower classes chosen apparently from among the more intelligent of the coolies. These 'poor people', as C called them, lived in the Ashram without wages, lithographing the *Ghadar,* and performing other functions."[157]

The working-class collective members involved in a labor of love might have been surprised to hear themselves described that way. Nor did they meekly accept Ram Chandra's autocratic and secretive behavior. He was drawing increasing criticism for his lack of transparency in accountability for German funds, as well as for his political views. There were accusations that he had appropriated thousands of dollars of the "national fund" for his personal use. Furthermore, many considered the new emphasis on German and Turkish interests in the Ghadar publications—at the expense of India's own—to be a betrayal of the integrity of their own goals. Many had had their doubts about the German alliance in the first place; these enemies of the enemy were not their friends, just another racist and imperialist power no more to be trusted than Britain beyond immediate strategic interest. Added to this were the corrosive actions of provocateurs and informants, with pervasive distrust leading to the murders of several suspected traitors.

C's true identity was Sagar Chand, a student from Lahore who had come to England in 1909, where he got involved with the India House "extremists" through a friend. The friend was Haider Raza, an India House habitué, Krishnavarma scholarship holder, and Chand's tutor in Persian and logic. C attributed the failure of his academic career at Oxford and the Middle Temple to "the life of dissipation" into which Haider Raza had "initiated him."[158] He remained an obscure figure until 1914, when he started writing seditious articles for papers in Punjab and energetically distributing the *Ghadar,* which his many "lady friends" helped him to post. In reality he had been feeding intelligence on the India House inner circle to the DCI from the beginning, having "lived a false life for over a year and won the confidence of the men he was hunting."[159] When he arrived in the United States, after making contact with Freeman and Gobind Behari Lal, he managed to allay Heramba Lal Gupta's suspicions about him sufficiently to make his way into Ram Chandra's inner circle in San Francisco, from where he passed detailed information to British intelligence.[160]

When Bhagwan Singh returned to California in October 1916 he was horrified at what he found, and resolved to reconvene the "real" Ghadar movement. He embarked on a campaign against Ram Chandra, and by February 1917 there were dual organizations printing dual papers. Ram Chandra claimed legal rights to the name *Hindustan Ghadar,* but Bhagwan Singh declared that his challenger, *Yugantar,* was the more genuine successor to the spirit of the original *Ghadar.*[161] Judging by the issues and excerpts available, he was correct. For example, the first number of the new *Hindustan Ghadar* said its purpose was to "disseminate general education, knowledge, culture and science," without mentioning revolution, India's freedom, or any of the other key planks of its predecessor.[162] The content of *Yugantar,* on the other hand, was very much like that of the earlier paper.[163]

The schism between these two leaders has sometimes been portrayed as a case of Hindus versus Sikhs. As played out in personal loyalties, this may have occurred *in effect;* in 1917 the Stockton and Vancouver Khalsa Dewans united to denounce Ram Chandra—whose alleged embezzling, and the death and imprisonment of mutineers, were now equated with "Hindu leadership"—and declare their opposition to the Ghadar Party in defense of Sikh orthodoxy.[164] Yet the Ghadarite Sikhs portrayed their own party as a secularist, rationalist alternative to the Khalsa Dewan. Perhaps more than anything else, the difference was between moderates and radicals; between aspiration to the values of the American mainstream as actually practiced—even unto adopting its racialist categories and markers of socioeconomic success—or in their idealized form, venerating in principle the libertarian texts legible to early twentieth-century radicals of any provenance, such as the Declaration of Independence. One aimed to acquire land in America; the other to liberate land in India. In short, there were two different expressions of nationalism, depending on whether the focus of identification, as well as the chosen vehicle of the desire for individual and/or collective freedom, was American or Hindustani.

SYNDICALISTS

The Ghadar movement is significant because it managed so early to connect two frames of reference—the history of race and class in the United States, and of colonization in what we would now call the global south—and to link the related grievance of racial discrimination toward a low-wage immigrant labor force to an explicitly anti-imperialist revolutionary program, rather than simply calling for inclusion in the existing society.[165] Thus the Ghadarites' galvanizing moment occurred precisely at the point where the politics of race, labor, and imperialism converged. The only other sector of early twentieth-century North American radicalism that was similarly able to articulate the concerns of labor, race, and imperialism was the Industrial Workers of the World (IWW or Wobblies), which provided the prewar Ghadar movement with its foremost interface with the left in the United States.[166]

Syndicalism may be defined as a form of radical trade unionism that peaked in the decades around the turn of the nineteenth to twentieth century. It was especially prominent in France, Spain, and Latin America, where it influenced important components of the Mexican revolution that were so compelling to Khankhoje and Har Dayal. Its foremost North American variant could be found in the IWW, a conglomeration of several radical unions into "One Big Union" committed to the ambitious vision of worker solidarity across all economic sectors, and to the ultimate abolition of the capitalist system through direct action. As a basic tenet, syndicalists bypassed the political sphere, seeking neither electoral advantage nor forceful seizure of the government. They insisted rather that direct action was to be applied at the point of production, and that its practitioners would do so in their capacity as worker-producers. Accordingly, the ultimate moment of transformation would be announced not by a coup but by a general strike to bring economic function to a halt, after which society would be structured as a horizontally interlocked federation of autonomous collectives in which the workers in each industry, not the state, would manage production and distribution. The trade union or syndicate would be the basic unit both of tactical resistance and of the future social organization.

The Ghadarites, too, by necessity, sidestepped electoral and parliamentary participation in favor of other tactics. In North America, this was because they were legally excluded from full participation; that indeed was part of their grievance. In India, of course, the rejection of parliamentary in favor of revolutionary methods was the hallmark of the extremists within the nationalist movement, from whom the revolutionary movement abroad had sprung. Without having set out deliberately to replicate the syndicalist manner or prefigure a future social arrangement, the Ghadarites' conditions of living and working in the United States did happen to be such that they functioned in de facto collectives, as work crews and *jathas*—miniature syndicates, one might say.

On the other hand, nation, not class, still retained its primary claim on the Ghadarites' loyalty. Furthermore, they pinned their millennial hopes on a mutiny, not a general strike. Nevertheless, the idea of a general strike (*hartal*), a boycott, or withdrawal of all participation in any production, consumption, and service sector of the economy associated with British rule was of course a pillar of the Indian anticolonial movement. It should be remembered that the Ghadarites' other main form of participation in the overseas imperial labor market was through military service. Thus for them a soldiers' mutiny *was* a workplace strike. From this perspective, focusing on suborning troops to mutiny or desert, as the Ghadarites did, was in effect much the same as encouraging workers to strike or engage in sabotage at the point of production.

All these traits helped make the Ghadar movement compatible with the IWW, which would provide the movement with important North American allies. Founded in Chicago in 1905, the IWW was almost exactly coeval with the modern Indian revolutionary movement.[167] Its presence in the agricultural, railroad, and lumber industries of the West Coast region corresponded neatly to the Ghadarites' distribution. Yet despite this overlap, and although the Wobblies were unique among American organized labor in their inclusivity of immigrant and nonwhite workers, evidence of Indian participation in IWW-linked agitation or strike activity is elusive, other than a tangential reference to the presence of "Hindu" workers at the Wheatland Hop Riot of August 1913.[168] One has to piece together bits of evidence that Indians were in communication with Wobblies, or that there was at the very least an ongoing proximity and/or affinity. To my knowledge the connection is not hugely significant from the American perspective. However, it must be recalled that the Indian laboring population was not large in gross terms and was concentrated in one part of the country. Even so there are some clues that indicate that contacts with the IWW had an influence on the Ghadarites.

Khankhoje relates his own first encounter with the IWW, initiating his life-long commitment to socialism. The young man had attempted to get a job in a lumber mill in Astoria around 1910, but the boss rebuffed him as a "black Hindu." Then he met an old Wobbly who helped him find work in an Oregon lumber camp. There, while living in a cabin in the deep forest, he and his fellow workers gathered around the fire at night to "[listen] to the lectures of the old labour leader who had got me my job. This was the first time I had heard of the labour movement in America and it was my first introduction to socialist thought."[169]

Again it was Har Dayal who most explicitly articulated the Ghadar movement's rapprochement with this form of American radicalism. He served as secretary to the Oakland branch of the IWW beginning in 1912 and lectured several times for them in their hall, including one speech called "The Future of the Labor Movement" that was covered almost verbatim in the *San Francisco Bulletin* of 12 July 1912. The speech, which he called his own "frank confession of faith," indicated the importance of the radical labor movement in Har Dayal's thinking of that period, and of labor conditions in fueling and shaping his community's political unrest. He began with a list of the obstacles facing the worker, and the prerequisites for winning industrial freedom:

> First, solidarity. Labor must think in terms of the whole world. . . . Should one nation acquire freedom, the rich of another nation will crush it. . . . For moral and practical reasons the labor movement must be universal.
>
> Second, a complete ideal. We want not only economic emancipation, but moral and intellectual emancipation as well. . . . No man will lay down his life for a partial ideal.

Third, good workers and leaders. The rich and respectable cannot lead us. . . .
We will have two kinds of leaders. First, the ascetics who have renounced riches
and respectability for the love of the working man, men like Kropotkin, the St.
Francises and St. Bernards of Labor. These will be difficult to find, for such renun-
ciations are scarce and such intellects are few. Secondly, we must have the sons of
toil themselves, who must take up their own cross and lead their brothers on.

Fourth, cooperation between the labor movement and the woman's movement.
The workers and the women are two enslaved classes and must fight their battles
together.

Fifth, constructive educational system. We want central labor colleges where our
young men can be taught, not by money, but by men. We do not want endowments,
because endowments, with their incomes, are another form of exploitation. . . .

Sixth, a feeling of actual brotherhood. The poor must love the poor. The shame
of labor is that the poor must accept charity from the rich. We are not so poor but
we can care for our own poor. . . . We must stand together.[170]

Har Dayal condemned parliamentarianism and parliamentary socialism,
which, he said, had ended in a blind alley in its strongholds of Germany and Bel-
gium; it was useless, he said, for labor to attempt to free itself using "the weapons
furnished by capitalism." But he had equally strong criticism for the other extreme, which he had previously advocated: "Terrorism," meaning propaganda by
the deed, "is a waste of force and gives the other party a chance for needless persecution. It provides martyrs, but the labor movement, which eschews terrorism,
will have its own martyrs in plenty. . . . A man who lives and acts in the interests
of freedom is himself living social dynamite."[171]

At another address in January 1913 Har Dayal was greeted with loud applause
upon entering the IWW hall in San Francisco (where the dogged Hopkinson
found himself quite unsettled by the ambient talk of "socialism, anarchism, and
all matters pertaining to political agitation"). After expounding on the current
efforts of Indian nationalist agitators, and the repression with which the British
responded to them, Har Dayal expressed his goal of "establish[ing] an association based on IWW principles for 'the benefit and uplifting' of the people of
India." Although this confirmed to Hopkinson that he was by no means barking
up the wrong tree in attempting implicate Har Dayal for his politics, he was nevertheless eager to make a quick exit from "surroundings [which] were composed of a
very questionable class of humanity . . . in the toughest part of San Francisco."[172]

Various Wobblies later popped up several times in the crevices of the so-
called Hindu-German Conspiracy. Har Dayal persuaded an IWW member
called Jones, who had become interested in the Indian movement while living for
a time in Assam (!?), to serve as New York liaison between Germans and Indians
in America. Ambassador Spring-Rice informed the secretary of state that the

"world-wide organisation" centered in Berlin was not only employing some Irishmen as agents but also making efforts "to affiliate some of the industrial workers of the world [sic], one of whom is now in Berlin."[173] Another, identified as an American anarchist or Wobbly named Jack or Jenkins, makes an appearance in M. N. Roy's memoirs, while a Foreign Office Memorandum mentioned that Har Dayal "was on intimate terms" with an IWW member named Anton Johansen, one of the accused in the 1916 California dynamite conspiracy case.[174]

The wartime repression, trial, and imprisonment of Ghadarites and Wobblies, then, followed a similar timeline, defined by the United States' entry into the war and its attendant legislation against dissidents. Taraknath Das formed an acquaintance during his two years at Leavenworth with fellow inmates William "Big Bill" Haywood, one of the IWW's founding heroes, and Ralph Chaplin, the movement's legendary artist. According to Das's biographer Tapan Mukherjee, Das habitually gathered with a whole group of IWW prisoners (ninety-three of whom had arrived there after the Chicago trial of 1918) "in a corner of the prison yard which they named the 'campus,'" to discuss politics, poetry, current events, the Russian Revolution, history, and Vedanta philosophy, in which Das held special classes in the evening.[175]

As it happens, yet another fellow inmate at Leavenworth was Ricardo Florés Magón, the Mexican transborder revolutionary leader and cofounder of the syndicalist Partido Liberal Mexicano (PLM). Although kept secluded, Magón was imprisoned at Leavenworth from May 1918 until his death in 1922. He had been active in Los Angeles since 1910. Ghadar had little presence in Los Angeles, although it was reported that Munshi Ram, part of the Astoria Indian Association prior to its absorption into the PCHA and later assistant manager in charge of correspondence and subscription records at the Ghadar Press under Ram Chandra, was assigned to go "preach sedition" there in March 1915.[176] Har Dayal had declared himself a supporter of the Magón brothers and their activities back in 1912. Khankhoje was also a personal friend of Magón's, whom he had met through a Mexican fellow cadet during his Tamalpais years.[177]

I have found no evidence to suggest that any Indians took part in the IWW brigade that marched to Baja to support the PLM that year, although Khankhoje and Pingle had long been entertaining a similar idea. Together they dreamed up a (perpetually thwarted) vision of a home base in Baja, first for training their guerrilla army outside the view of United States authorities and later as a place where "after the revolution, Punjabi farmers could till the soil."[178] The Indians' intimate association with the Mexican farm labor population in California, and their habit of looking to the Mexican border whether for refuge from United States law or for covert entry and exit when necessary, would have made such a thing plausible.

This eventuality didn't materialize, however, nor did Pingle and Khankhoje's later attempt at joining the battle to the south in 1911. After the Mexican Revolution broke out Khankhoje was eager to join in at the head of a force of Sikh veterans recruited in Oregon and California, as a sort of rehearsal for the revolt against the British Raj. But his putative squad, more experienced than he, advised him to cool his hot young head and scout things out first. His Mexican friends advised him to cross from Calexico to Mexicali, which he did. But once across the border he concluded with disappointment that his men were right; the plan was not feasible. It was a brutally violent situation in which bandits were abroad, and Spanish fluency was required—no place for a training exercise and too risky for the premature sacrifice of Indian blood, which must be saved against their own urgent cause.[179] Nevertheless, the border-crossing *revoltosos* of various factions involved in the Mexican Revolution from 1911 onward offered a constant background to the development of official American attitudes to the Ghadar movement, offering the immediate precedents for the legal discourse around the launch of military expeditions from U.S. soil, and providing the alibi for Ghadar's attempts to ship arms during wartime.

Perhaps the most significant political divergence between the Ghadarites and the Wobblies was their attitude to the Great War. Many North American and European syndicalists and anarchists, including Har Dayal's old friend, supporter, and *Indian Sociologist* printer, Guy Aldred, who spent several years in prison as a conscientious objector in England, expressed their anti-imperialism through staunch opposition to the war. Those who did take sides chose liberal Britain and France over militaristic Germany. But the Ghadarites, given their relationship to one of the major antagonists, saw the war not as a disaster but as a longed-for opportunity; they expressed their far more direct and personal anti-imperialism through an alliance with Germany against Britain. However, regardless of their feelings toward the war itself, the Wobblies and the Ghadarites may indeed have agreed on opposing the United States' *entry* into the war, since that was what brought them to grief as violators of neutrality.

Finally, aside from the tasks of resistance, both the IWW and the Ghadar Party occupied themselves with worker education and mutual aid, defense of free speech and civil liberties (necessitated by the repression of their other work), and cultural production. Both the IWW and Ghadar sourced a prolific wellspring of militant propaganda, newspapers, pamphlets, and volumes of singable poems in the 1910s and 1920s: where the IWW had the *Little Red Songbook,* Ghadar had *Ghadar-di-Gunj.* These iconic repositories of lasting inspiration arguably proved more of an influential contribution to the history of radical movements than the immediate instrumental results of any of their direct actions. And even these tangents were fortuitously entangled: American Civil Liberties Union (ACLU) founder

Roger Baldwin was among the foremost supporters of the Friends of Freedom for India in the 1920s, serving on its executive committee during the postwar antideportation campaign. The ACLU, of course, was a direct outgrowth of the IWW's wartime free-speech struggles.

Hopkinson had attended another of his quarry's lectures in early 1913, this one sponsored in some way, he reported, by the San Francisco Russian Revolutionary Society. Har Dayal opened with an apology for the presence of the American flag on the platform, for which he said he was not responsible, as he didn't believe in any government, and all flags were a "sign of slavery." He then proceeded to his planned remarks titled "The Revolutionary Labor Movement in France." At the . time, this would have referred to the syndicalist Confédération Générale du Travail (CGT). "Although he had not been in the United States very long," nevertheless "he had carefully studied the revolutionary movement in America, to include socialist activities and the IWW. This latter, he characterized as bearing the closest resemblance to the Anarchist Society of France of which, he said, he was proud to be a member."[180]

Despite the relationship of Har Dayal and his overseas comrades with European Socialists, and their awareness of some individualist anarchists, they had not engaged with this sector of French radicalism; after all, it was only in North America and not in France or England, that a working class–based popular movement became significant as a radical partner on the Indian side. The Indians politically active in Europe were primarily intellectuals and students from elite backgrounds; they interfaced most with a rarefied circle of other intellectuals and exiled professional revolutionaries, not with local trade unionists. Even so certain parallels with the traits of the Ghadar movement suggest themselves.

Bernard Moss characterizes French syndicalism as the domain of independent skilled artisans who were not yet alienated from the process and product of their labor and retained an attachment to their national tradition of republican radical democracy, in contrast to the thoroughly proletarianized and alienated factory workforce to whose working conditions Marx's more centralized and unified organizational model was most applicable. This syndicalist combination of libertarian and egalitarian principles strikes me as reminiscent of the Ghadarites' tendency, albeit stemming from different situational origins. In any case Moss also points out that differences in approaches to radical trade unionism were related to differences in the specific social conditions of labor, and not indicative of a universally applicable ideological principle. Though the Ghadarites' New World labors were of the more unskilled and alienated variety, their status prior to immigration had more resembled that of Moss's artisans, and even in the United States many still aspired to their own landholdings.[181]

But to return to Har Dayal's talk: he observed that the American revolutionary movement was far less mature than that of France and could learn much from both the successes and the mistakes of the latter. The moral of these lessons was, in a nutshell, "Love one another among the labouring-class, but hate, hate, the rich." He continued that such hatred, however, if expressed through dynamite, was liable to do more harm than good to the revolutionary movement, unless aimed very precisely at the assassination of despotic oppressors. He closed by inviting all interested attendees to come to meetings of his Radical Study Club, "which he had inaugurated in San Francisco for the purpose of teaching the people Revolutionary Methods."[182]

One can only speculate about what might have happened had the Ghadarite radical branch remained oriented toward their lives in the United States, rather than having their attention fixed, by the war, wholly on an immediate uprising in India. What if the war had taken five to ten more years to erupt, as Har Dayal had originally thought? Would they have left a deeper trace in the record of the radical labor movement and antiracist struggle on the West Coast? Might they, for example, have played a greater role in cross-border struggles carried out by Mexican syndicalist *libertarios?* They would have had ample opportunity.[183] Of course, they still would have confronted the repression of the Red Scare and an exclusionary immigration policy and thus might still have formed an exodus, though under different circumstances not of their choosing. But the war *did* happen; and, to repeat a cliché, it did change everything.

For one, it changed the course of revolutionary syndicalism, forcing its adherents to define their relationship to the nation and nation-state. In his magisterial *Fire in the Minds of Men* James Billington fits syndicalism into his overarching thesis of a rivalry between national and social forms of revolutionary thought. Of the precarious configuration of these formations on the eve of the First World War, he remarks: "Whoever controlled the banner of nationalism tended to determine the nature of the syndicalist legacy everywhere after World War One. In the United States, labor unrest was doomed by its opposition to the nationalist fervor that swept through America during and after the war. The social revolutionary intensity and the internationalism of the IWW (and the anti-war, anti-allied sentiments of many Germans and Irish in the labor movement) provoked a patriotic backlash."[184] These, of course, were Ghadar's main American allies.

But Billington was writing about the European context. For an Asian anticolonial movement, the choice between national and social forms was less stark. The Indian revolutionary lineage of which the Swadeshi and Ghadar movements partook likewise drew upon both.[185] Given the unavoidable primacy of the national liberation struggle, the question facing European revolutionary syndicalists—nationalism or internationalism?—then faced the Ghadarites as well, perhaps even more acutely. How they negotiated this crossroads would determine the road home—from San Francisco to Berlin, Berlin to Moscow, and Moscow to Lahore.

3

Enemies of Enemies . . .

The Nationalist Ghadar

FEELING LIKE A NATION, THINKING LIKE A STATE

It is a truism for theorists of nationalism (and even for common observers of the world) that the rhetoric of nationalism, and the emotionality of patriotism, increase drastically during wartime. The Great War introduced a hitherto unimaginable scale of conflict as the great empires collided and began ripping each other apart. National identities took over for the duration, breaking up the ideal of international class solidarity to the bitter disappointment of many anarchists and socialists.

For Indian and other anticolonial movements this effect of the war was even stronger. Nationalist rhetoric was the cornerstone of such movements in any case; besides, a colonized area is already by definition in a state of war, secured by foundational violence and subject at the best of times to conditions of low-intensity military occupation. The state's monopoly of force and its disciplinary regime are made more explicit and acute by their obvious external origin; hence the inescapability of the need for political liberation as the dominant theme of struggle in such a region (as distinct from the struggle's economic and cultural dimensions).

Furthermore, the war was ostensibly being fought, or so went the rhetoric, on the principles of democracy and self-determination for all nationalities—at least for those within the German, Austro-Hungarian, and Ottoman empires. This was a favorable environment for nourishing the slogans of Egypt for the Egyptians, Asia for the Asiatics, Home Rule, Swadeshi, Swaraj, Sinn Fein, Ourselves Alone, each expressing the fundamental notion that its claimants constituted a

People, and that a People must have an autonomous sovereign territory and a government of its own. While the war did not create such aspirations and identities, it intensified them to a pitch of influence and emotional power sufficient to absorb and bear the weight of all the other yearnings for social and economic emancipation and cultural transformation that had been on the rise over the past half-century. This was not overlooked by any of the main adversaries, who happily stoked insurgencies within one another's imperial possessions: the British cultivated the Arabs against the Ottoman Turks even as the Germans cultivated the Indians and Irish against the British, and the Moroccans against the French. Afterward at Versailles, the language of self-determination then drove not only the hopes but the subsequent bitter disillusionment of anticolonial movements, leading directly to the postwar upsurges of nationalist activity not only in India but in China, Egypt, and Ireland.

For the duration of the war, the strategy of the independence movement abroad, while still oriented toward armed revolt, was for all practical purposes anchored in the military and diplomatic logic of interstate power relations. Tactical realpolitik prevailed. It was a time for action, not for philosophizing. Thinking was about strategy and tactics, not about philosophy of liberation or analysis of oppression. Accordingly, propaganda was aimed more toward incitement to action than ideological persuasion, and tailored to whatever was needed to appeal to those one was trying to arouse, at least within the bounds of assuming a common immediate (though not necessarily ultimate) goal. Indeed, this pragmatism had always been characteristic of the Ghadarite approach; their philosophy of revolutionary praxis was by definition one of action, without which it made no sense.

However, now these tactics presumed nation-state units as actors. Internationalism was relevant here less as a principled ideal than as a geography of organization involving long-distance alliances, epic travels, and many covert crossings of lines. The revolutionaries worked through the German consulate system, with its outposts around the Pacific Rim, and sought to constitute themselves formally as a sovereign nation with diplomatic recognition. With damning accusations of anarchism continuing unabated, it seemed imperative to claim legitimacy by declaring oneself a government or authorized government representative—even if this meant only a few individuals wielding fancy letterhead and official-looking seals—capable of contacting world leaders and expecting to receive a hearing. By 1914 the India that the overseas revolutionists had in mind was clearly a secular, federated republic, though discussion of its future social and economic character remained deferred.

The revolutionaries abroad were well aware of predictions that Germany and Britain (and the United States and Japan, for that matter) were sliding glacially toward war. Indeed they were counting on it. But they had thought it would be much later, certainly not a mere nine months after the *Ghadar*'s debut. They had expected to have several years in which to mature the tasks of planning, educating, raising consciousness, preparing the ground. But with the conflagration unleashed in Europe, the Ghadar leadership saw a "golden" opportunity that, even if premature, could not possibly be refused.

THE BERLIN INDIA COMMITTEE

As the machinery of great power politics ground toward a seemingly inevitable collision, Germany had already been looking to the "Orient" as a field to draw on for opposition to its rival juggernaut, Britain. The referent for this vast and mysterious entity was, as convenient, either India or the so-called Islamic world— a significant elision adopted no less by Bolshevik Russia, or by Japanese, Indian, Egyptian, and Chinese Pan-Asianists themselves, than by German strategists. But strategy aside, Germany already had a venerable tradition of Orientalist scholarship and political interest, producing such distinguished figures as Baron Max von Oppenheim, who had a long history of archeological study and diplomatic service in Egypt and the Middle East, and Dr. Herbert Mueller, a Sinologist who had studied in China between 1912 and 1914. Mueller recalled that as early as 1904 at Berlin University he had "bec[o]me interested in the political emancipation movement in, what we called, "The Orient" at that time and I soon had many friends amongst nationalists and revolutionaries from Egypt, Turkey, Kurdistan, Persia, India, China and Korea."[1]

These strategists had determined that supporting Indian and/or Pan-Islamist anti-British unrest (between which there was understood to be significant overlap, although the two were obviously far from identical) was an important part of conducting their war.was In *Germany and the Next War,* published in October 1911, General Friedrich von Bernhardi indicated the German hope that the Hindu population of Bengal, "in which a pronounced revolutionary and nationalist tendency had showed itself, might unite with the Muhammedans of India and that the cooperation of these elements might create a very grave danger capable of shaking the foundations of England's high position in the world."[2] Plainly, despite the tendency to take the East as a single unit, German Orientalists at least were aware of the disparate religious, regional, and cultural affiliations within the Oriental world. Otherwise they could hardly have spoken of linking them up as a desirable new development, even if this goal was hindered by failure to fully understand the content and context of the differences among them, or their priorities. Nevertheless, the slippage or overlap of categories (along with the nature of the Indian national revolutionaries' relationships to Egyptian and Japanese movements) opened a door through which leftist, national liberationist, and

Pan-Islamist streams of anticolonial activity could flow in and out of each other in the 1920s.

By spring 1915 the German Foreign Office (Auswertiges Amt, or AA) had gathered most of the significant Indian radicals then active in Europe to form the Indian National Party or Berlin India Committee (BIC).[3] Indeed, both the Yugantar group and Dacca Anusilan Samiti had already approached Germany by 1911 on behalf of the Bengali movement, while Virendranath Chattopadhyaya had arrived in Berlin from France in 1914 to represent the international revolutionaries.[4] Other important participants from all quadrants of British India included Champakaraman Pillai,[5] Bhupendranath Dutt,[6] M. P. T. Acharya, Ajit Singh, and disenfranchised aristocrat Mahendra Pratap. Representing the North Americans were Muhammed Barakatullah, Taraknath Das, Bhagwan Singh, and Har Dayal.[7] Har Dayal was still presumed to exercise significant influence over the transatlantic movement, and one of the main reasons the Foreign Office wanted him was that they were very keen to incorporate the American Ghadarites. The California group was identified as a particularly valuable addition to the team, since they already had a well-developed infrastructure, mobilized support base, extensive propaganda machinery, and other situational factors such as the presence of large German and Irish immigrant populations in the United States, the latter of whose contingent of anti-British militants Germany was similarly interested in supporting. An article in the *Berliner Tageblatt* published 6 March 1914 and entitled "England's India Trouble" "depict[ed] a very gloomy situation in India," due to which "secret societies flourished and spread and were helped from outside. In California especially, it was said there appeared to be an organized enterprise for the purpose of providing India with arms and explosives."[8] As usual this was not altogether wrong, if exaggerated and not altogether right either.

In addition to the Indian committee, Berlin hosted similar Persian and Turkish groups. Indian activist Jodh Singh explained: "The object of the first named is to free Persia from European influence in general and create ill feelings against the British, in particular, and to assist the Indians in obtaining a republic. The object of the Turkish Society is practically the same."[9] Members of both groups also attended BIC meetings. But the BIC at first had little direct contact with the AA itself, communicating mainly through Oppenheim and Mueller, although Chatto and Har Dayal had clearance to attend meetings of the Foreign Office where "Indian matters" were discussed.[10] But while the German goal for India was to foment unrest that would destabilize Britain, integrating "all revolutionary organizations of America and Europe . . . under the control of the German authority," the better to effectively coordinate and "deploy schemes through other centres of authority in distant countries,"[11] the BIC's own stated goal for itself was first and foremost "establishing a republican government in India by any means."[12] As self-appointed "Supreme General Staff of the Indian Revolution" the committee was supposed to be an independent body, with the Indians making their own decisions about what to do.[13] Its members insisted that they must "represent India while negotiating with Germany on a footing of equality on the basis of mutual interest and not as a subordinate power begging for help," observed an intelligence report, and "seem to have continuously guarded themselves against being used as tools in the hands of Germany for her imperialist motives."[14]

In 1915 the AA established the Nachrichtenstalle für der Orient (News Agency for the Orient) to produce news and pamphlets in various languages for distribution to soldiers in Europe and the Middle East. The Germans hoped the members of the Berlin India Committee would serve as propagandists, translators, and compilers in this effort. By mid-1916, British intelligence had compiled a list of eighty-two papers and pamphlets "published by German agency or by societies subsidised by Germany" in languages including English, French, German, Dutch, Portuguese, Spanish, Italian, Turkish, Arabic, Persian, Malay, Tartar, Chinese, and four or five Indian vernaculars.[15] But "the production of anti-British literature" was only the first item in an agenda that the DCI compiled after the fact, in 1920.[16] Also on the list were "attempts to commit assassinations in England and allied countries, especially Italy," and "an attempt to endanger the lines of communication through the Suez Canal."[17] Meanwhile, some BIC members were tapped for additional training in explosives and sabotage, while others visited the captured troops in an attempt to "win Indian [POWs] from their allegiance," a task to be directed by Barakatullah.[18]

After Berlin the second major headquarters was in Istanbul, headed first by Har Dayal and later by the BIC's Dr. Mansur Ahmed. The Istanbul office was to be the hub for coordinating efforts in Egypt, Persia, and Mesopotamia. Plans for importing the revolt to India were deployed along the three major approaches to the subcontinent: over land from the northwest across Persia to the Afghan frontier, from the northeast across Siam to the Burmese frontier, and by sea from the Dutch East Indies.[19] Each of these three strategic initiatives was delegated primarily to a different segment of the Indian revolutionaries abroad: the northwestern land route to the Pan-Islamists and Europe-based nationalists, the northeastern land route to the California Ghadarites, and the southeastern sea route to the domestic Bengalis.[20] However, there were multiple connection points among the campaigns, and many individuals played a role in more than one area.

We will return later to the western approach, pausing here only to note one of the fruits of the German mission across Persia to Afghanistan: namely, the establishment of a self-designated Provisional Government of India in Kabul. Nirode

Barooah calls this provisional government in exile Barakatullah's "brainchild," as it was his suggestion that claiming a piece of land and achieving diplomatic recognition—that is, a state-to-state affirmation of sovereignty—would facilitate fund-raising by making it easier to procure war loans from other governments who opposed England.[21] From a strictly nationalist point of view, such recognition would be the very definition of freedom. Indeed, as Gobind Behari Lal put it, "The real significance" of the Berlin group was that "these Indian revolutionaries made great nations like Germany . . . recognize the concept of an Indian government in exile representing a free India."[22]

For now let us concentrate on the two entangled projects to India's east during the first half of 1915: one a gunrunning operation between Batavia and Calcutta; and the other, initial preparations for a Siam-based invasion across India's Burmese frontier. In order to focus on these projects we must first return to California, since it was through the Hindu-German Conspiracy trial in San Francisco, extending from November 1917 to April 1918, that the hidden events in East Asia entered the recorded narrative.

THE EASTERN FRONT

The BIC's East Asian initiatives were the ones most closely associated with the Californian branch of the movement abroad, second only to the initial mutiny attempt, which preceded any German role. East Asia was strategically important from the perspectives of both California and Berlin, due to the large number of Sikh and Muslim troops stationed in Burma and Malaya as military police, or as watchmen in Shanghai, Hong Kong, and the other British treaty ports of China.[23] There were also significant numbers of Indian laborers in the Philippines. Well before the war, in 1913, G. D. Kumar sailed from San Francisco for Manila, where he informed Taraknath Das in a letter that he was "going to establish a base . . . [to] supervise the work near China, Hong Kong, Shanghai. Professor Barakatullah is all right in Japan."[24] These cities, emerging as "subsidiary bases in the Ghadar network,"[25] were to serve as recruitment centers (garnering as many as six or seven hundred new activists),[26] propaganda distribution points, and intermediary links between San Francisco and India.[27] When C arrived in San Francisco in late 1914, several missions were already in the works: some to Shanghai via Japan to collect India-bound recruits; others to scout landing places in Java for arms and ammunition. Ram Chandra tasked C himself to go to Sumatra, where he was to contact the German consul for money and then go about the same tasks of recruitment, location scouting, and establishing contact with India.

Meanwhile, Bhagwan Singh nurtured a secret society in Shanghai until a few emissaries arrived from California to formalize a Ghadar branch there.[28] When he arrived in late spring or summer 1915 on the island of Sulu "in a small boat

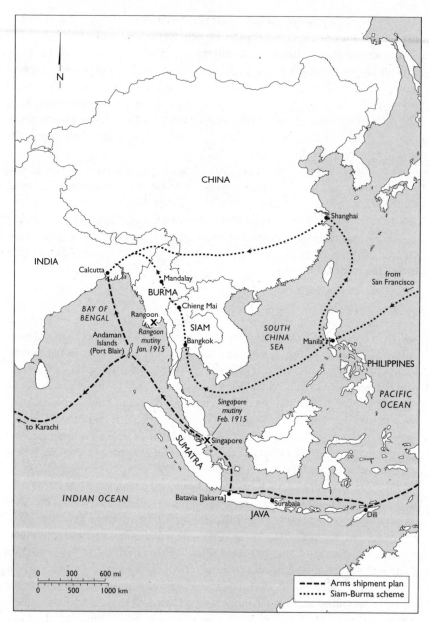

CHINA

INDIA

Calcutta

BAY OF
BENGAL

Andaman
Islands
(Port Blair)

to Karachi

INDIAN OCEAN

Mandalay

BURMA

Rangoon
Rangoon
mutiny
Jan. 1915

Chieng Mai

SIAM

Bangkok

Shanghai

SOUTH
CHINA
SEA

from
San Francisco

Manila

PHILIPPINES

PACIFIC
OCEAN

Singapore
mutiny
Feb. 1915

SUMATRA

Singapore

Batavia [Jakarta]

JAVA

Surabaja

Dili

N

0   300   600 mi
0   500   1000 km

- - - - Arms shipment plan
.... Siam-Burma scheme

MAP 2. Northeast invasion

laden with range-finders and other military equipments and maps," his destination was the Dutch East Indies.[29] Sent back to the Philippines after an arrest (for "trying to leave by an unopened port"),[30] he then proceeded to build Manila into one of the strongest Ghadar organizing centers in East Asia. In May 1915 the British consul at Manila wrote to the viceroy that Bhagwan Singh had turned up there accompanied by his friend Dost Mahommed, who was employed there as a watchman. Bhagwan Singh meanwhile had no apparent occupation other than propaganda work, distributing pamphlets to his countrymen, addressing small meetings, and collecting money for the cause. Many *Ghadar* issues had been posted from Manila into India, "wrapped well inside local papers and addressed not to the intended recipients, whose correspondence might be examined, but to unsuspected and inactive sympathizers, who would arrange for the transmission."[31] Those watching his movements reported him a frequent visitor to both the headquarters of the Indian Association of the Philippines and the local German consulate, which provided him with money.[32]

The German consul in Shanghai was supposed to be the anchor point for all Far Eastern operations, supervising the consulates in Bangkok, Batavia, and Persia.[33] In Hong Kong, the *Ghadar* of 29 August 1915 reported: "The American paper Gaelic [*sic*] . . . says that [there] the soldiers of the Indian army are trying to create a disturbance and that the soldiers are disobedient and turbulent to their officers. . . . They took all the Germans away to the south shore so that they could not have any intercourse with the Hindus. Later a telegram was received from Shanghai that somebody had thrown a bomb at the Governor of Hong Kong, and . . . escaped leaving no trace. Well done."[34]

The Batavia-Calcutta Scheme

Rash Behari Bose, Bhagwan Singh, and Abani Mukherjee had formed an independent council that sketched out a seaborne arms importation plan that they then presented to the German representatives in China (though they declined an invitation to a reception at the German consulate in Peking "owing to the fear of arrest").[35] A letter from the British consulate in San Francisco to the British Embassy in Washington, D.C., reported a plan "devised by Indians and financed by Germans" to ship fifty thousand rifles monthly from "a Pacific Coast port, not necessarily San Francisco," to a German-owned plantation in the Philippines, where the guns would be concealed inside hollowed-out teak logs or in plugged floating boilers for the next leg to Singapore via British North Borneo. There was no evidence that this ever got beyond the proposal stage.[36]

Simultaneously, Berkeley alum J. N. Lahiri arrived in Bengal from Europe in March 1915 bearing the separate offer of German aid to the circle of revolutionaries around Jatin Mukherjee. The Bengali Yugantar group then set up a fake import business in Calcutta called Harry & Sons to serve as a front for remittances and arms shipments. The scouts selected Dili on the island of Timor as the delivery point, and in April they sent a young emissary called Narendra-nath Bhattacharji—the future M. N. Roy, here going by the alias of Charles A. Martin—to Batavia as point man, at the BIC's suggestion. Jatin's cousin (and Dhan Gopal's brother) Jadu Gopal Mukherjee would then complete the cargo delivery inside Bengal. Confident that there were easily enough revolutionaries active in the province to take and hold the area—provided the British sent no reinforcements—they planned a three-part division of the shipment and dele-gated the operations to groups at Calcutta, Hatia, and Balasore. Each was to blow up the principal bridges on one of the three main railways. The Calcutta group was also assigned to seize the arsenals around the city, take Fort William, and sack the town, while the German officer slated to arrive with the gun shipment raised and trained an army in East Bengal.

But the entire ambitious program depended upon the arrival of the promised arms. The DCI was tracking the voyages of several ships, of which the most im-portant were the *Henry S, Annie Larsen,* and *Maverick.* A large part of the pros-ecution's case in the San Francisco trial rested on the details of these voyages.[37] The German ambassador in the United States, Count Johan von Bernstorff, wrote to Berlin in September 1914 announcing that he had found a German firm in San Francisco called Jebsen & Company that was willing to transport guns to India in a neutral ship. Military attaché (and chief German intelligence officer in the United States) Franz von Papen then passed along a report from New York that the American branch of the German arms dealer Krupp had managed to procure twenty thousand Spanish-American War vintage U.S. Army rifles equipped with cartridges, plus two hundred to three hundred automatic pistols; or, in other words, "eleven wagon-loads of arms and ammunition" to be loaded onto the char-tered schooner *Annie Larsen* in San Diego.[38] The *Annie Larsen* would take the cargo as far as the Socorro Islands off the Mexican coast, where it would rendez-vous with the *Maverick,* a repurposed tanker ship purchased from the Standard Oil Company. A German agent in San Francisco arranged with Ram Chandra to get a team of Indians aboard, laden with Ghadar literature and equipped with false identities. The weapons would be submerged in the oil tanks for the voyage to Batavia, where Bhattacharji would meet them, and the German consul would reveal further instructions. Unfortunately, through a series of mishaps the ships failed to make their rendezvous. The *Maverick* made for Java anyway, in hopes of meeting at some other point. The five Ghadarites burned their propaganda to save it from being searched by a British cruiser, and the weapons were seized when the *Annie Larsen* redocked in Aberdeen, Washington.

The testimony of supercargo John B. Star-Hunt, later a crucial witness in the San Francisco trial, offers us a glimpse of the voyage of the *Maverick.*[39] The cover story Jebsen had given when hiring the ship was that the *Annie Larsen* was carrying a "cargo of war material . . . for some belligerent faction in Mexico."[40] Star-Hunt had been skeptical, despite the fact that "American papers had taken the matter up" and there had even been "some sensational arrests of Americans and Mexicans" thought to be connected with the cargo. Jebsen also indicated vaguely that the *Maverick* was bound for a destination in the "Orient." Jebsen gave Star-Hunt two sealed letters, about which he appeared quite "anxious," with instructions to deliver them personally to a certain person on the other ship, and no one else. He also gave Star-Hunt an open letter containing enclosures with diagrams and instructions on "how to work the machinegun or a small Hotchkiss."[41]

The ship's multicultural crew included five mysterious "Persian waiters" claiming the names of Jehangir, Khan, Dutt, Deen, and Shamsher. Jehangir seemed to be the leader; Star-Hunt said that his real name was Hari Singh, though he didn't know the others'.[42] Star-Hunt described Hari Singh as "tall, big black moustaches, no beard, clean-shaven . . . very quiet and reserved in his manner; his age was hard to say, but I would say about forty years; he had evidently left India many (ten) years ago; he . . . did not speak English like an educated man, but read a lot of his own literature."[43] Then, recounted Star-Hunt, "when we were a couple of or three days out of Hilo," where they had stopped to take on fuel and supplies, "this man, Hari Singh, during a conversation referred once more to the literature he had destroyed at Socorro and said that it was the product of many of his countrymen who were in America and that he himself had contributed to it." Under the nom de plume Faqir, Hari Singh indeed was one of the main contributing poets to *Ghadar-di-Gunj*. Star-Hunt continued:

[Hari Singh] claimed to have the whole of [the literature] by heart and could repeat it without mistake. . . . He said that during the many years of his exile from India he had at various times written a good deal against the British rule in India. He gave me to understand that formerly he belonged to the Indian Army. He said that his home was in the far interior of the country, inhabited by ignorant classes, and that if he could only succeed in getting to them he could easily incite them to revolt against the British Government by promising to provide them with arms and ammunition. He . . . said that he knew the place we were bound for very well, and so did the other four, and that he could be of great assistance after we got there.[44]

At the appointed time as the ship neared Java, Star-Hunt finally read the top-secret letter from Jebsen that he had carried on his person all the way across the Pacific. It revealed the ship's true mission and gave instructions on how to proceed if encountering British warships or merchants: Act natural and confident; invite inspection; tell them the ship was being brought to Batavia to be sold or chartered for the China coast oil trade. The cases of rifles were submerged in one of the tanks, and the cases of ammunition placed in the other, though these were to be kept dry unless as a last resort. But under no conditions must the steamer or its cargo fall into British hands—better to sink the ship if the cargo was discovered and there was no escaping capture. A friendly boat was supposed to meet them at Anjer, but if for any reason they didn't make this rendezvous they were to proceed to Bangkok. And if there was no meeting there, they must press on to "Kurrachee." The password was "King George."[45] On the Sindhi coast the *Maverick* would be met "by numerous small friendly fishing crafts [which] together with the five blacks [sic] aboard would attend to the unloading and loading of the cargo. Two of the blacks should go ashore immediately on arrival and proceed in land to notify our arrival to the 'people'.... The remaining three blacks and the friendly natives would assist in burying the cargo."[46] Picks and shovels had been stowed on board. Even if no fishing boats met them, the two crypto-Ghadarites would still go ashore to notify someone, conceal and mark the cargo for later, and the ship would retreat to a neutral port.

In the end, Dutch destroyers escorted the *Maverick* to Batavia in July, searched it, and found it empty. Hari Singh and two of the others returned to San Francisco; the other two went to Bangkok, were arrested and sent to Singapore.[47] Meanwhile, as those on the other end waited in vain for the shipments, things began to fall apart piece by piece. A Chinese man named Ong Sin-Kwie [sic], trusted friend and former assistant of Emil Helfferich, chief German agent in the Dutch East Indies, had been delivering messages and money to Indians in Penang and Calcutta. Despite being "fitted out as a trader to sell batik and to buy gunnybags," he was taken ashore at Singapore, questioned, imprisoned, and threatened with being shot. He carried the Calcutta addresses written in invisible ink, ten thousand guilders in cash and ninety thousand more in checks. He didn't crack, though Helfferich said in a letter that his friend had "returned in a deplorable state."[48] He was allowed to return to Batavia with a promise to get his hands on more German money.

Then the British managed to procure the German telegraph and mail codes and began intercepting their communications. Even more damaging, several operatives turned approver. In August 1915 Harry & Sons was searched, resulting in some arrests. In September Jatin Mukherjee was killed in a skirmish during a raid of Universal Emporium, another branch of the faux trading company. The loss of his charismatic leadership was a heavy blow to the Bengali revolutionary infrastructure. And "Martin" had disappeared.[49] In October, two more Chinese were arrested in Shanghai in possession of 129 automatic pistols and 20,830 rounds of ammunition hidden in the center of bundles of planks, which a German called Nielsen had instructed them to deliver to Calcutta.[50] But the clincher in cracking the case was the discovery of a notebook on the person of Abani Mukherjee at the time of his arrest at Singapore on his way back to India from Japan, where he and Rash Behari Bose had been attempting to arrange for yet another gunrunning ship. The notebook was full of German and Indian names and addresses, including Nielsen's, where Rash Behari Bose was living at the time; and it indicated a scheme, now surely impossible, to wage war from bases in Tokyo and Shanghai.[51]

A final subsidiary aspect of this eastern Indian Ocean wing of the Indo-German collaboration was a proposal to divert a few nearby German ships, crewed with as many Germans as possible from Sumatra, to take the Andamans. After a quick stop to pick up machine guns and ammunition cached in the Nicobars (where it had been predeposited by a Swedish ship and also disguised as lumber), they would free the political prisoners at Port Blair, who by now included a good number of Bengali Swadeshi movement activists as well as a fresh batch of re-turned Ghadarites, and, it was thought, "men of the mutinous Singapore regiment," of whom we shall hear more later. The freed prisoners would then destroy the wireless station and form a rebel army to raid Rangoon, reinforcing those who were supposed to be massing in Burma. This group would be in charge of Chittagong and the mouth of the Hooghly. If things seemed to be going well, all the Germans in Siam and the Dutch East Indies would be conscripted to join the insurrectionary force.[52] This too never came to pass.

The Siam-Burma Scheme

There were great hopes for the potential of Burma as the third major prong of the BIC's global strategy, since aside from its location on India's northeastern frontier, it contained a small military garrison and a mostly Punjabi military police force likely to be sympathetic.[53] Moreover, a section of the Siam Northern Railway was under construction near the Siam-Burma border, where Punjabi Sikh contractors and laborers worked closely with German civil engineers. The frontier between Siam and Burma was a thousand-mile-long stretch of thinly populated jungle, with local inhabitants largely "Indian and Mohammedan," and thus an attractive region for smuggling arms or seditious literature.[54] When the activists arrived from the United States, they chose "places near the British frontier" such as Paknampho, "where a gang of 100 Indians was reported to be engaged in the manufacture of bombs under the supervision of two Germans"; or Bandon, located on a section of the Southern Railway staffed by Germans, where *Ghadar* consignments arrived weekly.[55] Indian residents in Siam were soon receiving a fortified diet of *Ghadar*'s "improved" version of the German fortunes of war, plus German-produced magic lantern shows.

Although the British consul at Bangkok had claimed that sedition was nonexistent in Siam before 1914, throughout late 1914 and early 1915 British observers noted a significant increase in Ghadar literature entering the country, as well as "an alarming increase in the import of sporting guns, rifles and ammunition, nearly all of which found their way to a mere eleven Malay dealers in the bazaar."[56] Then a secret message arrived on 2 August from the minister in Bangkok to the secretary of the Foreign and Political Department in Simla saying that the Siamese police had arrested three seditionists, from whom "considerable Hong Kong, Siamese and American currency bonds and many papers, books and clothings were seized." They were identified as Shiv Dayal Kapoor, Thakur Singh, and a third, who despite bearing a Persian passport issued in New York under the name Hassan Zade nevertheless "talks English well and Hindustani fluently, and has all the appearances of an Indian," and is described as "age 31 years, spectacles, height 5 feet 5 inches, wavy hair, forehead bald, black eyes and brows, a small moustache."[57]

A few days later Balwant Singh, a laborer from Canada, was arrested along with University of California students Darisi Chenchiah and Sukumar Chatterjee. More "incriminating" evidence was found at their house, namely, a secret code in Gurmukhi containing the sentence "Look sharp, we are delayed," and a letter in English asking for information on weights of packages for transport mules. Moreover, a "Browning pistol fully loaded" was unearthed in the room occupied by Thakur Das and Shiv Dayal Kapoor, "and a long knife under the bedding."[58]

The series of cases known to the juridical record as the Mandalay Conspiracy revealed something much bigger than a local Siamese intrigue. There were German and Turkish fingers in the pie, and those pesky Ghadarites were in it too—none of which can have been much of a surprise by that time. C made a statement in San Francisco titled "Object, Organization, and Fate of the Expeditions," which explained that "the main German object in the East is to bring about a successful revolution in British India and thus hasten the desired and expected collapse of the British Empire."[59] Within that larger goal he enumerated an ambitious list of action items: 'to foment trouble in China, Siam and the Shan states in order to distract the Allies' attention, to train and arm Indians in Siam, and so prepare a force to invade Burma, to co-operate with the Ghadar Party, organize a separate organisation in fomenting sedition, to assist Indians in India in organizing the preliminaries of a revolt, and in arranging the reception in India of the necessary money and arms." His list entitled "Principal Organizers of the Expeditions" included Heramba Lal Gupta (then designated BIC liaison to the United States), Ram Chandra and Godha Ram of the Ghadar Press, and German-Americans Albert Wehde and George Paul Boehm. He also named seventeen more who joined in Siam, one in Singapore, and three in Burma.

Gupta had met with Boehm in Chicago in March 1915 and asked the retired military officer whether he would be interested in training and commanding a force of ten thousand Indians in Burma to be ready when the gun shipment arrived on the *Maverick*. This force, in collaboration with the Burma military police (having been "seduced" to the cause by Ghadar literature), would take control of the country. Then, even if that failed to spark an insurrection in India, Burma could still serve as a northeastern base of operations, much like Afghanistan in the northwest. German agents in the United States and Mexico would supply weapons and money via the Far East.

The details of this plan came to light through, besides C, informers A, Z, and X.[60] A was Boehm;[61] Z may have been Shiv Dayal Kapur or Sukumar Chatterjee.[62] X, a German Secret Service agent, had in his possession detailed maps of the islands, photographs of the jail, and lists of officials, troops, police, and notable political prisoners, "which he said [were] written out for him in Berlin; the handwriting . . . turned out to be remarkably like that of Bhupendra Nath Dutt."[63] Assistant DCI Ker laid out his clues with the care of a detective story, including a notebook sketch of a ship with horizontal signal lights; color drawings of coded flags; slips of paper inscribed with destinations, arrival times, and number of revolvers; and twin notations found in the possession of Boehm and Kapur when arrested in Bangkok in August.[64]

But perhaps it might be most helpful to tell this rather convoluted story through the perspective of the eyewitness on whose testimony the case largely came to rest.[65] Within a couple days after Hassan Zade's arrest, it was confirmed that he was indeed an Indian, and that his name was Jodh Singh Mahajan. The British ambassador had had him confronted with a local resident of Persian origin, with whom he proved "unable to carry on any conversation."[66]

Born around 1884 near Rawalpindi, Jodh Singh had been educated in Amritsar and then employed by railroad contractors in Lahore, Calcutta, and Assam. After only a couple of months on the job, he absconded with a five-hundred-rupee check his boss had given him to deliver, cashed it, ran away to Chittagong, and then sailed for Canada via Penang and Singapore. He arrived in Vancouver in early 1907 and spent the next year working as a laborer in Portland. As soon as he was able to save a little money, he sent a check to his father, asking him to pay back the man from whom he had "borrowed" his passage. But the man insisted he owed a thousand.

"I then tried to get into the service of General Electric Company," Jodh Singh related, "but the Secretary of this concern, an Englishman, would not have me owing to racial prejudice. I, therefore, left Portland thoroughly disgusted, and crossed over to England." It was winter 1908. Jodh Singh spent three weeks in London casting about for a job until he went to India House "to see if they could fix me up." Here he met Har Dayal. "In reply to his enquiry I told him that I had to leave America, as I could not get any decent employment owing to race hatred. He, however, could not help me. He said that he, too was going to the States for study, but he did not tell me what he intended to study."

So Jodh Singh moved on yet again, this time to Berlin. During the two years he spent there, he recalled, "I used to get letters from Madame Cama in Paris, asking me to go over there and join their *Bande Mataram* staff, and assist them in their work." The movement matriarch also invited him to write something for the journal. "I already had notions of Home Rule for India" he admitted, "and Madame Cama's letters influenced my imagination further." But in ensuing correspondence he demurred, saying that while he was indeed a patriot in full sympathy with their cause, he was too busy working at present to write.

In October 1910 he sailed for Rio de Janeiro, where his intention was to set up a business serving the large number of Indian emigrants in Brazil; "later I began to think that it would be a good idea if I could only get them together and give them a general education, so that others would not be able to reproach Indians for being ignorant and uneducated." He and Niranjan Singh, a medical student newly arrived from Calcutta with a similar goal of improving the lot of Indians there, together approached the Brazilian government to facilitate immigration. But the response was not satisfactory. So Jodh Singh continued working for an overseas branch of his German employer, Siemens and Halske, and then for a string of other companies over the next four years.

Then, in February 1915, he received a fateful letter from someone calling himself "Mirza Hassan Khan" who wanted to meet him. He agreed to meet at Khan's hotel. The strange Persian claimed he had gotten Jodh Singh's name from Madame Cama. He was looking for a job; could Jodh Singh help? Jodh Singh agreed to do his best. When they met again a few days later Khan asked if he had heard of Ajit Singh. "I said I had read in *The Ghadar* paper of certain Ajit Singh who had come to Paris from Persia." The stranger then revealed that he himself was none other than that illustrious exile.

At this point Jodh Singh had been reading the *Ghadar* for about two months. After encountering it among the Rio de Janeiro Sikhs, he was interested enough to write to San Francisco asking to be listed as a regular subscriber. He also took up a collection from his Indian friends to send the Yugantar Ashram a donation of $25. Apparently Ajit Singh was sufficiently satisfied of Jodh Singh's sympathies and capabilities that not long afterward he tendered a proposal. Would Jodh Singh be interested in taking on a very important task? The catch was its urgency; he would have to resign from his job and leave immediately. Jodh Singh hesitated, wary of forfeiting the back pay owed him if he didn't give a month's notice. But Ajit Singh reassured him he would be taken care of financially. He could reveal no particulars of the job yet, but if they could meet in Berlin, all would be explained.

A fortnight later Jodh Singh was crossing the Atlantic on "Mirza Hassan Khan's" passport.[67] Chatto and Har Dayal received him in Berlin. Although Ajit Singh failed to arrive as he had said he would, over the next month Jodh Singh did meet with the "principal leaders of the society known as the Indian Revolutionary Society," including Dr. Hafiz, Dr. Prabhakar, Dr. Mansur, and Barakatullah. He attended a few of the meetings as well: "I remember one in particular . . .

attended by many Germans, Persians, Turks, and Indians." With Oppenheim presiding, "Har Dayal spoke at great length. The burden of his speech was that Indians must try with the help of Germans to establish a republic in India," in the cause of which, Har Dayal asked him afterward, would Jodh Singh be willing to go San Francisco to assist Ram Chandra? "I was to inform [him] that the German Government was ready to give financial help and that everything should be done to promote the object of the Ghadar party, that reliable men should be sent out to various places for getting Indians together and filling their minds with notions of independence and a republican form of government."

Jodh Singh was issued yet another passport (Ali Hassan this time, a name formerly used in Turkey by Heramba Lal Gupta's U.S. replacement Chandra Kanta Chakravarty) plus ship and rail fare to cross an ocean and a continent. On the way he was instructed to meet with Gupta in New York. Incidentally, when he disembarked there in late April, the German consulate first gave him the address of the *Gaelic American,* and he rang up Gupta from there to come meet him at the press. But when Jodh Singh passed on his messages, Gupta persuaded him that he might be more needed in Siam than at the Ashram. So Jodh Singh agreed to wait around in New York for a few more days to meet Wehde, the mission's financier. They met for dinner at a German restaurant, conferring in that language— which Jodh Singh had picked up along the way, plus English and Portuguese. He met Wehde again in Chicago, where he was introduced to Boehm, Sterneck, and Wehde's friend Jacobsen, who "seemed to be a great friend of Dr. Hafiz," whom Jodh Singh knew from Berlin. But Jacobsen made no bones about his country's interest in the matter, and it was not a commitment to anti-imperialism: "He said if the Indians were successful Germany would have a free hand in the Indian trade."

Once in San Francisco Jodh Singh "called on Ram Chandra at the Ashram, gave him the message from Har Dayal, and informed him of the change in my plans," backed up with a letter from Gupta to that effect. Through the eyes of the newcomer we glimpse the second phase of the operation: Ram Chandra "took me down to his place in Valencia Street, and showed me the Ghadar Press, where they print incendiary literature, and took me a few times to the exhibition to meet some Indians working there and whom Ram Chandra was inciting to join the revolutionary movement." The visitor learned "that the affairs of the Ashram were managed by four Indians, besides Ram Chandra, who was, of course, the leading spirit. . . . [The others] are all young men who look more like labourers than students."

Ram Chandra also wanted to give Jodh Singh some Ghadar publications to take with him, but he refused: what if he were searched? The editor then gave him an "open letter addressed to Bhagwan Singh in Manila," asking him to start a press in Siam and Batavia, and saying that some money was on its way to India, as well as preachers to Shanghai and Nanking, "as there is great demand for them." Unfortunately this letter too was seized, said Jodh Singh, who noted that the fact that Ram Chandra had already sent about a dozen letters to Bhagwan Singh, none of which seemed to have been received, which probably "indicated that their enemies were on the alert."

In the meantime, Ghadar members Sohan Lal Pathak and Harnam Singh Sahri had arrived in Bangkok in January 1915 bearing still more letters from San Francisco, to start making arrangements in Burma. Pathak had worked for several years as a peddler in Siam, then made his way to a pharmacy course at Corvallis University in Oregon by way of Hong Kong and Manila, just in time for the rise of the Ghadar movement.[68] Sehri had been deported from San Francisco for illegal entry while attempting to get arms for the *Komagata Maru* passengers. Since then he had been waiting at Yokohama, fearing to disembark in a British port lest he be arrested. Joined by five others, they crossed the Burmese border in late February or March and set up a base in Rangoon "for the accommodation and meeting place of the Ghadar Society" through which they hoped to smuggle arms, literature, and fighters between Siam and India. Then they traveled around the Sikh temples of Burma advocating their cause. They also set up a facility at Pakho for mechanical duplications of Ghadar publications, which were then sent to Burma through a confederate named Chalia Ram, aka Prince Charlie. Three new conspirators arrived that spring bearing messages and money from the German contacts in Shanghai.[69] In June a "large parcel of seditious literature" was seized in Myawaddy on the Burma-Siam border, which included two hundred copies of *Ghadar* in Urdu, Gurmukhi, and Hindi, plus a thousand locally produced leaflet copies. "One was a poem from the Ghadr, followed by a short piece of original composition, and the other, which was entitled 'A Message of Love to Military Brethren,'" was "a scurrilous attack on the British Government and the English."[70]

But this was a hiccup; more reinforcements were on the way from California. As Jodh Singh prepared for his departure amid a flurry of meetings and transactions, letters and contacts were exchanged, and arms and money stowed or received at the consulate. Some confusion was already apparent; whether this was a matter of fatal incompetence or cunning subterfuge remains unclear.[71] Nor was Jodh Singh told that the anonymous Bengali he had seen at the Ashram was his intended cohort Sukumar Chatterji until both were on board the *Tenyo Maro,* though Chatterji "was evidently looking out for me." He and his companion Chenchiah, said Chatterji, were also going to Manila, and Jodh Singh "was to help them with money." Sensibly enough, Jodh Singh replied that he "knew nothing about Chenchayya and, as I had no advice, I could not do anything for them. Subsequently, he himself came and saw me, but he did not tell me his purpose, nor did I tell him mine." According to Z, their assignment was to "do the preliminaries and recommend places and forests where all these operations are to be carried on . . . survey places and submit photos for approval," gleaning information from "the German railway officers on the line and their Punjabi overseers and surveyors."[72] But only when the ship docked in Manila did it become clear in Jodh Singh's account that he and Chatterji were each aware of the other's role in a shared mission. And it wasn't until the German consul at Manila (who also knew nothing about Chenchiah) was able to wire Boehm in San Francisco that they received confirmation that Chenchiah was indeed part of the plan and should be paid. (Jodh Singh gave him $100.)

And the confusion only increased; Jodh Singh saw hints of an ominous degree of disorganization. Boehm "complained that no details regarding the Siam expedition were settled when he came and that he had to do everything himself." The German consul, when they met, seemed oblivious to the mission, inquiring about the food situation in Berlin and how many prisoners of war were currently there. He and Boehm hoped Jodh Singh could help them identify the location of a place called "Chicacole" on the Indian coast. Jodh Singh consulted a map inconclusively. A telegraphed message had arrived from San Francisco that the arms shipment from Mexico was to unload at this "Chicacole," but the message was in code, and no one could quite figure out where was meant. (It seems that British intelligence knew the codes far better than the German and Indian participants did.) No shipment had been received, and they were starting to suspect—correctly—that it had been captured somewhere along the way. Moreover, when Jodh Singh visited the local *gurdwara* to give his letter to Bhagwan Singh, no one seemed able to find him. (It turned out he had left for Japan a few days earlier.)

Despite his growing unrest and doubts about Boehm's reliability, Jodh Singh left Manila with Chatterjee and Chenchiah on 26 June. Each carried a sealed letter for the German consul in Amoy. On delivering their messages, the bearers were told to proceed to Bangkok. Chenchiah was broke again and had to borrow another $50 from Jodh Singh, though his reluctant benefactor was by this time "getting hard up myself." In Swatow a rather suspiciously ingratiating and inquisitive Indian shopkeeper called Haroon helped them find lodging at a Chinese hotel. By now paranoia was justifiably rife. Prudently, they told Haroon no more than that they were on their way to Siam. At the hotel they found two other Indian guests (Thakur Singh and Balwant Singh), quickly "packing up to leave as they were suspicious of our being government agents." But in the course of conversation they all were able to soothe one another's nerves enough to establish that they were indeed on the same mission.

By the time they reached Bangkok on 17 July, any trust between the Indians and the German consulate had evaporated. The consul was standoffish and uncooperative; none of the promised arms or troops seemed forthcoming. And where was Boehm? It turned out he and Wehde were aboard the *Henry S,* which was "wandering about the Malay Archipelago in an aimless way."[73] The *Henry S* was supposed to bring five hundred of the five thousand revolvers in the shipment from Manila to Bangkok, and the rest to Chittagong.[74]

Moreover, though they didn't know it yet, Sukumar Chatterjee had turned approver.[75] Nevertheless, for the moment the team continued with the attempt to import mutiny across the northeastern border, or to rouse it among the troops stationed throughout East Asia. Some split up into several parties to cross into Burma, laden with "firearms, ammunition, explosives and instructions for making bombs . . . and Ghadar literature," with which they managed to induce three members of the Military Police Reserve Battalion at Pyaabwe to join them in their quest to "deprive the King Emperor of the sovereignty of British India."[76] In August two parties totaling twenty-two Indians and one American named Charles W. Allen, "all more or less connected with the Ghadr movement," were caught on the border and interned; the American was deported. The others scattered and headed for Siam. Those accused of infringing Siamese neutrality were deported to Singapore. Arrests and seizures continued throughout the summer and fall. Narayan Singh, who had come across the frontier from Siam, where he was working on the railway, was captured in a coffee shop in Maymyo five days later, carrying a copy of the *Ghadar* and a fully loaded pistol, which he tried to use against the police. Boehm was arrested in September in Singapore while en route from Batavia to Shanghai. Sohan Lal Pathak was arrested in August at Maymyo, "in the act of attempting to incite soldiers of the Mountain Battery of Artillery to murder their officers and mutiny and distributing Ghadar literature to them," and then hanged under the rules of the Defense of India Act.[77] Jodh Singh was detained in the Bangkok jail for about two weeks in early August, and then shipped to Singapore. The ministry at Bangkok telegrammed Simla in late October with the assurance "Operations continue with good results against revolutionary Indians in northern Siam." Eight Browning pistols, three thousand rounds of ammunition, and several Sikhs had been taken into custody, including the *granthi* of the Chiengmai *gurdwara,* "which place was an important centre of this movement."[78]

The Mandalay Conspiracy trial began in December 1915, with two additional special tribunals the following spring, and a supplementary case in the summer of 1917. Although Jodh Singh and his codefendants agreed that they would "defend ourselves as far as we could and not make any confession," in the end nine were hanged, and seven transported for life.[79] Jodh Singh turned approver and was not sentenced. Though we cannot know the precise circumstances of his actions, it was highly probable that he, like other approvers, was subject to torture or death threats. In any case we have not heard the last of him.

THE HINDU-GERMAN CONSPIRACY

The war did more than warp discourse and shape tactics; overshadowing the landscape, it also changed the material conditions in which the revolutionaries functioned under both British and American regimes, especially the practices of the empire related to policing, and to military personnel. In the preface to Ker's report, Director of Criminal Intelligence C. R. Cleveland frankly acknowledged that the war was proving quite convenient in making feasible enhanced powers of surveillance, policing, and punitive action against any "politico-criminal activity." Indeed, he commented, "the Great War has helped us a great deal in this endeavour." Cleveland explained: "At the beginning of [the war] we were severely handicapped by the breakdown of the Law Courts in Bengal, which had proved quite unable to deal with Revolutionary crime and criminals, with the result that there was no working system of punishment for the latter, while information was difficult to obtain and almost impossible to use." But now, "the combination of politico-criminal plots with enemy intrigue and aims enabled the police and executive authorities to use the special war powers with the most telling effect against the plotters, and our system of intelligence, prevention and punishment improved tremendously. One result of this was to give a great impetus to non-criminal political agitation which is now at a high level."[80]

The war thus served as an excuse for a crackdown on all kinds of radical and subversive activity and allowed an expansion of the state's legal use of force and special powers. The Ingress Ordinance passed in September 1914 gave port officers secret instructions that every returning Indian, "whether labourer, artisan, or student, was to be regarded with the greatest suspicion and even as a potential revolutionary." Those who rang alarm bells, whether confirmed revolutionaries or "reasonably suspected to be of revolutionary affiliations," should be intercepted and detained or interned.[81] This was the fate of over three thousand would-be Ghadar mutineers.[82] Even more sweeping, the Defense of India Act, passed in March 1915 just after the mutiny, allowed for detention without charge and special tribunals without a jury for political cases.

The Sedition Committee Report of 1918 then made recommendations, largely based on its summary of the wartime activities of the revolutionaries abroad, to retain the Defense of India Act provisions into what looked to be an equally restive postwar period. This was the "Revolutionary and Anarchical Crimes Act," commonly known as the hated Rowlatt Act after the justice heading the committee. In a letter to local governments and administrations on 19 April 1919, the secretary to the government of India counseled that a resolution be read to the troops explaining the act's object and scope in order to quell rumours and grumbling. "You, who have seen something of the world," they were to be told, "and who have helped to win the Great War, know the principle for which the Sirkar has fought, to promote liberty and to stop the oppression of the weak. You know the Sirkar would never pass an unjust and repressive law, such as this new Act is falsely represented to be." Surely they had heard of that nefarious plot supplied by German gold.[83] Such plots must be crushed. But loyal subjects had nothing to fear; the new law was aimed only at criminal force by outlaws "ready to rob, loot and murder peaceful citizens"—namely, innocents and Europeans—in their goal to "overthrow the King's government." Demonstrations against this legislation led to the Amritsar massacre, which then catalyzed the intensification of the independence struggle in the 1920s.

But natives of the subcontinent found themselves on the administering end of the state's monopoly of force as well. Indian troops such as those addressed in the message above were the backbone of Britain's campaigns in Mesopotamia and Egypt, while the Western Front rested on the muddy backs of Indian noncombatant laborers in France.[84] One result of such experience of the war was to douse the tendency to think about violence and blood sacrifice as ennobling and purifying (which had been typical of Swadeshi militance, Sorelian revolutionary syndicalism, and turn-of-the-century anarchist and nationalist propaganda by the deed). It also put to rest any conception of the West as vanguard of progress, giving the lie to its claim to a civilizing mission by revealing the "advanced" industrial world's annihilating savagery; and that of the United States as the cradle of liberty, poised as it now was to become a world economic and military power on the rubble of the older empires.

The United States' nationalist rhetoric had therefore also been significantly amplified in the course of the war, which was followed by an internal crackdown on dissent and radical activity corresponding to its new projection of power outward. This shift was visible in the conduct of the San Francisco Conspiracy trial in 1917–18, and the treatment of radical immigrants thereafter. It had always been the prudent policy of Ghadarites to avoid violating the laws of a country where they were working, and existing U.S. law contained no specific restriction on anything they had done as of yet.[85] Emily Brown points out that the Indians' Irish collaborators, and Mexican, Russian, and Polish groups, had all undertaken mobilizations to overthrow their home governments from U.S. soil; and that indeed there was still tacit acceptance of such a thing within the national self-image.

The United States' declaration of war abruptly negated Ghadar's legality. Even after the passage of the Espionage and Sedition acts in 1917, the violation would still have to be against the U.S. government and war effort, not against the British per se. But if German collusion could be proven in the Indians' attempts to ship arms from U.S. soil for use overseas in a conflict against an ally, then they could be indicted on violation of neutrality—or rather, conspiracy to violate neutrality. Thus without proof of a German role in ships leaving U.S. ports, and a link between those ships and seditious movements elsewhere, there was really not much of a case. With the Mandalay and Lahore Conspiracy Case statements now on the record revealing the byzantine details of arms shipments and mobilizations, there was incontrovertible evidence. And so it was the German connection that proved their downfall in North America and at the same time provided their main entry point into the U.S. historical record.[86]

The BIC first sent Heramba Lal Gupta to the United States in early 1915 as its designated liaison. Gupta was already familiar with the country, having paid a visit seven or eight years earlier "to study trade questions with a view to help[ing] the Indian nationalist industrial movement," and had helped coordinate some sort of revolutionary committee in New York. He went to Berlin at the beginning of the war. Now he was equipped with ample funds and instructions to put in motion a plan for moving men and arms in significant numbers to India, maintaining mailing addresses for the purpose in New York, Massachusetts, and Chicago, the latter under the name of Gomez, c/o Jacobsen.[87]

In addition to his work in the United States, Gupta had been advised to start recruiting in the West Indies, British Guiana, Trinidad, British East Africa, Java, and Sumatra. Trinidad was even named as a potential spot for an independent Hindustani republic.[88] Gupta in fact became fixated on the idea of rousing the Indian labor force in the West Indies, but this didn't bear much fruit, despite Bhagwan Singh's efforts in the region.[89]

Gupta was also asked to focus on Japan, where a number of Ghadar agents were already active. When the BIC was reorganized in 1916, Gupta relocated there and was replaced as Berlin-America liaison by Chandrakanta Chakravarty, who proved to be as controversial a figure as Ram Chandra, and if anything trusted even less in all quarters. He was continually requesting additional funds from Germany, little of which ever seemed to reach the activists in California, for the stated expenses of travel, guns, propaganda, and so on. Intelligence correspondence often described him as "oily" and "slippery," though nevertheless "a very dangerous man," and made much of his living situation, in flamboyantly exotic Oriental splendor, with German doctor and close friend Ernest Sekunna.[90] By zeroing in on this pair, intelligence gatherers were able to connect the dots to the German official (and designated United States arms coordinator) Franz von Papen; his secretary, Wolf von Igel; and Franz Bopp, the German consul in San Francisco, and thence to the San Francisco Ghadar group.

Even before U.S. President Wilson's declaration of war was made public, the assistant attorney general had authorized U.S. attorney John Preston to arrest Ram Chandra and his cohorts Chakravarty and Sekunna in New York, and their German collaborators, for a total of 105 indictments, of which 35 were Indians. The trial began on 12 November 1917 and dominated sensationalistic news headlines for months until it closed in April 1918. The scale of the trial was unprecedented: the *San Francisco Chronicle* reported that in the end it cost the British government $2.5 million and the United States government $450,000.[91] More than two hundred secret agents and other international personages were called as witnesses. In addition, sixteen defendants—ten Indian, six German—turned approver, and stipulations on admissible evidence regarding hearsay were relaxed so their testimony could be used against each other.[92]

The basics of the case, as presented in a note by the Northern District Court of California, First Division, clarifying charges in the case of *U.S. v. Ram Chandra et al.*, were these:[93] three violations of the neutrality law, for providing or preparing means for a military expedition against the territory or dominions of any foreign prince or state, colony, district or people with whom the United States was at peace; twenty-eight counts of conspiracy to violate neutrality laws, including the recruiting law prohibiting enlistment to fight in a foreign army against a nation with which the United States was at peace, and the military expedition law prohibiting organization of such a campaign against such a nation. Defining conspiracy, stipulated the court, required two things: first, two or more people planning together to commit any offense against the United States or to defraud the United States in any manner or for any purpose; and second, one or more people carrying out any act to effect the object of the plan. Consummation of said object was irrelevant and did not constitute a valid defense against the charge of conspiracy. On the neutrality violations, the immediate precedent was Mexico. Similar charges had been used against Huerta and Orozco during the revolution, but the trials weren't completed, due to the death or flight of the principals. The law against launching military expeditions had also been previously used against Irish Fenians circa 1866–67 and Cuban insurrectionists in the 1890s. But those trials were unpopular with the American public, and obtaining convictions had proven difficult.[94]

In mapping out the basic structure and program of the alleged conspiracy, the prosecution identified three centers of Indian organizing in the United States— San Francisco, New York, and Chicago—all in contact with each other and with German consuls and agents.[95] San Francisco was easiest to get a handle on, "for all they had to do was to get into touch with the Ghadar party. Most activists anywhere in the country going to or from India would pass through the strong and well-organized center, usually with a stop at the Yugantar Ashram.

The network's worldwide activities were coordinated via Berlin and included "elaborate and far-reaching machinery" in several categories that replicated the categories in the lists given in the Lahore and Mandalay trials: (1) propaganda; (2) dispatch of recruits; (3) dispatch of arms; (4) dispatch of money; (5) military enterprises in bordering countries (i.e., Burma; Afghanistan); (6) suborning of captured Indian soldiers; (7) "intrigue in China and Japan, designed to secure the assistance of political parties and, if possible, of the government in those countries."[96] Note that the evidence in the case triumphantly summarized above by the government advocate encompassed all activities of all branches of the revolutionary movement abroad, regardless of the type or degree of participation of the Caliifornia group in particular.[97]

Yet claiming complete separation would be as misleading as attributing all to Germany. And regarding the *degree* of autonomy, the juridical nature of the evidence (and a heavily partisan historiography) affects interpretation, given that the case for the prosecution was based on maximizing evidence of German involvement, and the defense on minimizing it. Furthermore, one of the great benefits of the conspiracy approach, from the prosecutorial perspective, is that weaving plausible relationships is enough; proving individual agency for any specific act that can be woven into the net is unnecessary so long as the agent in question can be woven into the same net.[98] I do not intend carelessly to replicate this tactic. However, if a historian, not a prosecutor, is assessing a movement, not a party, then it is appropriate to acknowledge the scale of the literature's influence, the scope of the partnerships, and the fact that many individuals of all religions and regional origins who participated in various German-backed projects had individual histories of involvement in Ghadar or close working ties with those who did. The web of revolutionaries abroad crossed and recrossed at multiple points; no thread could ever be completely disentangled from the others.

Nearly two years after the first Mandalay trial, Jodh Singh was summoned from India to San Francisco to testify as a government witness, as he was "a Hindu of more than ordinary intelligence and had a competent knowledge of the conspiracy," having been central to the events "detailed in these stories."[99] But when his turn came in the stand, he laid stipulations before the government that before giving his evidence he wanted certain pledges of leniency for the defendants. Had this after all been his intention from the start, in agreeing to testify? John W. Preston, the prosecuting U.S. attorney, refused the conditions; Jodh Singh refused, in that case, to talk. He was removed from the stand, arraigned as a defendant for his role in the Siam-Burma mission, and detained for the duration. The report commented laconically: "It was one of the dramatic incidents of the celebrated trial."[100]

But the most dramatic incident of all came right at the end. As the case proceeded, with the community under intense pressure and public scrutiny, the factional animosity and mutual recriminations escalated. On the very day the judgment was to be announced, 23 April 1918, Ram Singh of the Bhagwan Singh faction managed to smuggle a pistol into the courtroom, tucked inside his turban; an accomplice had passed it to him in the hall when he went out to get a drink of water. Just as Ram Chandra was "about to testify concerning the subversive activities of the organization," Ram Singh shot him point-blank as a traitor. The avenger was shot dead a few seconds later where he "stood calmly with the gun in his hand," by a quick-reacting U.S. Marshal.[101]

Fifteen surviving Ghadarites were found guilty, along with nineteen accomplices. They got prison terms ranging from a few months up to almost two years, the heaviest being twenty-two months for Taraknath Das, twenty-one for Santokh Singh, and eighteen for Bhagwan Singh.[102] To the British the sentences seemed absurdly light. But they were put on probation upon their release with the warning that if they returned to producing propaganda, they would be subject to deportation and delivered to the dubious mercies of the "hated British Government as you term it,"[103] and this, they were well aware, would be when their real punishment would begin. The campaign against deportation would be the first priority of the Friends of Freedom for India, formed after the war.

As for Jodh Singh, he had been confined to Alameda County Jail while awaiting sentence, but before it could be announced, the "subject . . . went hopelessly insane." With the ruin of his once-sharp mind, he was described as a ghost of his former self; Harish K. Puri suggests he may have been subjected to torture before arriving in the United States to testify.[104] By court order he was transferred in March 1918 to the California State Hospital for the Insane in Talmage and remained there for the next three and a half years. The government kept tabs on him through the hospital authorities; their physicians' opinion was that while his mind was irretrievably gone, "his physical condition is such that he will probably live to a ripe old age." (He was now in his early thirties.)

Back in Rawalpindi Jodh Singh's father, Sardar Singh, had learned of his son's fate from Lajpat Rai and initiated correspondence to the Ghadar office to locate him. "Dear Countryman," wrote Sardar Singh, "My anxiety about my dear son is adding to the infirmities of age. You will earn my heartfelt gratitude and good wishes if you very kindly [help me in tracing his whereabouts]."[105]

The government had no objection to relinquishing custody, since they foresaw paying the hospital $30 a month for the upkeep of this public charge for years to come, and plainly he was no longer any threat. A passport was secured from the British government, and Judge Van Fleet, who had presided at the Hindu-German Conspiracy trial, gave the order that the Marshal was to deliver the subject to his father's custody on board ship. "Sardar Singh has informed this office that he sails for India with subject September 3, 1921, and this information has been conveyed to the U.S. Marshal," his file confirmed. "Case closed."[106] I do not know how long "the subject" lived, or if he ever regained his mind.

4

. . . and Friends

The Republican Ghadar

SELF-DETERMINATION

Though the Germans were willing to fund schemes and initiatives, they lacked a nuanced understanding of the goals of their various benefactees. In an alliance formed of statist thinking, they were in starkest terms the enemies of the enemy. But the partisans of two other major national liberation struggles whom the Germans were supporting, running along timelines roughly parallel to India's, were genuine friends. The Indians gravitated easily toward alliances with Irish republicans in the United States and Egyptian nationalists in France. What is most striking about these interactions is their strong sense of solidarity by analogy, identifying their brothers in mutiny as ideological kin based on their shared political aspirations and structural positioning vis-à-vis the British Empire. Even while impelled by the immediate goal of their own national liberation, they saw themselves as counterparts to, even implicitly identified with, other national struggles that seemed to resonate in common cause with their own. They were, in a sense, speaking the same dialect of the language of nationalism: aiming for citizenship within a democratic republic, a prerequisite for which was collective political emancipation.

Again and again the three groups turned up in the same contexts. Delegates from all three countries were present at the International Congress on Subject Peoples held at the Hague in August 1907, where a proposition was introduced "that claims of subject nations for the management of their own affairs ought to be recognized, and the Indian and Egyptian representatives . . . spoke in support of it."[1] With the war came German sponsorship; both Irish and Egyptian activists maintained Independence Committees in Berlin, which were "always friendly with Indian nationalists and eager to join forces."[2] A DCI report for December 1918 noted that the BIC had sent a telegram to ex-Khedive Abbas Hilmi, "congratulating him on his arrival in Germany and expressing the hope that the victory of the Central Powers would soon liberate the enslaved peoples of Egypt, India and Ireland."[3] Despite their patrons' defeat, the anticolonial triple alliance was not abandoned after the armistice was signed. The New York–based *Independent Hindustan* frequently covered its sister struggles, while an anonymous member of the Indian Committee in Stockholm contributed the India chapter for a Swedish book on "England and her suppressed peoples with special chapters on India, Ireland and Egypt."[4]

Of course, none of the three struggles was internally unified regarding the tactics of resistance, or the institutional form envisioned for an independent nation. Among the varied voices contributing to each national discourse, the question was, then, which of them our particular revolutionists would identify as their counterparts, based on which commonalities. First and foremost, all three shared a dedication to the Mazzinian legacy of liberal constitutionalism, national unification, and republican democracy. In the case of the Egyptians, a further area of similarity with India was the presence of an Islamic cultural identity in the makeup of a composite homeland. Though it was the dominant element in Egypt, in significant distinction from India,[5] both could still be situated in relation to a transnational Pan-Asian or Pan-Islamist bloc.[6] In the Irish case, there was no element of cultural or religious continuity and no prospect of sharing membership in any pan-entity, unless it was the reluctant commonwealth of the British Empire's subject peoples.[7] And yet that was one of the most solid and enduring partnerships of all, perhaps indicating the triumph of principle over ascribed identity as the root of solidarity.[8]

EGYPT FOR THE EGYPTIANS

An article in the *Ghadar*'s first issue (1 November 1913) under the heading "A Storm Is about to Burst in Egypt, Drizzling Has Already Started" suggested that Egypt's awakening was a good sign for the Indian movement, since the "key of the Suez Canal is in their hands."[9] The Egyptians might well have thought that India's awakening was a good sign for themselves, given that the British interest in controlling the region was generally recognized to be motivated by strategic concern over protecting Britain's precious access to India.

As it happens, the first meeting of Indian and Egyptian nationalists came about when F. Hugh O'Donnell, an Irish Home Rule MP and journalist, and early advocate of solidarity among peoples subjected to British rule, introduced the India House habitués to Mustafa Kamil, the founder of the Egyptian nationalist party Hizb-al-Watan, during his visit to London in July 1906.[10] Later, Indian nationalists also developed warm ties with Kamil's successor, Mohammed Farid (Farid Bey), and journalist Mansour Rifaat, Paris correspondent of the news-papers *El Alam* and *El Akhbar* and founder in March 1914 of *La Patrie Égypti-enne,* organ of the Egyptian Emancipation Movement in Geneva.[11]

It is far from irrelevant here to draw upon the Urdu vocabulary of national-ism, which makes a distinction between *vatan* (often equated with the French *patrie*), which is based on attachment to a specific territorial/cultural home place, and *qaum,* which refers to a people, a community of social identification, belief, and practice, not necessarily linked by definition to territory. Thirdly, there is the category of *millat,* referring to a community of faith. These bases of loyalty, alle-giance, and identity need not always be in conflict, though the difference in em-phasis and proportion among the three is what distinguished the variants of Egyptian nationalism throughout the first quarter of the twentieth century.[12]

A string of the DCI's weekly intelligence reports between 1908 and 1911 allows a stop-motion peek at the developing cooperation between the two movements abroad.[13] In December 1908, the Indian nationalists then resident in Europe held a conference intended to serve as a counterpoint to the meeting of the Indian National Congress (INC) being held concurrently in Madras, the first since the moderate-radical split.[14] This gathering passed resolutions demanding complete freedom; calling for a comprehensive all-India boycott of British goods; and con-gratulating the Turks on their recent achievement of a constitutional govern-ment. A number of Egyptian nationalists were also present at this conference, and a joint decision was made to form an Indo-Egyptian National Association "to co-ordinate their struggle against a common enemy."

Informants gave details of a series of public meetings held that month. At the first, Rana spoke on the Indian desire for Swaraj, arguing that mere reforms would not be sufficient, and that self-sacrifice would be needed "for the attainment of freedom and the achievement of nationalist ideals." At the second, Bipin Chan-dra Pal declared the nationalist ideal to be "the acquisition of a United States in India, and after gaining that form of constitution the state would be divided into monarchies, and the princes of India would receive the homage due to them." (The moderate Pal's notion of a unity of Indian states as a collection of constitu-tional monarchies was at slight variance from the revolutionists' version of a fed-eration of republican democracies such as they would describe in the *United States of India* after the war.) At the third, before a majority-Indian audience of three hundred, one "noticeable feature" was "an attempt to create an entente with other oppressed nationalities, such as the Persians, the Young Turk Party, the Young Egyptian nationalists, and the Irish." Someone declared "on behalf of Egypt" that his country would make common cause with the Indians, even blocking the Suez Canal if need be.[15]

Much of the rhetoric at joint meetings was defined by the negative content of eliminating British occupation. (Immediate items from the Indian agenda included the commemoration of 1857 and the progress of the Savarkar case.) On the positive side, modernization, reform, and self-strengthening were on the table. Both Mustafa Kamil and the Indian revolutionists favored the separation of politics from religion, making the latter a matter of individual concern. The Hizb-al-Watan, dominant in the Egyptian national movement before the war, was pro-Ottoman in the sense that it acknowledged membership in a wider Pan-Islamic body, still identified with the Ottoman caliphate (though not inevitably so; Egypt made its own case for the title in the 1920s) while simultaneously expressing a passionate and particular love for a superlatively lauded homeland. Kamil's innovation was to begin moving the emphasis to the region, with its unique culture, history, and geography bonding members of different faiths.[16]

Excerpts from Kamil's fervid speeches on the love of his motherland make it easy to see how those who had come out of the Swadeshi movement with *Bande Mataram* on their lips connected with Kamil's approach. But within this approach a nonrationalist veneration of the *patrie* was still able to coexist *both* with calls for a liberal constitution and republican democracy *and* with membership in a broader cultural/spiritual solidarity, whereas these elements grew much more polarized in the 1920s. Again, the affinities are not so surprising; a similarly underanalyzed coexistence of multiple elements prior to separation, formalization, and polarization also reflects what I have observed of the prewar Indian movement abroad.

On 2 January 1909, some London-dwelling Egyptians hosted "many leading Indian agitators" covering a broad ideological range, including Chatto, Ganesh Khaparde, Pal, and (future British Communist MP) Shapurji Saklatvala, at a dinner at the Imperial Hotel. Khaparde submitted in his after-dinner speech that "the Egyptians and the Indians had much in common as regards the government of their countries and he hoped to see them united in order to prove that the Muslim did not differ from the Hindu."[17] Pal expressed his hope that Egyptian emissaries should come to India to "preach what Mustafa Kamil Pasha used to preach." His proposal for a new Indo-Egyptian Club in London was accepted unanimously among the nineteen Indians and fifteen Egyptians present. Next, the infant Indo-Egyptian Society held a small meeting on 15 February at the Grand Hotel, Charing Cross, at which twenty-two people were present to commemorate the first anniversary of Mustafa Kamil's untimely death. An Egyptian, Dr. Maaz, took the chair supported by Society Secretary A. K. Selim. A few other Egyptians made speeches, followed by Pal, who again urged that the two groups should "cooperate and work together to attain their goal," and gave examples of injustices perpetrated in the courts by the English against "the black races" when both "white and coloured men sought justice."[18] Finally, Haider Raza spoke on a "favorite subject" of his, namely, Hindu-Muslim unity in the spirit of nationalism, in which only cooperation would bring about the fulfillment of their desires.[19]

Over the next few years the two expatriate communities organized conferences together, contributed words to each other's journals, offered friendship and advice, and even inspired one another to militant action. For example, Rifaat's *El Alam* printed a speech by V. V. S. Aiyar with accompanying commentary, and Rifaat himself was a frequent contibutor to the *Indian Sociologist*.[20] Har Dayal and other Indians attended the Congress of Egyptian Nationalists in August 1909 in Geneva, as did a number of Europeans, including "many Germans and Frenchmen."[21] There was speculation too not only that Har Dayal was acting as Krishavarma's agent, but that even at this early date the Germans who were there had "promised many things and sympathized with the views of the Indian Nationalists."[22] The business of the meeting was unknown, but the informer did note that "a proposal to hold a Pan-Asiatic Congress in Europe was made in the *Indian Sociologist,* some time ago, and this may have been a preliminary attempt to carry it out." Here we may witness the extrapolation from Indo-Egyptian collaboration to Pan-Asiatic congress. Or perhaps, to put it the other way round, the Indo-Egyptian collaboration was based on the underlying awareness of the possibility of a Pan-Asiatic congress. The same slip from Asia to Orient to Islamic world to Peoples of the East, and back again from one to the other, was to recur after the war in the context of the Communist strategy for the colonized world in the 1920s.

A year after the initial series of meetings, another round continued to build on the same themes. At a gathering at Caxton Hall on 29 December 1909 attended by both Indians and Egyptians, a lineup of speakers ranging from Lajpat Rai and B. C. Pal to V. D. Savarkar all expressed more or less the sentiment that death was preferable to the deprivation of freedom. Savarkar actually "called upon the audience to rise in a body and die for their country's sake." Apparently not quite prepared for immediate martyrdom, the attendees settled instead on the goal of "work[ing] up a joint movement" by issuing a circular inviting enrollment in the Indo-Egyptian Nationalist Association in London.[23]

But the Indian and Egyptian revolutionists formed even closer links in Paris, "the most important center of young Arab nationalists in Europe,"[24] where Indian radicals were making an exodus across the Channel in the wake of the Dhingra and Savarkar trials. Ibrahim Nassif al-Wardani's assassination of the Egyptian prime minister Butrus Ghali Pasha in Cairo in February 1910 (for his alleged intent to sell Egypt's share in the Suez Canal to Britain) was thought to be inspired by Madanlal Dhingra's assassination of Curzon-Wyllie in July 1909. The Egyptian poet El Ghayati linked the two young avengers in a song for which he was promptly charged with sedition.[25] A telegram Krishnavarma sent to the khedive requesting leniency, reprinted in *L'Humanité,* was of no avail. Like Dhingra, Wardani was sentenced to death. And as Dhingra's final words had declared it his duty as a Hindu to strike a blow for the freedom of his country, Wardani died proclaiming that "God is One and ... Mahomet is his prophet and ... liberty and independence is a saying of God."[26]

The Egyptian National Party planned to hold its second congress in Paris in late September 1910. Chatto was reportedly spending entire days at the organizers' office at the Hôtel des Sociétés Savantes, while Madame Cama was seen receiving many visits to her Paris home by a man in a motor car, identified as "Farid Bey, the Egyptian revolutionist." Apparently Jean Longuet had introduced the two, and it was thought the pair were coordinating their respective upcoming nationalist conferences.[27] Writing years later in the Kirti, Agnes Smedley said of this conference that the Irish too were active participants in the effort, observing: "The Indian revolutionaries working in England and France worked shoulder to shoulder with the revolutionaries of Ireland and many Irish men and women were most reliable companions of theirs."[28]

The event had to be relocated to Brussels after the French government banned it, claiming it did not want Paris to become "the centre of an anti-British crusade." But on the eve of the delegates' departure for Brussels, there was an "Indo-Egyptian soiree" attended by "about 150 Egyptians and Indians and 25 Europeans, mostly French and German journalists. Notice of this was not given to the police."[29] The guests included two Egyptian secretaries of the upcoming congress, Loutfi Goumah (editor of the paper Egypt) and Hamid-el-Alaily, who the DCI thought was paying "too much attention" to the Indians.[30]

In Brussels, sure enough "violent speeches were made" just as feared, "denouncing Britain and condemning Roosevelt" for supporting British colonial rule in Asia.[31] The belligerent addresses naturally included one from Har Dayal, who "created a sensation by calling upon Egyptians to refuse to be enlisted in the Egyptian army."[32] El-Alaily presented a paper called "The Moral and Intellectual Aspects of the Egyptian Political Movement," of which Har Dayal also claimed to be the author. Rifaat read his own paper, titled "The Egyptian Army," the proofs of which Chatto had corrected.[33] Without knowing the precise content of this paper, one can make a reasonable guess, given that an ongoing theme in Ghadar literature a few years later was to urge colonial troops not to fight as mercenaries on behalf of imperial masters but rather to mutiny and offer their arms to the forces of emancipation. Just such exhortations were made to Indian troops in France, Mesopotamia, and the Suez region during the war, and in China in the 1920s.

After the conference, Indians in Paris remained in regular contact with their Egyptian counterparts; certain of them met regularly with Rifaat.[34] Chatto in particular was concentrating upon building two complementary unities: Hindu-Muslim and Indo-Egyptian.[35] Indeed, an Indian nationalism capable of solidarity with Egyptian nationalism would have had to be based on the principle of Hindu-Muslim unity. They tried to hold another joint conference in Paris in September 1911, but it too was forestalled by a French government ban, and it too moved to Brussels. Farid opened the meeting, characterizing it as "indeed a very well-advertised demonstration of anti-British fraternity between the Indian and Egyptian nationalists." The Egyptians reiterated the pledge to block the Suez Canal against British reinforcements in the event of a revolt in India, and in return the Indians pledged to prevent Indian soldiers being used to suppress nationalist efforts in Egypt.[36]

By spring 1911 the DCI had determined that the four current main strategies of the Indian nationalists in Europe were "(i) the dissemination of seditious literature; (ii) the export of arms to India for the purposes of assassination; (iii) working up the sympathy of the Labour and Socialist parties in England; and (iv) cooperation with the Egyptian extremists in making common cause against the British."[37] Moreover, noted C. R. Cleveland, with concern: "About this time, there seems to have been a considerable amount of cooperation with the Egyptian revolutionists."[38] At least in Paris, however, the collaboration could not continue at the same level of intensity for much longer because of the scattering of the Indian radical circle there.

But the partnership was renewed in Berlin. In particular the BIC enlisted the aid of their Egyptian colleagues in a mission to propagandize soldiers in the strategic Suez Canal region, to be coordinated from Istanbul, where their old friend Farid Bey helmed the German-backed Egyptian subcommittee, and Har Dayal the Indian one.[39] These old friendships were also reactivated in a rather anomalous Swiss-Italian assassination plot in summer 1915, through which yet again we can witness the networks of radical ideologues crossing and recrossing. The plan was to simultaneously assassinate a number of "leading figures in Entente countries," including the Italian king and prime minister, the French president and prime minister, the British war minister and foreign secretary (the Egyptians' bête noire Lord Kitchener), using ten timed bombs.[40] Made in Italy, the bombs were to be tested by the military in Berlin and then delivered to Zurich. The principals were Chatto and Abdul Hafiz of the BIC, plus an Egyptian medical student named Ali Eloui who was close to Chatto, and an Italian anarchist named Luigi Bertoni. But the secret leaked out, and they had to abort the operation.[41]

Rifaat left Geneva in some haste in autumn 1914, probably in connection with the seizure of some his papers by the Swiss police wherein he mentioned a "somewhat vague and wild . . . scheme of action against British India including the assassination of officials and extensive propaganda."[42] The ever voluble C later revealed that Rifaat had come to America in October, "taking with him a large number of pamphlets for distribution among Indians at San Francisco through whom he hoped to get into communication with the revolutionaries in India."[43]

Although traffic from Egypt to the United States cannot have been heavy at this time, in January 1917 the DCI's main agent in Europe requested that the Egyptian police pass on to him any "names of suspicious Egyptians going to America."

After the war, the affinity was renewed yet again. As the Egyptian Wafd and Indian Non-Cooperation/Khilafat mass agitations got under way, an editorial titled "British Barbarities in Egypt" appeared in the December 1920 *Independent Hindustan* listing a hundred killed in Cairo by machine-gun sweeps of a peaceful demonstration; rape and pillage in a number of villages; and collective punishments including houses burned and male inhabitants flogged. If any corroboration were needed to lend credibility to these allegations regarding the British character, the author referred the reader to comparable atrocities in Corke Park and Punjab.[44] Mohammed Ali Sarvar, a correspondent for the Egyptian paper *El Akhbar,* spoke on the Egyptian national movement at the 1920 convention of the Friends of Freedom for India in New York.[45] Taraknath Das, closely associated with this group, wrote an article on the "international aspects of the Indian question," divided between the January and February 1921 issues of the *Independent Hindustan,* which also contained extensive coverage of the convention. Of Egypt he said: "Everybody knows that Britain acquired the Suez Canal to control the route to India. . . . As long as India remains under British control, England can use millions of men against Egyptian aspirations as she has done in Turkey and Persia." "In fact," Das pointed out, "Indian soldiers conquered Egypt" and guarded the Canal Zone during the war, even while Britain's control of the Canal Zone enabled quick naval access to any Indian revolt. Thus the "bond of alliance between Egypt and India [was] growing," based not merely on idealism but on "mutual interest and self-preservation." Leaders of both would be meeting in India; how perfect it would be, Das suggested, if the Irish could come too. He continued: "We support with all our power the cause of Egyptian independence, and of an Indo-Egyptian alliance. . . . And Indo-Irish-Egyptian alliance is the nucleus of a world alliance against the British Empire."[46]

IRELAND: OURSELVES ALONE

In January 1909, at one of the Sunday meetings at India House, V. V. S. Aiyar made a speech "in which he compared the present state of India with that of Italy before the war of liberation." Aiyar observed of India: "Oppressed by foreign conquerors, its ambitions curbed by a despotic power and the liberty of the press taken away, secret societies were bound to rise as they rose in Italy under Garibaldi. These secret societies would lead to the cherished object of the nationalists, viz., absolute self-government. The more the government tried to suppress them the stronger they would become."[47] We have already seen how frequently the Indian national revolutionists invoked the unification of Italy and the names of its heroes. In this they were cousins of the same family; Young Ireland and the Irish Revolutionary Brotherhood also drew deeply on the Mazzinian tradition.[48]

Since the mid-nineteenth century there had been avid interest in the comparability of the Indian and Irish situations among British colonial administrators, on the one hand, and among Home Rule parliamentarians and nationalist militants, on the other. The former feared and the latter hoped that loss of control in Ireland might presage loss of control in India or vice versa, fatally destabilizing the empire; both sides were alert to this opportunity.[49] For example, Irish patriots took appreciative note of the Indian Mutiny of 1857, while a certain class of Indians watched the development of Parnell's Home Rule movement with great interest during the era when the Indian National Congress (INC) was taking shape. The Swadeshi militants then studied Irish rebels along with Russian revolutionists for applicable techniques and tactics of resistance, noncooperation, parliamentary petition, and direct action. The analogy between the literal meaning and substantive intent of Sinn Fein and those of Swadesh/Swaraj was repeatedly made.[50] Ramnath Puri noted in *Circular-e-Azadi* in 1908: "The king is no longer to us the representative of God in the country. We have come to know that people possess the right of appointing and dethroning kings." He then added: "Swadeshi is for India what Sinn Fein is for Ireland."[51]

But there was not yet unmediated contact between the two populations; direct communications were confined to exceptional (albeit exceptionally influential) individuals such as parliamentarian Dadabhai Naoroji. Furthermore, initially at least, the mutual interest owed more to the same instrumental mentality of "England's difficulty is our opportunity" than to any warm feelings of fraternal solidarity. However, among the immigrant populations of the United States the contact was direct and personal among the patriotic émigrés of both countries, and in this situation the friendship went quite a bit deeper than convenience.

There had already been some contact between sympathetic Irish and the India House community in London. Savarkar, for example, had shrewdly looked for allies in the direction of other oppositional and/or internally critical factions of British society: "Recogniz[ing] that the supporters of the free-India cause were on the periphery of British politics and were tied to international movements, . . . he exploited every facet of the radical press on a worldwide basis."[52] This included the Irish movement against British rule, which already boasted experienced agitators and an active press. But it was in the United States that the Indo-Irish partnership, which Das named "one of the most important and active alliances we have entered into," truly blossomed.[53] In fact, the presence of Irish nationalists in the United States who were "ready to take up any movement likely to embarrass the British Government"[54] was considered an inducement for Indian revolutionaries to base their activities there, and therefore another reason for the British themselves to want to forestall such activities.[55]

The British Home Office had introduced its intelligence apparatus into the United States in the 1860s, to keep an eye on the Fenians during the period of their initial attempts at revolt. But India was the first colony in which the British applied extensive surveillance mechanisms politically. In 1906, the government of India's Home Department then made arrangements with the British Home Office to pass on weekly intelligence on Indian affairs, so often linked to those of the Irish, from its New York agency.[56] Spring-Rice even worried that any public vocalization of Indian grievances—such as student agitation at Berkeley in the case of their countrymen being denied admission by the United States government—would stir up the Fenians. (He also feared lest the reason for such a denial of entry might have some connection to "the spread of anarchistic propaganda, and violent proceedings of the IWW," thus echoing the perception of a linkage between student politics, labor radicalism, and internationalist solidarity.)[57]

When Barakatullah and S. L. Joshi founded the Pan-Aryan Association in New York in 1906, inspired by Krishnavarma's example in London, they drew on the help of prominent Irish nationalists, including George Freeman (aka Fitzgerald), John Devoy, and others; the first meeting of the association was written up in the *Gaelic American* of 2 March 1907.[58] The association's stated goal was to bring India and America closer together by helping students come, learn, and then return home to spread the ideas of freedom and democracy they had imbibed abroad.[59] But even if that goal might be construed as innocuous, it got worse: "With the cooperation of the Irish nationalists, the Association started anti-British propaganda and, in a meeting held in New York, resolutions were passed repudiating the right of any foreigner to dictate the future of the Indian people. The speakers urged their countrymen to depend upon themselves alone and especially on boycott and Swadeshi." In addition to anti-British propaganda, the association favored unification not only between Hindus and Muslims, but between Indians and Irish in overthrowing British rule.[60] At one meeting, Mr. Bulmer Hobson of Belfast was the main speaker, addressing the audience on the "Aims, Methods, and Working of the Sinn Fein movement."[61]

Another early connection was brokered through Myron Phelps, a lawyer, gentleman farmer, and American supporter of the Indians in New York, who offered scholarships to "highly recommended Hindu boys" at various U.S. universities through his Society for the Advancement of India. Phelps also founded the Indo-American National Association (with Naoroji as president), with the goal of rousing joint American, English, Indian, and Irish support in a "united demand for justice," if necessary leading toward "open revolution in India to throw off the foreign yoke." According to the DCI's history sheet on Phelps his series "Letters to the Indian People" appeared first in the *Gaelic American* of 10 August 1907, and thereafter in M. P. T. Acharya's *Hindu* (Madras).[62]

The *Gaelic American,* founded by Devoy in 1903 and managed and edited by Freeman, was an early and outspoken sponsor of the Indian liberation project. Besides making possible the publication of Taraknath Das's *Free Hindustan* journal, it had links to that paper's close relative, the *Indian Sociologist.* Krishnavarma was said to be "unnerved" by a Scotland Yard detective's visit to the *Indian Sociologist'*s London office in September 1907 in the guise of a false *Gaelic American* staffer calling himself O'Brien.[63] After the *Indian Sociologist* was banned from importation into India by the 1907 Sea Customs Act, the *Gaelic American,* and another paper called *Justice,* began to print excerpts from it or write in a similar vein, with the result that they too were banned from importation into India as of May 1908. In the first two issues of *Free Hindustan* "the editor expressed gratitude to the *Gaelic American* for its service in the cause of Hindustan" and pledged that the paper would serve as a "medium to exchange our thoughts" with these Irish nationalists, on whom the future of the paper depended.[64]

Who was Freeman? According to C, he had once served in an Irish regiment but had been in the United States for many years.[65] Once the war broke out he began corresponding with Krishnavarma and was also reported to be "in intimate touch" with Heramba Lal Gupta. Freeman thus became, said C, "the intermediary between the Indians and the Germans with Gupta and also between the Irish and the Indians." Additionally, C reported: "The Germans pay Freeman for his paper and also for his services. When Irish are going to America and have no money, they wire to Freeman, and he meets the boat and claims them. I heard that the Germans pay Freeman well for Irishmen landing in America who are of military age and who will not join the army."

Freeman had written to Cama on 11 May 1914, predicting war: "I heard the other day that the German Government with the other members of the Triple Alliance has arrived at a definite decision as to when resistance will be made to the unqualified aggressions of the Triple Entente, and when that point is reached, the Triple Entente will have to back down or war will ensue. My information from Berlin of a little time ago foreshadowed this."[66] He also somehow managed to keep abreast of the latest developments in secret missions. A mutual friend of his and Cama's, named P. N. Dutt, alias Dawood Ali Khan, wrote to him from Kermanshah in southeast Persia near the border of Baluchistan on 3 August 1915, en route with a German expeditionary party, suggesting that if the war went on for a while maybe there would be time to put into action the ideas he and Har Dayal had hatched "on the banks of the Bosphorus"—though by this time Har Dayal had gone more or less AWOL. Dutt/Khan was finding the journey between Constantinople and Kermanshah "very interesting"; he had "had to make a midnight flight" from Bushire, in a pro-British zone, where Persian nationalists were hiding him. He would be leaving soon, but he asked Freeman: "Please send *Gaelic American* and other literature, if possible, to Kermanshah address."[67]

And who was Devoy? In addition to the journal *Gaelic American* he was also a founder of Clan na Gael, successor to the Fenian Brotherhood in the United States, which had staged several attempts to invade British Canada in coordination with uprisings in Ireland itself in the 1860s, and in effect functioned as the overseas wing of the Irish Republican Brotherhood (IRB). As an IRB member Devoy had been charged with fomenting a mutiny among Fenian members of the British Army. For this he was convicted for treason and sentenced to fifteen years' penal servitude from 1866.[68] He continued his resistance by carrying out prison strikes and later was involved in the ship *Catalpa*'s daring rescue of political prisoners from Australia in 1875. After a split in the Clan in 1879, Devoy was associated with the more militant "physical force" faction. All very Ghadaresque! Though it is impossible to know whether and how he and the Indian revolutionaries talked together about such things, the parallels cannot be entirely coincidental.

The similarity of the German mission of Roger Casement, another of Ghadar's Irish colleagues, certainly was not. A former civil servant of the empire from a moderate Protestant background, Casement's anticolonial convictions stemmed from firsthand observation of atrocities in Congo and Bolivia. Having arrived in Berlin from the United States on his mission of procuring military support, like Taraknath Das and Barakatullah, he too visited POW camps in Germany in search of Irish soldiers to recruit away from their British employer, as the Fenians had tried a half-century before.[69] His aim in Berlin was to secure a shipment of German arms for the Easter Rising in 1916. Directly paralleling its plan for India, Germany had promised the Irish insurgents arms and funds for the same purpose. Indeed, Franz von Papen, the German diplomat dealing with the Fenians in the United States, was also a key liaison for the Ghadarites. But again as with the Indians, the shipments (in a submarine bound for Tralee Bay outside Dublin) did not materialize at their destination. Thus this uprising was no more successful in the immediate term, and no less iconically inspirational to the 1920s generation of revolutionaries, than Ghadar's a year before.[70] The *Hindustan Ghadar* commented on that event in the 29 April 1917 issue: "In last April, 1916, a Ghadar was made against the English in Ireland. Also in the current month of April the English were much astonished to see the Irish republican flag fluttering on the Post Office buildings in Dublin.... On the 26th of April, the Irish celebrated the day of Ghadar, in every part of America. In the path of liberty, the ambition of the Irish is entirely praiseworthy."[71] Sooner after the fact, the paper had also chided its constituents on 3 May 1916: "Ireland rebelled when Sir Roger Casement was arrested but India remained quiescent when Gurdit Singh was shot, and no Englishman has been shot to avenge [his] death. Parmanand was arrested and sentenced to life imprisonment, but no Indian demanded the reason for such sentence without trial."[72]

Interestingly, Ghadar does not seem to have had any particular contact with James Connolly, through whom Socialism was incorporated into the Irish republican movement, as one might have expected, given the IWW link, as well as the fact that the references to Irish liberation and to Bolshevism in postwar Ghadarite literature tend to pop up more often than not within the same sentence. Connolly had also spent time in New York between 1903 and 1910, where he had been a member of the IWW and Socialist Labor Party, and had founded the Irish Socialist Federation. Was it no more than factionalism? The Indians were close to the IRB, which united with Connolly's Irish Volunteers only in the lead-up to the 1916 rising, in the fear that unless they joined forces he would do something precipitate on his own and ruin the timing of their own plans. Connolly did, however, pen an item entitled "The Coming Revolt in India" for his magazine *The Harp* in 1908, shortly after Cama's celebrated performance in Stuttgart:

> The appearance at the International Socialist Congress at Stuttgart of an Indian delegate, voicing the aspirations of the people of India for freedom, and the news items continually appearing in the capitalist press of sporadic acts of revolt in that country—harbingers of the greater revolt now fermenting throughout that vast empire—justify us in placing before our readers the following brief résumé of conditions....
>   British rule in India, like British rule in Ireland, is a political and social system established and maintained by the conquerors in the interest of the conquered.... The writer, *having had for some time exceptional opportunities of learning the real position of affairs in that country,* feels he is doing a service to the cause of freedom and humanity in laying before the readers of the *Harp* . . . the incipient rebellion which threatens the Indian Peninsula.[73]

When the Pacific Coast association was formed, the Ghadar publications likewise expressed a strong sense of solidarity with the IRB. The *Ghadar* predicted: "When the Hindu revolutionist comes up to the standard of the Irish rebel, then the British attacks will be answered."[74] And Ram Chandra related an anecdote in the *San Francisco Examiner* of 13 June 1916 in which "Mr. Gresham Stewart in the House of Commons . . . says: 'Five mutineers walking in the road [in India] said to a colonist: "Are you English?" and he said "No, I am Irish," and they said "O let him pass."'"[75]

In his work on the Irish role in the Hindu-German Conspiracy, Matthew Plowman portrays the Indo-Irish bond that long predated the German role, and then "survived the conspiracy and the war itself," as crucial to the functioning of the German collaboration. He even argued: "If this Irish and Indian bond had not preexisted . . . the conspiracy simply would never have happened"; and he hints, moreover, that without German meddling it might not have been botched as it was.[75]

Throughout, Plowman's strategy is to demonstrate that those Irish-Americans who were involved in the Ghadar/German affair were not just motivated by vague sympathy based on general anti-British sentiment. Rather, as activists deeply committed to the militant republican cause, they were aiding the Indians deliberately and with full awareness of the implications. It was only for political reasons, he claims, that the United States government and media downplayed the explicitly Irish republican element in the trial defense, and then even kept Irish-Americans off the jury. He further asserts that while the Indo-Irish collaboration was curtailed deliberately in the immediate lead-up to the war, this was because the Irish suspected their networks had been infiltrated by British intelligence, and wanted to insulate their Indian allies. Indeed, Plowman portrays the British infiltration of the Irish network as its initial wedge into the Indo-German puzzle. Charles Lamb, a British spy planted in the Irish organization in San Francisco during the war, told U.S. investigators that the conspiracy was driven by three brains: a German (Kuno Meyer, thought to be an alias of William von Brincken), an Indian (Ram Chandra), and an Irish (Larry De Lacey, who was jailed in connection with the Hindu-German Conspiracy Case, and in whose vault Ram Chandra allegedly "kept his most valuable Gadar Party papers").[76]

Even if the covert ties had been isolated, the Irish community in the United States did come through in support of the Ghadarites during the hard times of the conspiracy trial, as attested by none other than Mrs. Ram Chandra.[77] For example, Plowman credits American Fenians with furnishing Har Dayal's bail posting and Ghadar's legal defense. The clients of defense attorney and republican activist Daniel O'Connell, Plowman maintains, included Hindu-German Conspiracy defendant Moritz Stack von Goltzheim, who had endeavored with O'Connell's assistance "to collect funds from German Americans to publish the American *Independent,* which was used for pro-German and pro-Sinn Féin propaganda." Another attorney, "Sinn Féin diehard" George A. McGowan, defended Ram Chandra and von Brincken, who besides being one of the Ghadar Party's primary German contacts was also McGowan's son-in-law.[78]

In 1920, as national liberation struggles boiled over and veterans of the wartime uprisings in both countries began to emerge from jail, the long-standing covert alliance finally came into the open, linking the Friends of Freedom for India (FFI) and the Friends of Irish Freedom (a Clan na Gael front group) "through Devoy's publications."[79] The FFI recruited journalist Ed Gammons, due to his association with the Irish movement, to assist Surendranath Kar with its Indian News Service. Sailendranath Ghose, Agnes Smedley's partner in the related Indian National Party, put in notable efforts to strengthen the Indo-Irish link, "in which he is a firm believer."[80] The climax of the partnership came at the height of the FFI's antideportation campaign, which coincided with Eamon de Valera's controversial American tour of June 1919 to December 1920, which was aimed at garnering international recognition, particularly that of the United States, for the struggling Irish Republic.

But there was a schism within Irish republican circles in the United States after the war, placing Devoy on one side, and Ghadar collaborators De Lacey and Joseph McGarrity—who replaced Devoy as IRB liaison to the United States in the 1920s—on the other. The latter faction, which favored de Valera and his stance of no compromise on full independence, even broke into the *Gaelic American* office and seized Devoy's Clan-na-Gael membership list, intending "to rebuild the organization under their own faction."[81] Despite Devoy's support for the controversial Free State Treaty, seen by many as an unacceptable compromise, his paper continued advocating in its pages nothing less than complete independence (no partition, and no oath of loyalty to the crown) for Ireland, as did the Indian papers with which it had long been associated.[82]

When de Valera arrived in San Francisco in July 1919, Ghadar Party representatives Gopal Singh and Jagat Singh presented him with an Irish republican flag and a sword engraved with the words "Presented to [the] President of the Irish Republic by the Hindustan Gadar Party of America, San Francisco, USA. 21 July 1919."[83] The beleaguered president thanked them with the acknowledgment that the sword "represents the sacred idea of the struggle of both our countries for their freedom and the sword is really a sacred weapon when used for such a righteous cause," and assured them that the Irish people along with all the democratic forces of the world supported the justice of their endeavor.[84]

When de Valera returned to New York in February 1920, the FFI held an Indian dinner in his honor. His "vigorous and constructive . . . masterly speech" was recorded in the *Irish World* and the *Gaelic American* of 6 March 1920. He quoted George Washington but changed the words "Patriots of Ireland, your cause is identical with ours [America's]" to "Patriots of India, your cause is identical with ours [Ireland's]." More highlights from this speech follow:

> A nation is conquered only when it abandons its cause and gives way to despair. . . . The books tell us that Britain has plundered India. Of course, she has plundered India. What else is she in India for? . . . The books tell us that almost perpetual famine reigns in India. Of course, there is bound to be famine when an alien power's greed takes away all the wealth and all the food its forces can extract. . . . They [the British] will pretend to throw up their hands in horror at the deeds of their General Dyers, but the Dyers are the necessary instruments of that imperial system.

With such naked brutality, he continued, the world would now see through the hypocrisy of their behavior at the peace conference. Therefore: "We of Ireland and you of India must each of us endeavour, both as separate peoples and in combination, to rid ourselves of the vampire that is fattening on our blood. . . . Our cause is a common cause. We swear friendship tonight and we send our common greetings and our pledges to our friends in Egypt and in Persia and tell them also that their cause is our cause."[85]

In one sense any blow against the empire, any locus of resistance and unrest, was simultaneously a contribution to their own freedom; the liberation of *all* peoples subject to British incursion was seen as part of the mission. For oppressed fellow subject peoples of the British Empire this basis for solidarity was as strong, ideologically speaking, as it may have been arbitrary from the perspective of identity politics. Nevertheless, the Irish did balk at sending a force to Egypt to fight the British there, as the Germans had proposed to Casement. They insisted that their interest was solely in fighting in and for their own homeland, and for the moment remained impervious to the argument that a blow against Britain in a remote place would do just as well. (Can it be that there were more points of contact and continuity between Indians and Egyptians than between Irish and Egyptians?)

Not long after reporting this speech in the Indian News Service, Kar and Gammons wrote up a St. Patrick's Day parade attended by de Valera in New York, in which a contingent of Sikhs marched in green turbans. In Kar's words, it was "an imposing parade demanding the complete and unconditional Independence of India and Ireland. . . . The Indian republicans carried banners with mottos like: 'Up! the Republic of India,' '300,000,000 of India with Ireland to the Last,' 'President De Valera's Message to India: Our cause is a common cause.' "[86] The Indian News Service also reported on another less celebratory demonstration, in Philadelphia in September, "organized by Irish republicans against British atrocities," in which Indians were among the five thousand–strong crowd. Taraknath Das read a resolution in support of "the struggle of the people of India in their efforts and fight to establish a free and independent republic of their own," which the Irish Americans heartily acclaimed.[87]

When Terence MacSwiney died in prison the next month while on a hunger strike, having been condemned by a British military tribunal for his nationalist activities, Indian revolutionaries pledged to emulate him. *Independent Hindustan* of October 1920 included several articles on the martyrdom of MacSwiney, quoting in one the "immortal lines" of his "Battle Cry":

> Yea, reckon up the price for us,
> however great it be.
> We'll paint in our best of blood
> for Ireland's liberty.

"And may we add: Human liberty," the *Independent Hindustan* editorialized.

The December edition of the *Independent Hindustan* noted in its "News and Notes" section that "the Hindustan Gadar Party sends a telegram to Eamon de Valera" committing itself to "carrying out the principles and ideals in defense of which MacSwiney's blood has slowly been sapped by the British government."[88] De Valera replied in a telegram to the Friends of Freedom for India: "Only when we prefer death to bondage can our countries be free." Finally, in its February "Notes and News" section the *Independent Hindustan* included an item on a boycott of tea advocated by an "Irish Republican" pub in Chicago: when you drink a cup, it said,

> you drink the anguish, the bloody sweat of underpaid Hindoos and Ceylonese. You drink the bitterness of millions of people reduced to slavery and deliberately kept in a besetting ignorance. You drink the [filthy] greed of [England] who reaps rich profits out of the slavery of those upon whom she has imposed her will. You drink the blood of those who have died or will die fighting England in Ireland.
>
> Black Tea, aye, well is it named Black. Will YOU drink it?[89]

In the United States the friendship between Irish and Indians remained strong throughout the interwar period, with the Indians regarding their friends who had attained independent status—though not peace—in 1922 as a hopeful example for those who had suffered the disappointment of the called-off Non-Cooperation movement. (Maybe this was a mistake, since their independence also resulted in partition and massive bloody civil strife.) And so British intelligence continued to keep track of interactions such as the San Francisco visit of Syed Hussain and Nawab Syed Mohammed from Calcutta, who appeared at the Commonwealth Club and Civic Center in 1926 for a debate on the topic "Is British rule in India 'Satanic'?"chaired by Mrs. Frederick H. Colburn, who was "prominent in the past Irish activities." Their audience was reported as two thousand strong, "including 200 Indian students . . . many Irish and Germans, and judging from the applause which greeted some of the remarks, Communists."[90]

Outside the United States, the partnership was less solid in practice, even while the mutual sympathy was unquestionable. Proto–Irish Republican Army fighter Dan Breen mentioned in his 1924 memoir that he encountered Indian nationalists in London in late 1921, including none other than Gandhi, whom the die-hard militant Breen recalled as "the most intelligent man and the most implacable foe of Britain whom I have ever met," for all that he insisted that unarmed resistance was the only way that would work in India.[91] But Breen also met other Indians in London, "who favored armed revolt."[92] Interestingly, these very militants were purist enough themselves that when Breen "offered them my services in the hope of getting in one more blow for the cause of freedom," he related, "I got a rude shock when my advances were repelled, the reason proffered being that no Irishman could be trusted, seeing that his countrymen had abandoned the fight for the freedom of their own country." Breen doesn't name these particular Indians, but apparently their support for de Valera's faction had rendered them in effect uncompromising anti-treatyites. And perhaps they were projecting from their own factional struggle overseas, in which the Friends of Freedom for India and the Hindustan Ghadar Party, favoring complete independence, were bitterly opposed to Lajpat Rai's Home Rule group, which advocated autonomous dominion status within the empire.

The core idea of Ghadar was not accommodation but mutiny, a revolt of soldiers against commanders deemed to be unjust. An important feature that yoked together the various peoples of the British Empire was their incorporation into the apparatus of force that made the empire's maintenance and expansion possible. Many Irish served in the British Army in India; many Indians served in the British Army in Egypt. How diabolical, realized our heroes, that the peoples of the empire should be co-opted in order to keep one another in enforced subjection, while being made complicit in their own. This was why the suborning of military loyalty was key, present since the earliest leaflets: point 12 in the 1913 *Balance Sheet of British Rule* had condemned the fact that "using India's money and the lives of Indians, aggressions are committed in Afghanistan, Burma, Egypt, Persia and China."[93]

On 10 December 1924, Sean O'Ceallaigh, a veteran of the Easter Rising and then official Irish envoy to the United States, spoke on the theme of "India and Ireland" at a banquet in his honor in New York. His remarks reiterated the theme of a speech he had made as the representative of the Irish Republic to the opening of the League of Nations in Paris, in 1920—namely, the League's hypocrisy in serving as a tool of English and American imperialism. As examples he cited conditions "in Ireland where an English Army of occupation, 100,000 strong, led a campaign of terror and violence; in Egypt, where the revolution against English usurpation is very strong; in India where the resistance to English tyranny showed itself so menacing that the English troops recently went as far as to machine-gun for ten minutes a compact crowd of unarmed demonstrators."[94] At the same time he was attempting to form an association of the "oppressed peoples of the British empire," involving delegates from Ireland, India, Egypt, South Africa, and elsewhere, and he condemned any Irishman who served in the British Indian military or civil service. The Connaught Rangers, Munster Fusiliers, Dublin Fusiliers, Inniskillen Fusiliers, Royal Irish Regiment et al. "bore the weight of responsibility for England's horrid campaign." He ended his New York speech by proclaiming:

> We owe it to India because India's cause is Ireland's cause; it is the cause of right against might; it is the cause of truth and justice against hypocrisy, vice and tyrannical oppression. We Irish republicans, we Irish fighters for freedom in our own land . . . must feel under deep obligation to work for India, to preach for India, to fight for her and Egypt until both are free absolutely and forever from the tyrant's grasp. We owe a deep debt to both these countries, for has it not been largely by the work of Irish brains and Irish brawn and muscle that these two ancient peoples

have been beaten into subjection and have been so long oppressed? . . . May [India] soon burst her fetters and take her rank among the free republics of the earth.[95]

The language of O'Ceallaigh's speech is strikingly similar to the terms in which Ghadar literature during this period posed a challenge to the Sikhs on being co-opted into doing Britain's dirty work by fighting as mercenaries on behalf of the empire to hold in bondage those with whom they should rather stand as brothers against it.

In the *New York Call* on 31 August Kar claimed that the British Empire had expanded its territorial claims by 1,500,000 square miles since the Versailles treaty. And he continued: "Not only this. Violating every principle of international agreements and covenants, England has crushed the sovereignty of Persia and Afghanistan. Tibet and Chinese provinces are sacrifices for the security and maintenance of British supremacy over India."[96] INC spokesman V. J. Patel reiterated Kar's observations in the *Independent Hindustan* of October 1920:

> Britain is at this present moment engaged in military operations in various countries. The main brunt of these military adventures is borne by Indians. . . . Mr Churchill stated quite frankly the other day that the Government of India has now been warned to hold a further force in readiness to be despatched to Mesopotamia in case of emergency. *India herself is struggling to be free to regain her birthright,* and it is the iron of fate that India soldiers should help others in depriving the people in other parts of the world of their birthright.[97]

Surendranath Kar informed the Friends of Freedom for India in December 1920 that there were at the time 125,000 Indian soldiers in the British Army in the Near East, of which 83,500 were in Mesopotamia and northwest Persia, 8,000 in Constantinople, 14,000 in Egypt, and 18,000 in Palestine.[98] Thus both Irish and Sikh soldiers of this political bent developed a sense of responsibility to mutiny, and an awareness of their own importance as a linchpin in military cooperation.

In the end, ironically, the last major mutiny of the period on British Indian soil was not carried out by Punjabi Sikh soldiers, but by Irish ones, motivated by events back home.[99] The Connaught Rangers had a fabled history of colonial service: aside from intervals during which they served in the Boer and Zulu wars and in Sudan, they had been based in India since the time of the Great Mutiny of 1857, which they had helped to quell. During the Great War they were present on the Western Front, and in Persia and Mesopotamia—a range, incidentally, that was quite similar to the deployment pattern of Indian troops. When they heard news of the brutal reprisals of the Auxiliaries and Black and Tans against agitations in Ireland, three-quarters of a battalion mutinied at Jalandhar on 5 July 1920. But those events may not have been the only stimulus. The DCI reported in October that J. McLaughlin, ex-president of the Ancient Order of Hibernians, had expressed the desire to form an Eastern Society "with the object of sowing sedition in India among Irish and Indian troops." The report mentioned "an individual in Rawalpindi who is working quietly on Sinn Fein and Bolshevik lines."[100] In June a packet of sealed letters had been intercepted in Mexico, originating in New York and passing through the Ghadar Ashram. Inside was a bundle "in Gaelic colored with the Sinn Fein flag and destined it is believed for the Irish soldiers in India."[101]

Whatever their motivation, the Connaught Rangers met much the same fate as the Ghadar mutineers five years before: of sixty-nine rebels court-martialed, the *San Francisco Examiner* reported fourteen executed, forty-seven other death sentences commuted to penal servitude for life or less, and eight acquitted. Ever vigilant, Karr and Gammons reported on the mutiny, commenting in the India News Service of 15 January 1921: "The result of the Irish mutiny in India has done great good to the cause of Indian independence. The time has come when the Irish people who are struggling for . . . independence . . . should work with a wider vision and policy. They should see that all the forces in the world, which are opposed to British imperialism, should combine to achieve the goal."[102]

A Sikh league in Jalandhar held a meeting at the mutiny location to voice their condemnation of the British actions and "offered cordial cooperation for the success of the Republic of Ireland." The Ghadar Party convened another meeting in California, issuing a statement of "sincere appreciation of the invaluable services rendered by those Irish martyrs and patriots," which they intended to send "to all the Irish papers in the United States and to the press in general, and to the Irish societies."[103] The resolution was echoed by groups in Bombay and Calcutta, and by the INC then meeting in Nagpur; Ghadar announced that the Irish Progressive League in New York had responded to a letter from Nagpur "by assuring the Indian people of the ardent and unfailing cooperation of the Irish race in their fight for liberation," and sending copies to the Irish and British embassies and to the Indian groups in New York.[104] Ghadar Acting Secretary Bishan Singh wrote a letter of condolence, sympathy, and solidarity to their old friend de Valera, even as the FFI sent one considerably less supportive to King George: "Once more the British government, soaked in the blood of martyrs of many lands, hastens the glorious day of its downfall. We pledge anew our call to the millions struggling for life, liberty and pursuit of happiness in Ireland, India, Egypt, Russia and the Near East. Each martyr is a beacon in our onward march to imminent victory."[105]

In an article entitled "Irish Revolt in India," the *Independent Hindustan* declared: "We commend the action of the Irish soldiers who have laid down their arms in expressing their sympathy with the gallant Sinn Feiners who are sacrificing their lives for the cause of the Republic of Ireland." Nevertheless, the editor added a critical gloss:

Refusal to fight would have been far more effective, however, in the progress of revolutionary movements, had the Irish soldiers taken decisive action as a protest against the inhuman Punjab massacre and atrocities. The old imperialistic game has been to set one people against another. And the sooner the imperialism-infested people understand this, the nearer will be the emancipation of their countries from alien control. . . . We urge the people of India to take immediate action so that not a single Indian is sent to Ireland, Mesopotamia, Palestine, Egypt, Armenia, Persia, Afghanistan, China and Russia to fight for the British interests. Indo-Irish entente will be an effective weapon in destroying [the disturbing] British imperialism.[106]

ASIA FOR THE ASIATICS

The network of Indian revolutionaries abroad intersected with a third national—or a second imperial—entity during this period. This entity was Japan. But were the Indians' Japanese interlocutors enemies of an enemy, like Germany, their imperial patron, or friends, like their Egyptian and Irish nationalist counterparts? To answer this question we must examine the ground of commonality, and the changing substance of the link.

The Japanese victory over Russia in 1905 galvanized Asian national liberation struggles of the time, including the Swadeshi movement in Bengal, due to their sudden identification with the larger civilizational entity of Japan, which was now positioned as the champion in a simplified East/West conflict. Cemil Aydin's list of "Asian peoples" who shared this sense of an exciting turning point included Young Turks, Iranian constitutionalists, Indian and Chinese nationalists, and Vietnamese reformers. Mustafa Kamil praised the Japanese victory for its beneficial effect in rousing nationalist consciousness and anti-British resistance throughout Asia and Africa. However, Aydin also points out that this did not result in a deep or lasting alliance; Japan was less a partner for Asian peoples than a "metaphor of [Asian] modernity for Ottomans, Egyptians, and Indians" eager to discover the "secrets" of Japan's strength and success in challenging the Western powers. A very different relationship developed between India and Japan than the more symmetrical ties between India and Egypt, or India and Ireland. Unlike these countries, Japan was not subject to colonial influence; like Germany, it sought to rival Britain's empire, not to liberate itself from it.[107]

Still, at the same time as Rabindranath Tagore and Okakura Tenzin were lauding the transcendent spiritual and artistic superiority of a shared Asian culture, "students, revolutionaries, intellectuals and adventurers from all across Asia"—including Turkish and Arab students—had begun to flock to Tokyo in search of not spiritual kinship but modern technical training and proven-effective tactical models. The sojourn in Japan proved disappointing to the Indian rebels as a source of training, refuge, and aid, which why many of our future Ghadarite students eventually tried the United States. However, their time in Japan did enable them to establish tentative connections with other progressive Asian students and political activists in Tokyo, and to lay the foundations for later Pan-Asianist institutions and discourses. Some dissident Japanese of an antimilitarist bent (who were soon to be marginalized in their own society) collaborated with Indian and Chinese students to form the Asian Solidarity Society in Tokyo in 1907. Valentine Chirol of the *Times* claimed that Indians made occasional contributions to Japanese Socialist papers, but dismissed this as ineffectual, scoffing that "when [the Indian students] begin to air their political opinions and to declaim against British rule they are very speedily put in their place."[108]

Several of the Indian revolutionaries abroad who played significant roles in Ghadar's North American organizing and/or the Ghadarite mutiny of 1915, including Barakatullah, Taraknath Das, Heramba Lal Gupta, and Rash Behari Bose, also had connections to Japan. While the others arrived on the run and in hiding during the war, Barakatullah came first to Tokyo as a language teacher and newspaper editor in 1909; it was through him that Gupta, Bose, and others developed ties to Okawa Shumei, then an ally of Indian nationalists and the foremost ideologue of Pan-Asianism. Das, Bose, and others later contributed to Okawa's monthly journal *Nihon*, which appeared from 1925 to 1932. Despite or because of its radical nationalism, it also commented on wider Asian affairs—an Asia that, as defined in Okawa's influential 1922 book, incorporated India, Thailand, Afghanistan, Persia, Turkey, Egypt, Mesopotamia, Saudi Arabia, Tibet, and Siam. According to Cemil Aydin, the importance of Okawa's connections to Indian nationalism in formulating his Pan-Asian ideals at this stage cannot be overestimated.[109]

And vice versa, perhaps: the British Embassy at Tokyo learned of a surprising plan the year before the war broke out. A Japanese reserve officer named Shimada claimed that the Indians had recruited him to assist in raising a revolution headed by the Gaekwad of Baroda and using arms, ammunition, and ex-officers from Japan.[110] But at this point, Barakatullah's assistant Hatano (thought to be the first Japanese convert to Islam) turned informer. Among his revelations was a plot to poison high British officials in India and China, where Bhagwan Singh had already made the necessary preparations; Hatano showed his interlocutors "a sample bottle, labelled arsenic, in support of his story."[111] The attempt was foiled just in time. Even more interesting to the British investigators were Hatano's tips about the propaganda network: he provided the names of three "ringleaders of the seditious movement abroad" and a list of five hundred movement participants and recipients of seditious literature, scattered throughout North America, India, and East Asia.

It was within the same Tokyo milieu that the Indians first encountered Sun Yat-sen, the father of Chinese republicanism, whose successful 1911 anti-imperial revolution, carried out from a diasporic Pacific Rim, proved such a fitting tactical model for contemporary emigrant revolutionists. Sun's political principles were also more or less compatible with theirs at the time, combining moderate socialism with democratic republicanism. Sun thus proved to be an important mentor and model for Ghadar's revolutionary activities, and their friend and partner in Pan-Asian internationalism until his death in 1925.

Chenchiah spoke to Sun at some point during his tour of Siam and Burma in the summer of 1915. The veteran politico shared the impassioned student's opinion that British imperialism was the greatest enemy of the independence of other countries in the world; and that so long as the British ruled India they remained a global menace. The freedom of all weaker nations, he encouraged his son's Berkeley classmate, depended on India's "sacred and historical duty to help humanity."[112]

An intelligence report contained an Indian visitor's account of a conversation he had with Sun Yat-sen while in Japan:

> [Dr. Sun] asked me about the revolutionary movement in India. I told him that there was not much work being done outwardly, though at heart almost all the educated men were, more or less, dissatisfied. He has great hopes in the success of an Indian revolution and says that great forces are working out of India. He admires the Indians in Germany and has a high opinion of them. The British Government regards him . . . as their bitter enemy, because he stands for the freedom of India and they are trying to attack his character in their own defense.[113]

Sun then asked his guest for the name of another Indian "who was living in hiding in Japan, for whom he has much respect and whom he thinks to be a wonderful organizer." Sun was "much puzzled to understand how that man is still doing a lot in and from Japan, and if he remains there two or three years more, as he is now, he will create insurmountable difficulties in the way of the British Government. He left very much pleased when I said that I knew the man and talked a lot about his career in India."[114]

Perhaps the other Indian man Sun Yat-sen asked about was Rash Behari Bose. Fleeing India after the thwarted mutiny of 1915, Bose had married a Japanese girl named Toshiko Soma, the daughter of a Shinjuku baker who had sheltered him when on the run, "after two years on terms of closest intimacy with her."[115] While maintaining his covert connections to international revolutionary circles under the name Thakur, he also became a long-term collaborator in Okawa's political/intellectual work, contributing articles to his Pan-Asianist papers in the 1920s and 1930s. Sun's visitor continued: "It seems Dr Sun has seen Thakur in Japan, though he has not told me so. He says that the man is very strong [there] and his influence in giving encouragement to anti-British feeling in that country was extending."[116]

Of the revolutionists with links to North American Ghadar, Taraknath Das was the most prominent advocate of Pan-Asianism as a mode of discourse and vehicle of anticolonial struggle. Gupta and Das both arrived in Tokyo in 1916. Within forty-eight hours Gupta faced the threat of deportation, but managed to remain in hiding for months under the protection of the powerful ultranationalist secret society Kokuryukai, before returning to the United States.[117] But Das remained for the duration of the war, dispatched there by the BIC with the usual tasks of undertaking propaganda work, purchasing weapons, and organizing shipment points for moving arms and money into India by way of China.[118] According to one account, Chandra Kanta Chakravarty had instigated a Pan-Asiatic League as a way to garner Chinese and Japanese support but was prevented from going to Japan himself for fear of arrest. So he sent Das in his stead. Although the arms deal bore no fruit—one lead on a million rifles to be purchased from the South Chinese government was rejected when it was learned that they were archaic flintlocks and muzzle loaders—it did enable Das to set up branches of the Pan-Asiatic League in China and Japan, again proclaiming the motto of "Asia for the Asiatics."[119]

Das also interviewed Japanese politicians, gave lectures, and published two books, including a well-regarded analysis of Japan's geopolitical position and prospects called *Is Japan a Menace to Asia?* in which he argued that Japan's pursuit of its national interest in the Far East brought it into conflict with Britain and France. Thus Japan's only recourse from total isolation was to seek solidarity with the rest of Asia and its nationalist movements.[120] Das's second book was called *The Isolation of Japan in World Politics.* It also advocated the Pan-Asianist approach and prioritized racial categories (yellow and white) as the fundamental units of a great civilizational conflict.[121]

He later made several further trips to Japan and China to carry forward the Pan-Asianist collaboration, consulting with Bose and Sun while also remaining in touch with activists in North America. Near the end of 1917, a letter thought to be from Das in Japan was found in the possession of Sailendranath Ghose in New York. Das requested someone else to come as a representative to Japan; the ideal candidate would speak English and have a good character. He also warned Ghose against Roy and his apparently generous offers, because of Das's suspicions of Roy's sources, the Bolsheviks: "These people are the victims of Utopian ideas, which under no circumstance can materialise. It may be that I am wrong or am wanting in the full development of my ideas. But I cannot budge an inch from that I have received as a message from my intuition."[122] Overall it sounds as if Pan-Asianism was even becoming Das's overriding priority.

After his conviction in the Hindu-German Conspiracy Case, during his time at Leavenworth Das wrote extensive analyses of East Asian politics, even (when not busy cataloguing the eight-thousand-volume prison library) making policy recommendations to President Wilson wherein it is plain that Asia has become the paramount category in his thinking. In a letter to his lawyer Charles Recht on 5 September 1918, explaining the enclosed paper he had drafted on "Entente-American intervention in Siberia," he deliberately refrained from taking a stance vis-à-vis Bolshevism in his analysis of the "ultimate and probable political consequences" of such an intervention; his concern was rather with the fate of "the awakened New Asia." He hoped, through his paper, to correct what he felt was a perilous failure on the part of the Western "experts" and popular opinion to comprehend "Japanese national ambition, policy and psychology," thus crippling the government's ability to make valid policy. "As a loyal American," he said, "I like to do my share of service for the cause of Democracy in the best possible way. If I were free today, I would have placed before our government my services" in acquainting it with the matter of East Asia. Das saw the world falling into blocs, and he believed that the United States should seek to be close to the Asiatic bloc, as the best option "for the future peace and world progress." He closed on a conversational note, with kind thoughts for Agnes Smedley and Sailen Ghose, then in suspense over the pending outcome of their own trials, and thanked Recht for the candy and magazines.[123]

THINKING LIKE A *VATAN*, FEELING LIKE A *QAUM*?

For the duration and aftermath of World War I, both the political logic and the emotional force of nationalism predominated as the operative idiom for conceptualizing and expressing anticolonial resistance. Before and after, although the goal of national liberation never wavered, it was framed within a larger internationalist context of some sort.

In Ghadar's case, their patriotism—their devotion to the freedom of their *vatan*, like that of Mustafa Kamil's Egyptian nationalist party—was never in question. Without affecting that commitment, what is then subject to further consideration is the limit of their *qaum*—those with whom they felt themselves to be in solidarity and fraternity—and whether it was based emotionally in an ascriptive identity bound to a particular territory, or in an ethical commitment to a set of (possibly universalist) principles, that define membership if put into practice, and to a revolutionary ideology that appeared in various parts of the world.[124]

But the primary contradiction of Pan-Asianism in all its forms was based on racial or civilizational categories (East/West), not economic relations (owners/producers) as Marxists framed it, or political power relations (oppressor/oppressed, colonizer/colonized, master/slave) as national liberation movements did. And this civilizational contradiction was rooted in the idea of Asia as a vast cultural and spiritual entity in polar opposition to the modern materialist West, whose deepest imperative was the battle against domination by the latter, whether spiritually to transcend, or politically to conquer. Thus the struggle against British colonialism was not "merely," as Okawa put it, political or economic, but rooted in something supposedly even deeper and more fundamental: a civilizational genius that Japan, India, and even Egypt all claimed to exemplify in different contexts.

Bipin Chandra Pal spoke in compatible terms at a meeting in Manchester in July 1909, the same period as his pro-Egyptian speeches, to the effect that "India was of the Indians, *an eastern people. India could not be governed by western people;* it must be governed by people who understood the populace; India was the key to the world's prosperity; it held the key to Europe. If China with its 400,000,000 inhabitants and Japan with its inhabitants rise and are joined in their rising by India's millions no Czar, no Kaiser, no western nation could stand the shock of such an invincible force."[125]

Although such a civilizational binary did not characterize the Ghadarites' eclectic, modernist, libertarian-socialist style of thinking, its logic did provide the framework underlying some of their relationships of transnational solidarity. It also enabled the recurrent fudging together of Pan-Asianism and Pan-Islamism from both ends, by various people both inside and outside what German scholars and politicians, Japanese scholars and politicians, Egyptian Easternists, Bolsheviks, and Indian revolutionaries abroad alike have called the East, with the total of its variations stretching from the eastern Mediterranean to Japan, of which alternately Japan or an Islamic caliphate might be portrayed as the true and glorious manifestation in a given situation, conveniently overlooking the bits that fall out the edges in either direction. It made a certain sense for Okawa and his circle to count India and the "Islamic world" as part of their greater Asia, given the presence of substantial Muslim populations in parts of China, Indonesia, and India. But their formulation missed the point: rather than concluding that if such was Asia, then maybe Asia was too huge, complex, and internally diverse to assign it a unitary civilizational identity, the Pan-Asianist imperative was instead to squeeze everything south and east of northwestern Europe, however non-homogenous, into a monolithic civilizational unit.

A second implication of this East/West framing was its homology with the tension between rationalism and romanticism, on the part of Asiaphile Western critics of modernity and Asian nationalists alike, who in a sense were coproducing the notion of a civilizational binary (rendering European romantic antimodernism equivalent to spiritualistic Oriental anti-Westernism). The latter could thus, ironically, bolster their case by drawing on critiques of Enlightenment rationalism and industrial modernity that were internal to the West.[126] But this thinking too missed the point: instead of inferring that Asia must indeed be spiritually superior if even the westerners admitted their own decadence, they might have inferred rather that Western culture was neither homogenous nor synonymous with rationalism and industrial modernity; and that rationalists from Europe and Asia could form bonds of sympathetic communication just as antirationalists from Europe and Asia could, with neither rationalism nor anti-rationalism being solely identified with either side.

The assumption at the core of this philosophy—of a civilizational antipathy more fundamental than any *mere* political or economic structural or systemic inequity—leads us to the problematic of the postwar chapters, wherein the translation of our Ghadarite "core principles"—defined not by identitarian but by ideological commitments to liberty and equality—into and among all three languages of Communism, Islamism, and national liberation will become crucial to the development of the revolutionary movement abroad.

The German relationship was based strictly in realpolitik, and the Japanese in a combination of realpolitik and notional Pan-Asianism within which both Japanese and Indian cultural nationalisms were located (and to which each was sometimes equated). In both of these cases, it was questionable even at the time how much the relationship represented the Ghadar Party's own interests or the Ghadar movement's distinctive character. While Germany's imperial interests during the war had dovetailed with India's national ones, Japan's imperial (and therefore national) interests sometimes conflicted. Pan-Asian fellow feeling proved less strong than Japanese supremacism, which required formal adherence to the Anglo-Japanese agreement on which the guarantee of a free hand for each in its own sphere of influence depended. Japan would refrain from interfering with Britain's actions in India while Britain would do the same for Japan's in China, Korea, and Taiwan. Despite a good deal of support from the public, the ultranationalists, and a multi-party spectrum of parliamentarians, the Indians still worried that in the event of an uprising on their part, Japan's government would side with Britain and help to put them down, as indeed proved true in the Singapore Mutiny of 1915.

On the other hand, the Egyptian relationship was based on a compatible form of prewar nationalism that combined local patriotism and republican constitutionalism, located in the geopolitical context of anti-British resistance and a somewhat ambiguous relationship to the Ottoman Empire that was endowed with significance by the presence of an encompassing Pan-Asian/Pan-Islamic field. Its links to the Ghadar organization were not direct, but mediated through the individuals active in both locations. Beginning in the mid-1920s, shifts in Egyptian nationalist politics and in the politics of the Ottoman/Islamic world in which it was embedded reduced the breadth of opportunity for interaction with Indians in nationalist *and* khilafatist terms. The Ottoman caliphate was no more, and the liberal-secular republican constitutionalists then enjoying their brief moment of dominance in the Egyptian national scene were largely indifferent to other nationalist movements, nor were they very interested in other available forms of internationalism or transnational organization at that time.[127]

Meanwhile the Irish relationship—the one most central to the U.S.-based Ghadar movement and probably its strongest and longest alliance—was its closest contemporary analogue as republican nationalism similarly featuring a Socialist-leaning wing and an identical tactical approach. Lacking mutual identification with a transnational cultural entity, what was the glue, or the common element, for this relationship? Was the solidarity of an unwilling commonwealth enough? I think it was a deep ideological identification with what I suppose must be called the spirit of 1848. Ghadar's revolutionary commitment to national liberation locates it squarely and consciously within the tradition of post-Enlightenment romantic republicanism, drawing upon the precedents of 1776, 1789, 1848, and, above all, 1857. The perennial combination of the sacred texts of political liberalism with the veneration of martyrs and martyrdom lurked at the heart of the post-Enlightenment romanticism that fueled the republican national movements of both the Irish and Indians overseas, movements that set at least some of them along a road, far from home, not of purist chauvinism but of international solidarity.

Self-determination was as prominent a term as nationalism itself in the rhetorical vocabulary of the World War I era. And it was this principle that provided logical continuity between prewar anarchism, wartime nationalism, and interwar Communist internationalism. In March 1920 Santokh Singh, then living at the Ghadar Ashram after his release from prison and busy "reorganising the Gadar Party," wrote to N. S. Hardikar regarding a new constitution for the Home Rule League:

> My frank opinion is that India needs a revolution, political, social, industrial. An Independent India with social and economic problems unsolved does not appeal to my reason—but I am sentimental enough to say that I, in the hope of solution of the social and industrial problems a little later, would prefer a Hindustanee slave-driver to an Englishman. Self-determination is impossible so long as the Union Jack waves in India.[128]

After the war, there was something of a return to the larger framework for national liberation struggles, as was the case more often than not by far among the revolutionaries abroad, as contrasted with the domestic political scene. This kind of supranational thinking was not yet common among the people back home, *except* among Pan-Islamists, and perhaps some cosmopolitan cultural Pan-Asianists, until the return in the 1920s of diasporic leftist activists, for whom the category of the nation became less a primordial ethnic identity than a unit of class analysis at the geopolitical level. From there it was a short leap to the left.

5

Toilers of the East

The Communist Ghadar

A NEW ALLY

The results of the Great War, including the reconfiguration of the Ottoman, German, and Austro-Hungarian empires, combined with the Russian upheaval, drastically altered the conditions in which transnational anticolonial revolutionaries functioned at the global level and within both American and Indian domestic contexts. This is the moment at which it is generally said that Ghadar took a sharp left turn. However, it is perhaps more accurate to say that it forked, and that the radical wing, along with other sectors of the international Left, took a specifically Marxist-Leninist analytical and tactical turn. Prior to the war, that particular form of an institutionalized, rationalized, formalized organization, party and state, including its capacity to formulate and enforce dogma and to dominate the very definition of "left" itself, had simply not existed. Yet while evolving in form, the goals and ideals of Ghadar remained consistent with those of the prewar party. This formal shift expressed a painful self-critical awareness as the Ghadarites compared the Bolshevik success to their own apparent failure. Meanwhile, while the radical wing adopted a Marxist-Leninist approach and returned to India, the other faction embraced a more moderate Indian nationalism that served the goals of civil rights and ethnic pride within the United States.

"Turns" were taken by others as well, in the aftermath of the Versailles treaty. While the United States veered in a pronouncedly antiradical and anti-immigrant direction, Soviet Russia and the Communist International moved toward the zenith of their emphasis on anti-imperialism. Thus, after the war, not only did radicalism tend "left" (that is, hegemonically Marxist-Leninist), but this newly formalized left turned strongly anticolonial.

The national-colonial question occupied a prominent place in the debates of the foundational Comintern congresses of 1919 and 1920 until the Sixth Congress in 1928, when there was a drastic change in policy, away from any collaboration with bourgeois nationalist parties such as the Indian National Congress.[1] Communist parties in the colonizing countries were to support the corresponding anticolonial movements in their home countries' empires, recognizing this to be in their own best interest, lest their potential revolutionary force be sapped and their transnational class solidarity eroded because they were benefiting materially from colonial rule, having been co-opted as participants in exploitation. The analytical link between capitalism and imperialism then revealed a natural situational symbiosis between communism and Asian national liberation movements.

Even so, a global strategic analysis of this kind had to allow for two separate strategies in two different sectors of the world economy—the industrial West and the agrarian colonial East; or what might now be termed the Global North and South. According to the Communist analysis, while capitalism and imperialism (as its highest stage) were two faces of a coin, their differential locations within the structure of the global capitalist-imperialist system imparted a different proximate form to the primary contradiction between master and slave, oppressor and oppressed, exploiter and exploited. For the "Peoples of the East" the contradiction assumed the guise of colonizer and colonized rather than bourgeoisie and proletariat. This reintroduced the category of the oppressed or proletarian nation, analogous to the oppressed class in the global economic context.

From the Bolshevik perspective, national liberation in Asia was still seen as ancillary to European revolution, being a necessary ingredient to the world revolution, whereas so-called national revolutionists like Chatto and Barakatullah recognized world Communism as an instrument that could produce national liberation for Asian and/or Islamic nations.[2] Yet ultimately both components would be needed to comprise the desired goal; as always, the difference between the approaches was in emphasis and priority. Nevertheless the relationship (and occasional tactical conflict) between the anticapitalist and the anti-imperialist struggles—and hence of the relative urgency of eliminating foreign rule (even if it meant uniting classes) or initiating a domestic socioeconomic transformation (even if it meant dividing classes)—was a heatedly debated question for the Indian left throughout the 1920s.

Two separate channels for the importation (and interpretation) of Communism to India dated back to the factional rivalries among the revolutionaries abroad, extending from Berlin to Moscow by way of Kabul and Tashkent. One, which became the Communist Party of India (CPI), dominated until 1927 by M. N. Roy, established beachheads through Roy's contacts in Bengal, Bombay, and United Provinces.[3] The other, manifesting through Kirti and related groups based in Ghadar's Punjabi heartland,[4] remained distinct in leadership, temperament, and tendency, playing the Lancasters to the CPI's Yorks until their merger in 1942.[5] The postwar and post-prison Ghadarites, having embraced the new doctrines, now saw themselves as having a more "mature" level of political consciousness, through which they understood the causes for the failure in 1915 to be (a) treachery (exacerbated by poor security culture, which Rattan Singh attributed to lack of experience) and (b) failure to link the vanguard insurrection movement with the masses. Nevertheless, even the Ghadarites' extension of mobilization to soldiers and agricultural workers had represented a significant widening of the revolutionary circle. By contrast, the Bengali militants with whom the returned Ghadarites established contact when they arrived had at that time more conspiratorial experience but had never pushed their message beyond a narrow group of middle-class students. But the Ghadarites could claim to have developed a popular workers' movement with organic intellectual leadership.

Writing in 1928, DCI David Petrie expressed his "deep misgiving" that the "Sikh Comintern Group" among the dangerously "disaffected" Punjabis represented by far the most serious threat from Russian influence inside India.[6] Even Muzaffar Ahmed, a CPI founding member and Roy's lieutenant in Bengal, agreed that organizing did not really progress in Punjab until the Sikh revolutionists started returning from abroad.[7] The fresh arrivals were also joined by the original generation of Ghadri Babas, veterans of 1915 who, upon emerging from imprisonment in the various Lahore conspiracy trials, joined once again in building the communist and *kisan* (peasant) movements in Punjab along with "comrades young enough to be their children and even grandchildren," remarked Rattan Singh.[8]

Instructions from the Central Committee of the Third International to the western Secretariat in Berlin in May 1920 said: "The new fighting bases, which must inevitably start the movement for national freedom, are Egypt and India," and secondarily Persia and Turkey.[9] The Provisional Government of India in Kabul, fruit of the Turco-German mission, addressed a resolution to Lenin expressing the Indian revolutionaries' "deep gratitude and their admiration of the great struggle carried on by Soviet Russia for the liberation of all oppressed classes and peoples, and especially for the liberation of India." [10]

Lenin responded warmly:

I am glad to hear that the principles of self-determination and liberation of oppressed nations from exploitation by foreign and native capitalists proclaimed by the workers' and peasants' republic have met with such a ready response among progressive Indians who are waging a heroic fight for freedom. . . . We welcome the close alliance of the Muslim and non-Muslim elements.

We sincerely want to see this alliance extended to all the toilers of the east. Only when the Indians, Chinese, Koreans, Japanese, Persian and Turkish workers and peasants join hands and march together in the common cause of liberation—only then will decisive victory over the exploiters be ensured. Long live a free Asia.[11]

The argument was that the strength of the major capitalist powers (Britain, France, and the rising United States) depended on the markets, labor, and resources that their colonial systems provided. In the case of the Britain, its Indian possession provided not only a seemingly bottomless well of appropriable surplus but a specialized labor resource of army personnel crucial for maintaining military control of the rest of its empire, particularly South Africa, China, Persia, and Mesopotamia. Once the Comintern determined that liberating India would be the key to undermining Britain's global dominance, which would in turn be crucial in destabilizing world capitalism, it had to identify the local revolutionary vanguard. To whom could they look? There was no existing "large-scale rebel movement within the subcontinent," but they did spy "many active rebels among frustrated emigrés scattered throughout the world."[12] In other words, there *was* an Indian rebel movement with strong potential; it just did not happen to be resident inside India. Rather, it was clustered outside it around centers in Berlin, Kabul, San Francisco, Manila, and Shanghai.

Although official German support had faded, postwar Berlin remained an important hub for international radicals thanks to the organizational infrastructure put in place during the war. As of March 1919, the AA remained committed to paying 400 marks monthly to every Indian nationalist residing there as a "dwindling body of irreconcileables,"[13] either "until peace is signed or free communication with India is opened again."[14] In 1920 Berlin still hosted several active organizations of "Indian renegades," of which the "Indo-German Bolshevik Society," founded by former BIC officers joined by a new arrival called Dalip Singh Gill, was "reported to be the most flourishing."[15]

Gill was a Ghadar member from Patiala whose brother had been hanged as a dacoit. Rather ironically then, upon arriving in Germany near the end of the war he was arrested under suspicion of being a British spy.[16] The silver lining to the months-long jail stay that followed was the opportunity to strike up a friendship with fellow inmate and future German Communist Party (Kommunistische Partei Deutschlands) cofounder Karl Liebknecht.[17] Although Liebknecht was killed in the Spartacist uprising of 1918, Gill remained close to the infant KPD. In 1919 he bought a plane and flew to Russia to seek funding for a secret society among the Indians in Germany, with partial success. On his second flight he was shot down en route over Poland and captured, returning to Berlin on his release.[18] According to intelligence, "He asserts that he is being aided by Communists and nationalists," and "Some people, mostly Mohammedans, joined him," although it appeared his society, for which he claimed members in Sweden, Russia, Austria, Egypt, and Turkey, "took no part in politics."[19] Again all strands of anti-British resistance were accounted for; again I am less interested in the fact that the Director of Criminal Intelligence (DCI) dreaded the bogey of such a combine than that the empire's critics desired it.

The two major projects of the Third International for revolutionizing the tactically indispensable Peoples of the East were the 1920 Baku Congress, attended by over two thousand people of more than three dozen nationalities, among whom were fourteen Indians; and its eastern organizing bureau in Tashkent, in the newly proclaimed Soviet Socialist Republic of Turkestan. In order to implement these strategic objectives, it would be necessary to collect the Indian revolutionaries active in Europe, North America, and west and central Asia, in effect reassembling the same cast of characters (with a few notable additions and subtractions) that the German Foreign Office had recruited for the Berlin Committee at the beginning of the war. But at least initially, Bose suggests that beyond either the Berlin or Bengal groups, the Comintern found a third and "a more meaningful contact" with the "Ghadar revolutionaries outside India."[20] Just as the AA had, the Bolsheviks recognized this group's importance within international revolutionary circles as being far more than raw material: here was a solid group already politicized, organized, motivated, battle-tested, and sufficiently indoctrinated.

THE FRIENDS OF FREEDOM FOR INDIA

After the San Francisco trial, with the community fatally divided and the principals in jail or overseas, the Ghadar movement seemed silenced. Even those who remained at liberty found it convenient to lie low for a while, since, for any outspokenly political nonwhite foreigner, deportation was now a constant fear. This was the era of the punitive Palmer Raids, during which several thousand "radical aliens" were deported. Increasing restrictions on Asian immigrants were intended in part to catch any loopholes in Palmer. By 1917 the Asian Barred Zone was in place. In 1923 the Department of Justice started denaturalization proceedings against all Indians. In accordance with another law of the previous year, even the American wives of those subject to denaturalization would face losing their citizenship. Without citizenship, land ownership was retroactively precluded under the existing Alien Land Laws, which had gone into effect in 1920. This was a blow to the Sikh farmers who had been trying to build up agricultural livelihoods and claimed to have transformed the fertility of California's arid Central Valley with Punjabi farming techniques. Some attempted to retain the deeds to their land by putting them in the name of friends who were citizens, but this could backfire if the "friends" then claimed the land or the profit from the crops grown on it for themselves.

In the case of *U.S. v. Bhagat Singh Thind* (1922), the plaintiff—a U.S. army veteran and Berkeley alumnus who was friendly but not politically involved with several Ghadar members—tried to argue that South Asians were actually Cauca-sian, setting a precedent for racially based eligibility for citizenship. Stating that Thind was committing sophistry with the words of the founding fathers, when usage and common sense made it obvious that these words had never been intended to refer to dark-skinned Asians, the judge ruled that only those who showed the potential for complete assimilation, namely, "whites of European descent," would be considered. The final blow was the 1924 Immigration Act, which virtually banned Asian immigration for the next forty years.[21] Overall the situation of the Indians in the United States after the war was indicative of an important historical shift in the political and ideological makeup of American society, from identification with anticolonial rebellion to identification with im-perial power. In the words of U.S. Attorney John Preston, "This country is now realizing that we must teach the non-assimilable, parasitic organizations in our midst that while this is a land of liberty, it is not a country of mere license."[22]

Yet the Ghadarites had not lost hope. A 1919 intelligence report on disorders in Punjab—attempting to show that incidents of sabotage, raids, and riots raising slogans like "Maro Angrez" (Kill the English) and "Safed gosh mangta" (Demand white meat) were not merely sporadic bursts of violence but hints of an organized rebellion based on widespread antigovernment feeling—noted that when the Ghadarites in California heard such news through Japanese or Anglo-American contacts, their gratified response was to boast that they *had* after all "awakened India."[23] Supporter Bishen Singh sent a telegram to the jailed Bhagwan Singh and Santokh Singh in the wake of the Amritsar massacre encouraging them: "Cheer up. Revolution in India. Amritsar and Lahore under martial law. Many oppressors killed. Viceroy announced that the state of open rebellion against the authorities exists in these districts." Even though this was a bit of an exaggeration, it is per-versely heartwarming to think how it must have shored up the spirits of the prison-ers.[24] Indeed, letters written *from* jail revealed no sign of repentance, fumed the DCI. As of late October 1918, Hindu-German Conspiracy Case defendant Gopal Singh clung to the belief that "the message of Ghadr . . . sounds in the ears of hun-dreds of millions and not a few heads think and hearts feel." His greeting from jail continued: "The anniversary of the day when Ghadr first spoke in the new world of California is next week. Kindly accept our best wishes for a merry Ghadr day and a prosperous New Year. Yours for the freedom of India, Gopal Singh."[25]

Gopal Singh was one of three convicted in the case whose fight against depor-tation upon release became the first signature campaign of the Friends of Free-dom for India, the main vehicle for Indian political activity in the United States after World War I. According to Jensen the organization was born of a sugges-tion from Taraknath Das in a conversation with American socialists but was officially launched in March 1919 by Agnes Smedley and Sailendranath Ghose, themselves but recently imprisoned under the Espionage Act.[26]

Smedley later became famous for her role as a journalist in China, embedded, one might say, with Mao's Red Army. She was also later revealed to have been involved with a Soviet espionage ring based in Shanghai. But she cut her activist teeth as a passionate and indispensible contributor to the Indian struggle in New York and Berlin. Back in 1912, the budding radical had met Har Dayal in California and was swept up in the ideals of the Ghadar cause. After Dayal's departure she continued her acquaintance with Ram Chandra, while developing a close friendship with "his factional rival" Bhagwan Singh. It was the latter who sent her as a courier to New York in 1916 with documents for the BIC liaisons there, an errand that inserted her directly into the Indian militants' inner circle. Although initially she was close to Lajpat Rai, the two grew estranged as she gravitated more strongly toward the radical faction, who then asked her to maintain a safe storage point for their correspondence, literature, address lists, and the like. After leaving the country in 1920 she continued her involvement in Berlin and Moscow, while enmeshed until 1924 in a tempestuous and controversial common-law partnership with Chatto.[27]

Sailendranath Ghose had arrived in Philadelphia in January 1917, a veteran of the revolutionary movement in Bengal.[28] He immediately sent a telegram to alert Roy—whom he knew as Narendranath Bhattacharji, his errant comrade-in-arms—of his arrival and set off across the continent to San Francisco. At Nalanda House in Berkeley, Ghadar's Surendranath Kar "took him under his wing." Ghose also made contact with Ram Chandra via the German consulate and wired Roy, who was in New York. He paid Ghose's passage back across the country and offered him a room in his Bronx apartment. It was believed that Roy and Ghose had together absconded to Mexico by late May.

By November, however, as the Hindu-German Conspiracy trial was getting under way, Ghose turned up in San Francisco again, occupying a room taken there by Taraknath Das—who would himself be occupying a room in Leavenworth come spring. Das then wrote to Ghose from jail requesting that he publish an appeal to support Indian freedom in a Bolshevist paper in New York, addressed to the British Labour Party. Das instructed Ghose to approach editors Weinstein and Hourwich at the *Novi Mir*,[29] saying: "They will help you. Don't overstate our strength but encourage Russia to think about [imperialism and the population of Asia] and try to convince them that our cause is part of the world cause." (However, Das cautioned, Ghose must be careful not to sound like "an over-enthusiast imposing on them.")

The published appeal read, in part: "Let us hope you do your utmost efforts so that the political prisoners of India (Egypt as well) . . . be immediately released. Our aspiration is to achieve political, economic and industrial freedom of the people of India. . . . Long Live the Cause of Political, Economic, and Industrial Democracy in all lands and in all ages."

It was signed by Sailendra Nath Ghose, for the Indian National Party (INP).[30] The subsequent collaboration of Das and Ghose (identified in intelligence documents respectively as "the diplomat" and "the messenger") soon bore fruit, as they "styl[ed] themselves as Special Representatives of the Indian Nationalist Party" in close consultation with Bhagwan Singh's Ghadar faction. Bhagwan Singh, Das, and Ghose also introduced themselves in letters to Woodrow Wilson and to his secretary of state as "personnel of a Special Commission of the Indian National Party working for the Independence of India and for the establishment of a democratic federated republic of 315 million people."[31] Yet though the INP listed Rash Behari Bose as "Provisional President of the Supreme Council of the Indian National Party" and Jadugopal Mukherjee as "Chairman of the Foreign Relations Committee," it existed largely as no more than an impressive letterhead.[32] In March 1918 Smedley and Ghose were arrested along with four others under the Espionage Act for falsely representing themselves as diplomats representing a foreign government.

Instrumental in launching this nominal group were William and Marion Wotherspoon, left-liberal pacifists and long-time supporters of India, who offered their San Francisco home as mailing address and meeting place throughout the trial. This may have been where Ghose was first "infected" with the dreaded political plague of which there lingered a "prevailing atmosphere" in the house thanks to the sort of visitors that frequented the place, suggested a Justice Department report. Mrs. Wotherspoon and her sister Sarah Bard Field were prominent within the "local branch of the People's Council, an organization which accepted all the principles of Bolshevism,"[33] and—horrors!—there was even evidence that Mr. Wotherspoon had written to Trotsky and Lenin.[34]

It was certain that the Indian National Party had: a letter unearthed in a raid on Das's house was addressed on 12 November 1917 to the Workingmens' and Soldiers' Council of Russia c/o Leon Trotsky in Petrograd; in the letter, after observing parallels between the India of 1917 and the Russia of 1905, the INP stated its support for the Russian revolutionary government and asked for Russia's support for the Indian revolutionists on trial in San Francisco, as the British were negatively influencing the United States government against them.[35] This letter was cited as the pretext for arresting Smedley and Ghose, and for putting out a warrant for Das, who spent the rest of the trial in detention. An excerpt was printed in the *New York Times* on 19 March 1918:

> The hand of British Imperialism is long enough to have several scores of Indian revolutionaries arrested in the U.S.A. . . . so that the British Imperial Government will have the opportunity for taking vengeance upon its enemies by sending them to the gallows. We beg the Russian people not to forget us in our sore distress. We beg to proclaim before the world if in this war for the defence of the right of the people, India should be given her freedom. Long live the Russian Revolution.[36]

Military intelligence considered this clear proof that the "Hindu-German Conspiracy" had metamorphosed into a dangerous "Hindu-Bolshevik clique."[37] The Army Intelligence Department also intercepted a letter from Smedley to a Mr. H. Mitra (aka Ghose) c/o W. A. Wotherspoon in San Francisco, in which the writer said she had consulted with political cartoonist and Communist Party member Robert Minor regarding the means by which Ghose could travel from the United States to Russia.[38]

By June 1919 the DCI thought he had identified three "Indian gangs" involved in anti-British propaganda in the United States: Bhagwan Singh's Ghadar Party in California, Ghose and Smedley's INP, and Lajpat Rai's Home Rule League in New York, plus "another nucleus of sedition" in Mexico centered around Roy, who had fled there with his American wife, Evelyn Trent, and was soon to be "joined by others who have made even the United States of America too hot to hold them." Each group pursued its own methods, but all were in correspondence with each other and were "united in hostility to British Government."[39]

The Friends of Freedom for India, initiated by Smedley and Ghose following their stint in the Tombs (as the New York Halls of Justice and House of Detention were colloquially known), soon became the closest ally of the West Coast group, primarily through the vehicle of the antideportation campaign. For those affected, the charge of violation of neutrality was finally the one that stuck as previously leveled grounds for deportation had not: neither "moral turpitude," defined in 1917 as "an act of baseness, vileness, or depravity in the private and social duties which a man owes to his fellow man or to society" and based on implausibly vague allegations of sexual impropriety exercised by brown men upon white women;[40] nor anarchism, defined in 1918 as "those who believe in the forcible overthrow of the Government, or who are opposed to organized government, . . . believe in or teach the unlawful assaulting or killing of public officials or the unlawful destruction of property, . . . [or] become members of organizations advocating such destruction after entering the United States"; nor even the simple crime of still being present in 1919, when "all aliens convicted during the war who had been in the country too long to come under the old deportation laws" were now by definition deportable.[41] The high-profile cases deemed most urgent were those of Bhagwan Singh, Santokh Singh, and Gopal Singh. The first two were informed of the deportation orders while still serving their conspiracy sentences; Gopal Singh was detained by the Labor Department literally as he walked through the prison gate upon his release.[42]

Aside from this case work, the FFI's larger purpose as proclaimed on its letterhead was "to maintain the right of political asylum and to see that Hindu political prisoners and refugees in America get justice in the light of American traditions," and "to assist in the fair, frank and open discussion that the truth about India may be ascertained." Thus Kar crossed the continent at Das's invitation to serve as editor of the FFI's India News Service in New York, providing weekly information to labor newspapers and magazines.[43] Kar wrote to Gopal Singh "most heartily appreciat[ing the] thought and spirit with which you desire to entrust me with a part of the Works of a Great Cause to which we have pledged ourselves to do our humble share faithfully and intelligently," and acknowledging his consciousness of the deep responsibility of "serving my Motherland in cooperation with you all," a task that he would undertake with "the greatest joy . . . to the best of my ability."[44] His partner in this cause was Ed Gammons, on the choice of whom the new Ghadar Party president Harjap Singh had written: "Keeping in view the value of propaganda, it was decided that in order to run an English paper an experienced editor be taken from the Irish Party."[45] Chatto sent money from Berlin to help fund publication.[46] In addition, Smedley wrote to the Ghadar Party requesting that a member "furnish us with any news which he reads in the Indian papers received by your organization," by mailing weekly updates. Perhaps someone—one of the three defendants, for instance— would even be interested in joining the editorial board. "The policy of our news service is to furnish straight news," Smedley noted, "not editorial opinion or commentary. We choose from the Indian papers news which will be of interest to America. We wish as much labor news as we can get."[47]

However, Smedley's disavowal of editorial bias is unconvincing in context. This time, in addition to their Hindustani- and Punjabi-speaking constituency of potential revolutionary recruits, they had another audience in mind: the English-speaking American public of potential sympathizers. These were to be found among those Harish K. Puri identifies as "liberal-democratic and radical Americans,"[48] pacifists, and anti-imperialists, and in the labor movement, and of course the Irish freedom movement. The roster of public intellectuals connected with the FFI was distinguished: ACLU founder Roger Baldwin, Margaret Sanger, and Isaac Hourwich were on its executive committee, and *Dial* editor Robert Morss Lovett was its president. Free speech and civil liberties attorneys Frank Walsh and Gilbert Roe were its legal advisers; Roe offered his services pro bono for Indians fighting deportation. Walsh was also the chairman of the American Commission on Irish Independence. The board of directors included W. E. B. Du Bois, Upton Sinclair, Franz Boas, Sara Bard Field, and antiwar Socialist Norman Thomas. A "Hindustanee Advisory Board" consisted of Ghadar associates and other respected community members in both California and New York.

In a flurry of supportive editorials and articles in various papers FFI supporters posed rhetorical questions to the American public: Would you have deported your own founders for doing the same thing as these men? Would you have deported Lafayette, William Tell, Garibaldi (all names equally familiar to the readers of the *Ghadar*)? The *Commonwealth* remarked: "The accusation against [Gopal Singh] was none other than that he tried to do for the Hindus precisely that which Washington did for the Americans."[49] The *World,* a Socialist paper in Oakland, demanded: "Should these men be sent to India to be shot or to lie in prison for life for propaganda? *Liberty propaganda?*" Lovett commented in the *Dial:* "How far we have wandered from our former proud estate of political asylum. . . . Even ten years ago it never would have occurred to us to deny a Hindu refugee the right to say exactly that"—that is, to advocate the forceful overthrow of a tyrannical government—"if he thought it was true."[50]

The FFI also circulated a leaflet, signed by the Hindustan Ghadar Party (HGP), that read:

> President Wilson has declared many times that the right of any people to self-determination shall not be denied by any of the larger powers of government. Walt Whitman said of America, "I am the friend of every dauntless rebel." He took America as the typical land for the birth of Democracy and with the other poets he heralded the persecuted of the earth to seek refuge here. Gopal Singh, who is one of the young nationalists of India, took advantage of these high ideals of America and came here for the purpose of nourishing his aspirations for liberation.
>
> Has America ceased to live up to the hopes of its poets and orators? Can men be seized by powers not yet removed from monarchy and taken back to be murdered by "Commissions" without trial or semblance of justice? We hope not.

The leaflet then called on the conscience of "Liberty Loving people of America," appealing to their "sentiment of plain justice" and fair play: "Your voice has great influence in this Republic of yours. You are the nation. . . . Protest in every way possible against this outrageous treatment of men whose only crime is their love of liberty."[51] Anticipating the response, Ed Gammons expressed the confidence that "the spirits of the immortal Lincoln and of the great Jefferson seem to say: 'these libertarians of old India are safe on our shores.' America's traditions enshroud them."[52]

An ad for the FFI that appeared on the back cover of the *Independent Hindustan* for November 1920 offers its own interpretation of the American political legacy:

> *Our American Sovereignty must never be surrendered,* and in accordance with the Declaration of Independence and the spirit of the Constitution of the United States, it is our duty to see that *No One Usurps the Sovereignty of Other Nations.*
>
> Can a liberty loving American remain silent when inhuman brutalities, oppression, persecution and massacre are being carried out by the most militaristic nation in the world? Did we not make pledges to make the world safe for democracy? Do you know one fifth of the whole human race is struggling for freedom? What would you have done if someone spent millions of dollars to keep you ignorant?
>
> That is precisely what the British are doing in all parts of the world. You must know the truth.
>
> We, the American citizens, have organized the Friends of Freedom for India with a view

To maintain the right of asylum for political refugees from India
To present the case for the independence of India.

Smedley wrote several letters to Gammons and Gopal Singh in the fall of 1919 describing the growth of support in the labor sector in particular. There was to be a mass meeting at the Cooper Union in New York, at which union leaders representing ten major bodies would speak on the theme of "labor in India."[53] Kar and Gammons's news bulletin was being sent to over three hundred labor papers in America, as well as a hundred other magazines and dailies. A resolution was to be brought before the Women's International Labor Conference in Washington, D.C., as well as the International Labor Conference, at which Das was to have "placed literature about the cases in the hands of all the foreign delegates," including some from India for whom they hoped to hold another mass rally.[54]

Smedley and Morss Lovett also signed a letter to labor unions, containing the text of a suggested resolution they might endorse: "WHEREAS, the efforts of certain Hindus to gain freedom for their native land" had led to their imprisonment and threatened deportation, with the likelihood of permanent loss of life or freedom "for no other reason than that Britain's economic exploitation and political domination . . . may continue to go unchallenged," may it be resolved "that we, [the undersigned], emphatically protest against the flagrant violation of the spirit of Democracy involved in this denial of the right to asylum . . . and in conformity with the principle of self-determination of peoples, we demand that the persecution of these Hindus cease." Among the unions who submitted petitions on behalf of the three Indians were the American Federation of Labor (AFL), Chicago Federation of Labor, and Detroit Federation of Labor; in New York, the Micrometer Lodge of the International Association of Machinists, Ladies Waist and Dressmakers Union Local #25, and Paper Box Makers' Union of Greater New York; in San Francisco the Molders Union #164, Machinists Lodge #68, Millmen's Union #42, Office Employees Association #13, and Street Railway Employees #518; plus the California State Convention of the Sons of Irish Freedom.[55]

It was also suggested that each union create an India Committee to work with the FFI, which held its first national convention in New York on 5 December 1920, attended by the luminaries of the board as well as several delegates from India.[56] Kar addressed the attendees in no uncertain terms, apparently having discarded the prevailing caution in political speech:

We are convinced of one thing—that the evolutionary growth is impossible without revolution. Revolution in thought, revolution in ideas and ideals, revolution in action—revolution is necessary. . . . India is going to be free from British rule and autocracy as the Russian people have become from the czar, in spite of the conspiracy of the imperialists of the world. The Indian people want not only political independence, but also the kind of independence which will be permanent, only [if it is based on a] sound economic and social program.[57]

Peripatetic radical Amir Haider Khan gave Smedley credit as a driving force for the conference,[58] enlisting the aid of "various American liberal politicians, Irish, American and many other anti-British elements and individuals," and recruiting an unsung army of young American women (likely her feminist associates from the birth control movement) as a sort of "secretariat" who typed "innumerable" correspondence, circulars, and press announcements, gathered facts and literature for the convention, collected money, and set up meetings in connection with the event.[59] Khan further described these women as dressing "in the manner of upper class Indian ladies in beautiful sarees of various colors." As they circulated among the rows of conference attendees and throughout the corridors surrounding the meeting hall, they "enchanted and thrilled the sophisticated American visitors," who had not previously seen "the true-to-life Indian woman in her natural garments."[60]

The Indian men had likewise been rendered into Oriental splendor by the varicolored turbans Smedley, who "knew her America and the American people" (including presumably their susceptibility to the exotic), had persuaded them to wear. Khan says he chose a red one without knowing at the time the loaded significance of that color in the context of postwar America. Wearing such a thing, he said, was "like a red rag to a bull" for the "capitalist press and their agents in America." He also described another incident in 1918, while wearing a red tie he had bought in Brooklyn. His shipmates on the vessel where he worked teased him: "Ah, you Bolshevik, you ought to be deported to Russia! We don't want any goddamn Bolshevik here." He asked his friend Joe what they were talking about; Joe explained: "The Bolsheviks are certain people in Russia who are killing each other and destroying all good things such as religion, culture, home, family, in fact all the human institutions; their flag is red," and so Americans must hate red.[61] But perhaps he would not have changed his color choice even had he known. Khan reached New York via service in the British and U.S. merchant marines, met Ghadar members circa 1920 and thereafter began to distribute Ghadar literature at his ports of call. He later became a member of the Communist Party in the United States and returned to become a lifelong Communist activist in India, and after partition, in Pakistan.

Ultimately the three high-profile deportations were averted, but that apparent triumph was soured by the general "Alien Bill" passed in May 1920, which led to a "wholesale roundup" in which between seventy and a hundred ostensibly apolitical Indian seamen and steelworkers were shipped back.[62] Smedley wrote to Bishan Singh on 5 August that thirty-nine Indian workingmen were being held for deportation at Ellis Island. While she and Das had been "working 24 hours a day for a week" to secure a postponement, "the Department of Labor has practically acknowledged that a nation-wide raid is to be made of the Hindu workers." She added, however: "If the men are students they will not be deported." Pouncing on the loophole implicit in this class distinction, the FFI proposed starting classes for the workers. "It should have been done before this anyway," Smedley admitted. "I believe that educational work is far more constructive and more valuable in the long run than what we are doing."[63] She wrote again later to declare a victory in the case of one escaped seaman, Ram Sarup Singh. He was to be allowed to stay so long as he was enrolled in an institution of learning. So the plan, after getting him out of jail, was to get him into a school to be trained as a labor organizer. That way he would still have to leave in a year or two, but under quite different circumstances, to the benefit of the movement in India.[64]

Smedley herself left the country in December, frustrated with prevailing conditions and seeking better opportunities for revolutionary work in Europe. Kar also left for Berlin and Moscow, co-editing the Indian Independence Party's paper with B.N. Dutt until his death from tuberculosis in 1923. By spring 1921 there was no contact between the East Coast FFI and the West Coast HGP.

HINDUSTAN GHADAR 2.0

As prisoners were released, Ghadar reemerged from hibernation in a new form. Though its numbers were depleted and its activities constrained by the hostile environment, even a nominal reactivation of the party carried strong symbolic impact internationally. The pillars of this new incarnation were Rattan Singh and Santokh Singh. The latter had escaped arrest in Siam and returned to the United States only to be convicted in the San Francisco case two years later.[65] One of the last of the original core group, he now took up Har Dayal's old position as general secretary.[66] Rattan Singh had escaped attention and arrest during the San Francisco Conspiracy trial. According to Sohan Singh Josh, this had much to do with his honorable character; unlike some others of that period, he was "unassuming and worked quietly without hankering after publicity."[67] Until Santokh Singh's release in 1919 the party hobbled along, largely inactive yet saved from extinction by the fidelity of a few such "caretaker" leaders absorbed in the immediate priority of funding defense lawyers, paying bails, and other trial-related expenses. As ever, the Punjabi Sikh emigrant community gave generously. Now in March 1920 the Ghadarites moved back into the old Yugantar Ashram to take up again the work they did best: publishing revolutionary literature and propaganda.[68]

Like the FFI, they had the American Anglophone audience more clearly in mind this time around, to be informed and cultivated as potential supporters. The first organ to take on the task was the *Independent Hindustan,* under Kar's editorship. It was a 24-page "monthly review . . . aimed at the American public and educated Indians on the East Coast" and extending the work of the FFI's Indian News Service.[69] The first issue (September 1920) contained editorials sketching out "Our Aims" and "Our Plans," namely, to provide information about conditions in India under colonial rule and about the latest efforts to resist it.[70] As stated in the first editorial, "Actuated by a definite, determined and deliberate purpose, we are before you to interpret and inform concerning the revolutionary and progressive spirit which is guiding the destiny of India." Here too the cause of national liberation was mantled in a broader principle, as the editorial then beseeched: "Breathes there a man or woman with heart so dried and intellect so cracked who never rejoices over the prospect of a glorious day when the banner of freedom will be unfurled over Ireland, India, Persia, Egypt, China, Russia— over the suppressed and oppressed world?"[71]

Das wrote to Bishan Singh when the editorial appeared, offering congratulations and volunteering to contribute an article per month. He also "wish[ed] to suggest that in the paper you should have a separate section of 'Greater India' which will contain news from various parts of the world," and then signed off: "Bande Mataram to you. Fraternally yours, Taraknath Das."[72] The magazine's contents covered political developments in India, including the Non-Cooperation and Khilafat movements; the diaspora, notably North America, South and East Africa; and international affairs, keeping a sharp eye for events in Persia, the Philippines, China, South Africa, and especially Ireland and Egypt.[73] It kept assiduous tabs on labor struggles among the indentured sugar plantation workers in Fiji and tea workers in Assam, as well as trade union activity in Calcutta and Bombay, peasant and student movements, and the progress of women's rights in India. Always it emphasized Hindu-Muslim harmony and international solidarity, decrying the Indian military and financial role in maintaining British imperial power.

February 1921 included reprints from the *Lahore Tribune, Amrita Bazaar Patrika,* and *Gaelic American*—the latter on India's likely upcoming role as the "base of extensive military operations looking to the conquest of all Central Asia," and news briefs about Sikh soldiers of the Thirty-first Cavalry on hunger strike at Allahabad, students arrested by the British, the Soviet-sponsored Baku conference for Asian revolutionaries, and the establishment of the Tilak School for Politics in Lahore as the first school in India "to teach socialism and trade unionism," to train political workers in politics, economics, and social sciences, and to promote publication and a library for books in the vernaculars on these subjects.

The *Independent Hindustan* shut down operations upon Kar's departure for Europe. The *United States of India* was its eight-page successor; similar in appearance and content, it ran for five more years. An organ of this name and type had originally been Har Dayal's idea, hatched soon after he fled the country in

1914. In a letter to Ram Chandra he expressed his desire to return to San Francisco and work on an English monthly produced out of the Yugantar Ashram with a name chosen carefully to appeal to potential allies among both the native rulers of the princely states and the American public, flattery of whose egos he shrewdly guessed would be "good for our safety."[74] But wartime conditions precluded both his return and the publication. Now, following a planning meeting in Marysville and a reactivation of the trusty funding network, the first issue came out in July 1923. The lead editorial proclaimed that India was "coming fast to her political goal," namely, to achieve "the *United States of India* modeled after the United States of America . . . a free independent republican national state . . . of the people, for the people, by the people." This was reiterated even more explicitly in a note: "Our aim has been and now is the attainment for India of a form of government such as America has, with some modification befitting India. We want to have the *United States of India*."[75]

Continuing the themes and topics introduced by the *Ghadar, Yugantar,* and *Independent Hindustan,* the new magazine offered reportage and commentary on the full spectrum of anti-British activities as well as on the repression of these efforts. Labour and Conservative governments alike were condemned for colonialist policies responsible for outrages like the shooting of several hundred workers during the great Bombay textile strike of 1924 and the arrest of labor leaders in connection with the Kanpur Conspiracy Case.[76] Ample space went to China's freedom struggle and its relevance to the struggles of India, Egypt, and Ireland; editorials tackled such matters as the depredations of the opium trade and the role of British manipulation in outbursts of communal violence.[77] M. N. Roy was a guest contributor, as were members of a committee of French radicals and pro-Indian intellectuals led by Henri Barbusse.[78]

Despite the *United States of India*'s profession of admiration for American governmental structures, Sohan Singh Josh characterized its political tone as "cautiously pro-Soviet." This was consistent with the approach taken by Taraknath Das in a previous article in the *Independent Hindustan* entitled "International Aspects of the Indian Question":

> Imperialist Russia is gone. Revolutionary Russia is avowedly an enemy of imperialism in any form. She has given up her spheres of influence and extraterritorial rights in China. She has championed the cause of Persian, Egyptian, Turkish and Indian independence. She recognised the Irish Republic. She has entered into friendly relations with Afghanistan. And I can assure you that one of the principal reasons for the waging of war against Russia has been Britain's fear that Soviet Russia will inspire and unite with the Indian people to destroy the British empire.
>
> Under these circumstances, what should be the policy of the Indian people, Indian nationalist or revolutionists towards Russia? Our answer is: Friendship and alliance against the British empire.[79]

Das of course was no Communist; far from advocating Marxist ideology he was simply calling for a strategic alliance similar to the previous arrangement with Germany, for the moment replaced as "the greatest enemy of British imperialism and the British Asiatic Empire."[80] However, the core organizers of the secretive inner circle in California were indeed ideological Communists. Kar and Santokh Singh in particular had emerged as important articulators of Marxist theory. Santokh Singh, using his jail time (as it would seem many did) to read up on history and political economy, was one of the earliest converts and proselytizers. Josh quotes an intelligence report of November 1920 claiming "that Santokh Singh was advising the people to study the Marxian theory and learn Russian."[81] An inventory of Santokh Singh's library listed titles such as *Capital*, volumes 1–3, *Russian History*, volume 2, *Soul of the Russian Revolution*, and *Conflict of Colour*. Rattan Singh too had begun to read Marx and was passing it on, having "made many new contacts and . . . come into touch with many a communist working in the trade unions" in the course of his support work for the conspiracy trial and antideportation mobilization.[82]

Around 1920, the radical faction of Ghadarites in the United States decided to take the initiative in establishing direct contact with Moscow.[83] With the organization still facing financial difficulty and internal division, some in San Francisco, including Santokh Singh, talked of "leaving secretly for India to join the armed rebellion" that was supposed to "follow Gandhi's passive resistance movement." Kar was the first emissary, in early 1921. Then Santokh Singh was invited to attend the Fourth Congress of the Comintern in Moscow as a voting delegate from the Ghadar Party, with Rattan Singh as an official observer, in addition to the four delegates from India's still embryonic Communist Party based in central Asia. So in August 1922 the two left on a mysterious vacation, saying only that they were going to visit Taraknath Das in New York "on private affairs."[84] Kar was suspected to be already en route to Russia at Roy's invitation, where it was thought he hoped "to meet Barkatullah and the delegation from India and that he intends to arrange with Lenin for the supply of 'War material.'"[85] This, according to Rattan Singh, was when the party was truly revived as an anti-imperialist movement.

The Communist Party USA (CPUSA) gave the pair a document of confidence, "a sort of clearance visa or letter of introduction" affirming that the bearers "have been investigated by our party and we find that they are trusted members of the Hindustani Gadar Party." The document continued: "We request that every assistance be given them in passing through Russia and the neighbouring countries on their way to India."[86] Later American Communists helped spirit Moscow-bound Ghadarite trainees aboard vessels, using cloak-and-dagger maneuvers such as following a contact at a distance, having received a wordless sign, to a dock where they were sometimes obliged "to creep into dark holes in the ship below water level to escape scrutiny of the police."[87]

Nevertheless, despite such aid, the 1953 Senate Fact-Finding Committee on Un-American Activities in California failed in its aim of definitively linking the American Ghadar movement to international communism.[88] The committee had thought the party "a natural target for Communist infiltration": after all, "here was a conspiratorial, highly disciplined group that was fanatically dedicated to rid India of imperialist domination. Its members were scattered throughout Canada, the United States, Africa, Asia and South America. The Party was well financed and operated in secrecy. Clearly, it fitted in perfectly with Russia's postwar plans for the Communizing of Asia."[89] But although the Ghadar core personnel included "some highly indoctrinated Communists," of whom one would "occasionally . . . appear at a front meeting, in the Communist schools, or would receive some favourable attention from the Communist press in California . . . these occurrences are exceedingly rare."[90] For example, Munsha Singh, while not known to be a party member, was at the time of his service as Ghadar party secretary contributing articles to San Francisco's communist *Daily People's World.* Another unidentified *Ghadar* staffer was "surreptitiously teaching night classes at the Communist California Labour School in San Francisco—and at the same time assiduously circulated communist propaganda material among his Gadar Party contacts."[91] But most Ghadarites had no discernible connection with the official Communist apparatus in the United States, nor could the most prominent Indian communists be linked to Ghadar. In fact, the sister groups Ghadar and Kirti represented a stubbornly autonomous alternate left formation, distinct from the mainline CPI. The *Kirti,* arriving regularly from Punjab, was available for free distribution at *gurdwaras* and at the Yugantar Ashram, but its Comintern connection was not discussed.[92]

In 1925 Rattan Singh returned to impart the word fresh from on high to his HGP cadre. Dalip Singh made an appearance in the United States around this time, before returning to Moscow, where he was "understood to be . . . with the Central Bolshevik Committee."[93] The recommendations Rattan Singh conveyed from Moscow largely consisted in getting students from the United States to Moscow for education and training, after which they would have the option of remaining in Russia or proceeding to the task of mass movement–building inside India. So in spring 1926 Ghadar sponsored its first batch of students to the University of the Toilers of the East, a group that included Pritam Singh Kasel, Karam Singh, Harjap Singh, and Santa Singh Gandiwind. Harjap Singh reported that a second batch the following year consisted of seven Indian and seven black students.[94] Four more students made the trip in 1932, followed by at least two more batches within the next couple of years, plus other Ghadarites recruited from Canada, Argentina, East Africa, New Zealand, Fiji, and China.[95] According to a 1935 intelligence report there were sixty Indian students in Moscow at that time, not counting those who had already completed the training and had proceeded to their assignments.[96]

Amir Haider Khan was among the students in 1928. In his understanding, the Comintern wanted to help "all the colonial countries which had industrial workers to develop the communist parties in each of these countries. With this end in view, the Communist International was attempting to help for training some revolutionary workers who would become party organisers in their respective countries. Thus [they] got some students directly from the different colonial countries and some colonial students through the communist parties in different imperialist countries."[97] For example, the French Communist Party had sent students from Indochina, Morocco, Syria, and various other colonies. But neither the Communist Party of Great Britain (CPGB) in England nor Roy in India were making much headway. So the Comintern turned to the United States as a possible source of militant Indian workers.[98] The other sources of personnel were, according to Josh, the *muhajirin* plus "some deserters and prisoners from the British Indian Army in Iran and the Middle East"[99]—that is, the target audience of Ghadar's wartime propaganda efforts.

The first batch of travelers presented themselves as agricultural workers at the Soviet consulate in Montreal, since the United States had no legal diplomatic relations with the Soviet Union. For many of them this was no stretch, but it did not apply to all. For example, Prem Singh Gill had come by a familiar academic route: after studying at Lahore and then at Berkeley, where he was "greatly influenced" by the Soviet revolution, he volunteered to join the Moscow program along with six others in 1926. He later became an eminent scientist.[100] Jaswant Singh's trajectory was more unusual in that he worked not in West Coast agriculture but at the Ford Motor Company. Asked by a three-person commission why he had come to Russia, he responded that it was at Ford that he "came into contact with a Russian engineer who roused a desire in me to see the workers' raj and study there and then go to India to free the country. The Gadar Party has sent me here to receive education in communism." When asked his opinion of the American Communist Party, he replied: "I do not know much. I had some contact with a few comrades who took me as a party sympathizer. They told me that the Russian Communist Party had overthrown the czar and established a workers' and peasants' government. This increased my interest all the more."[101] Like Jaswant Singh, all trainees were sounded on arrival and required to fill out questionnaires, the literate assisting their less-schooled comrades. This process was intended to weed out British spies and to determine class background. One aspirant was sent back because his family owned too much land in Punjab.

What the students had in store was a year-long course of instruction on revolutionary history, political economy, historical materialism, strategy and tactics of proletarian revolution, and party building.[102] In general the university preferred "toilers" who were relatively young and at least moderately educated; many of the Punjabi laborers whom Ghadar sent were quite a bit older and illiterate besides.

Nevertheless, the "international department 'held high opinion about the Punjab comrades'" and admitted them anyway, in recognition of their proven record of sterling worth and revolutionary value.[103] As needed they were assigned a separate course of study, focusing on basic literacy—their first such opportunity in many cases—followed by the rudiments of Marxist theory. In Jawala Singh's words, they learned "what communism is; how man and society developed; how Marx and Engels worked out the theory . . . and about the Soviet revolution and Lenin's role in bringing it about." Raja Singh, who attended from 1932 to 1936, summed up his lessons as "how the capitalists exploited the workers and how accumulation of capital takes place and . . . that there were no four yugas (ages) but four stages of development of society" (although, Josh noted, he still could not list these stages correctly).[104] Instruction was in Urdu or Punjabi. Training for English speakers generally lasted for twelve months, and for speakers of other languages eighteen months.[105] Some stayed for a year, many up to four.[106]

In the characteristically damning tones of the prose of counterinsurgency, the California Senate fact finders fumed that "this academy of treason has produced some noted graduates," including their own homegrown Ghadarites. The report went on: "Graduates of this huge Red school are the real leaders of the world Communist movement, chosen because of their special talents for subversion, and intensively trained in Communist politics and ideology before they are given the special courses in train wrecking, street fighting, guerrilla tactics, underground organization, disruption of transportation and communication systems, contamination of food and water supplies, and the extremely refined and delicate art of espionage."[107] Despite this ominously sensational syllabus, in truth the course of training dictated that only after proper theoretical grounding were students to be given military training, and then a stint of factory work for practical experience. While this seems sensible for the petit bourgeois déclassé youth for whom the program was perhaps designed, one wonders if it was really necessary for the Punjabis, drawn from among a population of army veterans and lifelong agricultural laborers.

An extensive description of the school in Moscow is offered by Ernestine Evans, an American journalist who was in Russia in the autumn of 1921 and grew curious about the "University of the East."[108] The school had been founded a year previously at the suggestion of Broida, Stalin's assistant as Commissar of Nationalities, "whose difficult task is to harmonize the nationalist sentiments of the former subject peoples of the Russian Empire with the internationalist proletarian ideology of the Communist government, and still keep them within the Russian federation." Broida had suggested the school, Evans explained, "as one means of cementing the far-flung nationalities to Moscow."

In her article "Looking East from Moscow," Evans reported that there were 731 students at the school in 1921, including Tartars, Kirgiz, Turkomans, Turks,

Meshcheryaks, Uzbeks, Tadzhiks, Kazikuliks, Bokharans, Hindus, Persians, Arabs, Jews, Koreans, Japanese, Chinese, Osetines, Avars, Averians, Luzghians, Khivans, Liths, Georgians, men from Azerbaijan, Bulgarians, "and from somewhere and for some reason, one French student."[109] Predating the arrival of the Ghadarites by several years, Indian *muhajir* trainees Fida Ali and Abdul Kader said that "students from almost all Asiatic nations" were attending; Ferozuddin Mansur specified "many other Asiatic students, Persians, Bokharans, etc. but no Afghans." Mansur also reported that their classes were conducted in English, though Evans cited the use of ten different languages.[110] She also mentioned forty Chinese boys from Siberia who were kept busy learning Russian. *Muhajir* Rafiq Ahmad estimated that 10 percent of the students were girls. To be accepted, students had to hail from "the correct social and ideological background," meaning from worker or peasant families—in the Indian case, clerical occupations counted too—and they had to bear approval from a working-class or Communist organization. However, in academic experience they ranged from the functionally illiterate to the alumni of top European universities.

Evans observed a class taught by Evelyn Roy that "consisted in [her] reading aloud in English to eighteen Indian boys chapters from Raymond William Postgate's *Revolutions from 1789–1906*."[111] Evans remarked further: "A Korean who had attached himself to the class nodded sleepily from time to time. The girl read on in a fresh, eager voice. The boys asked a few questions about library cards. The class was over."

Evans also mentioned an interview she had with two Armenian boys who were collecting famine funds on behalf of the university to send to a Volga village. They were also sending rations of black bread, potatoes, and tea from the students' own allotments.[112] Evans asked the Armenians what nationality, among all those from which they had met representatives, they liked best. "They both replied with one voice sternly that they were internationalists and had no national favorites, but they roomed with young Turks from Azerbaijan, intelligent fellows, and they went about much with the Hindus who lived in the next house." Their version of the curriculum—in classes they shared with Chinese, Japanese, Bulgarian, and ten newly arrived Arab students—was "political economy, history of communism, history of Europe, history of human society, biology, geography, history of the cooperative movement, history of colonial development, problems of nationalism—and arithmetic." Evans said that she "laughed at the arithmetic, trotting along like a coachdog behind such a magnificent curriculum. My assessment hurt my visitor's feelings, and he said stiffly, 'We study what we need for the life.'" After completing the course, they planned to be teachers and to go "wherever there are groups of Armenian workmen."[113] In the meantime, they told Evans, they were happy in Moscow and often went to the theater. But their favorite extracurricular activity was attending weekly party conferences and discussions about what was happening in different parts of Russia. These happened in the social club room, where during this very conversation some multicultural fusion of music and dance was going on; later there might be chess, checkers, a lecture, or a play. It was far more crowded than "the library upstairs, with its Marxist volumes." Overall, "with its exotic assortment of students and its social club room," the place struck Evans as being "for all the world like the interior of the YMCA (in Trafalgar Square during the war.) The walls were covered with posters in chalk and paint, made by the students, posters announcing plays by the social club, posters calling for famine relief, posters for trade unions, all done in a primitive eastern style. It was not a very tidy university. Russia is not a tidy country."

Then-viceroy Chelmsford wondered in a 1934 letter to the director of intelligence whether suspected assistance from the Comintern to the Ghadar Party and others should be protested as a breach of the Anglo-Soviet propaganda agreement of 1929. This would be difficult, he was told, since it would require proving, first, that Ghadar students in Moscow represented the party and weren't just "individuals interested in communism"; second, that the Soviet government could be held responsible for actions of the Comintern; and third, that the Ghadar Party was indeed in league with the latter:

> Can we show that the Gadar Party's aims are of a communist nature. I do not think that we can show this. We can show that they are prepared to use communist methods in India and that they are connected with communists to whom they look for assistance; but we cannot show that the aim of the Gadar Party is the dictatorship of the Proletariat . . . nor that they will indulge in communist propaganda in the USA.[114]

Perhaps by 1934 that was the case, but throughout the early to mid-1920s, while various activists "shuttl[ed] between the USA, Moscow, Istanbul and Kabul," official chatter marked that the Ghadar Party in California was regaining notable momentum.[115] With the departure of Santokh Singh and Rattan Singh, Niranjan Singh Dhillon took over coordination of the radical faction.[116] They were rearming. Some were learning to make cartridges; earlier, Santa Singh Gandiwind in Holtville had received "a machine for this purpose," along with a supply of powder.[117] Bhagwan Singh returned in 1926, and with him back at the helm the group was once more "fervently spreading revolutionary ideas amongst the farmers and labourers."[118] Furthermore—indicating a touching concern for the workers' well-being—

> As regards the effect of the Ghadar propaganda among farmers and agricultural labourers, the Consul-General wrote that, left to themselves, these men would probably save up their money against their return to India but, worked up to a white heat of fanaticism by the revolutionary outbursts of local agitators, who were

kept in heart and pocket by the Ghadar party, they readily subscribed considerable sums of money to what they termed the "cause of freedom," and this money was sent over to the headquarters of the party in their native land, or was conveyed to Russia for the purchase of arms and ammunition for eventual use in India.[119]

A triangular circuit was now in effect between California, Moscow, and Punjab, with the Russia-to-India leg mediated through Kabul. This pattern was gradually revealed through intercepted correspondence written in a "secret cipher code."[120] The British consul-general at San Francisco wrote to the ambassador in Washington that the Ghadar Party officers were thought to be corresponding with the Soviet and Afghan governments as well as with the *Kirti* staff in India. At one point Secretary Nidhan Singh in California wrote to Gurmukh Singh in Kabul reporting on price lists for machine guns, automatic weapons, and such obtained from the agent of the California Arms Company; Ghadar in Kabul responded with a telegram requesting samples of hand grenades and machine guns to be sent via Paris as far as Aden or Persia, at which point they would take over. Later, the California party received a request from Kabul for "money for the purchase of a lorry." They agreed to send the price of a Ford, which should arrive in two months. During the first half of the year the party was "in low water," but by September, "when the pockets of the Indian farmers and labourers were well filled after the fruit picking seasons," they were able to collect thousands of dollars in California, of which about one-third was sent to India.[121] In January 1927 they got a letter back from Afghanistan thanking them for the truck and requesting also a cartridge-making machine such as the one they had in Holtville.[122]

In a memo regarding Ghadar's prospects for gunrunning in the Persian Gulf, officiating Political Resident Major T. C. W. Fowle reported that the Russian ship *Kommunist* had recently landed at Abadan, loaded with Browning pistols— typically the weapon of choice for Indian revolutionists, he noted, whereas rifles were more associated with the South Persian tribesmen—although there was also mention of "rifles and Thompson machine guns . . . such as used by the gangsters of Chicago." The Ghadar Party would need lots of organization and funds to pull it off, Fowle thought, but with their level of "zeal and energy" (plus the venality and corruption of Persian Gulf Customs) they just might be able to do it.[123]

But the Soviet strategy focusing on the Ghadarite base in Afghanistan was in flux. Once the Khilafat movement collapsed in 1924, the keystone for revolutionizing the Peoples of the East shifted from central Asia to China. At this point Soviet efforts to smuggle arms, ammunition, and explosives into India moved from the northwest to the northeastern frontier, which would depend more upon the collusion of Roy and his Bengali revolutionary network. After 1926, China was the destination of most Moscow-trained North American Ghadarites,[124] where Shanghai and Hong Kong had long provided a solid support base due to the presence of Sikh police and army troops.[125] Now they established links with the soon-to-be-sundered Guomindang and Chinese Communist parties, while joining Korean and Vietnamese activists in the newly convened International Union of Oppressed Peoples of the East. The formation—whose lead organizer, Ho Chi Minh, the Comintern had recently sent to China—first convened in Hankow in summer 1925. Dasaundha Singh, Genda Singh, and Shamsher Singh represented the Ghadar Party at the conference, which then provided a platform for their future work.[126]

But it was through a fortuitous fiasco that the reborn Hindustan Ghadar Party managed to open up its Chinese franchise. In 1925, Mahendra Pratap, a flamboyant, dispossessed aristocrat who had accompanied the BIC mission to Kabul in 1915 and had there been named figurehead president of the Provisional Government of India, arrived in New York to speak to his compatriots. Although an opposing faction warned him against "the Gadar gang,"[127] he declined to choose sides and visited San Francisco for two months as the guest of the Ghadarites. (Barakatullah had been after all his traveling companion across Persia and his colleague in Kabul.) Pratap was warmly received at his appearances; despite the Californians' own sharpened class consciousness, they seem to have succumbed somewhat to the glamour of royalty. According to Josh they were impressed with the fact that here was a genuine aristocrat on their side, and that he had made sizable sacrifices for the cause—sacrifice always providing bonus points for one's quotient of revolutionary legitimacy—as the British government had confiscated all his property. They were also, after a ten-year hiatus, growing restless once again for decisive action. So they responded eagerly when Pratap proposed a plan for a mission to Tibet and Nepal, in which they would scout a route for smuggling arms to India while he recruited the raja of Nepal to fight alongside them. Russia and Afghanistan would help. What he wanted from Ghadar was $30,000 and "six daring men" to come along. Evelyn Roy also did a separate organizing tour among the California Sikhs to encourage them to work among their countrymen staffing police and army in Shanghai and Hong Kong.[128]

Had the San Franciscans been familiar with Pratap's record and reputation, or known that their counterparts in Kabul had been against such a mission, they might have refused. But this was a new generation of activists, who lionized their predecessors—martyrs whose exploits had been immortalized through the Lahore and San Francisco Conspiracy cases—but were unable to benefit directly from their experience. This exposed them to the risk of falling into the same traps of impetuosity as a decade before. Nevertheless Pratap's "vehement denunciation of the British Government inspired confidence,"[129] and they outdid his request, producing $35,000 and seven men.[130]

The group bought tickets for Hong Kong and got off in Tokyo, where Rash Behari Bose met them and sent them on. By now they were having their doubts about the raja. Aside from the fact that he traveled second class while the rest rode in steerage, and that the checks he wrote them bounced, their anger grew as they realized he had no serious intention of carrying out the mission as stated. His behavior seemed more like that of a religious crank than a revolutionary, with his stated goal of spreading a universal "religion of love" by means of copious pamphlets signed with the ecumenical pseudonym Mohammed Peter Pratap Singh.[131] They felt disgusted, used, and deceived, and they were stranded in China. But they decided to stay and make the best of it.

By early 1926 the newcomers had "identified themselves with seditious elements in Peking";[132] they also taken guidance from Pritam Singh, then Ghadar's chief representative in Moscow, in undertaking the two standard Ghadarite projects: the production of a newspaper, and the subversion of the loyalty of the Sikh soldiers and police watchmen of Shanghai and Hankow. Dasaundha Singh's papers, confiscated upon his arrest near the end of 1927, specified several aims, including the development of a Chinese branch of the HGP to cooperate with the Guomindang against the British in Hong Kong and Shanghai; to form "Indian revolutionary units for service under Chinese military authorities"; and to disseminate appeals to troops, watchmen, and police for desertion or mutiny.[133] The Criminal Investigation Department (CID) also intercepted letters of cooperation and "inflammatory literature" passed between Chinese seamen and Indian trade unionists. Thus, when Smedley and Roy arrived in 1927, they found the Sikh community already mobilized, though subject to threats and deadly intimidation.[134]

Until 1927, Dasaundha Singh maintained his Guomindang (GMD) contacts and offers of Ghadar support, as the Comintern at that point was still recommending the Chinese Communist Party (CCP) should do.[135] A unanimous resolution proclaimed the following in February 1927, shortly before the massacre:

We, the Hindustan Gadar Party, sympathise with and endorse in its entirety the national program adopted by the Kuomintang Party of China in its national struggle for freedom from the domination of the foreign powers, and that we disclaim and disapprove of any and all acts of brutality committed by the Indians in the British service brought to China under brute force, to hinder in any way, shape or form, the movement for the national freedom of China.[136]

Even afterward, DCI David Petrie cautiously judged the bloody GMD/CCP split as a temporary setback to Bolshevism, but nothing to get complacent about. "In such a soil," he warned, "every foul weed is bound to take root. And Bolshevism will probably continue to flourish. . . . Similarly, the Indian revolutionary element will find a footing in disordered China and the Ghadar plotter and the Soviet emissary will join forces and exploit each other to his own advantage."[137]

The stated purpose of the *Hindustan Ghadar Dhandora* (Hindustan Ghadar Trumpet), which was brought out fortnightly in Punjabi, was to promote Indo-Chinese friendship and to persuade Indians resident in China to switch their loyalties from Britain to the Chinese cause.[138] Dasaundha Singh seemed to have found his niche in the newspaper: an intelligence report commented that he had "the makings of an inveterate propagandist." He sent a "frankly revolutionary 'Appeal to Indian Students'" to the *Bande Mataram* (Lahore); it also appeared in the *Akali* (Amritsar). He also wrote a "most objectionable article" titled "Let China and India Unite for the Holy Cause," which appeared in both the *Hindustan Ghadar Dhandora* and an Anglo-Chinese newspaper. The third issue of *Dhandora* proclaimed: "The dutiful sons of China are fighting for the freedom of their country. The freedom of India and the freedom of China have a close connection with each other. By the freedom of China the day of the freedom of India will draw near. . . . Oh! brave ones of the Indian army . . . it is [your] duty . . . to create a general mutiny";[139] or be no better than mercenaries, paid wages to fight people who are not their enemies. The 3/14th Punjabi regiment stationed in Shanghai seems to have received special attention aimed at "seducing" both Hindu and Muslim troops through conversation and literature, including the *Ghadar*.[140] In at least one instance the Sikh Artillery and the Mohammedan Police at Shameen refused to fire upon the Chinese when ordered to do so, and had to be shipped back to India.[141]

The Californians continued sending financial support as well as material for publication. The *United States of India* had printed several related articles including the following item in the September 1925 issue: "About 70 men of the British Indian police from Hong Kong left the service of the British government in a sympathetic walkout in favour of the Chinese workers as a protest against the ruthless methods used by the English in shooting down strikers and demonstrators."[142] Meanwhile a mass meeting of Ghadarites in Marysville, California, issued a cascade of resolutions to be forwarded to Indian newspapers against the "atrocities and butchery" visited upon Chinese workers and students by British invasion, and protesting the posting of Indian troops there.[143] But in 1926 there was an irreparable split between the radical and moderate factions. The *Ghadar* was still being published from San Francisco on a modest scale and circulated throughout British Columbia; as before the war, pamphlets and periodicals wended around the world to knit together the party's outposts, "wherever Punjabi workers resided in large number."[144] But the Communist or "Desh Bhagat" group (i.e., those committed primarily to continuing the fight for Indian independence, as opposed to those who wanted to enter the American mainstream) grew increasingly alienated from the community as a whole and indeed remained hidden to all but a tight core of activists.[145]

In the late 1920s a string of murders occurred in the California Sikh community. Though these were mainly related to land disputes and petty rivalries with no direct connection to Ghadar activities, the shadow of doubt fell on the Ghadarites nonetheless. They were also suspected, here with more validity, of involvement in the trafficking of illegal immigrants. This was a lucrative business for which the party's inner circle considered themselves well suited, having become skilled at smuggling their own people in and out of the country for so many years. Mexico had traditionally offered a refuge from the law, and a point through which to move literature, money, or weapons in and out. Throughout 1927 those vigilant in gauging activity among the North American Sikhs noted "a good deal of surreptitious crossing and recrossing of the border,"[146] such as that of Jagat Singh—believed to be among those directing the "secret work"—whose movements through Mexico, Cuba, and Turkey the CID had been tracking since 1920. Rattan Singh himself was smuggled across using an alias, in the efforts to "procur[e] further followers and funds in support of the . . . movement," until he ran afoul of U.S. immigration authorities, after which he jumped bail and absconded across the border.[147]

But when Teja Singh Swatantra arrived in 1929 to tighten up the ship, the local situation looked bleak. Despite his motivational efficiency, he tended to be authoritarian and domineering, and his attachment to conspiratorial tactics seemed to the new Communist Ghadarites to be inappropriately outdated, impeding the transition into the approved mode of mass organization. This was to be a recurring debate. Nevertheless, it appears he had a talent for inspiration, perhaps bolstered by his gifts as a Punjabi poet and by his taste for action.[148]

Prior to meeting the Ghadar leaders—Rattan Singh and Santokh Singh from America, plus Gurmukh Singh and Udham Singh Kasel, who had escaped across the border from jail in India post-mutiny—in Kabul in 1923, Swatantra was a preacher and Akali activist.[149] During the following year much of the group's international secret correspondence passed through him under the name of Ishar Singh.[150] But in 1924 he left to train at a military academy in Istanbul, where he then became an instructor at an automobile school and set up a front business through which to deliver cheap goods and Russian money via the Turkish envoy in Kabul. He was also "said to be amply supplied, with funds from America."[151]

In early 1930 Swatantra moved on to San Francisco and repeated the stratagem, starting up a Hindustan-American Trading Company as a cover for "shipping critical materials to the Gadar underground in India." He also traveled around California giving "impassioned lectures" and mobilizing trainees for the Moscow academy, from Stockton laborers to students from the Universities of Washington and California, while allegedly sharing his knowledge of concocting bombs and poisons.[152] He installed a new printing press at the Yugantar Ashram, encouraged the staff to buy an airplane, and gave flying lessons.[153] There were in fact improbably ambitious plans for an air force, with ten Russian-made airplanes to be supplied to Kabul courtesy of a joint Berlin-Moscow committee. The Provisional Government of India in Kabul was to send at least one plane to India "manned by a reliable nationalist and equipped with bombs, revolvers and

leaflets . . . to incite the rural population against the Government." Dr. Hafiz of
the BIC had arrived in Kabul along with "fifteen German and Russian engineers
and explosive experts." A letter from the BIC to Birendranath Dasgupta in Zurich mentioned that five Indians were learning to fly in Tashkent, and that in
addition Chatto wanted to bring over a friend of Dutt's who had "bec[o]me a flying expert in America before the war."[154]

Two years later Swatantra departed San Francisco "at the urgent request of
immigration officials" and journeyed to Panama (where he founded yet another
franchise of the bogus Hindu Trading Company), Brazil, and Argentina. His
most distinctive contribution thereafter was in Ghadarizing the East Indian
labor force of South America.[155] Indian revolutionists had been interested in this
region ever since Ajit Singh's efforts to establish centers in Brazil and Argentina.
Both Rattan Singh and Jodh Singh met with Ajit Singh in Brazil; Bhagat Singh
Bilga, one of the last survivors of the original Ghadarites and Moscow school
graduates, who emigrated to Argentina as a laborer in the 1920s and eventually
served as general secretary of the country's Ghadar branch, recalled that Ajit
Singh was the first person he met there.[156] At the time of Bilga's arrival there was
a well-established circuit of Indian laborers in South America, concentrated in
the railroads, refineries, farms, and factories of Mexico, Panama, and Argentina,
and sometimes passing through Cuba's sugar plantations. Bhagwan Singh's activities during the early part of the war had left behind a political center in Panama where Spanish-speaking "Hindus, Muslims and Sikhs all worked and lived in
unison" and where laborers would congregate for group readings of the latest
Ghadar and *Ghadar-di-Gunj*. And in the expanding industrial city of Rosario in
Argentina, Indian workers kept avidly abreast of current events and political developments back home thanks to a regular stream of newcomers. Gate meetings at
Rosario factories were addressed by "all hues of trade-union leaders including
communists,"[157] which perhaps contributed to the high proportion of Moscow
students arriving from that country—five batches of Punjabi-speaking workers up
until 1935, possibly totaling up to 70 percent of the Indian trainees in Russia.[158]

Both Swatantra and Rattan Singh made the rounds of the south, exerting their
persuasive powers upon the immigrants to "[make] them lovers of India's freedom," and signing up active party supporters. While both were "effective speaker[s]
and well aware of world politics," Rattan in particular was well acquainted with
many of the older workers through his long history with the movement, while
Swatantra was prone to supplement his rhetoric with instruction in the insurrectionary arts, thereby exceeding the party line but in the process inspiring
followers as much through personal loyalty as through the content of his political statements.[159] All of this exposed Swatantra to the accusation by some of his
own Moscow recruits that he was still "suffering from bourgeois-democratic illusions" with only a "vague and unclear" understanding of the mechanics of

world revolution or the functioning of a postrevolutionary "workers' and peasants' raj."[160] Rattan Singh insisted that what his colleague needed was to "forget . . . whatever he had read elsewhere and . . . learn new revolutionary scientific ideology" from the source.[161] So in 1932, despite his desire to return to India, Swatantra himself made the pilgrimage to Moscow, though he enrolled in the university unwillingly, convinced he already knew everything he needed to know. Despite his initial reluctance, Swatantra made himself useful in Moscow, translating Lenin's *Imperialism: The Highest Stage of Capitalism* into Punjabi and giving lectures in that language. He finally traveled on a false passport to India in 1934, and throughout the 1940s played a prominent role in the Kirti Party.

Swatantra left in his wake a core of committed organizers in the United States, including Nidhan Singh, who had worked on the *Ghadar* and was a defendant in the Hindu-German Conspiracy trial. An "ardent admirer" of Swatantra, he was later closely linked to Agnes Smedley. He became Ghadar Party president in 1930 and kept in contact with Sikhs in Russia, India, and Afghanistan, leading immigration authorities to tar him as "an undesirable anarchist." The case was dismissed when the League Against Imperialism and "its American counterpart, the International Labour Defence," rallied to his cause (though one suspects that the defense of "he's not an anarchist at all; he's a Bolshevik" cannot have been especially helpful). After two years he joined the trainees he had done so much to send to Moscow; much later (1951) he was elected to the Punjab Assembly on the Communist ticket.[162] Another committed organizer was Achar Singh Cheema, who arrived in California by way of Afghanistan in 1927 or 1928, and then proceeded to Moscow for training in 1932. He returned to San Francisco in 1934, touring the state with his "inflammatory propaganda" speeches. In 1935 he went to France, allegedly to meet with a French Communist agent, and following independence was thought to be "an active leader in the underground communist party in India."[163]

Despite this rearguard, Puri says that by the early 1930s, "all the Ghadarites"—by which he implies all the *real* Ghadarites, which is to say the radicals, who were now the Communists—had departed.[164] What was left was a platform for civic boosterism stumping for the economic success and political assimilation of the Sikhs within the American mainstream. Thus the cost of Ghadar's orientation toward international revolutionism was the weakening of its domestic role as a radical immigrant movement.

THE *KIRTI*

Rattan Singh and Santokh Singh left Moscow in May 1923, newly fortified with sophisticated theory and zeal for the cause, and ready to take up their work in India. To avoid British interception they took the long way around from Berlin through Persia to Kabul, where they established contact with Gurmukh Singh and Udham Singh, both of whom had escaped across the border after the attempted mutiny of 1915. Now, as the two new arrivals briefed Gurmukh Singh on the latest from Moscow, it once again became apparent that they differed on the desired approach. Gurmukh was a prototypical first-generation Ghadri Baba, with a suitably dramatic resume. He had been a "hero of the Komagata Maru and the Andamans struggle," which was carried out from inside the jail for the treatment of political prisoners. After escaping from a train while being transferred from the Andamans jail to a mainland facility in 1921, he had crossed into Afghanistan and eventually made the pilgrimage to the Soviet Union to study Marxism. He also helped to reorganize Ghadar in the United States in the early 1920s. Later he returned to fight underground in India, was jailed in 1936 and returned to the Andamans to complete his sentence, led a hunger strike, and ended up yet again back in Punjab jails. It had been his idea to send Swatantra to Turkey for secret military training, while Rattan and Santokh argued that Swantantra's services would be better used in organizing the peasants and workers of Punjab and running the new journal they planned to issue. But Gurmukh, like Swatantra, was still set upon the idea of armed conspiracy.

Meanwhile, Rattan Singh set up a stationery shop in Kabul as a front for keeping in contact with Soviet emissaries, while Santokh Singh proceeded to India to start an organ to "preach the new Marxist-Leninist ideology cautiously and carefully among the Punjabi people" in their own language. Udham Singh was to serve as liaison between India and Afghanistan, while both Rattan and Santokh maintained communication with California. But Santokh Singh was arrested en route to India and escorted the rest of the way in custody. Given the notoriety of his involvement in the San Francisco and Mandalay Conspiracy trials, his name itself was grounds for incrimination; his was the dubious honor of being considered sufficiently threatening to the stability of the Raj that Petrie decided: "There can be, I think, no question of his being permitted to be at large at the present juncture."[165] As "one of the leaders of the Sikh Ghadr Party in San Francisco, whose notorious history in that capacity, as well as the details of his implication in the Indo-China conspiracies in the United States of America in 1915–17, and of course his subsequent relations with Indian revolutionaries in Soviet Russia,"[166] he was detained at Amritsar subjail, then confined to his village under guard for a year on good behavior.[167]

Meanwhile, Rattan Singh was traveling through Europe and South America to organize new branches, writing letters as he went to update comrades on his activities—many of which letters were intercepted and used to build the case against him as the "outstanding figure in the foreign section of the conspiracy."[168] In 1925 and 1926 he was back in the Americas arranging the travel of Ghadar members to Moscow. He later resurfaced in India, where his "success in evading the police for six months," in India, remarked a government report, "stamps him as a person of more than ordinary resourcefulness."[169] Perhaps it helped that in addition to his gifts of quick-witted adaptability and "great persuasive powers," as Josh observed, "Comrade Rattan Singh was a smart, short-statured peasant" who "mixed up so unobtrusively with the people that nobody could suspect him of being a revolutionary. He wore very ordinary clothes—a khaddar kurta and chaddar, an old turban and ordinary shoes. He had simple habits and showed no trace of any European style of life"[170]—in contrast, perhaps, to his contemporaries the tubercular wordsmiths Santokh Singh and Surendranath Kar?

One of Rattan Singh's objectives in India was to seek an alliance with (and influence on) the Akalis, at Comintern request.[171] Gurmukh Singh and Udham Singh too had quietly crossed the border in 1923 with the same goal. Santokh Singh had already been in contact with Akali leaders, remarking in a letter to Dr. Hardikar: "My frank opinion is that India needs a revolution, political, social and industrial. An independent India with social and economic problems unsolved does not appeal to my reason. But I am sentimental enough to say that I, in the hope of a solution of the social and industrial problems a little later, prefer a Hindustani slave driver to an Englishman; self-determination is impossible so long as the Union Jack waves in India."[172]

As soon as he was at liberty, Santokh Singh lost no time in teaming up with fellow returnees Bhag Singh "Canadian," Hardit Singh, and Karam Singh Chheema to launch the *Kirti* in Amritsar. The monthly fulfilled a Ghadar Party goal for a Punjabi organ inside Punjab, cherished ever since Kartar Singh Sarabha had first attempted to set one up in 1915.[173] The managing editors previewed its purpose through advertisements in other papers a month before the first issue appeared in February 1926: "This journal will be the voice of Indian workers in America and Canada and will be dedicated to the sacred memory of those heroes and martyrs who awakened sleeping India . . . [it] will sympathise with all the workers throughout the world . . . the subjugated, weak and oppressed nations and subjugated India."[174]

Santokh Singh's intentions for the *Kirti* were threefold: to fight against British imperialism, to "present tenets and principles of communism in a simple and cautious manner" in order to prepare people to organize for "both their national and class struggles," and to rehabilitate and defend the legacy of the Ghadar movement, which he felt was underappreciated at home despite its contribution to the above goals.[175] Reflecting upon his experience in the North American movement, Santokh declared with reproach:

> It was to be expected that the national aims of the Indian workers living in Canada and America would be slandered by the alien bureaucracy through misrepresentations and falsehoods, but what about our national leaders? They also have either

misrepresented it, or have prevented it from being presented before the people in a helpful way. Now and then mention of the sacrifices of friends in Canada and America has been made, but with such restraint or circumspection that these in no way had encouraged their idealism. . . .

The *Kirti* will throw some light on this forgotten page of history.[176]

The cover picture of the first issue, portraying a proletarian corpse in full color, sparked some internal debate. In Josh's recollection the image was "not very inspiring." As he describes it,

A dead worker was lying on the funeral pyre, amidst factories, fields, etc.—the scene of his labours when alive—and surrounded with tools such as the hammer and pick axe, conveying the idea that either the deceased had succumbed to the hard work he had to carry out for the paymasters during his life time or [was] killed by the bullets of the imperialist police while on strike for higher wages. The hands of *Kirti* were placing a garland on his dead body.[177]

The Ghadar Party trainees in Moscow agreed that it was demoralizing. Their suggestion for a more optimistic replacement featured a factory worker holding a hammer and an agricultural worker holding a sickle, feet chained, facing each other and shaking hands.[178] Starting in May 1927, this image appeared on the title page against the background of a globe halved between smokestacks and farmland, crowned with a rippling red Communist flag. Josh believed this was the first time that symbol had been used in the Indian labor movement.

Not surprisingly, the Russian and British governments' reactions to the new publication fell at opposite poles. *Pravda* in February 1928 hailed it as "good news from the Punjab. They have a paper of their own to organise the peasantry."[179] But to the British, as expressed in Petrie's report, "the establishment of the Sikh communist paper *Kirti*" was both "highly objectionable" and "strongly revolutionary."[180] Most damning of all, "this journal has been consistently communistic and anti-government."[181] Petrie suspected there must be money coming in from Russian sources, though the CID traced its smuggled funding to "the Ghadar Parties of California, Panama, Fiji, Argentine, etc." Travelers entering India from North America were now searched on arrival.

In addition to serving as an organ for propaganda and political education, the *Kirti* was also meant to provide an organizing tool for mobilizing around immediate grievances. For example, the September 1927 issue announced a meeting to be held in Hoshiarpur over two days in October. The conference's statement of purpose called first for the formation of a strong worker-peasant party with branches in every district, to work for Indian national freedom. Its other points ranged in ambitiousness from "support [for] the Chinese liberation struggle and the Russian revolution" to demanding revenue exemption on smallholdings for the peasants, and an eight-hour day for the factory workers. It added a message of sympathy and support for the mill workers then on strike in Kanpur.[182] Resolutions at later meetings would combine the demand for nothing less than full independence with "local issues" like forced labor, lack of irrigation facilities, and, as always, relief from onerous land revenue.[183]

Santokh Singh's introductory editorial in the first *Kirti* touched on a few points by which we might construct a picture of Ghadar-Kirti ideology, presenting his thoughts on the use of force, internationalism, the nature of Communism, religion versus secularism, and social organization. While asserting the necessity for armed resistance and criticizing Gandhi's methods as ineffectual, he also made an effort to dissociate Communism from allegations that it was by definition violent: "A notion is current that communists stand for bloodshed. The reality is only this much that communists do not accept the principle of nonviolence. They consider it a good means to serve the needs of the time."[184]

Santokh Singh further took it upon himself to clarify misconceptions about Marxist theory in general: "Some falsely allege that the communist principle is 'what's yours is mine.' The truth is that they distinguish between personal property and individual ownership of the means of production. It is the latter with which they have something or other to do, not the former one."[185] Next, countering accusations that Communists were simply the pawns of the Russian government and other undesirable external forces, Santokh insisted: "The organisation of the Indian Communist Party is purely of an Indian origin. It is necessary to say that at present the work of the Communist Party will be limited to India and India alone. Our relationship with like-minded parties and the Third International is only that of sympathy and of proximity of mind. Indian communists are fellow-travellers and are in no way under them."[186]

Writing in the *United States of India,* the Hindustan Ghadar Party had taken similar pains to defend the independence struggle against attempts to discredit it with allegations that the people of India were no more than the pawns of foreign powers and that without these nefarious manipulations Indians would have lived quite contentedly under colonial rule: "During the recent world war, we were informed that it was the Germans who were agitating the Hindus; now it is the Russians, as if the Hindus themselves do not want independence. How the British Government of India lends false colour to the aspirations of the people of India!"[187] On the other hand, Santokh Singh encouraged readers to recognize the cognates of their own struggle in other parts of the world, rather than seeing India as an isolated exception: "The view of *Kirti* is that we should highly evaluate the sacrifices made by the freedom fighters wherever they may be living in the world. We should not see the oppressed peoples with [the same] spectacles through which the oppressors see them."[188]

Moreover, he added, "the programme of our freedom should be based not only on the conditions—social, economic and political—prevailing in India, but also take into consideration the situation prevailing in the world."[189] Power in the world, he said, was passing from the hands of the feudal aristocracy to those of the capitalist bourgeoisie. In the previous context the freedom struggle had not been so tightly linked to the working-class programme; but now, when it was the turn of the working class to take the reins of world power, any national freedom struggle's programme had for success to take account of the demands of the workers.

Santokh Singh's *Kirti* writings declared that "complete independence" and true *swaraj* would mean maximizing liberty and equality at all levels of the social structure, "from the democratically-elected village panchayat up to the top"; it would also require a "revolution in social ideas" based in critical thought, discarding the prejudices of sect and ethnicity and attachment to anachronistic traditions and blind rituals. Indeed, both editors emphasized again and again the interconnected themes of communism and workers' raj, internationalism, universalism, egalitarian mutual empowerment, and national liberation.

Echoing the original California *Ghadar* with its beloved poetry collections, the *Kirti* also became a showcase for working-class and/or anticapitalist Punjabi poets, aside from its polemical, organizational, and theoretical functions. Some poems painted pictures of wretched working conditions; others commented on current events. Gyani Gurmukh Singh Musafir, one of the contributors, won a prize for his poem "There will be workers' raj here one day."[190] Still, Josh reiterated: "Most of us [at that time] were just learning the A,B,C of Marxism! Poets like us had many illusions. . . . Some poets even expressed anarchist views in their poems."[191] Another indication, perhaps, of *Ghadar/Kirti*'s typically more libertarian leanings.

Santokh Singh meanwhile was engaged in a struggle not only against imperialism and capitalism, but against tuberculosis. He designated Sohan Singh Josh as his successor several months before his untimely death in May 1927—hastened, Josh implied, by his harsh passage through the North-West Frontier Province, capping years of driving himself to write and study while chronically deficient in proper food and sleep, compounded by bad jail conditions. Josh first came to Santokh's attention from a statement Josh made during the proceedings of the 1924–26 conspiracy case against the Babbar Akali leaders. He invited Josh to contribute articles for the journal starting in late 1926, and after some months, to take his place as editor in charge.[192] Josh recalled when Bhag Singh Canadian had asked him to meet with Santokh Singh in the Sikh Missionary Hall. The dying man was "pale and emaciated" with "a tremour in his voice," as he told his new editor-designate: "You are writing very hot stuff; go cautiously." In hindsight Josh took this to mean that Santokh Singh must be referring to his own experience with Ghadar's premature eruption in 1915, before the requisite groundwork had been laid. Josh decided thus that Santokh's "'Go cautiously' could mean nothing other than 'patiently organise the workers and peasants to fight their struggles, tell them who their friends [are] and who their enemies; and, perhaps, do not indulge in bombastic slogans.'"[193] (Though why this might not simply have meant the equivalent of "Watch your back and use wise security measures, because the police are always after us," I am not sure.)

In any case Josh did follow the practice of editorial anonymity, writing under several pseudonyms in addition to his own name, and contributing uncredited "leading . . . articles and monthly notes."[194] It was common to have dummy editors, he said, so as to prevent them from being quickly sent to jail.[195] When Rattan Singh paid a covert visit to attend a staff meeting, he but narrowly evaded a police interrogation on the way. The next day he disappeared, but the editors received messages that he had safely reached Kabul, along with a request that the *Kirti* be sent to a number of addresses in Europe and America, including the "Eastern University Library in Moscow."[196]

Gurmukh Singh and the other stalwarts in Kabul sent "very warm letters" expressing support for the new management, which were published in the September and October 1927 issues. Communist organizer Arjan Singh Gargaj noted that Josh's editorial regime introduced a marked shift in the *Kirti* propaganda toward scientific socialism, while also extending it for the first time well beyond Sikh into Hindu and Muslim readership, thanks to the introduction of an Urdu edition.[197] In April 1928, Bhagat Singh was invited to join the *Kirti* staff as Urdu editor. He vanished from sight after working in this capacity for only three months, but his articles continued to appear over a span from April 1927 to September 1928. It would fall to him, unparalleled icon of the 1920s revolutionary generation and direct heir of the Ghadarite tradition, to articulate more fully and systematically the combination of ideas and tactics that Ghadar had pioneered.

THE NAUJAVAN BHARAT SABHA AND THE HSRA

Everyone across the political spectrum wants to claim Bhagat Singh, who is portrayed with hagiographic hyperbole as an icon within the communist and nationalist pantheons, not to mention among Sikh militant separatists.[198] However, he should perhaps more properly be read in relation to the diasporic movement as part of an international rather than a regional frame of reference; to be specific, as the heir of Ghadarite ideas and practices, and the culmination of a synthesis that they had embodied in both ideological substance and tactical approach. In the Ghadarites' particular context, it was not only possible but quite reasonable to create something new and effective out of a broad range of elements, motivated by impulses toward pragmatism rather than toward orthodoxy either new or old. Thus, considering Bhagat Singh as a Ghadarite—and as a culminating rather than an initiating figure—may also shed some light on the nature of his own short life and meteoric political career.[199]

Ghadar's prehistory was also Bhagat Singh's, starting with the roles of his father, Kishan Singh, and especially his uncle Ajit Singh in the agitations around the canal colonies, circa 1907. This was also the year of his birth, while his father was jailed in Lahore, and his uncle in Mandalay. Prefiguring Ghadar's signature traits, the agitations associated with Ajit Singh's name—which had after all been floated first to lead the mobilization of the Pacific coast communities in 1912— were notable for their cross-communal unity as well as their militance.[200] Bhagat Singh was eight years old in 1915 when Ghadar attempted its uprising. The returned *baghis* often came to Kishan Singh's house for advice or money—he was a generous funder of their activities—and his young son eagerly listened in on their plans and debates. This is where the idealized Ghadar martyr Kartar Singh Sarabha was imprinted on him, and he began to consciously model himself on the man he proclaimed to be his "hero, friend and companion." Thereafter he always carried a picture of Sarabha in his pocket, and took one of his poems as a sung motto, the gist of which was "Easy to talk but hard to do; dedicate your life to the struggle."[201]

Bhagat Singh was a founding member of the Lahore-based radical student group Naujavan Bharat Sabha (NBS), and one of the core of the closely related Hindustan Republican Association (HRA). Also involved in the latter was Sachindranath Sanyal, the Bengal/Ghadar liaison of 1915. When Gurmukh Singh reestablished contact with Sanyal in 1924, he also took the opportunity to seek Ghadarite recruits for the HRA.[202] In 1928, joining forces at a symbolically freighted meeting at Jallianwala Bagh in Amritsar called at the invitation of the *Kirti* staff, the revamped Kirti Kisan Party and Naujavan Bharat Sabha together took a position at the forefront of anticolonial resistance in Punjab.

The Kirti Kisan Party was intended to serve as the northwestern counterpart to the Worker Peasant Parties (WPPs) based in Calcutta, Bombay, and Kanpur. Josh was elected general secretary, and M. A. Majid joint secretary; a five-member committee drew up rules and a programme.[203] The aims they framed in the party constitution were "to secure complete independence from British imperialism by every possible means, to liberate the workers and the peasants from every kind of political, economic and social slavery and to establish a United Socialist Republic."[204] The Kirti Kisan Party and other WPPs were to take up the tasks of mass organizing and consciousness-raising in accordance with Marxist orthodoxy as interpreted by Moscow, rendering the peasants and workers—those most superexploited by British rule—as the leading edge of the independence movement. Meanwhile, the new NBS manifesto (penned by Bhagwati Charan Vohra) was laced with evidence of its close intellectual and spiritual kinship with the Ghadar revolutionaries, allusions to Ghadar's history, and echoes of its documents. Among the various pamphlets distributed by the NBS tract society were works by Har Dayal and Agnes Smedley.[205]

Only a few months after the NBS/Kirti Kisan meet, the HRA too was radically reshaped. At a two-day gathering in Delhi in September 1928, members of revolutionary groups from across northern India decided to amalgamate into a nationwide federation. They also added a crucial S to their name: HRA now became the Hindustan Socialist Republican Association (HSRA) with an affiliated military wing, the Hindustan Socialist Republican Army. The HRSA's stated object, stated in a document authored by Sanyal, was "to establish a Federated Republic of the United States of India by an organized and armed revolution." The future Republic would be organized in accordance with a constitution to be "framed and declared by the representatives of the people at the time when they will be in a position to enforce their decisions." It would be based on universal suffrage and would demand "the abolition of all systems which make any kind of exploitation of man by man possible."[206] The goal for national liberation was no longer a minimalist program of expelling foreign rule, but "the adoption of a socialist republican state."

When the Ghadarites had proposed the United States as a model, they meant a democratic republic of freely federated states, though without yet explicitly specifying its economic mode. Nevertheless, Bhagat Singh's interpretation of their program, as gleaned from his reading of 1915 Ghadar veteran Ram Saran Das's book *Dreamland*, for which the author had requested him to write a foreword, was the following:

> They want to establish a socialist society. Meanwhile they have to maintain an army to defend themselves against the capitalist society. . . . The revolutionary armies shall march to other lands not to rule or loot the people, but to pull the parasitic rulers down from their thrones and stop their blood-sucking exploitation and thus to liberate the toiling masses. But, there shall not be the primitive national or racial hatred to goad our men to fight.[207]

While the end goal was noncontroversial, here yet again the debate about means recurred. Bhagat Singh's faction represented those who allegedly lacked the patience for the long maturation of revolutionary conditions through mass organizing and consciousness raising, insisting instead upon immediate action instigated by individuals and small groups. "Bhagat Singh wanted to do something very quick, through the use of bombs and pistols," said Josh; "something spectacular" that could "politically awaken the slumbering youth and students" and inspire them to "come forward to make sacrifices for the cause of freedom."[208] This was the implicit legacy of the pamphlets of over a decade before—Har Dayal's *Shabash!* and Bhagwan Singh's *Ailan-e-Jang*. The program of action outlined by the HRA in 1924 and further elaborated in the HSRA proposal of 1928 mirrored almost exactly that of the Hindustan Ghadar Party as formulated in 1913.[209] Its designated public activities were to start associations in the form of clubs, libraries, *seva samitis*, and labor and peasant organizations; to start weekly papers in every province propagating the idea of an independent republic; to publish booklets and pamphlets spreading news of current events and intellectual developments in other countries—all while still not disdaining to work through Congress and other such bodies. Meanwhile, in private, different departments would undertake the tasks of setting up a secret press for circulation of "such literature which cannot easily be published openly"; establishing regional branches throughout the country;collecting funds in as many ways as possible, ranging from voluntary subscription to forced expropriation; sending promising candidates for military or scientific training in foreign countries "so that they may . . . take charge of armies and ammunition factories at the time of open rebellion"; importing and/or domestically manufacturing arms and ammunition; infiltrating members into the army; generating public sympathy through retaliatory propaganda by deed when necessary; and maintaining close contact and collaboration with the revolutionaries outside India.[210] Plainly, Sanyal was drawing on the Ghadarite tradition of 1915, which had in turn drawn upon the traditions of Bengal's Swadeshi and London's India House. However, the HRA documents were not signed with Sanyal's name, but rather with the posthumous signature of "Kartar Singh, President."

But this time around, the revolutionist program was developing more nuance. For example, in fund-raising dacoities they would aim "as far as possible to loot government treasuries rather than individuals." Furthermore, actions were now to be designed less for direct, instrumental efficacy than for communicative potential. Every dramatic action would be followed with a declaration explaining its purpose. In other words, the propaganda factor would take precedence over the direct effect of the deed in itself. Educating the public consciousness would then be the measure of instrumental efficacy.

Bhagat Singh was implicated in the planning and execution of two such deeds: the botched assassination of Deputy Police Superintendent J. P. Saunders in retaliation for the fatal police beating of Lajpat Rai, and the throwing of symbolic bombs into the Central Legislative Assembly. Bhagat Singh and Bhatukeshwar Dutt were sentenced in June 1929 to transportation for life; only a few days after the Assembly bomb verdict was announced, the Second Lahore Conspiracy Case began, regarding the death of Saunders.[211] While in detention as under-trials, the defendants went on a hunger strike to demand better conditions for all political prisoners. Here Bhagat Singh got another opportunity for direct contact with Ghadarite elders; Baba Chuhar Singh, who had been sentenced to transportation for life in the First Lahore Conspiracy Case, often came to talk and offer advice. He also met Randhir Singh, the Ferozepur cantonment chaplain who had joined the mutiny in 1915, but the young atheist resisted efforts to reconvert him, despite allegations to the contrary.

When Jatin Das, one of the hunger strikers, died after sixty-three days, the leaked news of his martyrdom produced a spike in public sympathy for the prisoners (and many invocations of his Irish counterpart, Terence MacSwiney). This attention plus the long duration of the case meant that regardless of the outcome, in some sense the defendants fulfilled their intended objectives, since it offered an unprecedented opportunity to expound on their political ideals and goals before the public. In a joint statement the two Assembly bombers proclaimed: "We hold human lives sacred beyond words . . . and would sooner lay down our lives in the service of humanity than injure anyone else. Unlike mercenary soldiers of imperialist armies, who are disciplined to kill without compunction, we respect, and in so far as it lies in us, we attempt to save human life."[212] (The latter dig was a familiar tool in the Ghadar propaganda arsenal to shame and/or inspire Indians enlisted in the British Army into mutiny.)

Their sole purpose, they testified, was not to cause physical harm but "to make the deaf hear and to give the heedless a timely warning. . . . We have only hoisted the danger-signal to warn those who are speeding along without heeding the grave dangers ahead." Echoing Har Dayal in *Shabash!* Bhagat Singh had written in a similar vein in the *Kirti* under the nom de plume Vidrohi (Rebel). A "single deed," he argued, "makes more propaganda in a few days than a thousand pamphlets," and "one human being in revolt with a torch or dynamite was able to instruct the whole world!" He predicted that the course of the struggle would unfold as "one deed brings forth another, opponents join the mutiny, the government splits into factions, oppression intensifies the conflict, the concessions come too late, the revolution breaks out."[213] Both the bomb case statement and the *Kirti* had argued that the greatest effect of such a deed was not in what it accomplished directly but in what it inspired others to accomplish. Propaganda by the deed was in this sense a tool serving mass organization—not a substitute for it. This in fact aptly, if inadvertently, describes the Ghadar legacy itself. The movement itself was a great act of propaganda by the deed, in that the immediate effect of the 1915 uprising was not to overthrow the government but to awaken the next generation of revolutionists.

The death sentence for Bhagat Singh, Rajguru, and Sukhdev was announced on 7 October 1930; they were hanged on 23 March 1931.[214] Josh says that when the Indian workers in Argentina heard the news of the execution, they struck work for the day.[215] The California Ghadar Party issued a special *ailan* (announcement) in poster form in Punjabi and Urdu, featuring the martyrs' pictures, decrying the injustice of their death, and "call[ing] on Indians to take up arms against British rule."[216] As the three comrades marched to their deaths, record the hagiographers of the left, "the jail walls reverberated with the slogans" of "Long live revolution!" and "Down with imperialism!" If this tableau echoed that of Kartar Singh's trip to the gallows fifteen years prior, it was no coincidence. Bhagat Singh had replicated, amplified, and extended the role of his Ghadarite predecessor, and perhaps fulfilled it. The shifts in popular opinion, the world political situation, and level of domestic mobilization in the intervening years now enabled Bhagat Singh to be elevated to iconic status as a political catalyst in a way that had eluded the Ghadarites in 1915. The Second Lahore Conspiracy Case might then be considered the closing of the second Ghadar era, as the series of trials starting with the First Lahore Conspiracy Case and ending in San Francisco had concluded the first.

INDIA'S OTHER LEFT

The year 1929 was a difficult one for the Indian left as NBS/HSRA members were embroiled in the Second Lahore Conspiracy Case, and CPI members were rounded up in connection with the Meerut Conspiracy trial.[217] Among the thirty-two Meerut accused were returned *muhajirin* Shaukat Usmani and Abdul Majid, who was also involved with the NBS; and American Ghadarite Amir Haider Khan. All three had trained in Moscow. Despite the enforced hiatus, Kirti Kisan still managed to hold meetings in 1930 in Lahore and in 1931 in Karachi. But the various coalitions were disunited and argumentative; a rift was opening between Kirti Kisan in Amritsar and Naujavan Bharat Sabha in Lahore. According to Gurharpal Singh the Punjab unit, especially the "Ghadar-Kirtis, Moscow trained Ghadars," were stubbornly resistant to the CPI's attempts at imposing discipline, particularly regarding the fresh mandate for cooperation with the INC.

But what exactly was the substance of these differences between "Kirti Communism" and the CPI orthodoxy? Puri deduces that the former, judging by the articles they wrote and the alliances they sought, was endowed with "a peculiar flavour of romantic egalitarianism and valour of the Sikhs," with an "emotional attachment to the Ghadarite notion of revolution"[218]—that is, to the dramatic sacrificial gesture, the blaze of heroic bravado thrown out as a beacon in the darkness. Gurharpal Singh concurs that what he calls Ghadar-Kirti Communism was expressed through the particularistic medium of Punjabi Sikh culture, drawing upon communal categories to supplement a purely material class analysis, although both Puri and Josh identify the proletarianization that transformed their outlook in North America as a key component in Ghadar's rebirth, when fused with enthusiasm for an idealized radical democracy complementary to the traditional Sikh egalitarian philosophy. Gurharpal Singh further points to their rural, peasant-agrarian, vigorously anti-intellectualist and unfailingly militant identification, always insisting on praxis over academic theorizing, its exemplars having proven themselves through long records of action, in contrast to a doctrinaire party of young urban educated twits and babus. This view held that the

Ghadarite character of the former had come into its own only after shearing off the previous accretion of Bengali petit bourgeois intellectuals that had become attached to the leadership in California.

I find it less simple to unravel the elements of Ghadar's evolution from its pre-war (or pre-Revolution) days. Rather, I think that its category-defying flavor of radicalism stemmed precisely from its synthesis of elements, even if the original source of some of the ingredients had been left behind. Furthermore, the intensely patriotic and culturalist overlay—or, in the terms of the national-colonial question, an emphasis on the anti-imperialist rather than the anticapitalist aspect of the world revolutionary struggle—was characteristic not just of Ghadar-Kirti but of any of the movements among Oppressed Peoples of the East, from Azerbaijan to China, whose struggles for national self-determination were identified as crucial links in the world revolution's second front.

Writing in 1952 in the Royist journal *Thought* (Delhi),[219] Tilak Raj Chadha observed that this Punjabi communism of the 1920s had been in tension around two tendencies, symbolized respectively by Sohan Singh Josh and Teja Singh Swatantra.[220] Even as Rattan Singh, Santokh Singh, and Sohan Singh Josh piloted a course in the direction of systematic, class-conscious mass organization building, others, like Swantantra and Gurmukh Singh, remained unreconstructed adherents of the prior version, their revolutionary imaginations fired directly by memories of prewar Ghadar. Within the reborn HGP, and within Ghadar's sister/daughter organization Kirti, this contradiction between earlier and later phases was never fully resolved.Thus what the orthodox Marxist Josh saw retrospectively as "shortcomings and weaknesses" in Kirti's party line were perhaps nothing of the kind, but rather an illustration of the continuity in Ghadarite thinking across two decades, in which receptivity to Marxist-Leninist developments did not necessarily entail total rejection of other strains of revolutionism but retained certain characteristics associated earlier with both anarchistic and republican-democratic movements. An article on land redistribution in Russia in the March 1929 *Kirti* obliquely reinforces this genealogical impression. "Kirti Raj," Bhagwan Josh deduced from such articles, would resemble the Russia of the New Economic Program period, in which land tenure was based on peasant ownership, wherein peasants would work their own holdings more or less autonomously, and the working class would engage in small-scale commodity production while managing the state apparatus. There would be no wage labor or rent, and little to no land revenue payments. In this way, he said, the Punjabis echoed the sentiments of the Ukrainian peasantry.[221] The *Kirti* article also recommended that *panchayat* councils should determine local land distribution "in a brotherly manner"; cultivators would have the option but not the obligation to team up on the use of machinery; otherwise they could "sow their land, harvest it and consume it the way they want." As the article explained, "That is the reason why

Russian peasants are prosperous. They have got their own land, and they are to pay no revenue at all."[222] This more politically decentralized and economically mixed social vision makes Ghadar-Kirti communism quite legible as the ideological kin of a Makhnovian libertarian socialism.

Much of the basis for Ghadar's supposed transition from protocommunism and emotional utopian socialism to Marxism-Leninism proper was tactical: they abandoned the folly of secretive conspiratorial actions and individual propaganda by the deed for the wisdom of building a mass base and organizing among the workers and peasants. Yet Ghadar's very innovation had been its appeal to peasant laborers and its work of public education and mobilization, expanding the revolutionary base beyond a small group of students and intellectuals. Moreover, its main strategy was fomenting mutiny among the army, accompanied by the creation of large-scale popular uprising—not individual propaganda by the deed at all. Conspiratorial action was necessary only when repression made open organizing impossible; the United States was a desirable location precisely because free and open organizing, agitating, educating, speaking, and writing were possible to them there. Overall, the only mass they had neglected was that portion of the global Indian community that happened actually to be living in India—and this was due more to legal repression and censorship of mail than to any fault of their own. In short, what was lacking was not mass organization, but a connection between diasporic and domestic populations, whose politicization within the specificities of their sundered contexts was proceeding at different speeds. But the late 1920s were a different moment, the result of a chain of political events in India and in the world to which the Ghadarites themselves had contributed. And despite the changes in imperial formation and domestic mood, the continuities in the revolutionary program are striking, although the relative emphasis among its constituent elements was shifting.

Finally, the revolutionary generation of the 1920s, consisting of Ghadar's direct heirs and assorted cousins, has been assessed as equal parts "Marx and Mazzini"; that is, both nationalist and communist. Chhabil Das even alleged two *simultaneous but separate* factions within the NBS—one influenced by the Russian Bolsheviks, the other by the Irish Sinn Fein; of which one focused on "collecting arms and throwing bombs," and the other on "raising the consciousness of the masses, rural people, peasantry and factory workers."[223] Shiv Verma suggests that what differentiated the earlier revolutionaries from those of the 1920s was the shift from "Mazzini to Marx"; in other words, the two strains were subsequent rather than simultaneous.[224] However, in the context of the national liberation struggles in what would later be called the third world, these two were hardly mutually exclusive. Just as in the case of tactics, so in content: Marx was there from the beginning, and Mazzini to the end.[225] In any case it is convenient to be able to identify one's cultural characteristics and patriotic ideal with egali-

THE COMMUNIST GHADAR   165

tarian, substantively libertarian principles rather than with exclusivist, hierarchical ones. This makes it far more likely that the streams of national liberation struggle and social revolution can converge and reinforce one another rather than sap one another's strength by flowing crosswise. The Sikh Ghadar-Kirti communists attempted this identification, as did the Muslim socialists whom we shall meet in the next chapter.

6

"Dear Muhammedan Brothers"

The Khilafatist Ghadar

AN OLD ALLY

We have been tracking the evolution of a unique organization that shifted in form in a dramatically changing global context while still remaining consistent in its agenda and principles of progressive radical democracy, political libertarianism, and economic egalitarianism. But a constant counterpoint throughout this period was another movement without which we cannot understand Ghadar's ability to communicate and translate relevant concepts from one discourse to another, nor the internal diversity of rationalist and romanticist impulses, nationalist and socialist logics, that made this possible.

The DCI's report for December 1918 on the Indian National Committee in Berlin noted the text of a telegram to the Turkish ruler that had appeared in several German newspapers, signed by Bhupendranath Dutt on behalf of the committee. The message "congratulate[d] the Sultan on his accession to the throne and state[d] that thousands of oppressed and plundered Indians look up to the brave and chivalrous Turks and hope that they will listen to their cry for help." Just as there were two currents of communism flowing into the subcontinent, the intermingled springs that fed communist organizing in Punjab in the 1920s were twofold again: the Ghadar revolutionists and the formerly Khilafatist *muhajirin,* both channeled through the northwest in analogous tactical roles from the Kabul transmission point established during the war.

Long before the alliance with Germany and Turkey, and even before the formation of Ghadar as an organization, Indian revolutionists abroad had been making overtures to the Islamic world as ideologically defined, while also establishing a presence in its geographical domain. However, during the First World War, once the German/Ottoman alliance had become the hub for the Indian revolutionary movement, the Pan-Islamic approach became even more significant, reflecting the goals and preoccupations of this alliance. After the war, when Moscow displaced Berlin as the center of patronage, this pattern of relationships did not change. Both imperial Germany and Communist Russia identified the Muslim world and/or the colonial world—both vague and roomy categories between which there was much convenient overlap—as the British Empire's Achilles' heel(s).

To reiterate, it was the fluidity between the categories of Asia, Orient, Islamic world, Peoples of the East, and the colonized world—which in the contemporary parlance of both Europeans and Pan-Asianists could encompass everything from China to Anatolia—that enabled any one section of a corresponding Venn diagram to be equated with any other, even if a given point was not in an overlapping section. This is why it was possible for the Soviets to meld Pan-Islamism and Pan-Asianism to such an extent in their calls to the Peoples of the East (a tendency no less visible in Barakatullah's cumulative literary output). It also allowed various nationalisms and national liberation struggles, whether Indian, Egyptian, or Japanese, to be identified as standard-bearers of such a vast entity's success in the world, even if the interests of major components of it were in opposition to each other.

When the Comintern orators during this period called upon the Oppressed Peoples of the East they were referring, sometimes explicitly and sometimes by default, to the *Muslim* Peoples of the East, who had a key role to play in the united struggle against capitalism and imperialism. Moreover, they seem to have included India in these calculations as a Muslim country, or at least as a crucial part of the Muslim world. The Baku conference's fifth session, on national-colonial questions, offered this definition:

> What is the East? . . . We mean by the East today the countries of Asia and of the north coast of Africa, mainly Egypt. In particular, by the Muslim East we mean: Turkey, Persia, Baluchistan, Afghanistan, Bukhara, Khiva, and all the regions of Turkestan, India, and part of China. . . . Naturally, in such an extensive territory as this there is tremendous heterogeneity, an enormous exotic bouquet of nationalities, speaking a variety of languages, but they are all united by common features in their culture—by Islam.[1]

Another speaker, in his report on national and colonial questions for the session's Presiding Committee, equated the *Eastern* (i.e., Asian and/or Islamic) struggle with the Russian one, proclaiming: "In the giant struggle we have begun, the peoples of the East will henceforth be our loyal allies. For a war against Soviet Russia is a war against the revolutionary East, and vice versa, a war against the East is a war against Soviet Russia."[2] He described the response to news of the All-Russia Central Executive Committee's confirmation of the establishment of the new autonomous Tatar Socialist Soviet Republic as a "mighty echo throughout the many-millioned Muslim world, in Persia, Afghanistan, Turkey, and India. In the eyes of our Muslim brothers, the workers and peasants of the East, it was a fresh example of the great principles that underlie the national policy of the Russian federated republic. But this is not to the liking of the capitalist governments."[3]

Pan-Islamism had been developing in India since the late nineteenth century and was nourished as Urdu journalism grew more politically sophisticated, bringing news of world events impacting Muslim populations, such as the Crimean War, the British takeover of Egypt in 1882, and the French seizure of Tunis in 1881. Moreover, since Mughal power had disintegrated, Muslims in British India increasingly looked to the Ottoman sultanate for emotional sustenance as the greatest remaining Islamic world power. Thus they took any European encroachment on Ottoman territories, whether by Austria-Hungary in the Balkans or czarist Russia in the Caucasus, quite personally.[4] The two main goals of the Khilafat movement were to defend the independence and territorial integrity of Ottoman lands then being occupied and divided up by the victors of the First World War, and to work for the liberation of India from British rule. While the coexistence of these goals led to questions of where the primary allegiance of Indian Muslims lay, and whether their overriding identity was as part of an extra-Indian Islamic community or as part of an extra-Muslim Indian community, for leading Khilafatist figures of the time, such as the Ali brothers and Abul Kalam Azad, these identifications were complementary and not conflictual.

Though the Pan-Islamist narrative developed independently of Ghadar's, the two repeatedly converged and intertwined within the field of international Indian radicalism. What made it feasible, logical, and desirable for a movement that was predominantly Sikh in ethnic composition, and emphatically secularist in its political approach to religion, to interface with political Islam? There were several circumstances that created points of connection. First, just as the map of North American syndicalism tended to coincide with Ghadar's distribution on the West Coast, the constituency for Pan-Islamism occupied many of the same geographic niches—and had an analogous structural relationship to the British Empire—as Ghadar's operations and target audiences in east and west Asia. Before and during the First World War, the German Foreign Office wooed Islamist, tribal, and/or protonationalist oppositional elements in both British and French colonial possessions.[5] Moreover, the Ghadarite and Pan-Islamist political programs were articulated in response to similar conditions, sharing some common stimuli or irritants. They shared the immediate goal of opposition to British imperial rule in the "Orient," an opposition extended by implication to Western colonization and capitalism; and sometimes extending even further to encompass liberal modernity as a whole, with its materialism, consumerism, and industrialization. They also had recurrent rhetorical themes in common, such as condemning colonial rule and economic exploitation not only in systemic/structural terms, but also as a moral indictment of the manifest treachery, hypocrisy, and racial/cultural double standards of Western liberalism; plus a veneration of martyrdom. Some people were affiliated with both movements, slipping seamlessly from one to the other: most notably Muhammed Barakatullah, but also his Provisional Government colleague Obeidullah Sindhi and the radical students of the Hijrat movement.

Finally, each was a transnational orientation distinct from but not necessarily opposed to territorial/political nationalisms; a source of extraterritorial identity and loyalty, and a force of social cohesion in which sentiment or structure of feeling, not ascribed ethnicity, was key. Like Ghadar, the Khilafat movement could only really be imagined and enacted physically and/or mentally outside the country. While India's national liberation was an urgent goal, it was only a part of the larger purpose; the Indian nation-state did not necessarily correspond to the boundaries of the imagined community in question, nor contain the scope of its activities.

So while there were utilitarian reasons for such a collaboration at the tactical level, the interface between Indian diasporic anticolonial radicalism and Pan-Islamism, at least at those points where it was most sustained and successful, went beyond the utilitarian to a degree of substantive compatibility. The particular sort of Pan-Islamists most closely associated with Ghadar-related revolutionary nationalist activities before the war tended to be those who were sympathetic to liberal, secularist projects, as in Turkey or Iran, while those associated with Ghadar in its postwar Communist incarnation expressed forms of heterodox socialism in an Islamist idiom at the height of the Khilafat movement in the early 1920s. Those whose Pan-Islamism took a more traditional or revivalist form had a more tenuous or frictional relationship with the Ghadar revolutionaries. All of which serves to reinforce the notion that the discourse, idiom, or vocabulary of Islamism was, like the internally contentious discourses of leftism or nationalism, capable of expressing a range of ideological statements; and that Ghadar's organizers and ideologues in their most meaningful alliances remained consistent in ideology and praxis, even while appearing wildly omnivorous in their willingness to engage with various political actors. Although variations existed, to be sure, the difference was in language more than in substance. Ghadar's emphasis, and that of the Islamists with whom the Ghadarites worked, was on political self-determination, an ethic of comprehensive social justice, and economic redistribution on a global scale.

OVERTURES

Although the savagely Hindu revivalist flavor of much Swadeshi rhetoric kept Muslim involvement low inside India in the first decade of the twentieth century, nevertheless a few politicized Muslims, most notably Abul Kalam Azad, were connected to the Bengali revolutionary movement, especially among the less sectarian and slightly more internationalist Yugantar group.[6] Meanwhile in the European political hubs, Indian revolutionists were making overtures to liberal, progressive nationalists of Muslim cultural background. Friendships that would have been unlikely in Bengal or Maharashtra seemed possible in England. Take, for example, the case of young Rafik Mohammed Khan, son of a commander in chief of the Nabha State Forces, who won a scholarship in 1907 to study at the Royal Agricultural College in England. Over summer vacation of 1908, he fell into the company of "extremists" like (the very Hindu) V. D. Savarkar and his cohort in London. When Khan returned to school in the fall, he and his friend Harnam Singh "got into trouble for wearing the Mutiny badge"—a token distributed during the annual May 10th celebration held at India House to commemorate the anniversary of the great Ghadar of 1857. With his scholarship revoked, Khan withdrew from the school and enrolled instead at a dairy institute in Reading.[7] But during the next year's vacation he "renewed his intimacy with the advanced party in London, and took a keen and sympathetic interest in their doings." When Savarkar was under trial, Khan attended one of his court hearings and later visited him in jail. He also met with V. V. S. Aiyar and Chatto in Paris and was "regarded by the London anarchists as an important member of their organisation . . . completely under the influence of V. D. Savarkar."[8]

Indeed, the revolutionaries abroad allegedly took an interest in cultivating active alliances with extra-Indian Muslim constituencies in the hope that they might thereby entice Indian Muslims into the movement at home, by means of, for example, the "Persian question," meaning the recent constitutional transition in Iran amid the region's subjection to competing British and Russian spheres of influence; in other words, the revolutionaries abroad used Pan-Islamist sentiment as a motivation for Indian nationalism. This was one of the motives at the London "Muhammedan meeting" for reading the telegrams in which Chattopadhyaya and Madame Cama had solicited messages of solidarity from Persians and Egyptians protesting British interference in their respective homelands.[9]

Aside from the Bengali route to London and Paris, another important pathway led from the Punjabi agitations of 1907 via Persian exile into Ghadar and BIC circuits, only to be spliced back into the networks running between Istanbul and Soviet central Asia during and after the war. Ajit Singh, Sufi Amba Parishad, and M. P. T. Acharya were strong links in this chain. Ajit Singh and Amba Parishad had been the most famous of the agitators deported amid the 1907 crackdown on sedition.[10] They then relocated to Persia to establish an external political center. According to an article that appeared years later in a Turkish-language paper called *Najaf*, the British consul at Bushire had put out a reward of 1,000 rupees for the capture of "the Sufi." But he was alerted in time to flee along with Ajit Singh, by night in a heavy rain, with the help of a few sympathizers in the area. Ajit Singh, "who is reckoned as one whose aim is to secure the liberty of India," stayed there while Parishad went to Shiraz to teach in a sharia school and issue the *Hayat* newspaper, for which he "wield[ed] a powerful pen."[11] But this only attracted the disapproving attention of the British consul in Shiraz, and he was soon back on the wanted list. So he fled again, and his whereabouts remained unknown for some time.

A report of February 1911 stated that Ghulam Hussain, aka Thakur Das, had joined Ajit Singh and Amba Parishad in Bushire in October 1909, having previously been associated with the West Coast radicals in the United States. He was tracked to Constantinople, where he "sounded the CUP regarding Indian affairs";[12] then to Paris with Ajit Singh, who was then traveling under his Persian identity of Mirza Hassan Khan. He was sighted in December 1910, staying at Chatto's flat and working in proximity to Rana's office, plainly accepted as part of the Paris revolutionary circle, whom he sufficiently "persuaded . . . to believe that he is a very desperate fellow" that in August 1911 they entrusted him with a "mission . . . to preach sedition amongst the Sikh labourers on the Pacific coast."[13]

In fact Ajit Singh played a key role in guiding and facilitating the movements of many other revolutionaries around the world. For example, it had been his suggestion to send Jodh Singh to Brazil and, allegedly, Har Dayal to North America. It was also he who proposed to Chatto that they send Acharya to Constantinople as an emissary in November 1911. He could earn a living there, Ajit suggested, by teaching English, and he provided Acharya with letters of introduction to a number of his friends and contacts. According to the DCI's report, "One of the main objects of [Acharya's] mission seems to have been to carry out the scheme (which was discussed sometime ago by the Paris gang) of spreading disloyalty amongst Indian Muhammedans visiting Mecca and Karbala, and apparently he hoped to secure Turkish agents for this."[14] But he didn't get very far with the introductions. Two were out of town, and others didn't seem eager to help. The only one to bite was educator and journalist Saiyyid Mohammed Tew-fik, principal of the Persian School in Constantinople, translator for several Turkish papers, and editor of the *Shams*. He had also lived for a time in Hyderabad, and acted as a correspondent for several northern Indian newspapers on events in Turkey's war with Italy. He then went to Egypt, where "he associated with nationalists and posed as a leader of a widespread revolutionary movement in India." He "contributed a number of articles on Pan-Islamism and kindred subjects to Indian newspapers,"[15] and he produced essays in Turkish, Persian, and

Arabic calculated to "educate and mould the future destiny of the Asiatics."[16] He was also a friend of Ajit Singh, who had helped him in the past, and was described as "having the revolutionary spirit."[17] For the moment, though, Tewfik could give Acharya no more than a rather vague promise to go on the next haj, and in the meantime to write articles and encourage others to do the same, "arousing Indian Muslims to their sense."[18]

This was not Acharya's first frustrated venture into the potential of Islamist rebellion. In August 1909, he and Sukh Sagar Dutt left London for Gibraltar en route to Morocco, where they had intended to join the rebels in the Rif against the Spanish, "with a view to gaining experience in military practice" in their guerrilla techniques "and also to draw the attention of the Muhammedans in Morocco to the condition of their co-religionists in India." Acharya had been heard to say at that time that they might then proceed to Turkey.[19] But upon failing to reach their destination they were forced to abandon the idea. Dutt returned to London from Gibraltar in early September. Acharya, "the other would be soldier of fortune," made it as far as Tangier, where he got stranded and "was looked after for a month by a friendly Moor."[20] He wrote from there to V. V. S. Aiyar to say the plan wouldn't work. Not surprisingly, the British consulate in Tangier refused his somewhat inexplicable request for help and passage back to London. After all, aside from thirty shillings, "when these youth landed at Gibraltar they were in possession of a magazine rifle, a revolver and three hundred rounds of ammunition which were taken charge of by the Customs."[21] Aiyar instructed Acharya to return to Paris instead.[22] But this was not the end of Acharya's work in the Dar-ul-Islam. Later, through the auspices of the BIC, he participated in wartime propaganda missions to Baghdad and Suez, and then journeyed to Kabul and Tashkent, where he was at the center of the effort to reroute the emigrant Indian Khilafatist *muhajirin* toward their new mecca in Moscow.[23]

It is worth noting that in California, where nonsectarian unity was a foundational organizing principle from the very inception of the PCHA, no less than in northwest India and central Asia, it may have been the Khilafat cause that opened the door to widespread Muslim participation in Ghadar circles. At a 1912 mass meeting in Sacramento subscriptions were raised on behalf of aid to Turkey, then fighting a war in the Balkans.[24] One of the members of a four-man committee appointed in Sacramento to tour the country to drum up further funds and support was Nawab Khan.[25] He had previously visited San Francisco in the company of Thakur Das/Ghulam Hussain and met Har Dayal there and heard him give a lecture. Nawab Khan stated that, having been greatly impressed by Hussain and Dayal, his thinking had moved in their direction, and from then on he began to convince others as well.

A joint Hindu-Muslim meeting was held in Astoria, Oregon, to build harmony between the communities; the conveners planned to follow it up with

weekly meetings to read Indian papers and discuss politics. Har Dayal passed
through these meetings on his 1913 summer tour, during which the germ of the
PCHA idea solidified, and plans got under way to start collecting monthly subscriptions, publishing newspapers and books, and mobilizing the local communities. In other words, narrating from this angle suggests that a nascent Khilafat
sensibility—or at least an extrapolation from a Khilafatist priming of sensibilities for internationalist anticolonialism—was one of several midwives attending
the birth of the PCHA, which in turned spawned the Ghadar Party.[26] Furthermore, this attention to Pan-Islamic sensibilities may help to explain a new theme
that began to emerge in Ghadar circles: concern for the fate of the Ottoman
Empire. A note written in the margin of a copy of the *Ghadar* smuggled into
India reflects this concern:

> Chaudhri Sahib, act according to this and get others to act, too. Preparations for a
> mutiny are being made in America and Canada. You also should try to drive out
> the badmash white people and begin to work in secret. . . . Revenge for Turkey
> should now be taken. . . . Secretly all Europeans are against Turkey. Brother, if you
> come to other countries and see for yourself you will know how prosperous are
> countries which are independent. Therefore you are repeatedly enjoined to preach
> mutiny among the police and others as far as possible, and to unfurl the banner of
> liberty. . . . Hindus, Muhammadans and Sikhs should unite.[27]

In the *Ghadar* issues of 16 and 23 December 1913 Har Dayal commented approv-
ingly on the increasing participation of Muslims in the national movement,
although his biographer Emily Brown suspected this was hyperbolic wishful
thinking on his part. Intelligence claimed that the *Ghadar*'s "despatch to Hong
Kong, Singapore, Tientsin and North China was noted as early as March 1914,
and it is among the numbers issued shortly before this date that a special appeal
to Moslems may first be observed."[28]

Among the Sikh soldiers of the February 1915 mutiny were also "a few Muhammedans," including a farrier called Abdulla whose name appeared repeatedly in the statements of a core group of participants among the Twenty-third
Cavalry. He was "a strong man" who learned the rudiments of making explosives
along with Lance-Daffadar Wasawa Singh, a cavalry mate of Puran Singh, the
brother of Kirpal Singh the traitor. Another companion called Banta Singh recalled a conversation Abdulla had initiated with him, concerning what he called
the English/Turkish wars. Abdulla said that since the Turks had taken Tabriz from
the Russians, he himself would also go on doing damage to the English. What
would he do? asked Banta Singh. Abdulla said he had already cut one or two telegraph wires.[29]

Soon after the aborted uprising, a report was given to the Resident's office in
March 1915 that the *Ghadar* had arrived in Isfahan: Dr. Asadullah, a Bahai physician

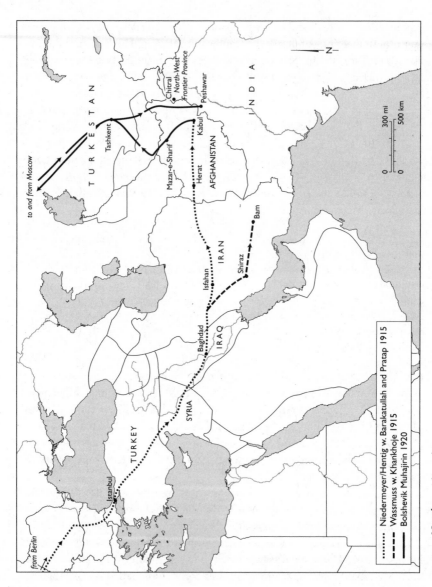

MAP 3. Northwest invasion

Niedermeyer/Hentig w. Barakatullah and Pratap 1915
Wassmuss w. Khankhoje 1915
Bolshevik Muhajirin 1920

from Najafabad, was receiving "several numbers in packets." Risaldar Malek Rab Nawaz Khan, officer-in-charge of the consular guard, reported that the doctor had passed it along to a *sowar* whom he saw reading something in "Persian print" (Urdu), saying: "If you want something to read, read this." It was the premiere issue of *Ghadar*.[30]

THE WESTERN FRONT

During the war the interests of the German and Turkish governments converged to a certain extent with those of Pan-Islamism and revolutionary nationalism.[31] These ties proved tenuous, due to the divergence of their ultimate goals: Germany was content to interfere with British access to India through Persia and Mesopotamia, whereas Turkey would have liked to consolidate its own territorial power in the region. Meanwhile, both Turks and Indians resident in Istanbul bridled at the overbearingly Hindu inflection of some of the nationalist activists. But N. K. Barooah suggests that despite the German disdain for the Hindu nationalist revolutionary "terrorists" who had made their appearance around 1907, there was nevertheless still "one section of the Indian people" whom they did support, namely the Muslim community, upon whom the AA counted as part of its wider "Orient policy" precisely because they were seen as being "under the spiritual influence of Turkey"—indeed to a degree considered bizarre by Muslims elsewhere in central Asia and Ottoman lands.

The very day the Turco-German agreement was signed on 2 August 1914, a German general wrote to the AA urging: "Attempts must be made to raise a revolt in India in case England becomes our opponent. The same should be done in Egypt." Persia too should be encouraged to take this opportunity "to get rid of the Russian yoke and to proceed together with the Turks."[32] The kaiser agreed: "Our consuls in Turkey and India, agents, etc. must get a conflagration going throughout the whole Mohammedan world against this hated, unscrupulous, dishonest nation of shopkeepers—since if we are going to bleed to death, England must at least lose India."[33]

In Istanbul, Enver Pasha was thinking similarly, and so an Ottoman member of parliament delivered a proposal to the German ambassador that they should move quickly to "organise the revolutionary movements in North Africa and Afghanistan by sending suitable German officers to those places."[34] So it was in Istanbul that the Berlin group established a new outpost with a brief to coordinate two major projects based on the mobilization of Pan-Islamist sentiment: first, the circulation of propaganda to Indian soldiers and pilgrims in the region, and second, an invasion into India from the northwest.

Har Dayal had proposed the basic outline of this program to the German consul general in Geneva, where he was staying with Egyptian nationalist journalist

M. Rifaat. Not surprisingly, his version emphasized the potential Ghadarite contribution. "Apart from the general unrest in India among all classes," he argued, "we have 10,000 Hindus in the United States and Canada and about 100,000 in China and the Malay Peninsula. The nationalist paper Gadar circulates among them, and they are just now very much agitated over the Indian question in British Columbia. At least a few thousand will respond to an appeal for immediate action, if German support [in the form of officers, arms, ammunition, bombs, planes, and wireless apparatus] is assured." They should focus all attention on Kashmir, he proposed, because its mountainous terrain and relative dearth of military personnel would favor the insurgents. An early success in establishing a liberated zone there had the potential to unleash waves of rebellion across the country and stimulate widespread actions by "young men ready for any sacrifice." He himself volunteered to make appearances in Constantinople, Mecca, Baghdad, and Kabul "to help the execution of this project, if it is accepted."[35]

Har Dayal arrived in Constantinople in September 1914 to set up a headquarters. However, there was already an established community of Indian Muslims there, with whom the Berlin-based revolutionists did not mesh smoothly, due to a sense of turf rivalry compounded by ideological differences. Among the leaders of this community were the Kheiri brothers, Abdul Jabbar and Abdul Sattar; the BIC had contacted them early on. Sons of a government official in Delhi, they had been educated in Beirut since the turn of the century and thereafter had made only a few brief visits to India. Jabbar, who taught Urdu at the University of Constantinople, bore a particularly strong antipathy to the nationalists, whom he perceived to bear a Hindu bias, and was very competitive with them in his quest for German patronage.[36]

The brothers had formed a society called the Hind Ikhwat-ul-Anjuman and were reported to have visited the Indian POWs captured from the British Army and held in Germany.[37] Since 1915 they had also edited the Pan-Islamist journal *Akhwat* or *Brotherhood* in Urdu and English.[38] The CID had snagged a few copies of their publications in England, and a few more in Mesopotamia, "where they were dropped in [the British] lines from enemy aeroplanes." Despite the editors' alleged antipathy to the Berlin group, the DCI reported that the material in the English version's articles "attacking the British Government in India" seemed to be mainly drawn from "Hindu revolutionary propaganda, though an occasional clumsy attempt is made to appeal to Muhammedan feeling. More interesting are the political notes, headed The Islamic World, which deal with Caucasus and anti-British developments in Persia and Afghanistan." In general the magazine was full of "religious and historical articles of great interest."[39]

Another weekly paper, called *Jehan-i-Islam* (Islamic World) and containing articles in Arabic, Turkish, and Urdu, was printed in Istanbul starting in 1914. Its purpose was to "discuss politics and try to promote intercourse between

Muhammedan countries," but its import into India had been proscribed under the Sea Customs Act due to its alleged "violently anti-Christian tone."[40] The Urdu segment was edited by Abu Saiyid, Har Dayal's friend and host in Constantinople and a fervently anti-British Punjabi Pan-Islamist. He had worked as a teacher in Rangoon, then traveled to Egypt in 1912, at the time of the Turco-Italian war. Though ostensibly there on business (selling Turkish caps), he commenced to "associate with nationalists." He also proceeded to Tripoli, "to circulate there a lithographed Urdu letter" regarding the Khilafatist organization for protection of the holy places, Anjuman-e-Khuddam-e-Kaaba.[41]

Har Dayal's proposal for taking over the *Jehan-i-Islam,* along with its Turkish War Office backing, and remodeling it as an Indian nationalist organ did not go over well with Saiyid's readership, nor did his attempt to dub the BIC office in Istanbul the "Bureau du Parti National Hindou."[42] Still, after the war declaration, Abu Saiyid's Urdu section included "a leading article by Har Dayal," written especially for the occasion, plus "virulently anti-British articles by the Egyptian Nationalist leaders" Farid and Rifaat, both friends of Indians in London and Paris since around 1908, and a speech by Enver Pasha making reference to Ghadar.[43]

But by fall 1915 Har Dayal was becoming a liability to his Indian colleagues. Taraknath Das (whom Nirode Barooah characterizes in favorable contrast to Dayal as "one of the serious-minded Berlin Indians in Constantinople" at this time)[44] was very critical of Har Dayal for his failure to cooperate with anyone else, his fickle attention, his insensitivity to local sentiments, and his apparent taste for being at the center of fanciful intrigues. He left Istanbul with no warning or explanation in October 1915, later claiming that far more than any Hindu-Muslim tensions, it had been German manipulation, untrustworthiness, and marginalization of Indian leadership in their own cause that had driven him out. Nevertheless, even after his abrupt exit, the plans that he had initially pitched to the AA went forward.[45]

The first of these efforts was highlighted in a memorandum from Chatto to Otto von Wesendonk, the German legation secretary who became the Indians' most important German interlocutor, in which Chatto "stressed the importance of propaganda among the Indian pilgrims in Mecca and among Indian soldiers in southern Persia, Basra, the Persian Gulf, and in France."[46] In January 1915, the first expedition embarked for Baghdad. The aim of the mission was to convince Indian soldiers at these sensitive postings to abandon the British Army and to raise a volunteer force from among their compatriot POWs and other locally resident émigrés. Even before the official declaration of war against Turkey, Britain had sent an expeditionary force consisting of a brigade of the Sixth Poona Division to seize Mesopotamian oil installations at Abadan. By November 1914 they had seized Basra and controlled much of the Tigris-Euphrates region.[47] This strategically critical corps was the target of the BIC's Baghdad team.

Once in contact with the Ottoman Ministry of War, they made for their intended operational base near Jerusalem, laden with "propaganda leaflets in Hindi and Urdu . . . to be smuggled to the Indian soldiers,"[48] materials designed to blend Pan-Islamic *jihadi* appeal with anti-British nationalism.[49] It was reported that when the British occupied Jerusalem, among the propaganda literature found at the University of Salahedin in Ayub "some . . . was of the Ghadar origin and some had been produced in Germany or Turkey by members of the Indian National Party."[50] The mission consisted of eight Indians, none of them Muslim, though all bore Islamic aliases, including Ghadar's original military strategist, Pandurang Khankhoje. Reaching Baghdad in May 1915, they set up a press to generate a weekly dose of subversive literature for the Indian soldiers. But despite the team's energy and commitment (for which they were commended by local German officials), the dynamics of the region doomed their efforts. First of all, many of the soldiers in the unit were Sikh or Gurkha and did not respond to Pan-Islamist appeals. Second, "Anglophile Arab notables" exerted too much influence within the provincial Turkish officialdom. Finally, local Indian Muslims no less than Turkish military brass harbored a strong distrust of these *kaffir* propagandists, "with their Muslim names and German money."[51] So the group dissolved in September after only four months. A second team was formed in April 1916, intending to reprise the same mission. With Dr. Mansur Ahmed from Berlin as group leader, this time they made sure to include Muslims, in hopes that this would increase the mission's success. But this attempt fell apart too, due to the usual combination of factional disharmonies.

When the British captured Basra, the sultan-caliph had called for a jihad on "all Christian powers opposed to Turkey," which was supported by fatwas from the Sheikh-al-Islam at Constantinople as well as statements from the Shi'a leaders at Najaf and Karbala.[52] But despite this broad endorsement, it did not automatically create a groundswell of Muslim support. On the contrary, the Iranians distrusted the Turks as much as they did the British or the Russians; the Egyptians were anti-British while other Arabs counted on British support against the Turks. In addition to these regional/national/ethnic divisions, some more pious Muslims also felt skeptical of an alliance with German infidels and Hindu idolaters.[53] In other words, true Pan-Islamic unity was a mirage beyond the power of any propaganda to embody.

In April 1915, a separate mission left for the Suez Canal Zone. The members of the team, some of whom would later join the second Baghdad mission, included the distinguished revolutionaries Acharya and Taraknath Das, along with some Indian POWs and two Egyptian revolutionary nationalists, Muhammad Husni and Muhammad Abd al-Halim Bey.[54] These two provided references for other Egyptian nationalist contacts to be activated, in hopes of collaborating toward some "sabotage work, if not a general rising, behind the British lines."[55] The

Egyptians too were invited to "harangue the [Indian] Muslim soldiers" in order
to "assist the Turkish offensive" in cutting off Britain's Red Sea passage to India.[56]
Unfortunately, since this proposal was dependent on when the Turkish army
would start a long-delayed trans-Sinai offensive, it failed to have much effect on
Indian troops in the area.

The team turned their attention next toward the prospect of Indian *hajis* circulating to Mecca and Medina. Chatto's December 1914 memo to Wesendonk had
"stressed the importance of propaganda among the Indian pilgrims in Mecca and
among Indian soldiers in southern Persia, Basra, the Persian Gulf, and in France."[57]
But the AA discouraged the idea on account of prohibitions on propaganda in
the holy places, not to mention the likely scarcity of pilgrims arriving during
wartime, and British screening of such pilgrims in any case. So the team remained stewing in aimless frustration in Sinai for the next few months.

Taraknath Das in particular had grown disheartened with their allotted task,
feeling (as did the Fenians, who had also been asked to campaign in Egypt) that it
was too removed from their primary objective. A member of the mission summarized the sentiment: "Active revolutionaries . . . were few in number," and therefore
"they should seek death only when effectively serving their national cause or where
their martyrdom would leave an impression on their countrymen; so why face
death without much purpose in that desert corner of the world?"[58] In August 1915
Das requested to be removed from this mission and at the end of the year "went to
Hebron to recuperate his broken health."[59] In August of the following year, upon
the failure of a major German offensive, Birendranath Dasgupta retreated to Istanbul also for health reasons, while the others were posted to Baghdad "to work
among the thousands of Indian soldiers taken prisoner upon the British defeat at
Kut el-Amara, and to incite them to join the Ottoman forces."[60]

Even though these missions bore no fruit, their German sponsors faulted neither the energy of the Indians' efforts nor the quality of their agitprop. Nevertheless, even years later, after the war, an *Independent Hindustan* item titled "British
Terror in the Near East," drawing on a report from London in the *Muslim Outlook* on the treatment of the Turkish population of Constantinople, claimed that
only the Indian troops stationed there were sympathetic to the Turks' plight:
"Apparently they [the Indian soldiers] are beginning to realize the gravity of the
situation of the principal defenders of the Orient against the West European
aggression. They themselves belong, of course, to the aggrieved Orient. Signs of
fraternization have more than once been suspected between Indian soldiers and
individual Turks."[61]

What was the substance of the BIC's message? The literature aimed at potential mutineers was a combination of typical Ghadar themes and motifs calculated to appeal to Khilafatists, demonstrating our prolific propagandists' habit of
tailoring materials for a range of target audiences. In this case, two simultaneous

messages were often implied: a reiteration of the call for Hindu-Muslim unity in the cause of Indian liberation, with the separation of religion from political and national matters; and an appeal to Muslims *as* Muslims, with their own distinct heritage and identity.

For example, one Urdu leaflet urged: "O Indian brave soldiers! Do not remain loyal to the rascal Englishmen! These tyrant English have been sucking the blood of our nation." It pointed out that the English impose heavy land duties, carry off money and crops, and pay Indian soldiers only ten to fifteen rupees per month, while the white soldiers get two or three times that plus rations, despite the fact that the Indians are made to do "the hardest work of war." The English spread disease and famine, lock patriots in prison and drive them to hard labor, incite the "Indian brethren to fight with one another," "outrage the modesty of Indian women," and demolish Indian places of worship—temple, mosque, and *gurdwara* alike.[62]

Even worse, the leaflet noted, "recently [the English] have shot down Sikhs, Hindus and Muhammedans in Egypt, Canada, Calcutta [a reference to the *Komagata Maru* incident, which is later described in some detail], and Delhi; have hanged them and have transported them." "Now," it exhorted, "take revenge upon them. Raise a mutiny and kill them. . . . Liberate India. Rule yourselves in India. Raise a mutiny and kill all the rascal English and those Rajas and Nawabs who are their friends and who oppress the Indians." In other words, to use an anachronistic term, compradors were considered no less the enemy than foreigners; this was not a national consciousness that was blind to class.

Still, with an eye to wartime realities, the pamphlet continued: "The Germans are not our enemies. They are our friends. The English are our enemies. . . . Do not fight for them. . . . At present, besides the Germans, the Turks, Persians, Egyptians, Afghans, Chinese, all these are fighting against the English. In short this is the time for raising a mutiny in India—Bande Mataram."

A little bit later: "Dear Indian heroes! . . . All the Indian soldiers, Rajputs, Sikhs, Pathans, Dogras, Gurkhas and Muhammedans, should throw down their weapons before the brave Germans and then uniting with the Germans should fight against the English so that India, Egypt, Persia, Malaya, Kandar, Afghanistan, Baluchistan and China be altogether freed from the oppression and slavery of the Feringhees . . . everywhere Swadeshi, i.e. Self-Government, may be established and all males and females may live in happiness and peace."

The leaflet then called upon the Indian military to take responsibility for its role in maintaining the empire: our "dear simple Indian sepoys have not only made their own country a slave but they have fought in Afghanistan, Nepal, Persia, Baluchistan, China and Africa and have shed their blood. But for whom? For the dacoit Feringhis, for the oppressive Englishmen and for the enemies of our country. We, the Indian soldiers, are making India and the whole world slaves. . . . Now what should be done?"

What should be done was that the soldiers must turn on them, "beat them out" from all those places (note here, incidentally, the astonishing deployment range of Indian troops), "free the whole world from the claws of the tyrannical and immoral Englishmen, establish . . . our own rule . . . eat our own bread with satisfaction and establish the honour and rights of our sisters and brothers in our own and foreign countries. . . . This is a good opportunity. . . . Be courageous. . . . When you have to die, die for the sake of the freedom of your country and your countrymen."[63]

Another leaflet called for Hindu-Muslim unity: "O good sons of Bharat, O braves of India—you are two drops of one and the same blood . . . you are two plants in the same garden; you are two fruits of one tree. . . . Both Hindus and Musalmans are the sons of the same mother. Alas! They have become devoid of good sense. Why do not Hindus and Musalmans unite? . . . Both Hindus and Musalmans are losing property and wealth."[64]

After all, the leaflet pointed out, the English were eaters of *both* cow and pig; both communities would benefit from a war of liberation. But due to the devious tricks of the English to divide and rule, now "brother is the enemy of brother, and relations behave like highwaymen." "O brethren," it urged, "for the sake of God, put faith in my words and do away with the bandage of treachery tied round your eyes and put on the garment of liberty. Raise yourselves to honour and dignity and restore your mother Bharat to her former grandeur and dignity."[65]

Perhaps it is little wonder that the persistent invocation of Bharat Mata and use of phrases like "Bande mataram," so closely associated with the Hindu Swadeshi extremists, put Muslim teeth on edge. Interestingly, there is no mention of Sikhs in this particular leaflet, and little in other Urdu texts, such as *Hamara Khana-jungi, Vartman Zamana* and *Mazhab Kya hai? Ghadar-di-Gunj,* on the other hand, was addressed directly to a Sikh audience. It continued in a religious vein (though one general enough to apply to readers of Gita, Koran, or Guru Granth): "It is all in the name of truth and justice, which, by the mercy of God, is the right path leading to heaven."

> Wake up, o ye youths, be you Hindus or Muhammedans—Don't you see that now even the Sultan of Turkey, feeling compassion on you has kissed his sword and has declared that so long as he has not released his children from their afflictions and restored them to happiness, he will not sheath his sword. He has published his orders everywhere, on every road and lane: "Awake, raise high the cry of mutiny; all should help me, Hindus as well as Muhammedans, and be martyrs in the cause of regaining liberty, for your sacred books order you to obey the commands of the emperor."

Strikingly, this call for unity did not only invite Muslims to join the cause of Indian national liberation, but also invited Hindus to join the Khilafat cause.

An Ailan-i-Jang (Declaration of War) asked its "dear Indians" to "just think a little, you and your country's state, what is happening to them"—that is, that they had once been among the richest and most fruitful and now were among the poorest. And, in addition to the crippling extraction of wealth and grain from the country, "[their] brothers in arms have been sent to the war in Europe." "What sort of astuteness is this," it asked, "that in battle the whitemen [sic] remain behind and in order to have them killed, place the Indians in front?"

After invoking the names of some devoutly Hindu nationalists, it addressed the "dear Muhammedan brothers":

> Today the English tyrants, and Russia and France, are fighting *your* Sultan of Turkey. Staring you in the face in the papers is an advertising announcing that the Turkish Empire will be wiped out. Now they have made a new Sultan of Egypt. Do you find this palatable that in front of your eyes the Muhammedan religion is being destroyed and you remain silent? No, certainly not. Dear brothers, now is the time; arise.

Finally, once again addressing Indians as a whole, it invoked a variety of martial communities and militant religious constituencies by name:

> Dear Indian brothers—Your days of pain are over. For the sake of Indians I am announcing to you that the war is commencing. In the whole of Hindustan war has begun; you too arise and deliver Hindustan from the bondage of slavery. Think! Brave Pathans, Turks, Moghals, Kshatriyas, their blood is in your veins.[66]

All would meet with the angel of death someday, somehow, so why not win the way to paradise in battle? "Rise and acknowledge your faith," it urged.

By now this message may sound repetitive to the reader. After all, it is no more than a minimal reframing and application of the same themes that appeared in the Ghadarite Yugantar Ashram publications *Wartman Zamana* (Modern Times), *Hamara Khanajangi: Iska Sabab aur Ilaj* (Our Civil War: Its Cause and Cure), and others. This, indeed, is the point.

In 1916, after the initial missions' lack of success, the BIC decided to reorganize (and Islamicize) the Istanbul headquarters with a new staff consisting of Dr. Mansur Ahmed, Abdul Wahid, Ata Mohammed, and Dr. Hafiz of the BIC, supplemented by some local activists. The committee would now be called the Young Hindustan Association, to be supervised by Abdul Wahid with full recognition by the Turkish government. But, as before, the reactions the association faced ranged from, at worst, fierce opposition (from Jabbar and his followers) to, at best, unhelpful indifference (from Ali Bey Beshhamba, who was in charge of the Turkish War Ministry's department dealing with Indians). Finally, by autumn of

1916, the BIC regretfully acknowledged that its Istanbul-based programme, despite valiant efforts, wasn't proving worth the trouble. They decided to wind down the operation.[67]

Meanwhile, however, efforts were under way in another direction. The second of the original plans was to send a mission to Kabul to secure the Afghan amir's cooperation in invading India at the crucial moment. The mission would travel by way of Persia, an area of considerable strategic significance for the Turco-German alliance because of its importance for their great enemy. Britain required a neutral Persia to facilitate its lines of support and communications to India. With the country overshadowed by Russian influence in the north and British in the south, neither the shah nor the constitutional government could project any power very far, while the intelligentsia and tribal leaders were divided as to which bloc they favored, often depending on whether their resentment of the Russians or the Turks was the stronger.

Through this volatile environment, the AA sent consular official Wilhelm Wassmuss (aka the "German Lawrence") on a mission in September 1914 to disrupt Britain's ability to function in the region by fomenting guerrilla warfare among the local tribes. His party was joined by "several disaffected Indians" of the BIC, namely, Khankhoje, Agarche, and Pramathnath Dutt, all recently recruited in the United States by Captain Kadri Bey of the Ottoman Ministry of Defense, who had come on a tour to scout for promising Indian revolutionaries.[68] In addition, some twenty other Indians bearing Persian identities and passports were reported to have left New York in spring 1915. Barakatullah may have been one of them, as he was sighted in Persia in June. All of these travelers were alleged to be in contact with German consulates.[69] While Wassmuss was busy encouraging tribes to harass the British and sabotage their oil installations, the three Indians planned to distribute propaganda among their enlisted compatriots in the area, and to establish contacts with allies back home, using Indian merchants in the Persian Gulf.

Although the tide of tribal support was turning toward the British by the latter half of 1915, Indian revolutionaries were involved in sporadic fighting in Iran until the end of the war. Cut off from communication and unaware of the collapse of the push for mutiny elsewhere, Khankhoje doggedly "battled on toward Baluchistan" across southern Persia.[70] In April 1916 he retreated under attack from a British-allied tribal chief to Shiraz—Amba Parishad's base—where he "was assigned the role of looking after the Ghadar soldiers who were to arrive from America, and eventually form part of their revolutionary army."[71] Amba Parishad and Kedernath Sondhi, a new arrival from San Francisco via Berlin, were captured and executed while fighting alongside the Turks in an Indian volunteer force in early 1917.[72] Khankhoje eluded capture several times to remain for the next few years in Persia, first working as a teacher in a Baha'i Bakhtiari tribal village and then in the service of a local sultan. He finally rejoined Chatto in Berlin around 1920 as part of the regrouped Central Committee, until beginning a new life in Mexico in 1924 as a celebrated agronomist and intimate of Rivera and Modotti.[73]

The Wassmuss mission never reached Kabul, nor did its simultaneous counterpart under Oskar Niedermayer, who was attempting to set up a base in Tehran with a team that also included some Indians. But after acknowledging that these bands were foredoomed because halfheartedly backed and shoddily equipped, the AA decided to outfit a real diplomatic mission to Afghanistan. Several days after Jodh Singh heard Har Dayal address a meeting in Berlin in April 1915, Chatto had escorted him to meet a prince—Jodh Singh did not recall his name, but doubtless Pratap—who was due to leave for Constantinople along with Har Dayal and two more intended operatives summoned from America to the Indo-Afghan frontier. This mission, scheduled to set off from Istanbul in May 1915, included two quite notable Indians: Mahendra Pratap and Muhammed Barakatullah, described as "a well-known Moslem anarchist and an Oudh talukdar who had been educated at Aligarh." Though W. O. von Hentig of the AA was supposed to be the actual leader of the expedition, it was hoped Pratap would contribute his aura as aristocratic figurehead, gauged to be impressive in certain circles susceptible to such things, while Barakatullah's presence would offer a measure of credibility calculated to appeal to Muslims in particular.[74] They went armed with powerful documents: the sultan provided a letter of introduction to the amir, the Turkish prime minister contributed letters for various princes, on "superfine notepapers," as Jodh Singh recalled;[75] and the Sheikh-al-Islam bestowed upon Barakatullah the text of a fatwa urging that Muslims work together with Hindus against the British.[76] The party of "six Germans, two or three Turks, and a Mullah, two Indians . . . 60 Arab soldiers from Bagdad [sic], one Persian and 50 transport mules" reached their destination in October 1915.[77]

Ultimately this mission too was unsuccessful in its stated goal; the amir was reticent, hedging his bets on the outcome of the war despite being offered permanent kingship of a large chunk of India if their side won. So the Germans went home, but the Indians remained in Kabul and set up the Hukumat-e-Muagita-e-Hind as a self-proclaimed Provisional Government of India (PGI) in exile (which Khankhoje referred to as the Ghadar Government). Pratap was named president, Barakatullah prime minister, and Obeidullah Sindhi home minister. The other officeholders were a mix of Ghadarites, BIC members, and *muhajir* students[78] These latter were but the latest of many subcontinental dissidents who had looked toward Afghanistan for decades, not only as a base for staging revolution but as a refuge for radicals on the run from British authority. The 13 January 1914 issue of the *Ghadar* touted Kabul as the place where readers could go to learn to manufacture rifles, boxes full of which they could then bring back for lavish distribution in Punjab.[79] Around the same time, the Yugantar Ashram in San Francisco had ordered Dr. Mathra Singh (alias Shamsher Singh) to arrange protection in Kabul for any Ghadarites who might need to retreat there in the course of carrying out the mutiny.[80] Mathra Singh himself had fled there after the failed rising of 19 February, as had Harnam Singh Kahuta, formerly Gurdit Singh's lieutenant on board the *Komagata Maru*. After serving a year of detention, Mathra Singh was named a "minister plenipotentiary" in the Provisional Government, and Kahuta a secretary. Mathra Singh was later arrested in March 1916 bearing a letter addressed to the czar from Mahendra Pratap as part of a diplomatic team consisting of a Ghadarite and a *muhajir*—himself and Mirza Muhammad Ali. They were transported to Punjab and included in the Third Supplementary Lahore Conspiracy Case; Mathra Singh was hanged.[81]

THE SILK LETTERS PLOT

"Times like the present bring to the surface secret and long forgotten currents," commented Sedition Committee chairman Justice Rowlatt in 1918.[82] In wartime Kabul several intermittently subterranean currents mingled at the surface. Only a few months before the arrival of the Hindu-German-Turkish mission, Maulana Obeidullah Sindhi arrived along with a party of three others to establish a cell for anti-British activity. Even earlier, in February of that year, fourteen or fifteen eager Khilafatist students from Lahore, led by Fazl Elahi, had left their colleges for Kabul "under the inspiration" of Obeidullah and Abul Kalam Azad. The role Azad played within India during the Swadeshi period was similar to the one I attribute to Barakatullah on a global scale—that is, he manifested a point of contact in a triangle of leftist, Islamist, and (in this case, Hindu-dominated) national revolutionists in and around Calcutta.[83] Azad had embraced both Pan-Islamism and anti-British nationalism in the course of his visits to Iraq, Egypt, Syria, and Turkey in 1908. He then established Pan-Islamist newspapers and societies circa 1912 to 1916, founded a training school for revolutionary youth as part of the Dar al-Irshad college he established in 1915 at his home in Calcutta, and maintained ties with the Yugantar group. Obeidullah and Barakatullah had then contacted him from Kabul upon the foundation of the Provisional Government of India, asking for his support. Azad and Obeidullah met secretly in Delhi with a tribal leader, Abdul Ahmad, in January 1915;[84] according to the 1918 Sedition Committee Report, the tribes had been preparing for an attack on British India since December of 1914, pursuing transfrontier contacts with "Muslim nationalists and Pan-Islamites within India."[85] In any case they offered support and hospitality en route to the famous "runaway students" who set out from Lahore with the intention of offering their services to the Turks in any capacity that might be required outside of "British soil" (i.e., India), whether as spies, messengers, soldiers, or preachers.[86]

Once in Afghanistan the students later identified as the first wave of *muhajirin* were placed in temporary detention, and then released under surveillance. Eventually some returned to India; others were captured by the Russians, who later handed them over to British custody.[87] The other students remained in Kabul until around 1920, when they were joined by new travelers in far greater numbers, destined to be present with them at the birth of Indian Communism among the Bolshevik-*muhajirin* in Tashkent, Moscow, and later in India itself.[88] We will return to these students, who, according to Muzaffar Ahmad, "engaged themselves not in holy war abroad, but in waging war upon British imperialism."[89] Still, for many among this group, before Communism came the Caliphate.

Even though the BIC mission from Istanbul had been unable to pursue the pilgrims, someone else could. At the same time as Obeidullah was heading for Kabul, his former Deoband mentor and political collaborator Mahmud Hasan was heading for Istanbul by way of Mecca along with ten followers, purportedly on haj. The Sands report on the Silk Letters conspiracy claimed that "in the course of the First World War . . . [Hasan had] conceived the idea of turning the Northwest Frontier Province into a pivot of anti-British resistance activity." Har Dayal and Barakatullah of course had floated the same idea on behalf of Ghadar and the BIC. British authorities suspected that Hasan's party was planning to consult there with Turkish officers and "that their journey was actuated by hostile feelings towards Governments,"[90] but had no solid information sufficient to detain them before they left India.

But DCI Cleveland's office wrote to Colonel C. Wilson, pilgrim officer at Jeddah, to alert him to a subject that might pertain to his jurisdiction: "a Mohammedan conspiracy which is now under enquiry in India." "This plot," reported Cleveland's office, "which is in some ways nebulous but in others practical, has an important ramification in the Hejaz, where resident and visiting Indians have been intriguing with Turkish officials."[91] They hadn't had the means yet, Cleveland's assistant continued, to get much intelligence on "the doings and sentiments of Indians in Arabia," but based on what letters they managed to intercept, it seemed that about half of them in the Hejaz "were actuated by anti-British sentiments in going there and were likely to bring treacherous influence to bear on Indian pilgrims"; and moreover, that the region was plainly "a breeding ground for fanaticism and disloyalty among the Indian residents and visitors." Thank goodness there was a friendly regime now that the sharif's rising had been successful; before that they had been dependent for information on the occasional loyal pilgrim passing through.[92]

In the end, Hasan was prevented from getting all the way to Istanbul by a conflict with the authorities in Mecca, but nevertheless Pashas Enver and Djemal were kind enough to meet with him there. They and Ghalib Pasha, the Turkish military governor of the Hejaz, signed letters known as the Ghalibnama, authorizing jihad, to be circulated throughout India and the border tribal areas along with other propaganda leaflets. Ghalib Pasha also signed off on a letter of authorization to be circulated by Hasan's party, stating:

> The Muhammedans in Asia, Europe and Africa adorned themselves with all sort of arms and rushed to join the Jihad in the path of God. Thanks to Almighty God that the Turkish Army and the Mujahidin have overcome the enemies of Islam. . . . It may also be known to you that Maulvi Mahmud Hassan Effendi (formerly at the Deoband Madrasa, India) came to us and sought our counsel. We agreed with him in this respect and gave him necessary instructions. You should trust him if he comes to you and help him with men, money and whatever he requires.[93]

The picturesque touch that gave the Silk Letters Plot its name when it was uncovered in 1916, when Hasan and four companions were captured by the British, and Ghalib Pasha became a POW,[94] was that the emissary bearing the correspondence between Obeidullah at Kabul and Hasan at Mecca, from whom the authorities intercepted the information, had sewn three swatches of yellow silk on which the plans were "neatly and clearly written" into the lining of his coat.[95]

Obeidullah had sent the plans along with a cover letter written to the emissary, Sheik Abdur Rahim, on 10 July 1916:

> (Please) have this trust conveyed through a trustworthy Haji to Hazrat Maulana at Holy Madina without fail. This is a work for which there is no harm in undertaking a permanent journey (even if it is necessary to quit India for ever). . . . After this you should try to come to me yourself. (Do this) for God's sake (as) there are many urgent works here. Come without fail. . . . It is necessary that the information may reach Hazrat Maulana on the occasion of the Haj.[96]

The silken documents summarized the basics of the German-Turkish mission to Kabul, the establishment of the PGI there, the presence of the runaway students, the circulation of the Ghalibnama, and "the projected formation of an 'Army of God'" to recruit rebels and mutineers within India while also pursuing diplomatic alliances among various Muslim rulers. Regarding the students, Obeidullah informed the Maulana that they alone were "the moving limbs in this work," noting that "some of them, after visiting the Durbar of the Caliphate, will come to you, God willing."[97]

Obeidullah also sketched out the structure for Al-Janud-Al-Rabbania, aka the Army of God, aka the "Troops of Liberation or Islamic Salvation Army."[98] This was envisioned as a "special Islamic Jama-at based on military principles"[99] whose goal was to create "a union between Islamic Kings." The Maulana was to be appointed president, "whose title is General or Al-Qaid in Military parlance, the real center being Medina,"[100] with secondary centers in Istanbul, Tehran, and Kabul, and third class centers in "Islamic countries which are under the influence of the infidels"; additionally, Europe, Africa, India, and central Asia were listed as in-tended "Spheres of Influence." At the apex of this army's chain of command were the Ottoman sultan-caliph, the sultan of Persia and the amir of Afghanistan, followed by field marshals, including Enver Pasha, Khedive Abbas Hilmi Pasha of Egypt, the sharif of Mecca, Nasrullah Khan of Kabul, the nizam of Hyderabad and the nawabs of Rampur, Bhopal, and Bhawalpur. There are also twenty-one lieutenant generals, nineteen major generals, twenty-nine colonels, ten lieuten-ant colonels (including four of the student *muhajirin*), five majors, two captains, and a lieutenant.

In addition to the detailed scheme for the organization of a liberating "Army of God," the PGI also planned to set up a printing press and money and muni-tions stockpiles in the North-West Frontier Province border region. Meanwhile, the Maulana in Medina was to cement an alliance between Afghanistan, Persia, and the Sublime Porte, "because this is the only way of inflicting an effective blow to the infidels in India."[101] By infidels, he meant the British; why not the Hindus? Significantly, Obeidullah intended his participation in "the other Anjuman called Hakumat-i-Moagita-i-Hind," that is, the Provisional Government of India,[102] to represent a deliberate attempt at Hindu-Muslim rapprochement—a theme also emphasized in the propaganda literature distributed to the soldiers.

Obeidullah felt that by working alongside and in unity with the PGI he could keep with him the "revolutionary elements among the Hindus."[103] He mentioned that the purpose of "this Jama-at," namely, the PGI, "is to liberate India." "The president of this," he continued, "is an Indian Rajah, who is staying at Kabul."[104] Beneficially, Mahendra Pratap was both "connected with the Arya societies *and* . . . related indirectly with the Indian Hajis."[105] Both the kaiser and the caliph had recognized him as a representative of India, having originally sent their own representatives with him to Kabul.[106] Pratap and Barakatullah then together "laid before the Amir the Indian question in support of the interests of the Hin-dus." "They both laid the foundation," Obeidullah emphasized. When they asked Obeidullah to join in their enterprise, he agreed, "with a view to safeguarding Islamic interests" therein.[107] In other words, via this institution, two separate transnational radical networks were brought to overlap, with nearly exact repeti-tion in the tactical plan of action.

The British were thrown into a minor uproar over the Silk Letters revelations, lavishing intelligence reports with lurid detail: in his report, C. E. W. Sands wrote of a conspiracy to overthrow the British government by means of "(1) Quranic teachings inculcated in such a way as to rouse Muslim religious passion and to paint India to be Dar-ul-Harb, (2) inciting the Frontier Tribe and Afghans to hostilities and reinforcing them with troops from Turkey."[108] For this purpose, Obeidullah had founded societies and schools and printed and circulated seditionist literature "inculcating Jihad."[109] This man's object was, in a nutshell, according to the 1918 Sedition Committee Report, "to promote a great Muslim attack on India, which should synchronize with a Muslim rebellion."[110] (Apparently there are other things, such as imperial paranoia over the inexorable militance and global ramifications of political Islam, that never change.)

A proclamation by the PGI was found on the frontier in the form of a lithographed circular bearing the signatures of Obeidullah as interior minister and Lahore student Zafar Hasan as secretary; Hasan was also ranked a lieutenant colonel in the Army of God. The proclamation opened with a bold self-introduction, saying in essence, "We're the ones you heard about in the Rowlatt report"; it then expanded:

> This government has instituted an order to establish a better government in place of the present treacherous, usurping and tyrannical government. Our Provisional Government has been continuously struggling for the last four years. . . .
>
> [It] has entered into a compact with the invading forces. Hence you should not destroy your real interest by fighting against them, but kill the English in every possible way, don't help them with men and money and continue to destroy rails and telegraph wires. . . .
>
> The attacking army guarantees peace to every Indian irrespective of caste and creed. The life and honour of every Indian is safe. He who will stand against them will alone be killed or disgraced.
>
> May God guide our brethren to tread on the right path.[111]

THE SINGAPORE MUTINY

Throughout the course of the war, there had been a continuous push and pull between the AA and the BIC over control of campaigns, choice of strategic focus, relative autonomy, and divergent objectives. Unsurprisingly, the Indians resented being used as pawns in German war aim, chafing at the denial of full access to the AA and at the unreliability of its promised resources. So in December 1916, as the fruitless west Asian efforts were being wrapped up, the BIC was reorganized so as to create greater Indian control and more direct contact with the German office, with Chatto as central figure on the Indian side and Wesendonk as main German interlocutor.

This led to a shift away from activating Pan-Islamism in the Ottoman lands, and toward the Pacific Rim; as previously mentioned, it also entailed the heaviest concentration of direct involvement on the part of the Californian Ghadar group through the third major initiative of the AA/BIC alliance: the importation of as large a quantity of weapons, ammunition, and American Ghadarites as could be mustered for a rebellion and invasion from the east. And yet Pan-Islamism was a factor on India's eastern front too, including the mutiny attempts Ghadarites helped to engineer at Rangoon and Singapore, which came closer to realization than any of those envisioned in the north and west.

Ottoman general Niazi Bey arrived in Batavia at the head of a small delegation in the early stages of the war and established contact there with the Turkish consul general, within whose jurisdiction "the 'Ghadr' was known to be reaching the island in large quantities."[112] Their "efforts were ably supplemented by numerous Sikhs, many of whom spoke English, and undoubtedly came from the United States, while others did not conceal the fact. Others also came from Chinese ports and Tsingtao."[113] Vir Singh was thought to be the first to receive and circulate Ghadar papers from America there, later adding others to the mailing list.[114]

In 1913, a suggestion from Abu Saiyid in Constantinople had led to the arrival of Tewfik Bey of the Committee of Union and Progress (CUP) to set up a consulate in Rangoon. And after Turkey entered the war, two veterans of the Indian Red Crescent Society's 1912 medical relief delegation to the Balkans who had stayed on in Turkey, by the names of Hakim Faim Ali and Ali Ahmed Gadiqi, arrived in Rangoon at the CUP's behest. They allegedly set about "forming a secret society among Muhammedans, whose object was to assist in subverting British rule." They collected subscriptions totaling 15,000 rupees, and "employed a well-known smuggler to collect pistols."[115] When "Hasan Khan" and Sohan Lal Pathak arrived from San Francisco to organize the Siam-Burma scheme, the two teams quickly established close collaborative ties.[116] In the "large batch of Ghadar literature" that the authorities seized at Myawaddy near the Siam/Burma frontier in June were letters addressed to Ali Ahmad and Faim Ali in Rangoon.

Sohan Lal Pathak continued his attempts to incite "sedition" in Burma throughout the summer of 1915 by appealing to the soldiers' sentiments as Muslims as well as to their anticolonialism. At the time of his arrest in the very act of "endeavouring to seduce . . . from their allegiance" the loyal men of the Mountain Battery at Maymyo—who "feign[ed] acquiescence" until they could alert their Jemadar and "by a clever ruse, the agitator was quietly secured"[117]—Pathak was carrying, in addition to three automatic pistols and 270 cartridges, a selection of papers, including the article "New Light and New Science" by the notorious Har Dayal; a copy of the *Ghadar;* a copy of *Jehan-i-Islam* ("a flagrantly seditious Mahomedan paper"); several copies of the sultan-caliph's fatwa, and elaborate formulas and supplies for making explosives.[118] When censors seized "large quantities" of literature entering Burma in early 1915, they found up to 104 covers containing copies of the *Ghadar* issue of 24 January 1915 (including 220 in Gujurati, 10 in Hindi, and 3 in Urdu) as well as six issues of Abu Saiyid's *Jahan-i-Islam* from Istanbul. Indeed, "the despatch of copies of the *Jahan-i-Islam* in bundles of the *Ghadar* newspaper," noted the Sedition Committee Report ominously, "seems to have been no accident."[119]

Even assuming these incidents were selectively emphasized, one gets the impression that when authorities intercepted revolutionaries carrying seditious literature during the war, they frequently found a mixture of Ghadar publications and Islamist propaganda. Despite the not insignificant difference between locating the ultimate source of one's political ethic in human reason or in divine decree, it does not strike me as too much of a thematic or stylistic stretch to combine the two here, with their parallel calls to heroic sacrifice and even glorious martyrdom; exhortations to cross-faith brotherhood in the service of united, mutual liberation; and unrelenting opposition to Britain as imperial aggressor anywhere in the world.

The men of the 130th Baluchis, a mostly Muslim regiment recently transferred from Bombay in November 1914 as punishment for assassinating an officer, thus became "contaminated . . . with the tenets of the Ghadar newspaper, and by January 1915 the regiment was thoroughly disaffected and ready for mutiny."[120] However, the danger was "nipped in the bud on the 21st January by the timely and drastic action on the part of the military authorities, who punished 200 of the plotters."[121] Then in February the Fifth Light Infantry, sent to Singapore to replace other regiments transferred to the Western Front in France, also mutinied.[122] Attribution was uncertain, though authorities suspected that there was a Ghadar connection, as two of those involved, Hira Singh and Gyan Chand, were later tried in Ghadar-linked conspiracy cases. The Sedition Committee Report thought that both the Fifth Light Infantry and the 130th Baluchis "had undoubtedly been contaminated by Muhammedan and Hindu conspirators belonging to the American Ghadar party."[123]

One of the participants—Mujtaba Hussain, aka Mul Chand, also implicated in the Mandalay case—had been in touch with Ghadarites in Manila before coming to Singapore to help "promote the mutiny."[124] A letter of his provided the first evidence of a Ghadar plot in Rangoon. Soldiers also visited and were visited by alleged Ghadarite Kasim Mansur, a "Pro-Turkish" Gujurati Muslim living in Singapore. Among letters he forwarded to his son in Rangoon was one containing an appeal from men of the Malay State Guides to the Turkish consul, declaring that they were ready to mutiny against the British and fight for the Turks; could the consul arrange to send a Turkish warship? The Singapore authorities, once they got wind of this, were quick to transfer the regiment elsewhere.[125]

Aside from this, "attempts were being made to tamper with the Military Police of Burma, a formidable force" of fifteen thousand men, recruited mainly from among Punjabi Sikhs and Muslims. A letter was found in the house used as Ghadar's Rangoon headquarters in which someone from the Sikh temple serving the military police in Moulmein asked Harnam Singh (alias Ishar Das), that "notorious Sikh Ghadrite from British Columbia," for money. Elsewhere the so-called Muhammedan Ghadar party of Rangoon were discovered to have "planned a rising on the occasion of the Bakr-Id in October 1915, when Englishmen were to be killed 'instead of goats and cows.'" The planners postponed the uprising to 25 December, because all the necessary preparations were not yet in place. But in November, before it could be pulled off, a separate Ghadarite plot was unearthed in the military police battalion at Pyabwe; "revolvers, dynamite and other things to be used in the mutiny were seized," and the chief conspirators interned under the new Defense of India Act regulations.[126]

On 15 February 1915, Sepoy Ismail Khan allegedly fired the first shot at the Alexandra barracks; other mutineers then seized a lorry that was being loaded, along with its cargo of ammunition.[127] They overpowered guards at the Tanglin barracks, released German prisoners of war, took the fort, killed some British officers, and marched seven hundred strong toward the city to rouse the police to their side. The mutineers clearly were not out to loot, wrote Ram Chandra, commenting on the rising in the *San Francisco Examiner* after the fact (13 June 1916), because they left empty or Dutch-occupied houses untouched and shot only Englishmen. The attack, therefore, was against "British power and British people." He also thought it worthy of notice that the mutineers went to an internment camp, shot the guards, broke the gates, and flung rifles to the Germans inside while calling out "Germans! Germans! Islam! Islam!"[128]

Brigadier General Ridout declared martial law and summoned aid from nearby Russian, French, and Japanese warships.[129] The fighting was "very severe" on the night of 15 February, "ditch to ditch, house to house, tree to tree," related Lieutenant Malcolm Bond Shelley of the Volunteer Rifles years later, rather in the manner of a ripping boys' adventure tale.[130] By the time reinforcements arrived two days later on a British sloop, forty-eight people had been killed, including a dozen British officers and at least that many civilians. The rising was finally quelled by a combination of Japanese reinforcements, regulars called up from the Malay State Volunteer Rifles, territorials of the Shropshire Light Infantry with their Dayak "native trackers," eager local civilians, and even some American missionaries who thereby earned unprecedented goodwill from British colonists, who had previously been less than pleased to have them around.[131] There followed 126 courts-martial, 27 executions by public shooting, 41 life sentences of transportation, and some other assorted prison terms.[132] Others were given the choice of imprisonment or transfer to East Africa. Most chose the latter; there they were "employed on lines of communication where they had a strenuous and anything but rosy time" and were mocked by other regiments as "Snake-Charmers."[133] The tracking down of six hundred mutineers throughout the area continued for three more weeks, leaving fifty-one still unaccounted for, thought to be either hiding in disguise or escaped well away.

Official reports were at pains to downplay not only the Japanese contribution to the pacification, but the anticolonial motivations of the revolt, ascribing the troops' refusal to obey orders to petty "jealousy and dissatisfaction concerning recent promotions."[134] The secretary of state for India stated in Parliament that it was merely a "regimental riot" and not really a mutiny at all, certainly not a "racial or religious rising against the British Government."[135] But the *New York Times* commentary pointed out that the troops had been showing signs of unrest since their arrival, and that the causes appeared much more "deep and complex" than a simple promotion grievance: "Suffice it to say that this was the very regiment, along with three others, that years ago started the great Sepoy Rebellion in India. Well has it lived up to its traditions!"[136] These traditions could hardly have been lost on either the Ghadar propagandists or the troops who responded to them, since the legacy of 1857 was so central for the national mythology of the revolutionists abroad. Bhai Parmanand himself later recalled in his memoir speaking to a gathering of two hundred Indian soldiers in Singapore, invoking the memory of 1857, and passing out copies of the *Ghadar* and the *Ghadar-di-Gunj*.[137]

But Sho Kuwajima adds another layer, locating the uprising not only as part of the linked series comprising the Great Mutiny, the *Komagata Maru*, and the Ghadar movement, but simultaneously within the context of the "'Pro-Turkish' or 'Pan-Islamic' feelings of Muslims."[138] This allows him to give a deeper interpretation to the contemporary authorities' dismissive reading of the mutiny as simple dissatisfaction with shoddy treatment. He sees it rather as a symptom of the Indian soldiers' increasing difficulty in finding any meaningful or positive reason to participate in the war, a difficulty he attributes to the influence of Ghadar propaganda reinforced by Turkey's entry into hostilities.[139] The wartime mutinies in Southeast Asia thus interwove both Ghadarite and Khilafatist ideologies, historical iconographies, and aspirations.

Lal Salaams

Ghadar and the Bolshevik Muhajirin

THE BOLSHEVIK *MUHAJIRIN*

A special appeal was sent out in December 1917, just after the Russian Revolution:

> Muslims of the East! Persians, Turks, Arabs, and Indians! All you whose lives and property, whose freedom and homelands were for centuries merchandise for trade by rapacious European plunderers! All you whose countries the robbers who began the war now want to divide among themselves! . . .
>
> Lose no time in throwing off the ancient oppressors of your homelands. Permit them no longer to plunder your native lands. You yourselves must be the masters in your own land. You yourselves must build your life as you see fit. You have this right, because your fate is in your own hands. . . .
>
> Muslims of Russia! Muslims of the East!
>
> In the task of regenerating the world we look to you for sympathy and support.[1]

In 1920, as the revolutionary regime strove to institutionalize its power, a Caucasian Turk gave a speech at a Bolshevik meeting in the central Asian city of Merv:

> Oh working Mohammedans! The Soviet Government has been formed to free you all. In future you shall breathe in peace. Are you aware that your fellow labourers in other parts of the world are being cruelly and shamelessly strangled in cold blood by the British—the greatest enemy of Islam? The British government is the same which has enslaved 70 millions of Moslems in India, which rules Egypt with fire and sword, which has wiped out Tripoli and dismembered the Turkish Empire.

And what could listeners do about this? he asked rhetorically. Well, for a start, one might win over the Indian sepoys. He closed with this exhortation: "Long live the working classes! Long live the Soviet and Lenin! Long live Islam and the true followers of Islam!"[2]

As had been the case in wartime between the Germans, Ottomans, Pan-Islamists, Ghadarites, and other assorted Indian national revolutionaries, now after the war Bolsheviks and Pan-Islamists identified each other as important allies in the struggle against Western imperialism, especially as manifest in its most advanced form, British capitalism. Those Indians still enmeshed in the revolutionary network abroad found themselves more often than not in a zone of overlap, in which they seem to have seamlessly spliced together some of the compatible threads from both sides.

A secret memorandum in December 1919 on "Defensive measures proposed for dealing with Bolshevism" made this judgment:

> There is no possible doubt that enemy agencies in Europe of various sorts—Germans, CUP, Egyptian Committee and seditious Indians—are working hard to write and to cause us every trouble in the East.
>
> There are two great sources of trouble. One is Islamic feeling to be played upon. The climax may be intended to come when the dismemberment of Turkey is announced. The other is Bolshevism. The military fortunes of which, though uncertain, are improving, and which is making extra ordinary efforts to dominate Central Asia and to penetrate to India.[3]

The geographical coincidence of the Muslim world and the Oppressed Peoples of the East also created convenient opportunities for rhetorical transference. A report summarizing this "serious menace" centered the Soviet policy for the East upon India as the linchpin of anti-British strategy, with Turkestan, Bokhara, Khiva, and Afghanistan counted in its sphere of influence, and adjacent states serving as corridors of propaganda.[4] The central Asia/Transcaucasus region had long been crucial for both Russian and British strategy in the never-ending Great Game of balance-of-power politics around the edges of the Ottoman Empire. It was no different now that the players had changed, especially as, even more than access to India, access to oil was becoming an ever more important factor.[5]

The Baku conference of 1920 was touted as the follow-up to the Second Congress of the Third International at which the national-colonial question had been elaborated in the famous interchange between Lenin and Roy. Delegates from throughout west, central, south, and east Asia converged in a massive gathering in the "vanguard" oil-refining center, where the majority-Muslim industrial workforce had just a few months earlier proclaimed the new Azerbaijan Soviet Socialist Republic. During the course of this mobilization, Soviet rhetoric explicitly called upon Muslims *as such* to play a role in the world revolution.

The other tactical component in the "liberation of Asia" to be directed from Tashkent was the training of military and political cadres from among the Asian nations in question, including an International Brigade envisioned as an irregular auxiliary force to the Red Army. It would include Indian British army deserters and Persian revolutionaries as well as Russian Communists. They were to exploit all opportunities, seeking any chance to neutralize or spark mutiny in the British Indian army, while arming and funding the North-West Frontier tribes toward anti-British revolt. A striking continuity links the strategy and tactics adopted by Ghadar in 1914, the BIC and PGI in 1915, the Khilafat movement in 1919, and the Comintern in 1920. This was the conjuncture at which Roy and the Soviets identified the *muhajirin*—the "exiles" or "migrants"—as ideal recruits, much as other eyes had lit upon the California Sikhs as a discontented and mobilizable mass.

The viceroy had already voiced his suspicions to the Army Department about a "common Bolshevik-Pan-Islamism programme for freedom of Asia," echoing a warning from his chief of general staff in Simla to the director of military intelligence that "everything points to an alliance between pan-Islam and Bolsheviks," which was further characterized as a "dangerous movement for the peace of Asia."[6] (Apparently peace and freedom were antithetical within the realms of the British Empire.) However, analysts predicted that if Bolshevism appeared in India it would not "propagate the particular doctrines associated with it in Europe." Instead, "it would be more likely to change its complexion and to ally itself with whatever forces of discontent or disorder it found in existence," and in particular, with the Pan-Islamism that was then "working upon the feelings of Mohammedans" in order "to arouse them against the Government" in reaction to the dismemberment of Turkey.[7]

From the other side, Pan-Islamism, like the Asian national liberation movements, was viewed in that conjuncture as an objectively revolutionary force positioned to strike a blow against the Western powers. As Roy recalled,

> Reports had reached Moscow that, responding to a call of the Khilafat Committee, thousands of Muslims, including many educated young men, were leaving India for Turkey to join the army of Kemal Pasha. It was a religious Pan-Islamist movement. But it gave me an opportunity to contact a large number of possible recruits for an army to fight for the liberation of India instead of for a lost cause.[8]

Lost, that is, because Kemal was fighting neither to reinstate the Ottoman Empire nor to defend the caliphate—both the spiritual and temporal power of which were soon to be abolished—but rather to construct the Turkish secular democratic-republican nation-state.

Another 1919 report on the Red threat to India cited a newspaper called *Independence,* owned by a Hindu and edited by a Muslim, that wrote much about

Pan-Islamist matters while also printing pro-Bolshevik articles.[9] In a Lucknow paper, the Urdu-Arabic *Albayan,* "a well-known Indian Pan-Islamist from England print[ed] an 'objectionable' article stating that 'prospects for freedom in India are better than in Egypt owing to the proximity of a friendly power, the Bolsheviks.'"[10] At the Khilafat conference in Bombay in May 1920, a resolution was passed to the effect that those present professed "every sympathy with the Bolshevik movement so far as it is consistent with Islamic principles."[11] But though most conference delegates favored using Bolshevism as a weapon against the British government, they nevertheless declined to pass conference speaker Maulvi Mohammed Fakir's additional suggested resolution that since the British press had compared Lenin to the Prophet Mohammed, "Mohammedans should not oppose Bolshevism in India or the rest of Asia."[12]

Less equivocal was Barakatullah, who wrote in the pamphlet *Bolshevism and the Body Politick,* circulated throughout India and central Asia: "Oh, Mohammedans, listen to this divine cry. Respond to this call of liberty, equality and brotherhood which Comrade Lenin and the Soviet Government are offering to you." Calling himself an "irreconcilable enemy of European capitalism in Asia whose main representative is the English," he then asserted that "in India have matured the same prerequisites of revolution which existed in Russia in 1917."[13]

Even the Kheiri brothers, Abdul Jabbar and Abdul Sattar, had been moving toward a rapprochement with socialism, visiting Moscow in November 1918.[14] Intelligence reported on Russian wireless transmissions: "[These] two representatives of the Indian Mussalmans from Delhi and men of learned professions . . . came here and interviewed our leader Lenin. They explained to him many things concerning India and the East." The two also delivered an address to the Soviet Central Committee in which they denounced British rule in India, which they too compared to the prerevolutionary czarist regime in Russia, and asked for Russia's friendship and support in their struggle for freedom. K. H. Ansari notes that they also "reveal[ed] some understanding of Marxist argument" in declaring that the true enemy of the Indian people was not the British per se, but British imperialism, which was the enemy of not only the Indians but also the British working class; and that "justice, freedom and socialism will be established on earth by the united efforts of all the oppressed peoples."[15] The response to their speech was warm and positive.

In April 1919 the two Indians, "who claimed to represent the 325 millions of India," read a paper in a similar vein before the All Russian Central Executive Committee:

Leader of the Russian Revolution, Comrades and Friends. Allow me to tender my thanks to you for personal happiness granted me in carrying to you the greeting from the Indian people and seventy million Indian Muhammedans. Allow me to give you greetings Russian people, and your Russian Revolution which has inspired us with new hopes and pointed out to us a new road to conflict.

They then described some of the depredations resulting from "the imperialistic and capitalistic English policy," with specific attention to the plight of workers and peasants, including both those resident in India and those "sent for some reason to other British colonies." But the Russian Revolution, they said, had "made a tremendous impression on the psychology of the Indian people" through its raising of the "war-cry, 'self-determination of the people.'" In conclusion they declared:

> Universal freedom will remain in danger so long as imperialistic and capitalistic England remains powerful. And her power rests on her Indian possessions and on the advantages she gains from the enslaved populations and industry of India. . . . We hope that our brothers of great unfettered Russia will hold out to us a hand in freeing India and the world.[16]

A February 1920 report mapped out the dangers of such a combination in sections titled "The Revolt of Islam" and "Lenin's Hand in the Game." One might have thought our Great War victory would have quieted them down, the writer lamented, but alas, no—on the contrary, "recent events in Egypt and India indicate that such intrigues have borne tardy but apparently dangerous fruit after the conclusion of the armistice." The risings in Egypt and India were surely just a "rehearsal for the expected revolt of Islam." The report identified Switzerland as the current "centre of Moslem intrigue" and suggested that "revolutionary events in India, Egypt and perhaps Afghanistan are not totally unconnected with such activities there"—activities in which the report also detected a whiff of Bolshevik intrigue.[17] In March, A. A. Mirza of the Islamic Defense League and the Workers' Welfare League in England was reported to be considering traveling to Russia in order to try to reach India as a Bolshevik agent.[18] By June apparently he had made up his mind, and the DCI noted that Mirza, "so long identified with Islamic Pro-Bolshevik agitation in England, has at last made his way to Russia" and then was reported to have been sent from Russia to Anatolia as "the bearer of important messages from Mohammed Ali of the Khilafat deputation."[19]

Additionally the CID was wary of a possible "League of Eastern Revolutionists and Young Turks." As usual, what was most significant to the imperial observers was the prospect that the "Indian, Egyptian, Turkish, Persian, etc. nationalists, who used to act independently, are now tending to combine together and join forces." For this they blamed the German Pan-Islamic Propaganda Bureau in Berlin (headed by erstwhile BIC coordinators Oppenheimer and Wesendonk), which had departments for Egypt, Turkey, Turkestan, Persia, Algeria, Morocco, and elsewhere with the goal of cultivating anti-French and anti-British sentiment in Muslim lands. But it seems that German intervention was superfluous; the former Sheikh-al-Islam, Nadjimeddin Mollah [*sic*], declared: "An Entente Cordiale has been effected between the Turks, Egyptians, Afghans, and Hindus . . . the peacemakers in Paris are cudgelling their brains how best to prevent new wars; they little suspect that a greater menace than the Germans hangs over Europe—it comes from Moslem Asia and Africa." One participant of the coalition announced that although "our new committee is comprised of Turks, Arabs, Hindus, Egyptians, Caucasians, etc.," the students in the major centers "will no more be called Turks, Egyptians, etc. but 'Moslems'—nationality no bar on membership." In other words, the sum of all fears was a convergence of the currents of Indian anticolonialism, Pan-Islamism/Khilafatism, and Bolshevism. The fact that such ubiquitous phantom entities have so often been imagined with fear as enemies does not negate the fact that they were also imagined with hope as vehicles of solidarity. In any case there was a good deal of contradictory information circulating both for and against the hypothesis of alliance between the Bolsheviks and the various Muslims of central Asia and the Caucasus.[20]

At Baku, the Soviet rhetoric made it very easy to conflate the three currents of Asian national liberation, Pan-Islamism, and Communism by harnessing them together insofar as they flowed in the same direction, that is, in throwing off Western (British, French, and American) military and economic domination. It is also clear that such rhetoric treats Islam less as a religion than as a nationality, to which the national-colonial theses applied; and whose adherents had the same rights to cultural autonomy, political self-determination, and territorial sovereignty as any other nation, with sensibilities, cultural practices, and traditions that had to be respected. In Lenin's words, "The activities of our Soviet Republic in Afghanistan, India and other Muslim countries outside Russia are the same as our activities among the numerous Muslims and other non-Russian peoples inside Russia."[21]

The 1917 appeal had made a call to support the Bolshevik government because it had pledged to guarantee for the first time freedom of national, cultural, and religious practice and access to education for Muslims within the czar's former territories:

> Henceforth your beliefs and customs, your national and cultural institutions are declared free and inviolable. Build your national life freely and without hindrance. . . . Know that your rights—like those of all the peoples of Russia—are defended by the full force of the revolution and its organs, the soviets of workers', soldiers', and peasants' deputies. Support this revolution and its authorized government.[22]

However, the Bolsheviks made no room for Islam as a faith, ideology, or institutional religion. Thus while they cultivated relationships with Khilafatists, they did not support the caliphate, and counseled Muslims in the central Asian republics against supporting it. While valorizing these populations as Oppressed Peoples, or as Soviet minorities unjustly discriminated against under czarist rule, they could still state (in a section listing caveats for dealing with "states and nations that have a more backward, predominantly feudal, patriarchal, or patriarchal-peasant character"): "It is necessary to struggle against the Pan-Islamic and Pan-Asian movements and similar currents that try to link the liberation struggle against European and American imperialism with strengthening the power of Turkish and Japanese imperialism and of the nobles, large landowners, clergy, and so forth."[23]

Initially, the Bolsheviks had been insistent on making material and moral assistance to such movements contingent on ideological correctness and "the acceptance of Bolshevik principles." This led to a compromise in 1919 with members of Turkish, Egyptian, Persian, and Indian organizations at St. Moritz and "reaffirmed in Berlin, Angora and Bombay" in which the assistees agreed, but only "so long as these principles do not clash with the principles of Islam." Eventually, however, realizing they were earning too much distrust from potential allies, the Bolsheviks relaxed their stipulations and decided to simply support the "Islamic National movement" regardless of mentality, while continuing to enjoy the effects of this movement's "unleashed power" against the economically precarious British empire.[24]

In a sense, then, their approach to this imagined quasi-nationality of Islam was analogous to the way they related to the nationalist movement in India. That is, they attempted to channel the energy of its more radical components while struggling to displace its bourgeois (Ataturk) and persistently feudal (sultan-caliph) elements.[25] Here again is the appeal of 1917 to the "toiling Muslims of Russia and the East": "The tsar's secret treaties for the seizure of Constantinople . . . are now declared null and void. The Russian republic and its government . . . oppose the seizure of foreign territory. Constantinople must remain in the hands of the Muslims. . . . We declare null and void the treaty providing for the division of Turkey."[26] In this way the Bolsheviks rejected the ideology of Khilafatism yet recognized its goals as compatible with their own.

At least, plainly there was enough overlap in the interests and desires expressed in both mediums that linking them together was not illogical. In the following excerpt from the culminating "Manifesto to the Peoples of the East" at the Baku conference the Bolshevik revolution is presented as the true holy war—a bravura transposition of concepts and fusion of language:

> Now we summon you to the first genuine holy war, under the red banner of the Communist International. . . . We summon you to a holy war for your own well-being, for your freedom, for your life. . . .

This is a holy war for the liberation of the peoples of the East, for the ending of the division of humanity into oppressor peoples and oppressed peoples, for complete equality of all peoples and races, whatever language they may speak, whatever the color of their skin, and whatever the religion they profess. . . .

Wage holy war for the liberation of all humanity from the yoke of capitalist and imperialist slavery, for the ending of all forms of oppression of one people by another and of all forms of exploitation of man by man! . . .

May the holy war of the peoples of the East and of the toilers of the entire world against imperialist Britain burn with unquenchable fire![27]

RAFIQ AHMAD'S UNFORGETTABLE JOURNEY

With Gandhi and the recently freed Ali brothers joining forces in 1920, the Khilafat and Non-Cooperation movements represented the closest domestic rapprochement ever achieved between Indian nationalism and Pan-Islamism, and also the high point of Muslim involvement in the mainstream Indian independence movement.[28] The Khilafat movement was also a major vector through which anticolonial radicals from India got involved in leftist politics in Russia and central Asia—a milieu that they shared with those others who had come the long way around by way of San Francisco and/or Berlin.

The Hijrat movement was an offshoot of the Khilafat movement whose partisans decided that India under infidel rule must be classified as Dar-al-Harb, and therefore that there was no recourse for Muslims to live and practice freely other than to quit India. They might be content simply to dwell elsewhere within the Dar-al-Islam, but they might also feel morally obligated to fight: whether to defend the sultan-caliph's realm or to launch rebellion against British rule in India directly. In 1915, as mentioned above, a small number of idealistic students had arrived in Kabul at Obeidullah's urging and joined forces with the Provisional Government of India. In 1920, thousands more *muhajirs* followed on their trail. Most were poor peasants, and many died on the way from hunger, cold, or bandit attacks. An influential minority, however, were militantly anti-British young men, educated and from service-class backgrounds. Eighty of these departed from north of Kabul in the spring of 1920, prepared to trek to Anatolia to pledge their services to the Khilafat.

During the course of this journey they were courted by the Red Army and attacked by Turkmen counter-revolutionaries. About half of them, having joined the former in defending a town from attack by the latter, were persuaded to transfer their revolutionary zeal from the caliph in Istanbul to the revolutionary regime in Moscow.[29] Receiving military and political training under M. N. Roy's direction, first in Tashkent (which had just been established as the Comintern's Eastern Bureau), and then at the Moscow University of the Toilers of the

202 GHADAR AND THE BOLSHEVIK *MUHAJIRIN*

East, these ex-Khilafatist *muhajirin* were the first to declare a Communist Party of India (CPI), in Tashkent 6 November 1921. Some of them went on to distinguished careers as lifelong party stalwarts.[30]

Initially the trajectory of these *muhajirin* was relatively remote from the usual Ghadar circuits. This was in part due to their loyalty to Roy, who had in effect polarized himself from the various Kabul- and Berlin-based revolutionaries. Although he had started his political career in the Bengal revolutionary movement, was assigned to receive Ghadar's arms shipments from the *Maverick* and *Annie Larsen,* and then upon his arrival in the United States had mingled with the radicals in California and New York, he had parted company with that lineage when he fled the United States for Mexico in 1916. Nevertheless, the physical and mental migration of the *muhajirin* from Kabul to Tashkent to Moscow—in which, Ansari argues, these devout Indian Muslims' discovery of "similarities between Islamist and Bolshevik ideology ... eased [the] transition to socialism"[31]—was facilitated by agents such as Acharya and Barakatullah. But perhaps the best way to access this section of our web is again through the eyes of a participant.

When the twenty-three-year-old Rafiq Ahmad left Delhi on foot in 1920, he was one of hundreds of student radicals among the thousands who set out at the height of the Hijrat movement. He and his brother Kabir were the sons of a retired schoolteacher in Bhopal, where Rafiq himself was in the private employ of a nawab.[32] I do not know what the political or religious leanings of the Ahmad household were, nor how the brothers became interested in attending the 1920 Khilafat conference in Delhi. What is clear is that they were deeply affected by the conference proceedings, throughout which the "Hijrat question" was a topic of heated discussion.

This topic was merely the latest installment in a perennial debate concerning whether British India was technically to be identified as part of the Dar-al-Islam or the Dar-al-Harb, the realm of war. If the latter, there would be no other correct recourse for observant Muslims than to choose one of two options: to stay and fight against infidel rule, or to emigrate to Islamic sovereign territory, and perhaps (though it would not be required) to launch the fight from there.[33] Encouraged by offers of land and livelihood from Amir Amanullah Khan of Afghanistan, about thirty thousand poor peasants relocated there, motivated as much by hope of economic opportunity as by faith, only to come to grief at the hands of marauders and brigands.[34] By summer 1920 five Hijrat offices had opened throughout India; twenty-five thousand travelers left in August alone. Of a cumulative total of sixty thousand, though, two-thirds returned to India, and many more died on the road from Peshawar to Kabul. Of those who survived, many dispersed throughout either central Asia or the Ottoman territories.[35]

It was a minority group who became the *muhajirin* of our story.[36] One of these, Shaukat Usmani, believed that although the primary motivation for the mass of *muhajirin* was either religious conviction or economic aspiration, joining the exodus also offered that section of the intelligentsia disillusioned with the INC's Non-Cooperation program—which seemed to them incapable of achieving *swaraj* (self-rule)— an "opportunity" to "[go] abroad and [study] the methods adopted by other countries in the struggle for independence," methods that could presumably then be applied at home. I cannot say whether this motive is ascribed anachronistically, added years later when Rafiq Ahmad was recording his memoir. Nor do I have any evidence of the degree and character of Rafiq Ahmad's political views prior to the journey. In any case, the *hijrat* message at the conference apparently inspired the Ahmad brothers sufficiently that they decided to head straightaway on foot to Afghanistan rather than going home.

So off they went with a friend or two via Gujranwala, Rawalpindi, and Peshawar to the Afghan border. There they were detained by a Mr. Eden of the CID, who searched and questioned them but found no "objectionable material" on their persons. However, Rafiq did recall: "We plainly told him that we did not want to live under British rule. He told us that we were free. I invited his attention to the handcuffs and asked 'what kind of freedom is this?' At this he smiled and ordered the handcuffs to be removed."[37]

At night they snuck across a wire fence with a guide sent by the imam of a nearby mosque and spent the night in an inn near the border. A guard informed them that that was where the British and Afghan powers confronted each other. Rafiq noted that there were three pukka roads with checkpoints consisting of cement, electric wires, and armed guards on the British side, but on the Afghan side, only a rough path with a single watchman in a tent and a ramshackle customs post. Seeing this, the brothers had doubts about their putative patrons. But a wizened local called Abdul Raheem, perhaps reading their misgivings, assured them that "in war what counted was the internal determination and not the outer pomp and show."[38] Their next stop was Dacca, where a senior officer advised them that despite it being the eve of Ramadan they should skip the fast because of the "long and difficult journey" that awaited them; and then Jalalabad, where Rafiq was stunned by the devastation wrought by British bombardment in the recent Anglo-Afghan war; and finally, to Kabul.

They were greeted with a "passionate and powerful lecture" by the amir, expressing sympathy for the hardships of their journey so far and making claims that struck Rafiq as dubiously grandiose, such as the vow that "the sword of the Ameer will not return to its sheath" until and unless the Khilafat-e-Usman were reestablished. But rather then sending them off westward, he reiterated the offer of land and jobs. They said they hadn't "come looking for land and jobs but for JEHAD [*sic*]."[39]

Nevertheless, they were sent to Jabal-us-Siraj, a settlement forty miles from Kabul, which Usmani described as consisting of five hundred houses in a lovely green valley, protected on three sides by mountains and fertile with almond trees and vineyards. The *muhajirin* were told to stay there in a guesthouse co-occupied by a family of Menshevik refugees. After two months as "state guests," they were to come back to choose occupations in their new home; the offer was open to join universities or the army.[40] In the meantime, while waiting, they elected an "exile committee" with Akbar Khan Qureishi as president, whom Usmani considered "a man of extraordinary ability and perseverance." With the help of this committee they arranged sports and activities, including drills and military exercises with sticks as practice rifles, under the efficient guidance of the ex-soldiers among them.[41] In fact, so proficient did they appear that the Afghan army invited them to join up on the spot. But it would not approve their desire to launch a fight against British rule from Afghan territory across India's northwestern frontier, which from the *muhajirs*' perspective, pointed out Usmani, was the whole point.[42] They declined.

By summer of 1920, there were 180 *muhajirin* at Jabal-us-Siraj. Our two narrators were among the first caravans; Rafiq tells us that when news of their arrival in Kabul reached India, it sparked a new rush of eager departures. But as their numbers grew so did their restiveness, and their disillusionment with the apparent obstructionism of an Afghan monarch who did not seem to have any intention of facilitating their quest.[43] In the robust phrasing of Rafiq's traveling companion from Delhi, Mohammed Khan, "You may tie us to the cannon mouths, tie us to the feet of elephants, but we will not go to [Jabal-us-Siraj]." This was their state of mind when they received an invitation to come to tea at the Russian consulate with Acharya, his colleague Abdur Rab, and PGI official Maulana Obeidullah Sindhi.

Rab was a Peshawari scholar who had worked in the British Embassy at Baghdad at the beginning of the war. Once Turkey declared for Germany, and the British abandoned the city, they left him behind "in the hope that he would take advantage of his being a Muslim to smuggle information" to them.[44] But instead he threw in his lot with their enemies. After the war he went to Ankara, then Kabul. In 1919 he accompanied Barakatullah from Kabul to Moscow; according to Ansari, "[Rab] was to play a major part, not just in winning the support of the Bolsheviks [for the Indian cause], but also in drawing the attention of the Muhajirin to the Soviet system."[45] However, Abdur Rab's relations with the Bolsheviks cooled as they judged his politics (and those of the *muhajirin* who gravitated to his faction as opposed to Roy's) to be fundamentally more nationalist than socialist; Roy, as self-appointed arch-Communist, dismissed Rab as a Pan-Islamist and/or a nationalist at heart. Rab relocated to Turkey in the mid-1920s, where he remained largely distanced from Indian political activities, married a Turkish woman, and eventually died.[46]

In 1920, however, Rab and Acharya were at the center of Indian organizing in Kabul, at least until they had a falling out with Obeidullah and Barakatullah over tactics: the latter, sensitive to British perceptions, did not want to antagonize their Afghan hosts by working too openly with the Soviet delegates there, whereas Rab and Acharya favored more overt opposition to the British whether the Afghans approved or not.[47] So the irreconcilables decamped in February 1920 along with a few other "fellow socialist-minded exiles" to shift their recently founded Inquilab-i-Hind, or Indian Revolutionary Association, to Tashkent. By March their initial membership of 27 had swelled to 115; they sent 7 delegates to Baku and published materials to inform Indians about the Russian Revolution.[48]

Before their departure they presented a proposal to the *muhajirin:* Come with us to Russia, "where a great revolution has taken place and the government is in the hands of the workers. [You] may see many things and learn if [you] go there." What should the *muhajirin* do? Rafiq for one was amenable to the proposal, recalling: "We wanted to reach this land of revolution as soon as possible." It certainly seems possible that writing in retrospect he too is prematurely anticipating his own leftist conversion. On the other hand, it may be that both his interest in revolutionary Russia and his attraction to the Hijrat movement were equal expressions of his penchant for social justice, whatever the vehicle.

Usmani implies that even at this early point there were several opinions among the dwellers in the valley. Most, he said, would have been content to remain at Kabul, having satisfied their purpose of quitting an India under infidel rule. But a few, "fanatics" in Usmani's estimation, were dead set on fighting for the caliph in Anatolia. Finally, there was a third faction, about forty strong, whom Usmani describes as "tried souls whose hearts were burning with the zeal of patriotism." Their prayers," he said, "were the prayers for freedom. They owed allegiance to none except to mother Liberty." These would become the Communist *muhajirin.*

Eighty men accepted the offer and sent a request to Amanullah Khan for leave to embark toward Anatolia. Although the amir replied unequivocally that anyone leaving "without permission would be shot down," they loaded their luggage on their backs and made a grand exit from Friday prayers behind a commander who "took a black flag in his hand and moved forward with the slogans of AL-LAHU AKBAR [*sic*]."[49] They headed out up the steep Panjsheer Valley. Usmani described fording swift, chill streams in a file, with the taller of them foremost, linked by hands on shoulders and turbans tied to waists; a horse was swept away, along with the luggage it bore.[50] They quickly lost their bearings in the mountains, but somehow—Usmani credited Akbar Khan Qureishi's courage and Abdul Majid's "fine management" skills—they crossed the Hindu Kush, climbing through landscapes of great drama. Usmani described the trek: "[We crossed] rugged hills, dales, fast flowing ice-cold rivers, and the awesome desert.... Ravines and caves took on the shape of open-mouthed dragons. ... At places the mountain paths, cut into the steep sides, were so narrow and hazardous that [even] walking in single file was virtually impossible."[51] They breakfasted on bread and cheese washed down with tea or snow, or local melons; some days they accomplished fifteen-hour marches without food. Once they descended into more populous areas, they would send someone on ahead to arrange tandoori bread and tea at a local inn, pooling their cash to pay for the food.

In Mazar-e-Sharif they met a Turk who had been in the Ottoman army during the war but was captured by the Russians and sent to Siberia; now he was trying to get home. The band of *muhajirin* gave him Indian clothes and the name of one of their fellows who was no longer with them. This new Sarfaraz, who spoke Russian, Turkish, and Persian, seemed likely to be a useful improvement over the old one, a tailor who had been detained by Afghan officials in connection with "some blot on his character."[52]

At last they crossed the Oxus from Afghan territory into Russian Turkestan, newly proclaimed as an Autonomous Soviet Socialist Republic.[53] They were met at Tirmiz by a welcoming committee consisting of a band and a Red Army detachment with an honor guard for "the revolutionaries from India," raising shouts of "Long live the solidarity of the oppressed people," "Long live the free people of India," and other slogans, "which being in Russian we could not understand," reported Usmani. "But assuming that they were cheering us, some of us cried 'Bande Mataram,' while our orthodoxy replied with 'Allah-O-Akbar.'"[54]

The commander made a speech, saying in effect that all the wealth, land, and houses of liberated Russia belonged to all the oppressed and working people of the world. They were entitled to all local rights and could be assured of support from the workers and peasants of Russia in their fight for their country's freedom. As smiling Red Army soldiers escorted them to their lodgings in a military barracks, the crowd "surged forward to see us," with women and children shouting revolutionary slogans in Turkish and Russian. The road-weary Indians felt ashamed of their bedraggled appearance, some shoeless, but a solicitous officer arrived to offer the services of a cobbler, tailor, and washerman. Even better, samovars awaited them, along with raisins, tobacco, white bread, and butter. Sheep were at that very moment being slaughtered and cooked by Bokharan chefs.

Were Rafiq Ahmad's heart and mind beginning to be won over by the warm reception? If so, the Bolsheviks were succeeding in their intent. But not all of Rafiq's cohorts were affected in the same way. His account is a bit unclear on this point, but Usmani states plainly that the group was by this time divided about equally into two factions. He himself was embarrassed by the bad impression he feared the intra-Indian discord was making on the Russians, and deplored the "fanaticism" of "our Pan-Islamist section,"[54] who he said were "cursing like lunatics" and insulting the Russians as kafirs. Usmani's response to these kafirs, though, was wonder and "bewilder[ment] to find white people addressing us as comrades." But they quickly "understood one another" to be deeply united across the color line by "revolutionary comradeship." He recalled: "For the first time in our lives, we were seeing Europeans mixing freely with Asians. . . . We were convinced that we had come to a land of real equality."[56]

Here they stayed from July to August of 1920, enjoying their fill of free cinema while awaiting the riverboats that would take them on the next leg. Once recovered, the young men grew restless again. Half of them were eager to see postrevolutionary Russia, while the other half were angry at the Russians for trying to dissuade them from attempting to reach Anatolia through hostile territory. Claiming that as fellow Muslims they were not afraid of the insurgent Turkomans, they insisted on leaving against their hosts' advice. The left-leaning faction, says Usmani, reluctantly agreed with the Russian president of Tirmiz that they had to go along too, to prevent the Indian public from believing any rumor that the Russians had killed them for being Pan-Islamists should the expedition come to grief.[57]

Sure enough, shortly after embarking in two small boats, they were detained by Turkomans in a riverside village who attacked them with sticks, looted their baggage, hung on the masts of their boats, and insulted the Koran—an odd detail for Rafiq to include, given the circumstances. Sarfaraz tried to tell the attackers that these were "Indian migrants, on HIJRAT [sic] due to the intolerable and barbarous treatment of Britishers." The Turkomans retorted that they liked the British (the anti-Soviet Basmachi rebels were indeed receiving British funding) and accused the band of being infidels, Jadedis,[58] and Bolsheviks.[59] They locked the *muhajirs* inside an inn for a week. Rafiq had a light head wound from a boy's sword. To bear their captivity, some of them read the Koran and did Namaz. Yet the locals remained convinced against empirical logic that they must be Bolsheviks, scoffing: "Look even kaffirs do it."[60] How could they have behaved in such a reprehensible manner? Rafiq wondered. By all accounts the hostility of the Turkomans, contrasted with the warm reception of the Russians, was no small factor in persuading some of the *muhajirin* to switch allegiance.

The prisoners waited as the council of elders debated: should they be executed singly or killed en masse? They attempted to resign themselves with dignity to their fate, reassuring one another that they were dying in the line of duty, serving India's cause.[61] But this was not after all to be the day of their martyrdom: they were saved by the "miracle" of a barrage of shelling from a Bolshevik steamer coincidentally passing on the river, unaware of their presence. Captors and prisoners huddled together under two more days and a night of bombardment, during which Rafiq impressed his captor with his "Persian stories of Muslim prophets."[62] At last the Turkomans cut their fetters and evacuated, leaving them at liberty but relieved of their possessions. They spent the day laboriously scavenging for food and searching for one another. By nightfall, sixty-nine had regrouped; eleven had been killed.

Together they reached the Russian fortress at Kirki on the banks of the Oxus. They explained who they were, with an Afghan merchant helping to translate.

Once the story was verified by radioing to Tirmiz, they were again welcomed. "Two big barracks were provided for us, and once more we knew what comfort was and, moreover, what freedom meant," declared Usmani: "Plenty of rations, good food, friendship and revolutionary literature to read!"[63] When Kirki came under attack, thirty-six of them offered to join in the defense, to the delight of the Russians. They were given guns, ammunition, and battle stations. For a week the *muhajirin* held the river approach to the fortress against three thousand attackers, thwarting a few close shaves through cunning subterfuge and extreme vigilance. Afterward, the Russian commander informed them that "the attack of the counter-revolutionaries was successfully met and [now] we were to launch a counter-attack. . . . We could drop out of this counter-attack if we chose, but . . . our participation would make them happy." They accepted. After the successful attack, they received yet another warm Red Army welcome. Flowers were thrown at the railway junction amid shouts of "Long live the defenders of Kirkee," "Long live the Indian comrades," and "Long live the international solidarity of the workers of the world."[64]

By now, however, the group's factional differences appeared thoroughly crystallized. Those who shared Rafiq's and Usmani's interest in "this land of revolution" wanted to go to Tashkent, only recently designated as the headquarters for the Comintern's Eastern Bureau, where Roy was waiting to welcome them into his revolutionary training school. Others had not abandoned the urgent goal of reaching Anatolia. Some, having had more than their fill of adventure, just wanted to go home. Nevertheless, those bound for Turkey or India still agreed that a stop in Tashkent would allow them to gather strength, supplies, and passports.

The train passed through the city of Bokhara, recently seized from its recalcitrant amir and established as a People's Soviet Republic alongside Turkestan.[65] Here the passionate sympathy of the Young Bokharan "Jadedis" (i.e., the modernists, or the progressives, as against the supporters of the mullah and amir) to the Indian plight made a strong impression on the *muhajirin*. When they arrived in Tashkent two or three days later, Abdur Rab was there to meet them and escorted them to their spacious rooms in India House. Now Rafiq Ahmad offered some glimpses of the factional "tussle" between Roy on one side and Rab and Acharya on the other: Abdur Rab said they should join the existing party (i.e., his and Acharya's Indian Revolutionary Association), form a provisional government (which already existed in Kabul), and get aid in that capacity from the Russians. Roy said they should form a proper Communist Party ("so that he could achieve an international position," scoffed Rafiq later). To date Roy was the Third International's Secretary for the Far East and a member of the Executive Committee of the Comintern but was not recognized as the representative of the Indians. Rafiq tried to query Rab further about his specific plans but was rebuffed, with Rab saying he could tell only formal members about his programme.[66] He also called

himself "Father of the Revolutionaries," a claim for which Rafiq saw no justifica-
tion. On the other hand, "we told M. N. Roy also that we would not join any party
unless we were convinced about the correctness of its line of action." (Again, this
sounds like veteran communist Rafiq's words in young *muhajir* Rafiq's mouth!)

Impatient with the whole quarrel, and annoyed with both leaders, Rafiq asked
to be sent back to Afghanistan. It was "very cold . . . impossible to do anything"
worthwhile in Tashkent; there was snow all around; he was sick, and he had swol-
len feet. But Roy suggested instead that if he wanted a task he should join Usmani
in Andijan, where he had been sent on a secret mission, scouting for a possible
route across the Pamirs into India and looking for contacts among Kashgari rebels, who opposed their British-backed khan. Rafiq took up the challenge; upon
wrapping up Usmani's operation, he came back to join Roy's school: "We were
given regular military training along with political education. . . . Some were getting air force training."[67] Meanwhile the infantry class was trained in "theory and
practice of musketry and machine guns," and also a little on "field guns." According to Rafiq's classmate Habib Ahmed, "The object of putting us through these
courses was said to be to fit us to serve our country or to serve in the Bolshevist
army, whichever we preferred. We were not told that it was to fit us to fight against
the English."[68]

Outside of class, they were assigned two-hour guard-duty rotations. Many of
them cheated on their shifts, admitted Rafiq, sometimes feigning illness or moving their watches ahead to tap the next guard early: "The military officers felt
disgusted. . . . At that time we did not feel anything but later we used to feel
ashamed of ourselves."[69]

The frigid houses were lit by kerosene lamps and candles; a stove in the base-
ment had only enough wood to light for short periods twice a day when cooking. A
committee of three was appointed to organize the allotment of rooms and the few
available cots and to avoid conflict over who got the warmest ones. They "readily
agreed" with Roy's suggestion that "preference should be given to those not in good
health and also to the aged," since there were a couple of "greybeards who had
joined the crusade for the defense of the Khilafat." Usmani noted further: "It was
a miracle that they had survived the hardships of their journey over the snow-
peaked Hindukush."[70] Roy remarked that "as a matter of fact, about a dozen young
men of the company [soon] proved to be very helpful" in mediating complaints
and quarrels, such as the common grievance of some people going through the
tobacco stock too fast. We may witness here the budding of good communist organizers. In the meantime there was plenty of debate and discussion among these
young men poised between ideologies, on pressing questions such as "Why are the
Russians against religion?" and "Is the meat in Tashkent halal?"[71]

Roy distinguished between the "educated few," the protégés whom he hoped
to cultivate, and the "ignorant majority," on whom he more or less gave up.[72]

Even regarding those he considered worthy of cultivation, he claimed that he was not initially planning to turn them communist, but to train them as leaders for a national democratic revolution with the "minimum level of political conscious-ness" necessary for that task. However, some of them initiated an ideological conversion far beyond his own stated tactical preference. (In any case Usmani later claims Roy's denial was calculatedly disingenuous, and that the whole thing was exactly as he planned.) A few of them were eager to start a Communist Party for India and declared one immediately on 17 October 1920. Mohammed Shafiq, an "intelligent and fairly well educated young man" who had come from Kabul with Acharya, was elected secretary.[73]

After only a few months the Tashkent operation was shut down on account of the Anglo-Russian trade agreement, which stipulated that Russia refrain from supporting anti-British activities within its territories. Suffering economically, the Russians needed the deal. The British refused to negotiate unless the Indian revo-lutionaries left central Asia. So school and command center shifted operations to Moscow under new names and forms, and the infant emigrant CPI was affiliated with the Comintern in 1921.

During the train journey from Tashkent to Moscow, Rafiq was able to view the full panorama of the harsh times: with famine abroad, hungry people clung to the passing train in hopes of food. Red Army soldiers went rationless as they guarded storehouses of grain against burning by British agents whose funds were "flowing like water" to the various central Asian counter-revolutionaries. Once in Moscow the *muhajirin* were starstruck by the glamour of the city. Usmani praised its glit-tering art and architecture, its "spires, colored domes and brilliant pinnacles," and its inseparable fusion of East and West. The *muhajirin* toured the Kremlin, the Kolomna motor and engine factory, children's colonies and kindergartens, and model humane prisons.[74] A few days after arriving, they enrolled at the University of the Toilers of the East, aka the University of the Toiling Masses of the Eastern Autonomous and Associated Republics. More also joined the Communist Party.

According to Abdul Majid, when they first arrived "there was no arrangement for instruction, . . . we just used to go to an office and read newspapers." But later, classes were held at the Hotel De Lux, where quite a few notables of the interna-tional left were also lodged. In this new phase of their education, Rafiq said they learned history and political economy and received training in the organization of labor and the development of industry. Habib Ahmed listed history and social-ism, including agrarian-colonial questions, as the principal subjects of the six-month course. "The object which the Russians had in educating us," Sultan Ma-jid explained, "was that we should on return home work for the overthrow of the British Government. We neither refused or accepted this mission." Abdul Qader concurred that they were being instructed with "the object to defeat capitalism and work for the overthrow of governments run on that principle," including presumably the one imposed upon their own country. Ferozuddin Mansur observed that the immediate goal was the "training of Eastern peoples in the propaganda of socialism in the East."[75]

Ferozuddin also remarked: "We were all taken to the University with the intention—on the part of the Bolsheviks—of being trained as communist propaganda agents. We were selected because of our education and made to change our names," so that the British wouldn't be able to trace them. "We were repeatedly told in the lectures at the University that as communists we must, on our return home, work for the good of our country on communist lines viz: for the overthrow of the present Government and the establishment of a communist one." Akbar Shah agreed: "The Bolsheviks educated us as propagandists. They told me and all the others to speak well of Bolshevism when we get to our homes. I have been trained in the Aviation class at Tashkent also. The theory of propaganda which the Bolsheviks want spread is that all men are equal and that this equality can only be given practical effect by a world revolution in the cause of which the money now in the hands of the rich will be divided among the poor." But he expressed some reservations about the realism of this utopian vision: "I do not think this argument will carry much weight with the local Zamindars and I do not intend to preach it. . . . In Moscow I did not mix in Russian Society, but there seemed to be the same distinction between rich and poor as everywhere else. A loaf of bread cost thousands of roubles but there were crowds of people driving around in motor cars."[76]

After their final exams (which Sultan says they passed, and Abdul Majid says most of them failed),[77] there was a celebration in their honor, according to Rafiq, which was attended by Chicherin and Zinoviev. Trotsky sent his regrets. The Soviet luminaries pledged all aid to the Indians in their next tasks. In fact, some of the *muhajirin* had already started disappearing mysteriously, and Rafiq and his friends suspected they had been sent to India. Late in March 1922 a party of ten (the third group to leave, according to Habib and Ferozuddin) finally left Moscow with an itinerary leading from Tashkent via Kharok in the Pamirs to Chitral on the Indian border.[78]

For part of the way by train they were to accompany a 250-strong division of the Red Army, which paused occasionally along the way to deal with Enver Pasha's counter-revolutionaries or their suppliers. At Takht-e-Suleiman, the last railroad station before the mountains, they purchased horses, camels, and food for the crossing. Unfortunately, while crossing the Amu Darya, two horses loaded with army machine guns were swept away. In fact, by the time they reached the Murghab-e-Russ fort near the Chinese border, most of the horses and half the camels had expired, leaving them with a paltry stable of four camels and one horse. Although four-fifths of the Red Army were going on foot by this time through similar attrition, an officer gave Rafiq a new mount, and the others received camel replacements. Rafiq mentioned that in addition to the animals they were also given sugar as an aid to breathing in high altitudes.[79]

They then followed the river to the Karakorum range through an uninhabited landscape of swampy ground, "soft like clouds," and passed into the Altai, hampered by snow. After spending a night in a roofless army post in the plain of Pamir, they moved downhill to a Russian camp set up in front of an Afghan fort. A treaty was in force allowing both Afghans and Russians to make use of the market unmolested. Rafiq's group stayed there a week in a bungalow while unbeknownst to them the army's CP unit was "busy making arrangements for our journey." Then one night Rafiq, Habib, and Majid were summoned, given shoes and local dress, a bit of cash, and a letter for someone called Suleiman, and told they would be starting in the early morning.[80]

They set out on foot down the Amur Valley, and by evening they reached a village at the foot of the mountain, again flanked by Russian and Afghan forts facing opposite sides of the river. Their host in the village offered the use of his guest room, and then promptly informed the Russians at the fort that he had spies staying at his place. Arriving with their squad commander, four soldiers held the trio at gunpoint. They rose to their feet, surprised. Rafiq said that unwittingly his hand went to his gun and removed it from his side. He asked, in Russian, "Don't you know us?" at which point the commander luckily did recognize them and asked if they needed anything. Majid admitted that some tobacco and matches would not go unappreciated. The commander brought these, along with a ration of tea and sugar and the advice not to trust the local border folk. "I won't ask you where you're going," he said. "I don't want to know." Then he took his leave.[81]

The four comrades left again in the early morning and reached the house of the mysterious Suleiman, "the only big house in the pass." Their host ushered them inside, read the letter they bore, and addressing Rafiq as Farooq without missing a beat, informed his servants that the travelers were visiting goldsmiths. In private, Suleiman told them he could supply a guide for a price of four pounds, and carefully explained the route. They rested at the house all day and departed that night, crossing the river on camels back into Afghan territory. The mountains in those parts, reported Rafiq, were 22,000 feet high, treacherous with deep gorges, some with solid-seeming crusts of snow concealing the drop. There was no grass or trees, only rock slopes, and the constant danger of being shot or arrested. On this moonlit night Rafiq feared their black clothes would be visible against the snow, but they crept along behind the cover of the ridge with food and bedding on their backs. They heard dogs barking and, at one point, someone on horseback looking for them.

Their new shoes felt no better than walking barefoot. Although breathing proved difficult (despite the sugar), they needed speed to reach a cave where they could spend the night. Finally, Habib Ahmad could no longer walk. "Leave me to my fate and you all go ahead," he urged his companions. Refusing to leave him, Rafiq and Majid divided his load between themselves to give him some relief. But a little while later Ferozuddin was also forced to "[declare] his helplessness," so the remaining fit pair divided up his load too. There was nothing for it but to proceed, trying to follow the footprints of the guide in the snow, who had gone on ahead.[82] The path was narrow, along a deep gorge. They tied ropes to the waists of Habib and Feroz to help them walk, only to be faced with a slope so steep that they had to go down on their rumps. They slid down wrapped in bedding, having realized that they needed such wrapping to protect themselves from those above who were sending pebbles tumbling down onto those below.

Next was a snowy valley, clear for passage. The guide assured them that it was safe; the army would not come through there. So they walked through the pass. The weather was overcast, and it was still snowing. They made a tent out of their blankets and sticks and sat huddled inside. When the snow on the top got too heavy, they stood up together to throw it off, and then sat back down. It snowed all night, but there was sun in the morning. Forward march. By evening they had come to a place of stone slabs and flowing water, where they spent the night. The guide said they were approaching the border. On the other side of the next mountain would be Chitral. They climbed all day, sometimes on all fours for the steepness, and reached the ridge in the early evening. Before them was a smooth downslope with a cave at the bottom, where the guide made a fire, and they slept "very peacefully and comfortably, but hungry because we had exhausted our supplies."

Feroz and Habib by now were losing their toenails to frostbite; their companions carried them piggyback to spare their bleeding feet. They had left the snow behind, but the cold was intense. Someone fell through a thin layer of ice into the waist-deep river. Ahead was a forest, the first trees they had seen. The guide made bread from flour and river water, baked on a flat stone, and then pointed them toward the pass into Chitral, indicating that the Indian border was as far as he went. Still, they kept each other's company as far as a village, where they purchased food from a house owner. They ate it on the spot with his family, gobbling fast and furiously. "Everyone was in a hurry to eat as much as possible," recalled Rafiq. "The wife of the owner was on my right side and sometimes used to push me aside and eat and sometimes I used to push her aside. In a few minutes the food was finished."[83]

There still remained several more days of travel, during which they managed to hire horses for Feroz and Habib and began to encounter other travelers on the road, such as a group that said it was on haj to Mazar-e-Sharif. Our comrades decided that such a pilgrimage would make a fine cover story if need be. By the time they stopped in Chitral, they looked so travel-worn and weather-beaten that people took them for beggars and offered them money. They spent the night at an inn in the market, where they found new clothes to replace the lice-ridden ones they were wearing, and because they "urgently needed Indian dress so that we may not be considered outsiders." Maybe it was the tailor who told on them, Rafiq speculated, but in any case, somehow the local inspector heard about them. They were called in for questioning by a private secretary. He was an Afghan student who received an English newspaper; when he noticed Habib reading it, he "realized that we were educated people," which may have raised an alarm. "So he behaved politely with us, but sent us before the political agent just the same." Now was their chance to use the Mazar-e-Sharif story. Apparently it was plausible enough that the ruler of Chitral offered them each fifty rupees and something to wear, but not plausible enough to avert all suspicion.[84]

Rafiq's account here is a bit confusing. Were they being detained? Were the Chitral authorities already in touch with the CID? Did the travelers know yet that they would not make it home free? When they told the agent about their journey he was quite surprised; he had thought the road impassable. Unfortunately for our quartet the Peshawar intelligence bureau chief was less sure. Superintendent J.M. Ewart claimed in his deposition for the Peshawar cases that the Pamir route had already been scouted and assessed, and the entry point into India was watched. The Bolsheviks had long been trying to make use of this route he asserted, but it had become possible only with recent developments, namely the death of Enver Pasha in summer of 1922, and the subsequent collapse of the rebellion that had simmered in the Ferghana area from 1919 to 1921, in collusion with the British consul general in Kashgar. Moreover, Ewart noted, the 1922 expulsion of all Indian seditionists from Afghanistan had closed that more usual route to them and pushed them toward this one.[85]

The four *muhajirin* were free to move about the city but only under guard. Then they were escorted by mule to Peshawar, and there the journey ended in their arrest. The guards were polite and apologized as they removed their handcuffs. They were brought for meals at the ironically named Hajee Hotel, the owner of which recognized Rafiq from the outward journey to Kabul a year and a half before.

The police report stated that Rafiq Ahmed, Habib Ahmad, Ferozuddin Mansur, Abdul Majid, Sultan Muhammad, Abdul Qader, and Fida Ali Khan were all intercepted at Chitral trying to enter India via the Pamirs after an absence of two years,[86] during which they had received "training in revolutionary propaganda at the Tashkent Propaganda School and the Moscow University for the Workers of the East." There was clear evidence that they had been sent back as "secret Russian agents and propagandists of revolution."[87]

Was this true? Shaukat Usmani stated years later in a letter that while returning to India via Persia or via the arduous route through the Pamirs, some had been in contact with revolutionaries in Bengal and the United Provinces, and also with the tribal militants in the North-West Frontier who had hosted the Lahore students in 1915, and to whom arms were now being sent "in sufficient quantities." "The modern bombs, which exploded against the British in the period after 1921, had the original prescription from the USSR brought here by one of our group," he noted. Some were also in touch with Abul Kalam Azad.[87]

They were placed in jail and forbidden to communicate with one another. Nevertheless, another prisoner, with feet in chains, managed to approach Rafiq, threw him some tobacco and matches, and let him know that Majid and Feroz were close by. They exchanged small messages—"Don't worry," "I am also here"—and eventually learned that five others were in the Peshawar jail too. As it turned out, they had been sent separately in their various small groups, now reunited in unfortunate circumstances.[89]

The chief commissioner of North-West Frontier Province recommended to the foreign secretary in Delhi that preferably they should be incarcerated for a long time in separate jails. Simply letting them free on security of good behavior would not be enough, because "the work for which they have been trained and sent to India is such that they could carry it out secretly without running the slightest risk."[90] They were to be accused under Section 121A of the Indian Penal Code for the crime of conspiring against the king-emperor. One or two were to be offered pardon for turning approver.[91] They were tried in a series of trials over the next two years known collectively as the Peshawar Conspiracy cases—the first in a series of famous anti-Communist trials throughout the 1920s.[92]

These were precisely the overlapping (or conflicting) identities that the *muhajirin* had to negotiate for themselves. Given the nature of the sources, it is difficult to interpret which of these loyalties took precedence at each stage of the journey. In the various statements given at Peshawar, the factual details about the trip from India to Afghanistan to Tashkent to Moscow and back through Soviet central Asia to the Chitral border are consistent with each other. The travelers' true motives, intentions, allegiances, aspirations, and beliefs, on the other hand, are impossible to verify. How much of the Bolshevik affiliation of those arrested at Chitral was due to genuine conviction, and how much to expediency? Had their ultimate commitments changed drastically over the course of the journey, or had they remained consistent, though transposed into a different mode and idiom, as I have argued was the case for the Ghadar Party? Beneath the opposition that Usmani sets up between modernity and tradition, rationalism and mysticism, was their conversion to Bolshevism a fundamental break from their identification with the Khilafat movement, or a continuation of the impulses that had led them on Hijrat in the first place? A transposition or an antithesis? As Nikki Keddie points out in her portrait of Jamal ad-Din al-Afghani's thinking, what may have seemed like inconsistency in his rhetoric over time is undergirded by a single consistent purpose, namely, instrumental opposition to British imperialism.[93] Here too the critique and the imperative for resistance are not in question; only the mode and rationale vary, according to a pragmatic search for inspirational efficacy.

A telegram from the consul general in Meshed to the foreign secretary in Delhi, reporting on some Turkey-bound militants captured in Persia, read: "To me all expressed penitence, but an informer who speaks Russian states that ex-Lance Daffadar of 6th King Edward's Own Cavalry by name Ghulam Ahmad has been extolling Russian freedom in Russian which he speaks fluently."[94] Another telegram of 24 May 1922 from army captain G. L. Stratton in Mussoorie to his adjutant-general in Simla included a translation of a letter Stratton had gotten from a Serb who had encountered a young Indian at a British consulate hospital (location unspecified) where they had both been convalescing. The Indian was to be sent back to India and placed under some sort of probation. But in the meantime he had struck up an enthusiastic conversation in Russian with the Serb while they were waiting for their medicine, saying: "There is a very good Red Army in Russia, the best in the world. Russia is a free country." The Serb reported further: "He told me he had been through the Indian propaganda courses in Tashkent and Moscow and was allowed absolute freedom while there. He was chiefly enraptured by the freedom he received in Russia." The Serb asked the Indian: "You of course do not want India to have such 'freedom' as is in Russia?" The reply: "We should be happy without the English. Now in India it is always revolution and it will be until the English go." The Serb then said: "If you speak like that in India it will go badly for you." He replied: "At first I will speak badly about Russia, and after I will go back to Russia, as Russia is a good place to be in."[95]

Approver Abdul Qader, even while allowing his questioners to glimpse the mechanisms of the organizational assignments that many of his companions had denied point-blank, nevertheless implied that the indoctrination imparted by their patrons was weak:

> All our training was revolutionary, and we were all told to do revolutionary propaganda on our return to India and to keep in touch with each other and to communicate with Mohammed Ali in Kabul.[96] Shafiq is another of the chief workers of the revolutionary party and, if we got in touch with him, we should also be expected to work under him. He has made several secret journeys to India and may be in India now for all I know. . . . This was our training but all the time we really wished to get home. I do not think that any of the batch of boys with whom I have come are convinced Communists but they do, according to their conversations while I have been journeying with them, intend to join in political movements against the British Government. Habib Ahmed, Abdul Majid, Rafiq Ahmad and Feroz Din all talked in this way.[97]

But if forty years later when he recorded his memoir Rafiq was still a close comrade of Roy's lieutenant in Bengal, Muzaffar Ahmed (who refers to him fondly as Rafiq Bhai), his leftist commitment was more than passing. Although he declined Usmani's invitation to the Sixth Comintern Congress in 1928, he remained a faithful party member at least until 1967, when he wished the Soviet people his best in a congratulatory message on their fiftieth anniversary and expressed his wish that he could be there personally.[98]

Of the other Bolshevik *muhajirin* that we have been following, some did drift out of active politics. But others remained active for years to come in the young CPI, the Naujavan Bharat Sabha, and/or the Kirti communist grouping in Punjab. Indeed, Muzaffar Ahmed credited the returning *muhajirin* as one of the two main catalysts for the growth of "real" communism in that region, the other being the returning Ghadarites from North America.

Ferozuddin Mansur took on the editorship of the *Kirti*'s Urdu edition in 1928 after Bhagat Singh went underground. He also made an Urdu translation of a booklet of Usmani's; the latter described him as "a good comrade," despite his habit of "publishing everything under his own name." After independence and partition, Mansur headed up the new Communist Party of Pakistan. Abdul Majid was one of the central organizers behind the formation of the Naujavan Bharat Sabha in 1926. Around the same time he started an Urdu weekly from Lahore called *Mehnatkash* (Labor).[99] Becoming a member of the Executive Committee of the CPI after attending the domestic founding conference in Kanpur in December 1925,[100] he also served as a secretary and, later, vice president in the Kirti Kisan Party, and a member of the committee appointed to prepare its rules and programme.[101] He too was arrested in connection with the Meerut case in March 1929.

Aside from those captured and tried in the Peshawar Conspiracy cases, other *muhajirs* had undertaken errands to Mongolia, Bokhara, or Turkestan. As of April 1925, there were ex-*muhajirs* in Moscow learning aviation,[102] writing or translating propaganda materials into Urdu,[103] or touring Russian factories to deliver speeches about India.[104] Among the original runaway students of 1915, both Iqbal Shaidai and PGI officer Zafar Hasan collaborated with Teja Singh Swatantra on his Istanbul front business, and on his efforts there toward Sikh-Muslim understanding. Swatantra and Hasan "prepared an agreement on which the signatures of Obeidullah and the representatives of the Ghadar and Akali parties were to be obtained," and Swatantra wrote an article in July 1926 entitled "The Akali Movement and Hindus and Muhammedans," which Hasan then dispatched to the *Mussalman* in Calcutta.[105] Their erstwhile leader, Fazl Elahi Qurban, finally returned to India from Russia in 1927, made contact with communists and other revolutionists in Calcutta, and within a few months was arrested and sentenced to five years' rigorous imprisonment.[106] I have no information on how he spent the 1930s, but in 1946 he represented the CPI on a propaganda tour of California and gave speeches in San Francisco, Sacramento, Fresno, and

Stockton, advocating collaboration between Ghadarites and Soviets.[107] Back in India in 1947 he teamed up with Swatantra to launch the short-lived (three weeks) Pakistan Communist Party as an attempted successor to Kirti as an autonomous regional counterweight to the CPI in Punjab.[108]

Usmani sums up:

> This travelogue, this piece of history, this journey, is not a pilgrimage without politics. We had started on our journey because of the political situation in our country. The entire country was in revolt. The foreigners, the British imperialists, had made our lives impossible. There was not a single soul in India who did not feel the urge for freedom. . . .
>
> Thus, we, the *Muhajireen,* who had faced all sorts of hardships through the mountainous territory of Afghanistan, were not adventurers or self-seekers. We had an ache in our hearts . . . and we had faith in all those who had declared their support for the Indian freedom struggle.[109]

The form and articles of this faith, it seems, were less important than the quality of commitment to its pragmatic political object.

The Khilafat movement collapsed as a significant political force in 1924, when Ataturk abolished the institution of the caliphate and Soviet policy for revolutionizing the East shifted from central Asia to China. After this, those who had been participants in this stream of activism polarized: the radical anticolonialists tended secular and left, while those emphasizing religion tended toward the new focus of Pakistani nationalism. Khilafat committees continued to meet for several years but grew increasingly marginal to the main currents of national liberation and social change.

One can only speculate about what might have happened if the caliphate had continued; if a synthesis—or at least an alliance of convenience—had remained vital and viable for a longer time between left and Islamic movements. Even in the malleable moment prior to the post-Khilafat polarization, did the Moscow and Tashkent alumni become progressive Marxists by rejecting their religion, by switching allegiances completely from one box to another? Or did they retain their religious identities within and through their Marxist one? If the latter, was this a purely cultural/ethnic identity, or did it also play a role in their ideological expression? Or was it possible for them to continue to view their mission through all three lenses simultaneously? Insofar as they did, was it only because of youthfully fuzzy revolutionary impulses, more emotional than reasoned, or conflicted ambivalence during a transitional period? Or was it a consciously chosen stance? For Barakatullah and Obeidullah, both instrumental in starting the *muhajirin* off on their journey to Tashkent and Moscow, the latter was true. Both of these respected activist scholars elaborated ways to interpret Islam and socialism as eminently compatible.[110]

TWO SOCIALIST ISLAMISTS

Even if we adjust for the imperial paranoid obsession with the dreaded bugbear of a Muslim-Bolshevik combine, it is important to recognize that Ghadar's interface with Pan-Islamism after World War I occurred largely through the medium of Communism, which often provided the vocabulary and organizational vehicle for the aspirations they had in common. Nor is it coincidental that the deepest and most lasting collaborations and interactions between Ghadar's postwar manifestation and Pan-Islamism were with those strands in which the latter was most closely engaging with contemporary socialist ideas. There were other points at which the alliance did not take, namely, where the goals and principles of the Islamists in question diverged especially drastically from those of the Ghadar and BIC partisans. W.C. Smith would have said that this was a reactionary Islam suited for the aristocrats and their persistent feudal-clerical social order, just as there was also an Islam articulated to suit the aspirations, needs, and self-image of the liberal bourgeoisie, progressive relative to the aristocratic one but only to the point that it rose to dominance, and from that point bound to defend the stability of the status quo. Now at last there was an Islam for the socialist, the worker, peasant, or modern intellectual. So it was not a commonality of Islam but a commonality of certain social and political aspirations, whether expressed in a Marxist or in a Islamist idiom, that was operative in this particular web of alliances.

Even by 1913, the Khilafat activist Mushir Husain Qidwai, one of the founders of the Anjuman-e-Khuddam-e-Kaaba, had been inspired to write a hefty pamphlet on "Islam and Socialism" in order to show "by authentic quotations from the Qur'an and Hadith, that Islam was the first of all religions to establish a state on Socialistic and Communistic principles." Qidwai, while noting that "Mohammed's socialism . . . was [ethical], while 'modern' socialism was 'materialistic'" also believed that socialism, insofar as it had yet been implemented, had been beneficial to the world, and that its global success would amount to "a triumph of Pan-Islamism." Qidwai was educated in England and had been acquainted there with Har Dayal and Krishnavarma, who, as Ansari points out, were by that time "already convinced of the value of revolutionary socialism for India's freedom struggle."[111]

However, Aziz Ahmad has credited Obeidullah Sindhi as "the only political thinker of any considerable calibre to come directly in contact with Russian communism at an early stage."[112] Born a Sikh in Sialkot in 1872, Obeidullah converted to Islam at a young age and became a disciple of Mahmud Hasan of the Deoband school in 1889. Apparently, however, he developed into as much an influence on his teachers and colleagues as they on him. In 1909 he founded the Jamayat-ul-Ansar (which the Silk Letters report suggested "may be called the Deoband Old Boys' Association"). He started another group in 1912 called Jamayat-e-Hizbullah, as a sort of missionary society; according to the Sands report, many of the names in the society's 1,700-strong membership list "had such remarks against their names as 'prepared for any sacrifice.'"[113] The same year he took charge of a Deoband affiliate in Delhi, where he advocated a synthesis of the Aligarh and Deoband traditions, introduced English-educated teachers, and "put into circulation newspapers of advanced political views," whatever that might mean. He "propagated the Pan-Islamic sentiment" during the Balkan and Italian wars and made the acquaintance of key Khilafatists including Muhammed Ali, while some of his colleagues adopted swadeshi cotton apparel.

After his political activities obliged him to resign from Deoband in 1913, he founded his own madrassa in Delhi called the Nizarat al-Mu'arif, stressing a militant line through his teaching and his two books, *Talim-i-Quran* and *Khalid-i-Quran*, published in 1914 and 1915. Then in June of 1915 he disappeared. As it turned out, he was busy with a covert mission, "selected by Mahmud al-Hasan . . . as an anti-British agent provocateur" to set up a network of contacts and allies among the frontier tribes throughout Sindh and the Peshawar district, with the ultimate aim of kindling anti-British uprising in NWFP and the "independent territories," in connection with the Silk Letters affair. He then proceeded via Quetta and Kandahar to Kabul by October 1915, where he joined up with the Lahore students and the Turco-German-sponsored BIC mission. In his new capacity as home minister in the Provisional Government, he maintained communications with Hasan in the Hejaz, still pursuing authorization for his campaign. After this approach—and the illusion of Pan-Islamic unity—was thwarted by the Arab uprising in 1916 and by Hasan's subsequent arrest in Arabia,[114] Obeidullah's thinking seemed to move in a more nationalist direction.

He also had links to the leftists. For the next few years he remained closely aligned with Barakatullah and kept an eye on Russian developments from Kabul. Among Obeidullah's party was Muhammed Shafiq, future founding "Secretary of the Indian Communist Committee" in Tashkent. There, according to one of his *muhajir* comrades, Shafiq was "greatly relied upon by the Bolsheviks and their allies (Roy etc) and was to organise revolutionary propaganda in India and link it up with Obeidullah's gang in Kabul."[115] Obeidullah's nephew Abdul Aziz was also among the founding group of Bolshevik-*muhajirin* at Tashkent. In Moscow he roomed with Fida Ali, who confessed to the authorities upon his arrest that "from [Abdul Aziz] I learnt that Maulvi Obeidullah and his party were engaged purely on revolutionary work (Inqilab) and that all the bombs thrown in 1920–21 in the Peshawar District were sent by Obeidullah through Mulla Bashir of Chamarkand who found Mohammedans and others actually to throw them."[116] In 1920 Obeidullah too traveled to Russia, and in 1922 to Turkey, where his nephew joined him. In 1926 he declared himself to be connected with the Ghadar Party, and expressed the desire to learn Russian in order to read Lenin in the original.[117]

In 1926 he also visited Istanbul and Milan as the guest of Iqbal Shaidai. With Roy's blessing he later based himself in Milan, where he hosted a rendezvous between Obeidullah and Roy's "henchman" Muhammed Ali Sipassi.[118] Incidentally it was reported in February 1926 that Rattan Singh was also in northern Italy, "associating with disaffected Indian Muslims and with a representative of Syrian rebels against the French."[119] Shaidai's connections to Obeidullah and Swatantra angered Roy, as noted in a classified document: "The Ghadar conspirators are known to be working with the Soviets quite independently of M. N. Roy and to have allied themselves with Obeidullah, who was recently sent to the Hedjaz by the Soviets. This has annoyed M. N. Roy, who is reported to have transferred Iqbal Shaidai from Italy to France because he was collaborating with Swatantra the Ghadar agent at Constantinople."[120]

After parting from their Italian host, Obeidullah and Abdul Aziz proceeded to the Hejaz at the Comintern's expense.[121] There followed "years of exile and scholarship" in Mecca; Obeidullah did not receive permission to reenter India until 1938. Back home, in the few years remaining until his death in 1944, he developed a program of composite, federative nationalism for India, and a synthesis of Western and Islamic culture that he propagated through his theological school, Bayt-al-Hima. He also founded a small party that, though officially under INC auspices, contained his blueprint for an independent socialist democracy along these lines to be reached via an evolutionary, nonviolent path (in contrast to his earlier militance) in the regions that would soon comprise West Pakistan.[122]

Although tracing his theological lineage to Shah Waliallah, Obeidullah's own political philosophy as it developed would not have been sanctioned by his predecessor. Spiritually he was something of a syncretist, recognizing truth in Judeo-Christian as well as Hindu scriptures while still criticizing the latter for their limited "cultural-national" scope, by which they compared poorly to the universal scope possible within Islam, as in, for example, Sufism.[123] Also, despite his anti-British (composite) nationalism, he entertained deep misgivings about the liberal bourgeois Congress, whose dominant elements he identified not only with "Hindu revivalism" but with "Hindu capitalism," which "appeared to him as the antithesis of Islam."[124] This is a telling conflation of religion and economics, wherein Islam for Sindhi becomes aligned with socialism. The enemy of my enemy . . . is myself?

Obeidullah was no antimodernist; he embraced technological and military innovation and material progress and approved of the communist revolution in Russia, so far as it went. Nevertheless, in his judgment this type of atheistic materialism allowed for only a limited and partial understanding of true emancipation. He suggested that the Bolsheviks had gotten it only half right—the rejection of Western capitalism's pursuit of material wealth, exploitation, and economic maldistribution—but missed the half that offered a constructive alternative, which could be found in the moral content provided by Islam. "Muslims will have to evolve for themselves a religious basis to arrive at the economic justice at which communism aims but which it cannot fully achieve," he said. "Atheistic communism can bring to the Muslim masses only an emancipation of an imperfect and alien variety."[125] Lacking moral compass, Soviet Communism therefore threatened to become a form of imperialism in its central Asian and the Caucasian territories. As a corrective to this tendency, he suggested that "theistic socialism would give the peasant and the labourer a much fairer deal in life than a purely materialistic communist state."[126] Obeidullah also made connections between the techniques and institutional formations of Communism and Islam, considering the disciplined Leninist revolutionary party as comparable to the original form of the *jama'a* (i.e., the active, organized religious society as it had existed in Muhammad's day), and of course the Marxian social revolution as atheistic analogue to the theistic jihad in all its myriad forms—offensive and defensive; personal, psychological, cultural, literary, political, and military.[126]

But by far the most important interfacer of Pan-Islamism, communism, and the Indian national liberation struggle was Muhammed Barakatullah "Bhopali."[128] In fact if this unique figure had not existed, I might have been tempted to invent him. He single-handedly embodied the overlap between the Bolshevik and Pan-Islamist networks, utilizing the connective tissue of the Ghadar infrastructure to do so. This was evident even to his contemporaries. A foreign office report of 1915 observed: "It would appear that Barkatullah [sic] was a sort of connecting link between three different movements, namely, the Pan-Islamic, Asia for the Asiatics, and the Indian sedition. The common aim of all those movements was, of course, the release of Asia, in which was included Turkey, from European domination."[129] German diplomatic attaché Otto von Hentig, leader of the mission from Berlin to Kabul, wrote that "Barakatullah was first in line a nationalist and then a Moslem. . . . [Obeidullah] also was first concerned with the liberty of India and then with fighting for Islam."[130] I am not so sure that these political identities could be so easily separated and prioritized for either person; in fact, each exemplified the ability to translate his political ideals and aspirations among the three languages, consistent in fundamentals though shifting in emphasis.

Barakatullah was born between 1859 and 1864 in Bhopal. "A very clever youth," he studied Arabic, Persian, Urdu, and Muslim philosophy at the Madrasa-i-Sulemania and left home at the age of nineteen to serve as a tutor in Khandwa and Bombay. Much impressed after meeting Afghani there, he embarked for England in 1895 to teach Arabic in the Oriental College at Liverpool University. There he made the acquaintance of a fellow called Nasrullah Khan from Kabul, who happened to be the brother of the amir of Afghanistan. Barakatullah's first political activity ever to be reported on by British intelligence was then over the next few years to send, through his friend, a weekly newsletter on England's affairs to the amir's agent at Karachi. By 1897 he was reported to be attending meetings of the Muslim Patriotic League in London and helping to edit a newspaper called *The Crescent* and a magazine called *The Islamic World*.

In 1903 he made the voyage to New York City. Here he first drew notice at a meeting of the United Irish League in October 1906, where he ventured a question to the featured speaker, nationalist journalist and Home Rule MP T. P. O'Connor:

> Mr. M. Barakatullah of Bhopal, India, would like to ask Mr. O'Connor as a repre-
> sentative of the Irish Parliamentary party, whether, in the event of the Indian
> people rising against the oppressive and tyrannical rule of England in India, and
> in case England should concede Home Rule to Ireland, Mr. O'Connor would be in
> favour of the Irish people furnishing soldiers to the British Army to crush the In-
> dian people.[131]

O'Connor's answer is not recorded here. Around this period Barakatullah co-founded the Pan-Aryan League, an "association of doubtful loyalty," with P. L. Joshi. Throughout 1907–8 he continued to evidence "a considerable interest in Indian politics," presenting some anti-British lectures in New York in which he also advocated Hindu-Muslim unity and suggested the "formation of a league between the peoples of Ireland and of India." Acting upon the latter, he maintained a friendly connection with George Freeman of the *Gaelic American*, assisting him with publication of *Free Hindustan*.[132]

In February 1909 Barakatullah left New York for Tokyo, to serve as professor of Urdu or Hindustani at the University of Tokyo's School of Foreign Languages. Both Freeman and Joshi had been keen for him to apply for the post and had asked Cama and Krishnavarma to pull some strings from Paris to help him get it.[133] In Tokyo, he then met an Egyptian ex-army captain and Pan-Islamist called Fadli Bey from whom he took over the publication of the English-language monthly *Islamic Fraternity*, with funding from the Ottoman government,[134] as well as assistance from his protégé, Hasan U. Hatano, thought to be the first Japanese convert to Islam. In its pages Barakatullah "occasionally adopt[ed] a rather militant Pan-Islamic tone." British intelligence noted: "As a Muhammedan, he was not in sympathy with the extreme Hindu nationalists, who, while professing to aim at 'India for the Indians,' really want 'India for the Hindus.'"[135] At the same time it was under Barakatullah's editorship that the paper shifted away from a purely Pan-Islamist focus and more toward anti-British anti-imperialism. Indeed, a memo to the British Foreign Office suggested that the Indian movement in Japan only really got under way with Barakatullah's arrival from New York.[136] Barakatullah, like Taraknath Das, later adopted the slogan "Asia for the Asiatics"; it might even be said that Asian self-determination was the connecting principle of

Barakatullah's Pan-Islamism, his Indian nationalism, his Ghadarite anticolonialism, and later his socialism.

In the June 1911 number of *Islamic Fraternity*, he announced his intention to travel by way of St. Petersburg and Odessa to Constantinople and Cairo, "the centre of the Khalifate and the centre of Islamic learning," respectively. He would then return to Tokyo by mid-September, after which the paper would continue as an annual.[137] In the September number of *Islamic Fraternity*, issued during his absence under the management of Hatano and F. Schroeder, an anonymous writer signing as "Plain dealer" predicted, as paraphrased in an intelligence report, "a great Pan-Islamic Alliance that may be formed some day, including Afghanistan which he calls 'the future Japan of Central Asia.'" The report continued: "He said all that is needed is a leader, who 'will arise in Central Asia, probably in Afghanistan. . . . The firing of an Afghan gun will give the signal for the rising of all Islam as soon as she is ready.'"[138] The next report stated that upon his return in October 1911 Barakatullah addressed a meeting of the "Asiatic Society of Japan" on the subject of "his visit to Constantinople and the war between Italy and Turkey"—an event considered to be one of the catalysts for invigorating the Khilafat movement in India. Barakatullah also wrote a piece for his paper in 1912 on "the Christian combination against Islam," in which he described Kaiser Wilhelm as the linchpin of war and peace in the world, since he was the only Western power to have "maintained . . . the Ottoman Empire." Thus, insofar as Barakatullah's Khilafatist readership heeded his words, a possible opening was being set up for the direction of the Ghadarite alliance to be fulfilled two years later.

The trip had also marked an intensification of Barakatullah's focus on national liberation. He renewed his contact with Krishnavarma and other revolutionists in Europe and kept in frequent touch with them after returning to Japan. Soon he was the chief transfer point for the dissemination of revolutionary literature, including the *Indian Sociologist* and other journals from Europe and North America, while offering a way station for Indian revolutionaries passing through. His own publications flowed in the opposite direction, reaching Indians throughout east Asia, and India itself through Singapore. Stressing the importance of speaking to audiences in their own vernaculars, he produced pamphlets in both Urdu and English.[139]

But Barakatullah's assistant betrayed him. For some reason Hatano revealed to the British Embassy the tidbit that Barakatullah was receiving funds from the sultan of Turkey and the amir of Afghanistan, and provided a long list of names of people "in the movement or to whom seditious literature could be posted" in multiple countries around the Pacific Rim. He also "state[d] in conversation that [Barakatullah] received sympathy and support from a Mr. Freeman, an Irish American, resident in Seattle, and editor of a paper called the 'Gaelic American.'" He surrendered blocks and plates used to print the seditious pamphlets, and asked for a secret interview, begging for anonymity as a witness for his own protection. The British ambassador at Tokyo commented that he seemed to want to separate himself from Barakatullah, "with whose plans he was no longer in sympathy." He offered his services to the government of India as an informant, apparently in hopes of regular pay, and even offered up the *Islamic Unity* as a "secret organ" with the promise to "gradually modify its tone until it became pro-British."[140]

He did not get the chance to do so. Just as they were later to press U.S. authorities to neutralize Ghadar in San Francisco, the British government exerted greater and greater pressure on the Japanese authorities to eliminate this annoyance. And the Japanese authorities finally caved, suppressing the paper and dismissing Barakatullah from his university post in 1914.[141] It was then that he threw in his lot with the Ghadar Party, whose paper he was already receiving in Tokyo; Sohan Singh Josh said that he well "knew the situation developing in California."[142] Barakatullah and Bhagwan Singh, both of whom were "undoubtedly very seditious people . . . mixed up in the general revolutionary propaganda of Indians abroad, and especially with the 'Ghadr' people of America and Canada," sailed together from Yokohama on 6 May, just in time to address the *Komagata Maru* passengers.[143] Soon after reaching North America they appeared at a mass meeting of Indian revolutionaries in Portland. The new arrivals then comprised two-thirds of the "Big Three" along with Ram Chandra, traveling up and down the coast to address gatherings and helping to pick up the slack on the West Coast after Har Dayal's hasty departure. Once hostilities broke out, Barakatullah relocated to Germany to help initiate the Berlin committee.

A pair of letters to him from Har Dayal were of great interest to the intelligence community. In the first, sent in January 1915 from Geneva to Zurich, Har Dayal wrote: "My respected and worthy Maulvi Sahib, may your kindness ever increase. Accept Bande Mataram and salaams." He then asked Barakatullah's opinion on whether they should sever ties with Krishnavarma, as the Ghadar Party should pursue a united policy, and invited him to contribute articles (whether under his own name or otherwise) for a proposed English-language magazine in the United States. The second letter came from Hamburg to Berlin. In this letter, Har Dayal told of meeting 250 Muslim employees of a shipping company, on whom Barakatullah's influence, he felt, would be very beneficial:[144]

> Your coming here is essential, as it will have a very good effect on them. Several of them can be prepared for doing good work by influencing their religious feelings. Please come at once for a few days. . . . Tarak's lectures in Bengalee have had a good effect. Please move for inviting Professor Otto to tea on Saturday on behalf of the Indian Committee. With compliments from your servant, Har Dayal.

Barakatullah's next stop was in Istanbul to help coordinate the Egyptian and Mesopotamian propaganda missions before joining the von Hentig mission to

Kabul and heading up the PGI. Here he stayed throughout the war. Then in May 1919 the tireless traveler went as Amanullah's trusted "ambassador extraordinary" to Moscow in an attempt to formalize Afghan-Soviet relations.[145] At an intimate meeting Barakatullah, Pratap, and company discussed the regional situation with Lenin, including the possibility of rendering aid to Afghanistan under Britain's shadow. Josh asserts that Lenin was quite impressed with Barakatullah (though not with Pratap), appreciating the Bhopali's keen knowledge of Middle Eastern politics; he wrote to Soviet foreign minister Chicherin to be sure that the Indian's Persian pamphlet "Appeal to Muslim Brothers," on that community's relationship to Bolshevism, got published.[146] Barakatullah was equally impressed by Lenin, remarking that he was "the embodiment of these progressive forces of mankind which are longing to show their worth." "[Lenin's] name," Barakatullah asserted, "will be written across our times."[147] After this encounter he made several tours of the eastern Soviet regions, giving speeches in support of the new regime. Already an outspoken anti-imperialist, he now made himself known as a supporter of the Soviet Union, and an admirer of the principles of equality enacted by the Russian Revolution, which he saw as the best concrete step taken yet toward enabling other liberation movements in Asia.[148]

At about the same time, the viceroy sent a telegram to the Foreign Department, part of a series of such messages "indicating Afghan-Bolshevik connection." This communication reported that the Eastern Propaganda Department was up and running in Tashkent, and that Barakatullah was involved. It relayed: "Bravin . . . asks Barakatullah should be reminded that he promised to write a pamphlet on 'Bolshevism in the Koran'; that his work be expedited and 100,000 copies printed in Persian and Hindustani, and sent urgently by special courier."[149]

Yet Barakatullah continued to distinguish his own ideology from that of the Communists. Ansari believes that the reason "he never claimed to be a Bolshevik . . . was probably because he could not free himself from the psychological attachment to Islam," noting that "his views on most temporal matters became almost identical with those of the Bolsheviks." But I wonder if perhaps Barakatullah did not feel the need to adopt the identity of Bolshevism because he was able to find all of its substance that he thought important already within the discourse of Islam as he interpreted it.[150] In any case, Barakatullah maintained the limitations of the parallel, insisting in an interview with a *Pravda* correspondent: "I am not a communist nor a socialist, but my political program at present is the expulsion of the English from Asia."[151] The Pan-Asian sentiment reflected the Comintern's tactical concern with the Oppressed Peoples of the East. He added: "I am an irreconcilable enemy of European capitalism in Asia whose main representative is the English. On this point, I coincide with the Communists, and in this respect, we are your natural allies."[152] In other words, like Mir-Said Sultan-Galiev, who had welcomed the Afghan mission to Moscow on behalf of the Revolutionary Council, he had reversed the primary and subsidiary contradictions of capitalism and colonialism.[153] He continued:

> I only know one thing, that the well-known appeal of the Soviet Government of Russia to all peoples, calling upon them to struggle against capitalists (and for us, *capitalist is synonymous for the foreigner, more accurately, the Englishman*) has created on us a colossal impression. Even bigger impression was produced by the annulment by Russia of all secret treaties imposed by imperialist governments and the proclamation of the right of peoples, however small they may be, to self-determination.[154]

However, he did not recommend to his coreligionists that they should "convert" from Islam to communism (as the *muhajirin* had), but rather that they should recognize the communists as their greatest friends and allies and should pledge to reciprocate by making every effort to support the revolution and hinder counter-revolutionary forces. Therein, he insisted, lay their greatest chance at freedom from Western imperial rule, and from the capitalism that was its primary mode of domination and exploitation.

In a pamphlet entitled *Bolshevism and the Islamic Body Politick*, thought to be written en route from Afghanistan to Russia, completed in Tashkent in March 1919, and eventually distributed throughout India and central Asia in several languages,[155] Barakatullah "sought to justify a fusion of these two antipathetic creeds."[156] He began by ambitiously outlining the history of world civilization; the development of the division of labor, law, and government; the origins of inequality; the emergence of war, despotism, and imperialism; as well as the steps taken toward progress as kings were replaced by representation, constitutionalism, and democracy. He also identified key principles for equality and the development of individual potential based in public, collective property—a precedent he found in Jewish, Christian, and Muslim scripture and tradition, as well as in Marxism. He lamented the fall of Muslim states due to mistakes, abuses, and despotisms. But now, he said,

> there is no cause for despair. . . . The administration of the extensive territories of Russia and Turkestan has been placed in the hands of labourers, cultivators and soldiers. Distinction of race, religion and class has disappeared. Equal rights to life and freedom are given to all classes of the nation. But the enemy of this pure and unique Republic is British Imperialism which hopes to keep Asiatic nations in a state of eternal thraldom.

Therefore, he urged,

> The time has come for the Mohammedans of the world and Asiatic nations to understand the noble principles of Russian socialism and to embrace it seriously and enthusiastically. They should fathom and realise the cardinal virtues taught by the new system and in the defence of the true freedom they should join Bolshevik troops in repelling attacks of usurpers and despots, the British.

He also suggested they send their children to Russian schools to learn modern science and technology. He then announced the annulment of treaties, cancellation of debts, withdrawal of troops, and promotion of Oriental self-determination and Turkish integrity, all of which were proclaimed in the Bolsheviks' 1917 message to "Muslims of the East." Then he concluded with this exhortation:

> Comrades and brothers, let us tell you, we are bent upon acquiring an honourable peace, we have inscribed on our banner our intention to give to the oppressed nations of the world liberation and justice. We expect, oh Mohammedans residing in eastern countries, every one of you sincerely to follow this righteous path and to give active assistance to the realisation of our object.[157]

A note made on the British government's filed copy of the leaflet read: "It at once appeals to the Mohammedan poor and even middle classes, just the sort of people Barakatullah and his Bolshevik advisers wish to draw into their net."[158]

Again, much of what Barakatullah professed at this stage sounds quite similar to Sultan-Galiev's notion of "Muslim national communism," which in effect recognized Asian/Islamic national liberation and communist revolution as two sides of the same coin while simply reversing heads and tails.[159] Whether or not there was any continued contact or influence between the two, Sultan-Galiev's ideas left a mark on the curriculum of the University of the Toilers of the East between 1921, when it was founded, and 1924, when its staff was purged;[160] and the toilers in training were certainly exposed to these ideas. Barakatullah befriended his young fellow Bhopali Rafiq Ahmad in Moscow, and Chatto and Acharya advised Usmani.[161]

Barakatullah remained in Soviet Russia until 1922. By this time he could no longer return to Afghanistan—although Alexandra Kollontai said that Barakatullah was "regarded by the Russian Communist leaders as one of their most trusted agents for Afghanistan and India," and that he received reports and funds from centers in Java and San Francisco.[162] Amanullah had moved closer to the British, banished the PGI from Kabul, closed down the Ghadar headquarters at Gurdit Singh's stationery shop, and arrested some of its denizens. So Barakatullah went instead to Berlin to help Chatto and others in reorganizing the new Indian Independence Party (IIP) and Russian Relief Committee, of which he was often credited as a guiding force.[163]

He also began printing another weekly, called *Al Islah,* and produced an Urdu pamphlet on the Khilafat question to be distributed in India.[164] Despite being banned from France, and accused by the British of spreading Bolshevik propaganda, he was in Geneva in 1925–26. He also served as the Hindustan Ghadar Party's official representative at the League against Imperialism conference in Brussels in 1927. Then he returned to New York City to reunite with his old Irish friends, and to San Francisco as the guest of the Ghadar Party. In California, the original heart of the network he had done so much to ramify, he succumbed to diabetes in 1927. His gravestone can be found in Sacramento.

But perhaps a more appropriate local memorial is the "Proclamation of Liberty," which Barakatullah is thought to have written in 1913 or early 1914, an intriguing exemplar of the synthesis of ideas that are so characteristic of the Ghadarite political profile.[165] Like Har Dayal's *Shabash!* it begins and ends with the bomb "thrown by a plucky Indian youth at Lord Hardinge—the embodiment of a monstrosity called the Indian Government," an event that Barakatullah identifies as a harbinger of "regeneration for Asia and salvation for the globe." He invokes the liberal traditions of American political and intellectual history while enhancing the meaning and scope of the act by locating India's struggle at the center of not just a global but even a cosmic struggle:

> It was an echo of the boom of the cannon fired by the American Patriots one hundred and thirty-six years ago on the battle field of Massachusetts at the same hated foe which, as Emerson declared, was heard by all the tribes of the earth. The influence of the latter, though considerable in developing the material resources of the new world will pale in comparison when the effect of the former will galvanize the human race with cosmic forces playing into all realms.[166]

Barakatullah then gives a nationalist nod to Hindustan's ancient cultural splendor and material wealth, now reduced to famine and penury by the "Anglo-Saxon system of rapine and plunder [which] has become a fine art, a science," thanks to that race's innate "predatory instinct," enhanced over two millennia by "the refinement of hypocrisy, which sharpens the edge of brutality." But he does not stop at lamenting the draining of India's blood. Barakatullah understands that "the undisputed control over and the irresponsible possession of [the] inexhaustible resources [of] Hindustan has not only enabled England to treat 315 millions of Indians as slaves—strangers at home and of no status abroad"—here was Ghadar's original, proximate grievance of discrimination faced in North America—"but it has also placed in her hand power to do mischief everywhere in the world."[167]

Barakatullah segues now into a Pan-Islamist's-eye view of England's imperial scope:

> It is a matter of common knowledge that England gave Morocco to France, Tripoli to Italy and divided Persia between herself and Russia. The Balkan war has also been the outcome of the Anglo-Russian intrigue. These are however, the preliminary steps only to her cherished designs for destroying all Islamic kingdoms in the world and subjugating the Asiatic Continent with the co-operation of Russia and France.

Barakatullah knew well the secular scope of Britain's economic and geopolitical power, but in the incidents he selects here to highlight, he echoes the Khilafat movement's specific litany of provocations against the transnational body of Islam.

Switching from a Pan-Islamist to a Pan-Asianist lens, he quotes extensively from a speech made by Lord Morley assessing the state of the world in summer 1912, wherein Morley enumerates how all the East "from Adrianople to Peking" is disintegrating into chaos but for bastions of stability in British India, French Indochina, Japan, Russia, central Asia, and Siberia, while Ottoman Turkey, Persia, China, and Afghanistan roiled with internal factionalism and lawlessness. Aiming to reveal the power-hungry mendacity of the Secretary of State for India's claim that European rule was the only escape from Oriental ineptitude, Barakatullah even accuses Morley of psychological manipulation, using autosuggestion to keep the East willingly subordinate to colonial rule by publicly repeating such blatant lies.[168]

Besides, he challenges, how much stability and contentment could there really be in British India, when the bomb incident eloquently spoke otherwise? The days of the Raj were numbered. Barakatullah then rehearses the development of Indian resistance to British presence from the days of the East India Company (EIC) through the Mutiny through the crowning of the Queen Empress to the founding of the INC.[169] But Hindus lost their faith in English liberal political principles once they "worked hard and surpassed the Englishman in examination tests" only to find that promises of equality in civil service employment had been false. Next to go were illusions of the binding justice of the law. The swaraj movement had initially striven to remain lawful, until the deportation of Lajpat Rai and Ajit Singh demonstrated that "the will of the Englishman was the only law in India." Once all political activity right down to the shouting of Bande Mataram was outlawed, freedom of speech and press banned, and an "army of spies" unleashed throughout the country, scruples about legality no longer applied to tactical choices. Lawful boycott and unlawful bombing both went forward. Even so, this revelation of British hypocrisy had a useful effect, he points out, with early sensitivity to the register of colonial psychology: "Out of his disappointment in Englishman [sic] sprang up his hope through his confidence in self. . . . He discovered the enormous force that was about him and the utter helplessness of Englishmen in India, if even the millionth part of the force was properly handled."[170]

But then the frame changes yet again, this time into political theory: "'What is the government?'" the hypothetical disappointed swadeshist asked himself.

"It is an organization," he answered himself. "Then, let me create an organization of my own people, which one day may over-power the alien organization that is oppressing everybody," he continued. "But the British government has money and army of spies to destroy my organization," he paused for a moment. "There is no lack of money and men in the country," he argued. "I must force the rich to contribute large sums to the national fund and must establish a more efficient intelligence department than that of the alien government to watch its activities," he soliloquized.[171]

And so to business: "The patriots, then, went out revolver in hand to the millionaires of the town" to make their demands, expropriating funds from the rich to operate the struggle. These were often university graduates "obliged to wear disguises and wander all over the district armed with deadly weapons to . . . exact contribution from the wealthy of the place for the national work." Barakatullah assures us that "the latter, yielding to the force of the argument [if not just yielding to force!], often paid the sum willingly; for he knew, after all, the spotless character of the one playing the blackmailer." The money thus gathered was indeed "handled in the most honourable way, in issuing revolutionary literature in various languages secretly, in giving scientific education to the youth of the nation, and in preparing young men for fighting the enemy in the coming war of independence," or in gaining abroad the technical skills necessary for postindependence administration.

True social bandits, these patriots: the way to "hoist England in her own petard" is to "tak[e] a leaf out of the . . . book" of the Macedonian and Thracian "*he duck* or patriot-outlaw"—the very haiduks who inspired Hobsbawm in *Primitive Rebels*. And it was they who "[kept] alive the tradition of liberty," along with "the folk-poet, the schoolmaster . . . the monk and the priest."[172] Sometimes the "brigand of the folk-songs" even turned out to be the monk in disguise. Barakatullah mentions the famous monasteries of Mount Athos, from which emerged "many of the pioneers of the present war of liberation" in Greece. "The abbot's cell was an armoury" in Ivan Vazov's novel *Under the Yoke,* and "chance had made him a monk instead of a guerrilla leader."[173] There is an implicit resonance here with the *sanyasis* of *Ananda Math.*

To conclude, Barakatullah turns back to the Hardinge bomb and its value. It was first and foremost, he says, an answer to the challenge of a government that "having defied all moral considerations" insisted on ruling India "by force against the will of the people." However, "the bomb indicates that the people can meet force by force. It also points out that the people are going to take India from the grasp of alien foe, and that they will not ask the tyrant for concessions any more." This was a message sent not just to the rulers or to the witnessing world, but in particular to the Muslims of India, who had for too long been "hypnotized" into betraying their community "for a mess of pottage" in the form of government patronage just as the Ghadarites had taken the Sikhs to task for their history of military loyalty.

But this "[Hindu] bomb-thrower set an example of manliness, sacrifice and devotion to the service of our common Fatherland." Let Indian Muslim patriots then join in the movement "for the liberation of our beloved motherland, by instituting their own secret organization aiming at the same goal." That is, an organization like the Yugantar group, perhaps, as Abul Kalam Azad had tried to do? But the Muslims of India not only shared national parentage with the Hindus of India; they also had "brethren and sisters in the Faith" elsewhere whose suffering Barakatullah lays at the door of England: "Let the events in Tripoli, Persia and the Balkans serve as an eye-opener to them. Let them reflect upon the fact how the Balkan nationalities, that were at daggers drawn at one another for centuries passed [*sic*] sank their differences when they found an opportunity to strike at the common foe. The Indian Muslims have to avenge themselves upon England for two wrongs, (1) to the people of India and (2) to the Muslims abroad."[174] Here, precisely, were the two complementary goals of the Khilafat movement: Indian national liberation in particular, and the integrity and autonomy of the caliphate as a whole.

In closing, Barakatullah comes full circle, back to the principles of the American Declaration of Independence, which for that matter might just as well be a variant translation of the "Proclamation of Liberty":

> So let us take a solemn oath that we will not rest until we have driven the British out of our glorious country. Let our motto be: 'Life, liberty and the pursuit of happiness are the birthrights of every child of man'; 'No nation has a right to govern another nation'; 'No good government by aliens can ever be a substitute for self-government.'[175]

Thus Barakatullah seamlessly interweaves the slogans of Enlightenment political liberalism with invocations of Pan-Islamic sentiment, internationalist political analysis, militant Swadeshi nationalism, a glorification of social banditry and propaganda by the deed, and perhaps even a hint of socialistic economic redistribution—his is a Ghadarite document if ever there was one.

Epilogue

The arc of Ghadar's narrative paused for breath but did not stop at the threshold of the 1930s, with the Meerut and Lahore Conspiracy cases, the deaths of Bhagat Singh, Rajguru, and Sukhdev, and a new round of struggle in the Chittagong Armoury raids and the Civil Disobedience movement. Although Ghadar-linked activists were doing their work through other names and formations, even in 1931 British intelligence issued an alert that rehearsed a pattern that had remained remarkably consistent for fifteen years: vague warnings were sent out that plans were afoot for a Russian-sponsored invasion of Punjab from the northwest, timed to the coordinated eruption of massive internal upheaval. And sure enough, just as so many times before, "it was noted that the Kabul branch of the Gadar party was making persistent endeavours to secure arms, large scale maps of India and adjacent countries, hatching schemes for mobilisation and concentrating on military information regarding the North-West Frontier."[1]

The northeastern variation on the Ghadarite theme was reprised even more loudly during World War II in Subhash Chandra Bose's Indian National Army, recruited from among the Indian POWs in Southeast Asia for an invasion of liberation across the Indo-Burmese border, after he had sought patronage from Germany and Japan. This was a tactical legacy; the ideological thread could be traced via the League Against Imperialism to the postwar Non-Aligned Movement, framing the commitment to Third World solidarity in the same logic of national liberation plus culturally appropriate socialism that had characterized the alumni of the Moscow University of the Toilers of the East.

Other Ghadar veterans continued this work even more directly and immediately. One of a very few North American Ghadarites from a scheduled caste

(Chamar) background, Mangu Ram channeled his experience in a unique direction as one of the architects of the Punjabi anti-Untouchability movement Ad Dharm in the mid-1920s.[2] In 1909 at the age of twenty-three, he took a job his father had arranged picking fruit in California through a labor contractor who paid his passage, which was to be reimbursed from his first wages, after which he would send the money home to his family. Over the next four years he spent time in various work camps throughout the Central Valley, often employed by émigré landowners from the same families who had been the zamindars of his village at home.[3]

But everything changed when he encountered Ghadar.[4] Fired by the movement's dream of social equality, he became a full-time worker in the San Francisco office. In 1915 he joined the five-man team that would accompany the hazardous *Annie Larsen/Maverick* expedition. After an odyssey that included the witnessing of a volcanic eruption in Hawaii and two eleventh-hour escapes from execution, he made landfall in the Philippines, where Ghadar comrades kept him safely hidden until the end of the war. Though the danger had passed, he chose to stay on in Manila working for a contractor to an American garment factory.[5] A 1920 intelligence report then identified him as one of the "leading Indian revolutionaries" contributing to "the disloyalty of many of the Indian residents in the Philippine Islands." At a meeting in Manila, he and other speakers predicted a Bolshevik advance on India, on which those hopes previously invested in a German victory must now rest; they also spoke of "the risings now occurring daily in Turkey and Arabia." They agreed to collect all the available funds and literature their countrymen throughout the Philippines had received from San Francisco, to send on to the troops and peasants in India.[6]

When Mangu Ram returned to India himself in 1926, he found that his years abroad had changed his bearing to the extent that he now passed for a person of higher caste. "For sixteen years abroad he had enjoyed a life in which he was treated as an individual rather than as a Chamar," remarks Mark Juergensmeyer, noting that while the Indian community in North America faced external racism, they were internally egalitarian to a degree unheard-of within India. Moreover, "the camaraderie of the Gadar movement . . . provided a standard of fellowship and equality that Mangoo Ram believed to be applicable to all societies. His social expectations had risen definitively."[7] But his individual escape from the strictures of the caste system made him even more sensitive upon his return to its collective injustices. Juergensmeyer observes: "By the time Mangoo Ram reached Punjab he was convinced that there was need for social change, and wrote to Gadar party headquarters in San Francisco about the difficult conditions of the Scheduled Castes in India, announcing that their freedom was more important to him than that of the nation itself." The party leaders then assigned him the task of "the uplift of the Untouchables."[8] Despite tenuous contact with other

Ghadar veterans in Punjab, Mangu Ram retained his "respect for the party, and considered himself to be carrying on Gadar goals in Ad Dharm," of which he was the charismatic prime mover for the first several years of its existence.[9]

The assassin of O'Dwyer, author of the Amritsar Massacre, can also be counted as a Ghadarite.[10] Udham Singh (aka Muhammed Singh Azad, to indicate both freedom and communal unity) was born around the turn of the twentieth century and raised in an Amritsar orphanage. He served in the British Army in Mesopotamia and East Africa, worked on the Uganda Railway, and then sailed to the United States via Mexico. After working for seven years in California, Detroit, Chicago, and New York, he signed on as a seaman and carpenter for an American shipping line under the false Puerto Rican identity of "Frank Brazil" and traveled extensively throughout Europe and the Mediterranean. He finally disembarked in India in 1927, only to be arrested shortly thereafter. He was first fined in Karachi for alleged possession of obscene postcards, and then in Amritsar under the Arms Act, for possession of unlicensed weapons, including "two revolvers, one pistol, a quantity of ammunition and copies of the prohibited paper, Ghadr-di-Gunj." The police reported: "While in America he appears to have come under the influence of Ghadar Party and to have been affected by its teaching." Over the years he had made the acquaintance of Lajpat Rai, Kishan Singh, and the latter's son Bhagat Singh, "whom he considered his guru and 'his best friend.'" Now the report recorded that Udham Singh had stated his intentions "to murder Europeans who were ruling over Indians and that he fully sympathised with the Bolsheviks, as their object was to liberate India from foreign control." He was given five years of rigorous imprisonment.[11]

Casting about after his release, he turned up London in 1934. He was next reported to be living with a white woman in the West End, picking up periodic work at film studios as an extra in crowd scenes. On several occasions he was heard to have expressed "extreme views" and even to have "boasted that he had smuggled arms into India." Yet he could not be linked to the meetings of the known London extremist groups. As of November 1939, his last known job had terminated, and he was receiving monthly unemployment benefits under the name Singh Azad. One morning in March 1940, Azad went out to see a Paul Robeson film in Leicester Square, but the cinema was not yet open. He then wandered restlessly to the India Office to see about an exit visa, but the person he needed was out, and he did not want to wait and left. It was then that he noticed a sign advertising a meeting of the East Asia Association and Central Asia Society at Caxton Hall, where Percy Sykes would be giving a talk on Afghanistan. Azad went to the meeting, and it was there that he shot O'Dwyer.[12]

Azad was hanged in July, with his last words expressing pride in dying for his country and eagerness to follow in the footsteps of Bhagat Singh, consciously echoing his beloved friend as he in turn had echoed Kartar Singh. The police report remarked that he was not, as listeners might assume, insane; rather this is what those Indian revolutionists do, namely use passionate "poetical compositions" as political propaganda, "in which truth is subordinate to the flow of language" in a "farrago of British barbarisms." Azad's last words—which Ghadar, which had funded his appeal for clemency, must not get hold of lest they publicize him as a martyr—were written in English, Urdu, and Gurmukhi, and the "sentiments expressed [were] typical of the half-educated Ghadar revolutionary": namely, that he would rather die than live under British terror, and that his people would rather not exist than remain under English imperialism. The people of India must use the "profits and produce of the country" for their own benefit "without class or creed prejudice." He accused the British of bringing degeneration, saying, "Don't ask me, just read your history." He then spat at the judge, gave a shout of "Inquilab," and proclaimed his readiness for death.[13]

Udham Singh's portrait was thereafter to be seen prominently displayed at meetings of the Indian Workers' Association (IWA), established in 1937 by Ghadar supporters in Coventry. Within a few years the loose, decentralized formation linked branches in most of the major cities of England. These branches advocated for the rights and social welfare of Indian workers during the Second World War, provided a way for Indians to participate in the British labor movement, campaigned for the freedom struggle, and raised funds (as did the interwar American Ghadar Party) for the Desh Bhagat Parwarik Sahaik Committee in Amritsar to support the families of Ghadar and Akali political prisoners. Although factionalized and much reduced in membership by the end of the war, the IWA continued to support independence while protesting against partition and was revitalized by a further influx of immigrants in the later twentieth century.[14]

But Ghadar's influence—its Ghadar-di-Gunj, its "echo of revolt"—continued to resonate long after independence. The Kirti Party, and later the Lal Communist Party, espoused a heterodox socialism that resisted the diktats of CPI correctness and retained characteristically Ghadarite elements of romantic idealism. It should perhaps be no surprise then that when the party once again fell apart in the 1960s along fault lines submerged for thirty years, the surviving Ghadari *babas* gave their blessing to Charu Mazumdar and the Naxalites. The first elected leader of the new Communist Party of India (Marxist-Leninist) (CPI-ML) in Punjab was a veteran Ghadarite from Argentina by way of the Moscow school, Bujha Singh. The new Far Left party in turn recognized solidarity with an autonomous overseas wing founded in 1969 in England and Canada that called itself the Communist Ghadar Party of India and listed its main goals as anticapitalism and opposition to neocolonialism in India and antiracism and the struggle for immigrant rights in the West.[15] After all, this very struggle—the recognition of immigrant rights—had been the experiential entry point for the majority of Ghadarites in the United States.

Bhagat Singh Bilga himself kept the flame burning along with his comrades at the Deshbhagat Yadgar, the Ghadar memorial archive in Jalandhar, until his death in May 2009 at the age of 102. Since returning to India from Moscow in 1934, he had weathered several imprisonments as a lifelong communist activist and spoken out powerfully against sectarian violence in Punjab during the violent height of the Khalistan movement in the 1980s, and more recently against economic neoliberalism. He died in England, where his son served as president of the Birmingham IWA; its memorial was hosted in the name of the Shaheed Udham Singh Welfare Trust.[16] Continuity prevailed.

For Rattan Singh, this was a story of "simple peasants who became revolutionists and dared to raise the banner of armed revolt at a time when our foremost national leaders could not think beyond 'Home Rule.'"[17] Shiv Verma paraphrased Bhagat Singh's assertion that the Ghadar movement was the first to articulate a positive revolutionary content, a vision for transforming society beyond just rebellion against British rule: initially as republican democracy embracing the French revolutionary fundamentals of liberty, equality, and fraternity, to be given form in a federated United States of India inspired by the American political blueprint, but eventually requiring socialism as the prerequisite for equality and the highest form of substantive democracy, with the elimination of economic exploitation, not just political subjugation, as prerequisite for liberty.[18] Our patriotic heroes were demonstrably willing to stake their lives on their beloved country's freedom. But the deities on whose altars they made their sacrifices (and here I'm adopting their own language of *qurban*, of *sarfaroshi ki tamanna*)[19] were liberty and equality, not a personalized god or nation. They sought liberation from oppression for all people, on principle, including their own.

Closer contact with the international scene also enabled them to participate in and contribute to a richly cross-fertilized radical discourse that was less easily available to their fellows inside British India, at a moment—sometimes termed the first round of globalization—when advances in communications and transportation technology enabled such cross-fertilizations to occur at an unprecedented pace. A. C. Bose suggests that once released from traditional "social restrictions and allegiances," they found conditions in the new places conducive to a rapid transition to "progressive" attitudes well ahead of those of their more sedentary countrymen.[20] Now that the revolutionists were in conversation with new allies and interlocutors in multiple contexts, the causes they saw themselves serving expanded from the nationalist to the trans- or internationalist; while the forms of radicalism that they most resembled and with which they most closely engaged shifted, along with the proportional emphasis among the component elements—elements whose presence nevertheless remained consistent.

As a prewar American movement, Ghadar bore the marks of utopian socialism and syndicalism. As a wartime global movement, it appeared determinedly nationalist. As an interwar Indian movement, it was communist. This plurality of elements—the result of the richness of the conjuncture, both material and discursive, that attended Ghadar's birth—is what enabled it to find points of affinity in both strategy and ideology with a number of different and ostensibly irreconcilable movements. Ghadar was not protean, but it did contain multiple potential attachment hooks, receptor sites, or interfaces.

Within the larger revolutionary movement abroad, Ghadar can be viewed in a number of ways. Most narrowly defined, it was an organized party based among a close-knit group in California, eclectic in their alliances but unwavering in their goals, supporting a dedicated core of peripatetic activists of whom many were martyrs of the cause. But it was also a concept of mutiny and revolt, mutable and adaptable; it was the broadly decentralized radical network inspired by this concept; and it was a magnificent underground society of switchboard operators, transmitting information and ideas between different networks, translating them in the process from one coding system to another. Thus it created a semivisible connective tissue filling the negative space of geographical, chronological, and philosophical gaps in the history of the Indian freedom struggle.

Ghadar was a missing link located at a key branching point in the intellectual history of revolution, by which the politics of militant anticolonialism in the early twentieth century polarized after a storm-tossed hiatus into both far right and far left radicalisms in the 1920s. Yet it was a synchronic as well as a diachronic link, providing a stable yet dynamic synthesis of elements that remained internally logical and consistent across times, places, contexts, and idioms; and which were never mutually exclusive, but only at times ascendant and at other times latent or oppositional. Pinning Ghadar down is only simple if we select the most restrictive definition, artificially isolating it from its various inflows and outflows, neglecting to periodize its evolution over time, and ignoring its internal variations and debates, the complexity of its composition, and the richness of its texture over time. We thereby do it an injustice. Rather, it seems appropriate to apply to the Ghadar movement—and to the revolutionary movement abroad as a whole—the fable of the blind men and the elephant, in which one thought he was feeling a wall, one a tree trunk, one a rope, and one a snake, depending on which portion of the great beast's body he happened to have touched.

NOTES

INTRODUCTION

1. *Ghadar,* 11 August 1914, quoted in virtually every work on the subject. This version translated from Muhammed Irfan Khan, *Barkatullah Bhupali* (Bhopal: Irfan Publications, 1969), 122. Also in Brown, 197; Sareen, *Select Documents,* #17; Isemonger and Slattery, 28; Gould, 204; Khushwant Singh, 21; and other excerpts in Mathur, 46–47, 50; Brown, 196–97. For full accounts of the Ghadar movement, see first and foremost Harish Puri, *Ghadar Movement: Ideology, Organisation, and Strategy* (Amritsar: Guru Nanak Dev University, 1993); and Sohan Singh Josh, *Hindustan Gadar Party: A Short History* (New Delhi: People's Publishing House, 1977–1978). Detailed intelligence reports were compiled by F. C. Isemonger and James Slattery, *An Account of the Ghadr Conspiracy, 1913–1915* (Lahore: Superintendent Government Printing, 1919); James C. Ker, *Political Trouble in India, 1907–1917* (Calcutta: Superintendent Government Printing, 1917); and Rowlatt Sedition Committee Report of 1918 (Calcutta: Superintendent Government Printing, 1918); these are followed closely by T. R. Sareen, *Indian Revolutionary Movement Abroad* (New Delhi: Sterling, 1979); and A. C. Bose, *Indian Revolutionaries Abroad, 1905–1922, in the Background of International Developments* (Patna: Bharati Bhawan, 1971). There are numerous other accounts, although aside from Puri they contain little in the way of analysis: A. B. Ganguly, *Ghadar Revolution in America* (New Delhi: Metropolitan Book Company, 1980); Khushwant Singh and Satindra Singh, *Ghadar 1915: India's First Armed Revolution* (Delhi: R & K Publishing House, 1966); L. P. Mathur, *Indian Revolutionary Movement in the United States of America* (Delhi: S. Chand, 1970); Gurdev Singh Deol, *The Role of the Ghadar Party in the National Movement* (New Delhi: Sterling Publishers, 1969).

2. Bose, *Indian Revolutionaries Abroad, 1905–1922,* 10.

3. Emily Brown, *Har Dayal: Hindu Revolutionary and Rationalist* (Tucson: University of Arizona Press, 1975), 78–79.

4. Bose, *Indian Revolutionaries Abroad, 1905–1922*, 11.

5. Actually the call said (Puri, 94, quoting Harnam Singh Tundilat) that India would soon be emptied of white troops, who would be off fighting on German battlefronts; therefore, "Hindustanees should proceed to India forthwith." This of course overlooks the fact that there were never very many white troops in India in the first place, and that it was Indian troops who would be "emptied" from the country to the fronts in Africa and the Middle East.

6. Rattan Singh, *A Brief History of the Hindustan Gadar Party* (San Francisco, 1927), 25–28 (SANA Box 4:3). This firsthand account relates that Sohan Singh Bhakna went on a hunger strike for six weeks; years later Bhagat Singh, visiting him in Lahore Central Jail, beseeched him not to do it again due to his age. Sohan Singh Bhakna retorted: "What if the body has grown old, a revolutionary never gets old." Indeed, he was released in 1930 after fourteen years in prison and survived to organize many another day. See also Neeti Nair, "Bhagat Singh as Satyagrahi: The Limits to Non-Violence in Late Colonial India," *Modern Asian Studies* 43.3 (2009).

7. Valentine Chirol, *Indian Unrest* (London: Macmillan and Co., 1910), 146.

8. Bose, *Indian Revolutionaries Abroad, 1905–1922*, 35.

9. Ibid., 8. O'Donnell killed Carey as a traitor for implicating his codefendants in the Phoenix Park murders. Kanai Lal Dutt killed fellow under-trial prisoner Narendra Nath Goswami as an approver in the Alipore case against the Swadeshi movement militants. Documents in the Life of Sri Aurobindo, The Assassination of Narendranath Goswami, in Bengal Government File on the Assassination: Confidential No. 1876-C, dated 31 August 1908 (www.sriaurobindoashram.org/research/show.php?set = doclife&id = 15).

10. Their postwar Friends of Freedom for India colleague Ed Gammons associated them with the "great libertarian" tradition; Roy referred to their revolutionary offspring as "20th century Jacobins." In other words, they favored the radical-democratic rather than the bourgeois-republican side of the post-Enlightenment revolutionary family, replicating its evolution toward socialism in only a few years. On the FFI, see Tapan Mukherjee, *Taraknath Das: Life and Letters of a Revolutionary in Exile* (Calcutta: National Council of Education, 1998); Janice MacKinnon and Stephen MacKinnon, *Agnes Smedley: The Life and Times of an American Radical* (Berkeley: University of California Press, 1988); Ruth Price, *The Lives of Agnes Smedley* (New York: Oxford University Press, 2005); and of course Smedley's own *Daughter of Earth* (New York: Coward-McCann, 1929).

11. *Boston Daily Advertiser*, 10 October 1916 (Sareen, *Select Documents*, 145–46).

12. L. P. Mathur, *India Revolutionary Movement in the United States of America* (Delhi: S. Chand, 1970), 44.

13. The phrase was popularized by Dadabhai Naoroji in his 1901 book *Poverty and Un-British Rule in India*.

14. Rattan Singh drew an implicit contrast to the Swadeshi period in emphasizing that this was "no ordinary terrorist movement" and commenting that "more than a conspiracy: it was a whole movement," meaning that Ghadar marked an unprecedented expansion from secret cells into mass-scale organizing.

15. Quoted in Joan Jensen, *Passage from India* (New Haven, CT: Yale University Press, 1988), 177–78.

16. Foucault's concept of governmentality ("On Governmentality," in *The Foucault Effect: Studies in Governmentality*, ed. Graham Burchell, Colin Gordon, and Peter Miller [Chicago: University of Chicago Press, 1991]) is applied by Gyan Prakash, *Another Reason* (Princeton, NJ: Princeton University Press, 1999); Patrick Joyce, *The Rule of Freedom* (New York: Verso, 2003); and Timothy Mitchell, *Rule of Experts* (Berkeley: University of California Press, 2002).

17. I am using this term in Bakhtin's sense in *The Dialogic Imagination* (Austin: University of Texas Press, 1981), salted with Raymond Williams, *Marxism and Literature* (Oxford: Oxford University Press, 1977) on the notion of emergent or oppositional formations (with reference to what he calls structures of feeling); or Foucault's notion of subjugated knowledges in *Power/Knowledge*, ed. Colin Gordon (New York: Pantheon Books, 1980).

18. Behrooz Ghamari-Tabrizi, "Foucault, Orientalism, and the Iranian Revolution" (lecture, University of California, Santa Cruz, 25 February 2008). See also his "Contentious Public Religion," *International Sociology* 19.4 (December 2004): 504–19.

19. Israel Gershoni and James Jankowski, *Egypt, Islam, and the Arabs: The Search for Egyptian Nationhood, 1900–1930* (New York: Oxford University Press, 1987). Their definition of intellectual history is applied to a discussion of the various broader identifications and solidarities possible for Egyptian nationalists during the period contemporaneous with Ghadar's development, according to different logics of Ottomanism/Pan-Islamism, Arabism, Egyptian cultural/territorial exceptionalism, and so forth.

20. Incidentally, presuming heteroglossia within each discourse is also the key to escaping the anxiety of colonizing influence and derivativeness, which so often comes up when dealing with the kind of connections I am arguing for here. If there are compatible strands in both "West" and "East"— Amartya Sen in *The Argumentative Indian* (New York: Farrar, Straus and Giroux, 2005), for example, points out the examples of rationalism in Indian intellectual and cultural history, countered with examples of European mysticism— then there is no need for Indian cultural purists to reject a political movement as inherently Western. The connections can be seen as a bilateral meeting of counterparts rather than passive mimicry, as is often suggested. However, we must always be very careful not to ignore or falsely neutralize the power gradients of asymmetrical interactions.

21. Gershoni and Jankowski, viii. They elaborate: "We believe that context can explain much but not all of the history of ideas: ideas are not merely echoes of social processes or forces. . . . Although the historical context is vital to explaining the origins and much of the evolution of a system of thought, it cannot fully account for the specifics or the quality of a complex body of speculation. Once set in motion by society, thought has its own internal dynamics. Just as ideas cannot be analyzed exclusively in terms of themselves, neither can they be understood only as a product of external circumstances" (x). Which is also to say that a given set of circumstances will not automatically produce the same experimentally replicable (rational) reactions, let alone guarantee the ways in which people explain and justify them.

22. Rattan Singh, 8.

23. Ker, 100.

24. On the early years of Indian Communism, see G. Adhikari, *Documents of the History of the Communist Party of India*, vols. 1–3 (New Delhi: People's Publishing House, 1971–1982); M. Persits, *Revolutionaries of India in Soviet Russia* (Moscow: Progress Publishers, 1983); Gene Overstreet and Marshall Windmiller, *Communism in India* (Berkeley: University of California Press, 1959); Sanjay Seth, *Marxist Theory and Nationalist Politics* (London: Sage Publications, 1995). On developments in Punjab in particular, see Bhagwan Josh, *Communist Movement in Punjab, 1926–47* (Delhi: Anupama Publications, 1979); Gurharpal Singh, *Communism in Punjab: A Study of the Movement up to 1967* (Delhi: Ajanta Publications, 1994).

25. Brown, 74.

26. Kim Stanley Robinson, *Red Mars* (New York: Bantam Books, 1993). Tom Stoppard uses a similar conceit for the nineteenth-century Russian radicals that populate his historical play cycle *The Coast of Utopia* (London: Faber, 2002), as Herzen, Bakunin, and all their comrades and rivals seek to cross the stormy seas of revolution to that undiscovered country.

27. Lamin Sanneh, "Time, Space, and Prescriptive Marginality in Muslim Africa: Symbolic Action and Structural Change," in *World History: Ideologies, Structures, and Identities*, ed. Philip Pomper, Richard H. Elphick, and Richard T. Vann (Oxford: Blackwell, 1998).

1. GHADAR IN AMERICA

1. On the indentured labor diaspora generally, see Thomas Metcalf, *Imperial Connections* (Berkeley: University of California Press, 2007); Madhavi Kale, *Fragments of Empire* (Philadelphia: University of Pennsylvania Press, 1998); Hugh Tinker, *A New System of Slavery: The Export of Indian Laborers Overseas, 1830–1920* (New York: Oxford University Press, 1974); and Khal Torabully and Marina Carter, *Coolitude* (London: Anthem, 2002).

2. On the social experience and politicization of the Punjabi immigrant laboring community, see Joan M. Jensen, *Passage from India: Asian Indian Immigrants in North America* (New Haven, CT: Yale University Press, 1988); Karen Isaksen Leonard, *Making Ethnic Choices: California's Punjabi Mexican Americans* (Philadelphia: Temple University Press, 1992); Bruce LaBrack, *The Sikhs of Northern California, 1904–1975* (New York: AMS Press, 1988); N. Gerald Barrier and Verne Dusenbery, eds., *The Sikh Diaspora: Migration and the Experience beyond Punjab* (Delhi: Chanakya Publications, 1989); S. Chandrasekhar, ed., *From India to America: A Brief History of Immigration: Problems of Discrimination, Admission, and Assimilation* (La Jolla, CA: Population Review Publications, 1982); H. Brett Melendy, *Asians in America* (Boston: Twayne Publishers, 1977); Edna Bonacich and Lucie Cheng, *Labor Immigration under Capitalism: Asian Workers in the United States before World War II* (Berkeley: University of California Press, 1984); see also the documentary *Roots in the Sand* (Jayasri Majumdar Hart, 2000).

3. According to Immigration Department records, 45 "East Indians" or "Hindus" as they were called regardless of sect entered Canada in 1905, 387 in 1906, and 2,124 in 1907. For the United States the figures for these years were 145, 271, and 1072. In 1908, 2,623 entered Canada, and 1,700 the United States, the highest numbers yet according to Harish Puri, *Ghadar Movement: Ideology, Organisation, and Strategy* (Amritsar: Guru Nanak

Dev University, 1993), 17, 31. Rattan Singh estimated over 15,000 Indians in America and Canada, which could mean either that his guess was less scientific and more generous, or that he was going by probable undocumented numbers rather than official immigration figures. The following year Indian immigration dropped to almost nothing in Canada, while the United States continued to receive several hundred Indians per year until the war began, and numbers dropped. These numbers are from LaBrack; see also Darshan Singh Tatla, *A Guide to Sources: Ghadar Movement* (Amritsar: Guru Nanak Dev University, 2003), 174–75.

4. Jensen, 170–71 (see also 95, 99, 107, 114–5, 118–19, 151). Statistics provided are not always very clear on whether numbers refer to people entering in a given year, or cumulative arrivals; or even whether numbers refer to just Canada, just the United States, or all of North America. Nor is it always clear how many people in the count stayed on and how many left and were replaced. See Isemonger and Slattery, 52; Ved Prakash Vatuk, *Thieves in My House: Four Studies of Indian Folklore of Protest and Change* (Varanasi: Vishwavidyalaya Prakashan, 1969), vi, quoting a note from the Delhi Criminal Investigation Department in late 1914, which gave a number of 6,000–7,000 Indians in North America, evenly divided between the United States and Canada, of whom 200–300 were university students.

5. Commerce and Industry Department, Emigration A Proceedings, December 1914 #4. Dady Burjor's report quoted in Puri, 24.

6. See P. N. Chopra, ed., *Indian Freedom Fighters Abroad* (New Delhi: Criterion Publications, 1988).

7. David Petrie, *Developments in Sikh Politics, 1901–1911* (Amritsar: Chief Khalsa Diwan, 1972). Petrie also suggested that encouraging orthodoxy among the Sikhs would be a good way to promote troop loyalism. This was where the Sikh Sabha was most influential.

8. Puri, 36–37, quoting from Home Department Proceedings, 1909.

9. "Memorandum on Matters Affecting the East Indian Community in British Columbia," Public and Judicial Department, 6/1137/1912. Summed up in a letter from Secretary of State for India to Home Department, 26 February 1909 (IOR).

10. Vatuk, vi. Compare Puri's figures: $1.25–$2 as laborer, $2.50–$3 as foreman, $3–$4 or even $5–$6 on an eighteen-hour workday in harvest season—wages that Vatuk compares at a rate of three rupees to the dollar to the monthly pay of a schoolteacher, and Puri (27) favorably to that of a soldier in the British Indian army.

11. Jensen, 41, quoting Tuly Singh Johl in an interview with the author on 28 May and 24 August 1975.

12. Puri, 44.

13. Others were scattered at schools throughout the West and Midwest in Chicago, Corvallis, Seattle, Portland, and Iowa, among other places. According to the estimate of Taraknath Das, quoted in Jensen, 171, there were thirty in Berkeley in 1910 and a total of a hundred in the country in 1911. Gobind Behari Lal—who himself had arrived in late 1907—estimated anywhere from fifty to a hundred at Berkeley circa 1912. Gobind Behari Lal, "A Note for the UC Study Project," (unpublished manuscript, San Francisco, 1973) (SANA Box 4:8). See also James Campbell Ker, *Political Trouble in India, 1907–1917*

(Calcutta: Superintendent Government Printing, 1917; repr., Calcutta: Editions Indian, 1973), 208.

14. Lal, "Note for the UC Study Project."

15. Ibid., 31–32.

16. Ibid.

17. Ibid., 32.

18. Jensen, 170–71, drawing on Sarangadhar Das's articles in *Modern Review* 10 (December 1911) and *Indian Review* 11 (June 1910). Darisi Chenchiah's "History of the Freedom Movement in India: The Ghadar Movement, 1913–1918" (unpublished manuscript) (SANA Box 4:3), is comparable. Chenchiah said that wages for agricultural work were the equivalent of about 400 rupees a month. One could spend 100, save 300, and come out of the summer with a net gain of 1,000 rupees.

19. Emily Brown, *Har Dayal: Hindu Revolutionary and Rationalist* (Tucson: University of Arizona Press, 1975), 86–87.

20. Reproduced in Sareen, *Select Documents on the Ghadr Party* (New Delhi: Mounto Publishing House, 1994), 4 [henceforth Sareen]. It is unclear whether the parenthetical originates with Chima himself, is a later police gloss, or was added by Sareen as editor.

21. Gobind Behari Lal's account, written for the government of India's History of Freedom Movement Board, 1955; printed in Sareen, 20.

22. Jensen, 171.

23. Mathur, 30. See also Jensen, 164–65. According to Jensen, Detective W. C. Hopkinson blamed the students for politicizing the Sikh workers, which was the reason for his interest in tracking the activities of people like Taraknath Das and Har Dayal.

24. Brown, 87.

25. Herman Scheffauer, "The Tide of Turbans," *The Forum* (New York) 43 (June 1910) (SANA Box 1:6). This particular marker of racial/ethnic stigma was specific to the West Coast. Jensen (171) points out that in the Northeast a turban could have a certain social cachet, whereas in the South and Southeast, wearing a turban could prevent an Indian from being taken for an African American and thus treated even worse. Again note that the class positioning of East Indians led to drastic differences in their racialization, and the potential ability to assimilate or "pass."

26. The extensive literature on this theme includes Buhle and Georgakas; Cheng and Bonacich; and, more broadly, Alexander Saxton, *The Indispensable Enemy* (Berkeley: University of California Press, 1971); Dana Frank, *Buy American: The Untold Story of Economic Nationalism* (Boston: Beacon Press, 1999). Most stress that the antipathy of white laborers toward Asian workers was fundamentally an economic and not a racialist conflict. Legislation against Asian immigration included the Chinese Exclusion Act (U.S.), 1882; the Japanese Immigration Protection Law (U.S.), 1896; the Chinese Immigration Act (Canada), 1903 (raising the head tax to a prohibitive $500); and the Gentlemen's Agreement with Japan (U.S.), 1907.

27. Rattan Singh, 6.

28. Puri, 60, quoting Jwala Singh; see also Jensen, 42–45.

29. Home Department, Political, Deposit, October 1910 (Sareen, 6). These statements were vehemently refuted by Myron Phelps.

30. Jensen, 144.

31. Ibid., 147–48.

32. Ibid., 141. The reasons given were that they were unassimilable and that they wanted to exploit American resources. Incidentally, the report also noted that while the problem on the West Coast was Asians, on the East Coast it was new southern European entrants, deemed inferior to previous northern Europeans. I am not sure how southern Europeans compared with Asians in this estimate.

33. Puri, 39–41.

34. The following information is compiled from Chopra, 142–43; DCI 10.4.1909, B, June 1909 #108–114; Secret, Foreign Directorate of 27.8.1915, D, October 1915 #43.

35. I do not know if this was considered a decent rate or not. If not, perhaps this was the origin of his reputation as a swindler.

36. (Secret) Prog. #19, DCI 30.11.1907, B, January 1908 #19–26.

37. Ibid.

38. The following information is compiled from "Subject: Position of Indians in Canada: History Sheet of G. D. Kumar," B, April 1912, #82; Chopra, 92.

39. Ker, 217.

40. Puri, 50. Puri quotes Sohan Singh Bhakna's comment that Kumar's speeches were mainly "social reformist in nature," emphasizing, for example, community welfare and renunciation of alcohol and casteism.

41. One veteran of the Tenth Bengal Lancers (and the secretary of the Khalsa Diwan), Bhai Bhag Singh, publicly burned his honorable discharge certificate following a resolution of October 1909 pledging that no members of the Executive Committee of the Sikh Temple of Vancouver would bear any uniform, insignia, or medal; it was no badge of honor but rather marked him as a "slave to British supremacy." Isemonger and Slattery, 9.

42. *Free Hindustan*, Home Department, Political, B, *Proceedings*. DCI weekly reports ending 15 June 1910.

43. Ker, 210–11.

44. Puri, 50.

45. Isemonger and Slattery (11) said the deportation was in connection with an attempt to sell real estate; reasons given elsewhere were violation of the continuous voyage statute, or entry under false pretenses.

46. Isemonger and Slattery, 11.

47. Mathur, 20.

48. "Subject: Position of Indians in Canada: History Sheet of G. D. Kumar," B, April 1912, #82; Mathur, 20.

49. Information compiled from Tapan Mukherjee, *Taraknath Das: Life and Letters of a Revolutionary in Exile* (Calcutta: National Council of Education, 1997); Chopra, History Sheet of Taraknath Das; Gould, 182–99.

50. Jensen, 167.

51. Prog. #78, DCI. 20.6.1908, B, July 1908 #72–81.

52. Puri, 49. Its language seemed to be aimed at the educated Indian revolutionary intellectuals, like the Paris/London group, or even for the benefit of a white audience, as Canadian government agent William MacInnes suggested in his Report of 1908 (cited in

Puri, 136; Gould, 187–88), rather than at the Punjabi laborers, the majority of whom could not read English. One possible implication is that there were already significant ties among the politically active components of both populations, or that there was tight coordination between the issuers of the *Swadesh Sevak* in Gurmukhi and *Free Hindustan* in English.

53. "Memorandum on Indian Revolutionaries Abroad," Home Department, Political, A, August 1915 #216 (Sareen, 57).

54. Chopra, 49–50.

55. Secret, Foreign Directorate of 27.8.1915. D, October 1915 #43.

56. DCI weekly reports ending 15 June 1910, Home Department, Political, B, *Proceedings*, August 1910.

57. Mathur, 19, 27.

58. See the biography of Khankhoje by his daughter Savitri Sawhney: *I Shall Never Ask for Pardon* (New Delhi: Penguin Books, 2008), which is based on his memoir in Marathi, located among the collection of private papers at the Nehru Memorial Museum and Library.

59. Brown, 136.

60. Sawhney, 77.

61. This is the account of Sawhney, 85. Khankhoje later told Puri in an interview that it had a membership five hundred strong and that future Ghadar Party officers Sohan Singh Bhakna and Kanshi Ram, a labor contractor for the lumber industry, were leading figures, though Sohan Singh later said he had no recollection of this particular organization. Puri, 59: interview with Sohan Singh Bhakna, 26 November 1968. Perhaps the discrepancy stems from a difference in the interpretation of memory, which in turn could be related to Bhakna's early resistance to Khankhoje's leadership.

62. Sawhney, 80–81; 62, 92.

63. Ibid., 105.

64. Ibid., 95–96, 105.

65. Although Parmanand had made a similar suggestion to Har Dayal—perhaps at Das's behest?— and arrived with him in Portland in 1913, Gobind Behari Lal suggested it was Teja Singh who invited Har Dayal to come to California (Brown, 126). Sohan Singh Bhakna said in his autobiography, *Jeevan Sangram* (Jalandhar: Yuvak Sewak Prakashan, 1967), 39, that they had first thought of inviting Ajit Singh, and Isemonger and Slattery too mentioned (15) that Har Dayal himself had favored a proposal to recruit the lauded veteran activist (then allegedly "sitting idle in France") to come "tour the country and inculcate revolutionary ideas into the minds of all Indians resident in America." But Ajit Singh was soon to be quite busy elsewhere.

66. Secret, Foreign Directorate of 27.8.1915, D, October 1915 #43.

67. (Secret) Prog. #19, DCI 30.11.1907, B, January 1908 #19–26.

68. Isemonger and Slattery, 13–15. Here too there are varying accounts of the precise details. In his introduction to Isemonger and Slattery's report, Vatuk gives Kartar Singh credit for making the first meetings happen (vii). Puri's notes (68) attest to various conflicting evidence.

69. Isemonger and Slattery, 13.

70. Rattan Singh, 9. These same three names are also given as the members of a "secret commission" appointed at the initial meeting. Puri (74–76) says it mainly was involved in fund-raising and newspaper distribution and that its covert nature was greatly exaggerated.

71. Isemonger and Slattery, 15.

72. Ibid., 13–14.

73. Lal, "Note for the UC Study Project," 34.

2. THE SYNDICALIST GHADAR

1. Lal, "Note for the UC Study Project," 35.

2. Sir Cecil Spring-Rice, British Ambassador to the United States, to U.S. Secretary of State, 15 February 1915. Home Department, Political, Deposit, January 1915 #43 (Sareen, 70). The packet of "voluminous papers" contained an account of the efforts to foment rebellion in India, including court documents from the Lahore Conspiracy trials, supplemented by reports from the crucial intelligence source known as C.

3. Spring-Rice to U.S. Secretary of State, 15 February 1915 (Sareen, 72–73).

4. Rattan Singh, 9.

5. Puri, 69.

6. Josh, *Baba Sohan Singh Bhakna*, 38. But Gobind Behari Lal (quoted in Brown, 140–41) dated the public debut of the term "Ghadr movement" to October, at a dinner meeting held in San Francisco for American sympathizers just before this more private one, seeking political and financial support on the anniversary of the partition of Bengal. Since the first number of the *Ghadar* came out on 1 November 1913, either the date given for the in-house meetings must be too late, or the plans were already under way in other private meetings not mentioned.

7. Chenchiah "History of the Freedom Movement in India: The Ghadar Movement, 1913–1918" (n.d.) (SANA Box 4:3).

8. Mathur, 54; Brown, 145. The quote is from Har Dayal's lead article, "Our Name Is Our Work," in the first issue of the paper. See also Gerald Barrier, *The Sikhs and Their Literature* (Delhi: Manohar Book Service, 1970), 101.

9. Bureau of Immigration of the Department of Labor, Record Group 85, Hindu Situation, 1914–26, File #9.10.3, vol. 47, pp. 4325–30, National Archives and Records Administration (NARA). Lal made this statement in his testimony at an examination regarding his application for naturalization in 1916.

10. Mathur, 56; Padmavati Chandra, interview by Mark Juergensmayer and Vidya Rasmussen, New York City, May 1974, transcript (SANA Box 4:1).

11. Rattan Singh, 9–10.

12. Puri, 160–63.

13. Lal, "Note for the UC Study Project," 31.

14. Isemonger and Slattery, 17–20. They counted the weekly run thereafter as 2,500 Gurmukhi and 2,200 Urdu. But Mathur (26) says 25,000 Urdu. Is someone omitting or adding a zero?

15. Lal, "Note for the UC Study Project," 37.

16. Ibid., 42.

17. Isemonger and Slattery, 37. Rattan Singh (10) said that the twenty-five members who lived there were paid an allowance of $2 per day.

18. Vatuk, introduction to Isemonger and Slattery, viii.

19. Isemonger and Slattery, 38. A friend of Jwala Singh's, he took part in the bomb experiments at the latter's farm and left the United States in August 1914 to join the mutiny.

20. Isemonger and Slattery, 38. Hari Singh wrote poetry for the *Ghadar* under the name Fakir; he later joined the *Annie Larsen/Maverick* arms shipment mission.

21. Lal, "Note for the UC Study Project," 45.

22. *Ghadar*, 1 November 1913.

23. Record Group 118, Work Papers and Evidential Materials, U.S. vs. Bopp, Ram Chandra et al. (NARA); Secret, Foreign Directorate of 27.8.1915, D, October 1915 #43 (A. C. Bose, *Indian Revolutionaries Abroad, 1905–1927: Select Documents* [New Delhi: Northern Book Centre, 2002], 82 [henceforth Bose]).

24. *Ghadar-di-Gunj* #1 (SANA Box 2:9); Barrier, 99.

25. Mathur, 36. Even so, Anglophone audiences would remain as important for their work as Hindustani/Punjabi speakers.

26. Brown, 145–46.

27. He also referenced the work being done in South Africa, where Indians would no longer "tolerate living as a disgraced community," though he did not mention Gandhi. Ghadar had a presence in South and East Africa, on which see Zarina Patel, *Unquiet: The Life of Makhan Singh* (Nairobi: Zand Graphics, 2006); "Note on Sedition among the Indians in British East Africa," Deposit, June 1916 #5 (Bose, 227–29); "Sedition among Indians in British East Africa until 1916," Foreign Political, July 1916 #74 (Bose, 229–33).

28. See also Bhagwan Singh's *Yugantar*, 1917 (SANA Box 10:7–8).

29. According to Chenchiah (see note 7 above), Har Dayal had even given a speech upon the launch of the paper, calling himself "a disciple of the Russian revolutionary movement" and urging supporters to mark "the lessons they could learn from it."

30. *Hindustan Gadar*, Yugantar Ashram, San Francisco, 9 December 1913–July 1917 (SANA Boxes 7:20–22, 8:1–10, 9:1–5). See Puri, 79–80, for issue numbers; Urdu serialization started 8 November 1913, and Gurmukhi 23 December.

31. *Ghadar*, 23 December 1913.

32. Isemonger and Slattery, 35; Lahore Conspiracy Case Judgment.

33. Brown, 150, quoting from Balshastri Hardas, *Armed Struggle for Freedom* (Poona: Kal Prakashan, 1958).

34. Record Group 118, Work Papers and Evidential Materials, U.S. vs. Bopp, Ram Chandra et al. (NARA).

35. Lahore Conspiracy Case Judgment (Part III: On the Revolutionists in America), A, October 1915 #91.

36. See, for example, Frederic Mackarness, *The Methods of the Indian Police in the 20th Century* (San Francisco: Hindustan Ghadar Office, 1915) (SANA Box 2:29).

37. *Balance Sheet of British Rule in India* (SANA Box 1:24); Isemonger and Slattery, 33–34. The *Balance Sheet* appeared regularly on the front page, and also as a separate leaflet in Urdu, Gurmukhi, Gujarati, Hindi, and English.

38. *Angan de Gavahi* (San Francisco: Hindustan Ghadar Press, 1915) (SANA Box 1:18, 19).

39. Lal, "Note for the UC Study Project," 37.

40. *Balance Sheet of British Rule* (SANA Box 1:24).

41. From Cleveland's list of Ghadar Press publications, a Gurmukhi pamphlet that "purports to give a true account of the arrest and deportation of Bhai Bhagwan Singh Granthi from British Columbia and calls upon Indians to rise up and kill the English." Political, A, June 1914 #110–111.

42. SANA Box 1:26–29.

43. *Nim Hakim Khatara Jan, Navan Zamana, Naven Zamanen de Naven Adarshya* (SANA Box 2:1).

44. *Barabari da Arth* (SANA Box 1:33); *Social Conquest* and *Meaning of Equality* (SANA Box 2:3).

45. See Cleveland's list of Ghadar Press publications (Bose, 96–98): "The whole pamphlet is in metrical form and is highly seditious."

46. According to Darshan Singh Tatla, *A Guide to Sources: Ghadar Movement* (Amritsar: Guru Nanak Dev University, 2003), poems were contributed anonymously by Harnam Singh Tundilat, Kartar Singh Sarabha, Munsha Singh Dukhi, Wasakha Singh, Bhagwan Singh, Bela Singh, and others; several of these wordsmiths could hardly be called uneducated. Were they deliberately adopting an "earthy" style then, or were there other unlettered poets at work as well?

47. Ved Prakash Vatuk, *Thieves in My House* (Varanasi: Vishwavidyalaya Prakashan, 1969); Vatuk, "Protest Songs of East Indians on the West Coast, USA," *Folklore* (Calcutta) 7 (October 1966).

48. Isemonger and Slattery, 10.

49. Chenchiah, 5.

50. Barrier, 99–119; *Ghadar-di-Gunj* #1–7, 1914–1931 (SANA Box 2:9–14).

51. Barrier, 104–6, poem 1. Note that the above are not the complete poems, just selected couplets.

52. Barrier, 106–7.

53. Ibid., 107–8.

54. Ibid., 108–11.

55. Ibid., 111–13.

56. Home Department, Political, *Proceedings* #210–219, A (Secret), September 1914; Har Dayal in *Ghadar*, 11 August 1914; Record Group 118, Work Papers and Evidential Materials, U.S. Attorney, CA, N. Dist. Neutrality Cases: U.S. vs. Bopp, Ram Chandra et al. (NARA).

57. Isemonger and Slattery, 20; Puri, 85.

58. Isemonger and Slattery, 21. They also report 104 intercepts, including 86 copies of *Ghadar*, 6 addressed to soldiers on 7 February; 387 letters and 4 packets including 331 *Ghadar* copies, 15 for soldiers on 13 February.

59. Isemonger and Slattery, 22.

60. Ibid., 21–22. Date of letter probably early 1914.

61. Isemonger and Slattery, 24–25.

62. Ibid., 23.

63. Sawhney, 116–18.

64. Brown, 52. See Carl Glick, *Double Ten: Captain O'Banion's Story of the Chinese Revolution* (New York: McGraw-Hill Book Company, 1945); Eugene Anschel, *Homer Lea, Sun Yat-sen, and the Chinese Revolution* (New York: Praeger, 1984).

65. Brown, 151–52, drawing indirectly upon Khankhoje's diary.

66. Sawhney, 71–73.

67. As recalled by Chenchiah (2–3), the radical students too—lacking any sort of experience or military training, unlike Khankhoje and his Chinese advisers—dove into strategic debate: Should they go province by province? Where should they start? Kashmir and the North-West Frontier Province had mountains suitable for guerilla warfare, they thought, and it would be easy to rouse the masses there because there was a blatantly yawning "social, religious and economic inequality between ruling class and ruled" (2). Perhaps they could achieve a Republic of Kashmir by 1925, and then use it as a base for expanding the liberated zone province by province! (3).

68. Isemonger and Slattery, 36.

69. For full details of the *Komagata Maru* episode, see Malwinderjit Singh Waraich and Gurdev Singh Sidhu's thorough compilation of materials in *Komagata Maru: A Challenge to Colonialism; Key Documents* (Chandigarh: Unistar Books, 2005); Hugh Johnstone, *The Voyage of the Komagata Maru: The Sikh Challenge to Canada's Colour Bar* (Delhi: Oxford University Press, 1979); Isemonger and Slattery, 40–45; Sedition Committee Report, 146–49. See also the documentaries *Continuous Journey* (Ali Kazimi, 2004) and *A Time To Rise* (Anand Patwardhan, 1981).

70. Puri, 33.

71. Prog. #260, DCI 28.7.1914, B, August 1914 #259–262 (Bose, 95); Waraich and Sidhu, 92, 120 (Annexures to Lahore Conspiracy Case Special Tribunal Judgment).

72. According to Waraich and Sidhu, 232 (Annexure to Lahore Conspiracy, Special Tribunal, Second Supplementary Case), this was the organ of the United India League in Vancouver, which met every Saturday at 7.30 pm.

73. Prog. #260, DCI 28.7.1914, B, August 1914 #259–262.

74. Brown, 195.

75. For details, see Jensen, 135 (drawing on the Governor General's Correspondence, vol. 211 in Public Archives, Canada); Waraich and Sidhu, 69–80.

76. In addition, two European police officers, two Punjabi police officers, and two bystanders were killed; twenty-three passengers plus six European and five Punjabi police were wounded. Waraich and Sidhu, 126–62: an extremely detailed report compiled by Chief Secretary to Government of Bengal, #9236 P. 12 October 1914 (Confidential). Khushwant Singh's final count, drawn from Home Department, Political, *Proceedings* #345–369, June 1915, and Home Department, Political, *Consultations* #1-B, March 1915 (Khushwant Singh, appendix, 67), included 222 imprisoned, 19 killed, 21 wounded, 9 escaped, and 62 who boarded trains to Punjab. Twenty-nine disappeared and remained unaccounted for but were presumed dead, except for Gurdit Singh, who reappeared, went to jail, and later escaped to rejoin the Ghadar work. Most of the *Komagata Maru* internees were released only after the mutiny was considered broken, almost two years later.

77. Waraich and Sidhu, 276 (*Komagata Maru* Committee of Enquiry to Secretary of GOI, Home Department, Report #4465-A, 3 December 1914 [Calcutta: Superintendent Government Printing, 1914]).

78. Isemonger and Slattery, 47

79. Isemonger and Slattery (48) note that the gathering was also addressed by Barakatullah, Bhagwan Singh, and an otherwise unspecified "Muhammadan named Mahmud."

80. The Fresno *Republican* of 23 September 1914 reported that "350 Hindus gathered in a mass meeting . . . yesterday noon, and for six hours listened to speeches. . . . As a direct result . . . many Hindus will leave San Francisco Saturday, on the Manchuria for India." Ker, 224–25.

81. Ker, 224–25.

82. Puri, 92–93; Isemonger and Slattery, 49.

83. Mathur, 75–76; Isemonger and Slattery, 49; Puri, 95.

84. Jensen, 191. An exception to the small group trend was the *Tenyo Maru*, departing San Francisco 21 October with over a hundred who had been refused entry at Vancouver, plus fifty more California Sikhs (191–92).

85. Isemonger and Slattery, 54–55; Ker, 225. The *Portland Telegram* reported on 7 August 1914: "Every train and boat for the south carries large numbers of Hindus from this city, and if the exodus keeps up much longer Astoria will be entirely deserted by the East Indians. The majority of the Hindus employed at the Hammond Mills have gone and the balance are preparing to depart in the immediate future." Isemonger and Slattery, 58.

86. Chenchiah, 5.

87. Isemonger and Slattery, 50.

88. Isemonger and Slattery, 51, 59–64, 64–67. Various ships made stops in Honolulu, Yokohama, Nagasaki, Hong Kong, Manila, and Shanghai.

89. Isemonger and Slattery, 51.

90. Jensen, 192; Mathur, 75–76. A hundred were kept jailed (including Jawala Singh), and seventy-nine were released on security.

91. Sedition Committee Report, 149–50.

92. For lists of ships and passenger numbers, see Mathur, 75–76; "Memorandum on Indian Revolutionaries Abroad," Home Department, Political, A, August 1915 #216 (Sareen, 11); Puri, 97; Khushwant Singh, 68–71; tables given in Tatla (129–32), from Home Department, Political, A, *Proceedings*, September 1914 #211–224.

93. Home Poll 671–84 Part A 1915: Banta Singh's statement.

94. Tatla, 129; Isemonger and Slattery, 58.

95. Rattan Singh, 5. Isemonger and Slattery (58) reported 1,050 Indians returned from North America and the Far East between August 1914 and the first quarter of 1915, followed by 263 over the remainder of the year (based on counting names on ships' manifests?).

96. Isemonger and Slattery, 51–52.

97. Ibid., 53. Besides—alas for the inscrutability and cunning of Orientals—with "little or nothing by which to differentiate between individuals [!] it was necessary to proceed on the assumption that all were potentially dangerous" (101).

98. Puri, 95.

99. Khushwant Singh (68–71) gives these numbers: 18 passengers put under house arrest from the *Tosa Maru*, arriving in Calcutta 19 October 1914; 31 under house arrest from the *Sailun Maru*, arriving 31 October; 30 under house arrest from the *Edgware*, arriving 7 March 1915; 7 arrested from the *Ansterley*, arriving 9 March 1915. Rattan Singh (15) says that of the returned, 400 were jailed, and 2,500 interned. According to the Sedition Committee Report (155), by February 1915, of over 3,000 returning emigrants 189 were interned, and another 704 restricted to their villages. Puri (97) says that 5,000 of the 8,000 arrivals quietly "returned to their families and farmlands."

100. Account of Nawab Khan in Isemonger and Slattery, 75.

101. Isemonger and Slattery believed it likely that arrangements had been made in advance from America to secure the cooperation and guidance of the "Bengali anarchist party," (76), i.e., the Yugantar faction surrounding Rash Behari Bose and Sachindranath Sanyal.

102. Isemonger and Slattery, 75–90; Tatla, 133; DCI's weekly reports on movements and activities of Ghadarites in the Punjab, Home Department, Political, B, *Proceedings*, December 1914 #27–29; "Administrative and Police Reports on Movements of the Ghadarites in the Punjab," Home Department, Political, Deposit, *Proceedings*, January 1915 #43.

103. Isemonger and Slattery, 105.

104. Ibid., 95–96.

105. Ibid., 132.

106. Sedition Committee Report, 155.

107. Isemonger and Slattery, 84, 91; Ker, 336; Sedition Committee Report, 153.

108. O'Dwyer (198) notes that Bhai Parmanand had in the British documentation been misleadingly attributed the role of "link between the disaffected section of the Hindu intelligentsia and the Sikhs of the Ghadr Party." Brown (200–201) suggests that Pingle or Kartar Singh better suited that description. O'Dwyer and Brown are talking about the link between the Hindu intelligentsia still inside India and the returnees; I might also point out that in the United States the original Ghadar Party itself was the link between the Sikhs and the disaffected Hindu intelligentsia.

109. Isemonger and Slattery, 110.

110. Ibid., 107. Actually, although Bose had been central to the plan, the man who had actually thrown the Hardinge bomb was Basanta Kumar Biswas, and he had just been hanged. Though the bomb expert remained unseen by all but Bose, Pingle, and Ram Saran Das for the duration of his stay, the authors reported that it turned out to be a chemist called S. C. Lahiri.

111. Isemonger and Slattery, 110.

112. Ibid., 47–48; Lahore Conspiracy Case Judgment (Part III: On the Revolutionists in America), A, October 1915 #9 (Bose, 89).

113. Isemonger and Slattery, 95–96.

114. Reuters reported on 5 July 1915 that a German ship interned at Naples at the outbreak of war was found to contain an impressive array of "half a million revolvers, a hundred thousand rifles, 200,000 cases of ammunition, 2 hangars with 4 biplanes fitted with wireless apparatus and maxims, a thousand aeroplane bombs, 14 field guns, hundreds of

tons of cement, and 2 complete wireless stations" along with unidentified "important military documents." Isemonger and Slattery (88–89) speculated: "The unusual number of revolvers in the consignment would seem to indicate that the arms were meant to assist some revolutionary movement rather than to equip any proper military force." The Ghadarites perhaps? Or their counterparts in the Irish Citizen Army?

115. For more details on some of these incidents, see Isemonger and Slattery, 76–83; Sedition Committee Report, 152.

116. Called *chavies,* these were "the traditional weapon of the Central Punjab dacoit," rigged up by Gujar Singh. Isemonger and Slattery, 88–90.

117. Isemonger and Slattery, 77.

118. Rattan Singh, 7.

119. Detailed reports in Ker's list of dacoities and murders (337); Isemonger and Slattery, 111–18.

120. Ker, 336; Isemonger and Slattery, 107–9.

121. Isemonger and Slattery, 108.

122. Ker, 336: "Doctor Mathra Singh then asked us [Mula Singh and Parmanand] to bring one part potash (chlorate of potash), two parts mansle (Sulphide of arsenic), one part sulphur, one half part sugar and three or four minims of sulphuric acid in a well corked phial"—which they fetched from the bazaar. For missiles (Ker said) they might pack the casings with nails, small knives, or rifle slugs.

123. Isemonger and Slattery, 128. These included copies of *Ghadar-di-Gunj* and *Ghadar Sandesa* in Urdu and Gurmukhi, and *Ailan-i-Jang* in these languages plus Hindi.

124. Rattan Singh yet again portrayed Kartar Singh "as the model revolutionary organiser" (16). "Brilliant and resourceful, with unfailing presence of mind," when he audaciously walked at night into cantonments dressed as an officer, so convincing was his confident self-presentation that the guards saluted him. (Remember he was supposedly nineteen years old at the time!)

125. Rattan Singh, 15–16.

126. Isemonger and Slattery, 105–6.

127. Ibid., 121.

128. Ibid., 147. Hira Singh had formerly been a Hong Kong watchman, discharged and banished in 1914 as an alleged ringleader in sedition. From there he had gone to Saigon and Bangkok (where he again "delivered seditious lectures" to Ghadar sympathizers) as well as Singapore, where he took part in instigating mutiny among the Fifth Light Infantry.

129. Isemonger and Slattery, 83.

130. Ibid., 127.

131. Rattan Singh, 1.

132. Sedition Committee Report, 154.

133. Isemonger and Slattery, 124.

134. Hardas, quoted in Brown, 199.

135. Though a staunch Ghadarite, Randhir Singh (unlike many of the returnees) was also more traditionally devout. When he made the case for mutiny he emphasized the point that the government was interfering with their religion—another Akali Dal opening. He

was imprisoned for his role in the mutiny and many years later met Bhagat Singh in jail. Although the younger revolutionary revered him as a Ghadari *baba,* he was not receptive to the old priest's attempt to reconvert him to God, despite some hagiographers' assertions to the contrary.

136. Isemonger and Slattery, 123.

137. O'Dwyer, 202–6; Sedition Committee Report, 154.

138. Rattan Singh, 18–19. Two hundred were arrested in the ensuing "manhunt."

139. Shaukat Usmani, *Historic Trips of a Revolutionary: Sojourn in the Soviet Union* (New Delhi: Sterling Publishers, 1977), 6.

140. Isemonger and Slattery, 124–25.

141. Ibid., 127.

142. Ibid., 129.

143. Hardas, quoted in Brown, 200. A conflicting account says Sanyal was not even informed of the change of plan, and so when his men came out on the 21st not the 19th, they naturally got no signal to go. They were nevertheless tried in a separate Benares Conspiracy Case (Ker, 346).

144. Isemonger and Slattery, 131.

145. O'Dwyer, 19.

146. Ibid., 198. Isemonger and Slattery (131–39) provide details of later murders, raids, and attempted sabotages, lasting until August (O'Dwyer) or September (Rattan Singh, 18).

147. O'Dwyer, 198; Rattan Singh, 19. Isemonger and Slattery (123–30) said ten at Lahore were executed for knowing about the mutiny and not telling, and four at Meerut were executed for taking part in it.

148. Sedition Committee Report, 157–59; Isemonger and Slattery, 140; Evidence and Judgment, Lahore Conspiracy Case, Home Department, Political, A, *Proceedings,* October 1915 #91; Evidence and Judgment, First Supplementary Lahore Conspiracy Case, Home Department, Political, B, *Proceedings,* May 1916 #219–221 (NAI). Tatla (135–48) gives tables on verdicts of all related conspiracy cases.

149. Isemonger and Slattery, 146; Khushwant Singh, appendix.

150. For lists of sentences, see Lahore Conspiracy Case Judgment, A, October 1915 #391 (Bose, 84–89); Rattan Singh, 22–24 (SANA Box 4:12); Khushwant Singh (appendix); Isemonger and Slattery, appendices C-G; Sedition Committee Report, 157. There seems to be concurrence that 28 were hanged in all, though Tatla's tally of 142 for all Ghadar-related cases comes to 46 hanged plus 70 transported.

151. Isemonger and Slattery, 97.

152. Ibid., 103.

153. Ibid., 105.

154. Ker, 100 (my italics).

155. These included Munshi Ram, treasurer; Godha Ram, Urdu editor; Gopal Singh Sohi, Punjabi editor; Hari Singh Fakir, assistant editor (later led the *Maverick* team); Sundar Singh Ghali, office secretary; Ram Singh Dhuleta, Mahadev Aboj, Imamdin, Nidhan Singh, and Bishan Singh Hindi as general staffers.

156. B, October 1915 #206–338. "Sedition in the Far East: Reports on the Movements of Bhagwan Singh" (Bose, 261–66).

157. Deposit, May 16, 1916; "German-American Conspiracy in America" (Bose, 209).

158. History Sheet of Sagar Chand, D, January 1916 #7.

159. Popplewell, 130, and 143 n. 32, quoting Cleveland in a note of 12 July 1915 titled "The Dissemination in Siam of the Seditious Indian Newspaper 'Ghadr.'"

160. Deposit, May 16, 1916; "German-American Conspiracy in America."

161. Political, A, June 1914 #110–114. Cleveland's list of Ghadar Press publications indicates that the *Hindustani Ghadar* was identical with the earlier *Ghadar* "but was renamed to show that it aimed at raising a mutinry in India only, at the time when Lala Har Dayal came into bad odour with the American government."

162. *Ghadar* and *Hindustan Ghadar* issues from 9 December 1913 to 8 July 1917 (SANA Boxes 7:20–22, 8:1–10, 9:1–5).

163. *Yugantar* issues June to October 1917 (SANA Box 10:7–8).

164. Popplewell, 245; Home Department, Political, B, *Proceedings,* February 1917 #552–555. See Tatla, 149, on the conflict between the Khalsa Diwan Society and the Ghadar Party.

165. As an American story Ghadar fits into a literature of of Asian-American and immigrant activism that includes Paul Buhle and Dan Georgakas, eds., *The Immigrant Left in the United States* (Albany: SUNY Press, 1996); Ronald Takaki, *From Different Shores* (New York: Oxford University Press, 1994); Fred Ho, *Legacy to Liberation: Politics and Culture of Revolutionary Asian/Pacific America* (Oakland: AK Press, 2000).

166. On the IWW, see Joyce Kornbluh, *Rebel Voices: An IWW Anthology* (Ann Arbor: University of Michigan Press, 1968); Melvin Dubofsky, *We Shall Be All: A History of the Industrial Workers of the World* (Urbana: University of Illinois Press, 2000); Salvatore Salerno, *Red November, Black November: Culture and Community in the Industrial Workers of the World* (Albany: SUNY Press, 1989); Paul Brissenden, *The I.W.W: A Study of American Syndicalism* (New York: Russell and Russell, 1957); Deborah Shaffer, Stewart Bird, and Dan Georgakas, eds., *Solidarity Forever: An Oral History of the IWW* (Chicago: Lake View Press, 1985).

167. In their introduction to *Revolutionary Syndicalism: An International Perspective* (Aldershot, Eng.: Scolar Press, 1990), Wayne Thorpe and Marcel van der Linden periodize the life span of revolutionary syndicalism as roughly 1900–1940. This more or less describes the Indian revolutionary movement abroad as well, though with a seven-year lag if we start with Swadeshi extermism and end with independence.

168. Hyman Weintraub, "The I.W.W. in California, 1905–1931" (PhD diss., UCLA, 1947).

169. Sawhney, 83.

170. Brown, 110.

171. Brown, 110–11, quoting the *San Francisco Bulletin,* 8 July 1912. (As an example of such a man he mentions Francisco Ferrer.)

172. Brown, 132.

173. Spring-Rice to U.S. Secretary of State, 15 February 1915. Home Department, Political, Deposit, January 1915 #43 (Sareen, 69).

174. Sareen, 58; Mathur, 79. For an eloquent autobiographical portrait of another questing immigrant radical's sojourn with the Wobbly comrades, see Dhan Gopal Mukerji, *Caste and Outcast* (1923; repr., Stanford, CA: Stanford University Press, 2002).

175. Tapan Mukherjee, *Taraknath Das: Life and Letters of a Revolutionary in Exile* (Calcutta: National Council of Education, 1997), 150–51.

176. Isemonger and Slattery, 38.

177. Sawhney, 72.

178. Ibid., 100.

179. Brown, 137; Sawhney 93–94.

180. Brown, 133.

181. Bernard Moss, *The Origins of the French Labor Movement, 1830–1914: The Socialism of Skilled Workers* (Berkeley: University of California Press, 1976). On French radical labor of the time, see also Barbara Mitchell, *The Practical Revolutionaries* (New York: Greenwood Press, 1987); Peter Stearns, *Revolutionary Syndicalism and French Labor: A Cause without Rebels* (New Brunswick, NJ: Rutgers University Press, 1971).

182. Home Department, Political, B, *Proceedings,* #5–17.

183. This question was stimulated by a talk entitled "American Labor and Imperialism: Friends or Foes? The Twentieth Century Experience" by David Montgomery at the University of California, Santa Cruz, on 11 October 2007.

184. Billington, 440.

185. Compare Charles Bertrand's comment on Italian prewar revolutionary syndicalism in Thorpe and van der Linden, 146: "The outbreak of war created turmoil within the USI. The Mazzinian and Masonic traditions that promoted nationalism and republicanism in Italy had permeated the revolutionary syndicalist movement. The coming of war forced the members of the USI to choose between antimilitarism and the republican nationalism of Mazzini and the Freemasons." In other words, as compared to other forms of industrial unionism, revolutionary syndicalism had affinities with certain forms of nationalism associated with Mazzini and the Masons.

3. THE NATIONALIST GHADAR

1. Letter to A. C. Bose, reproduced in *Indian Revolutionaries Abroad, 1905–1927: Select Documents* (New Delhi: Northern Book Centre, 2002). In fact, one of Mueller's "most intimate friends" from India was a chemistry student from Assam with connections to the Bengali extremists.

2. Sedition Committee Report, 119–25.

3. Ker, 240–41.

4. Bose, xxvii.

5. Champakaraman Pillai was of Tamil origin but had been adopted and raised by a a progressive and eccentric Englishman, Sir Walter Strickland, who had lived in Italy and elsewhere in Europe since 1899 and was vehemently anti-Christian and anticolonialist. Pillai initially approached the German consul in Zurich, where Pillai had studied engineering and now chaired an "International Pro-India Committee," with an outline of the Indian revolutionary movement, and a request to distribute anti-British literature in Germany. The consul agreed to inform his government, and they liked the idea so much that by October they invited Pillai to work with the German Foreign Office. P. N. Chopra, ed., *Indian Freedom Fighters Abroad* (New Delhi: Criterion Publications, 1988).

6. Bhupendra Nath Dutt was the brother of Vivekananda, a veteran of the Bengali movement, as part of the Maniktola Garden circle, and editor of the paper *Yugantar.* He was jailed in 1907–8 for writing seditious articles, and then went to New York. At the start of the war he offered his services to the German Embassy in Washington, D.C., and was sent to Berlin, where he became an important member of the BIC, serving as treasurer, and later as president and secretary. He was accused in absentia in the San Francisco Hindu-German Conspiracy Case. Home Department, 1924, File #404 (Bose, 323–25).

7. Har Dayal arrived in Switzerland after a covert flight from the United States in March 1914, facing possible deportation as an accused anarchist. Barakatullah then invited his old colleague to Berlin in 1915. Mueller said of him later in a letter to Bose: "Har Dayal came later and was viewed by some of his countrymen with mistrust. In any case he was an intelligent man and of a type somewhat akin to Chatto's but without the latter's deep humanity." Mueller to Bose, 145 (see note 1 above).

8. Ker, 239.

9. Statement of Jodh Singh, 23 January 1917, File #9.10.3, Record Group 60, Reel 3. Department of Justice 8445, part 3 (Bose, 196).

10. Jodh Singh said that Har Dayal and Chatto "had considerable influence with the German Government and are the only two Indians privileged to take part in the deliberations of the German Foreign Office," which were kept secret from the other members (see note 9 above).

11. "Indo-German Plots"—Extracts, "Bengali Revolutionaries Abroad, 1900–1920," W. Bengal Paper #83 (Bose, 135).

12. Jodh Singh (see note 9 above).

13. Bose, 95; the group appears as the Indian Revolutionary Society in L. P. Mathur, *Indian Revolutionary Movement in the United States of America* (Delhi: S. Chand, 1970), 78.

14. "Indo-German Plots"—Extracts, "Bengali Revolutionaries Abroad, 1900–1920," W. Bengal Paper #83 (Bose, 135).

15. Ker, 247.

16. DCI, Deposit, 23.8.1920, August 1920 #110 (Bose, 344); Sedition Committee Report, 119–20.

17. Ker, 246–47.

18. Sedition Committee Report, 120.

19. Deposit, May 16, 1916; "German-American Conspiracy in America" (Bose, 212–14).

20. Sedition Committee Report, 119–25.

21. Nirode Barooah, *Chatto: The Life and Times of an Indian Anti-Imperialist in Europe* (New Delhi: Oxford University Press, 2004), 64 n. 8. Letter from Barakatullah to Har Dayal, 24 November 1914.

22. Emily Brown, *Har Dayal: Hindu Revolutionary and Rationalist* (Tucson: University of Arizona Press, 1975), 182; from a taped interview with the author.

23. Ker, 260–69; Popplewell, 270. The latter says there were 500 Sikh and 50 Muslim Indians among the Shanghai Municipal Police, plus 175 watchmen (unspecified sect)—and all loyal.

24. Ker, 217.

25. "Memorandum on Indian Revolutionaries Abroad," Home Department, Political, A, August 1915 #216 (Sareen, 58).

26. Mathur, 58.

27. Spring-Rice to U.S. Secretary of State, 15 February 1915. Home Department, Political, Deposit, January 1915 #43 (Sareen, 74).

28. These were Shiv Dayal Kapur, Kishan Chand, and Atma Ram. Ghadarite Tahl Singh was already there making arrangements for transporting volunteers to Siam/Burma. Mathur, 80; Sareen, 62. Details of all arrangements in "Organisation of the Hindu-German Conspiracy," Record Group 118, Reel 4, U.S. Attorney, CA, N. Dist. (NARA).

29. W. Bengal Paper #83, "Bengali Revolutionaries Abroad, 1900–1920" (Bose, 133–41).

30. "Confidential Memorandum from Acting Vice-Consul," #206–338, "Sedition in the Far East: Reports on the Movements of Bhagwan Singh" (Bose, 263).

31. B, October 1915 #206–338 (Bose, 262). Letter from British Consul in Manila to the Viceroy, 19 May 1915.

32. Senate Fact-Finding Committee, *Seventh Report on Un-American Activities in California* (1953); Home Department, Political, A, "Memorandum on Indian Revolutionaries Abroad" (Sareen, 62). Ker (270) even suggests that Bhagwan Singh was so indispensable in East Asia that the fact he remained at Manila instead of getting involved in the Siam-Burma affair is one reason why things went so wrong there.

33. Ker, 48; confirmed by informant A. Spring-Rice to U.S. Secretary of State, 15 February 1915 (Sareen, 66).

34. Record Group 118, Work Papers and Evidential Materials, U.S. vs. Bopp, Ram Chandra et al., *Ghadar* extracts (NARA).

35. Bose, 137. According to the "Report on Bengal Revolutionaries Abroad," W. Bengal Paper #83 (Bose, 138), it was the seizure of Abani' Mukherjee's notebook that really scotched the Bengal arm of the plot.

36. B, June 1917, Files #521–532, "Alleged Smuggling of Arms into India by German-Indian Plotters: Memorandum" (Bose, 219).

37. On the *Annie Larsen* and *Maverick* voyages, see Sedition Committee Report, 122–25; Ker, 248–50; Record Group 118, Works Papers and Evidential Materials, U.S. Attorney, CA, N. Dist. (NARA).

38. Ker, 248–50; Popplewell (238) says eleven thousand rifles and five hundred revolvers were transported from New York to San Francisco.

39. Star-Hunt's statements made at Singapore, 8–16 May and 5 August 1916. Records of Trial, Record Group 118, U.S. vs. Bopp, Ram Chandra et al. (NARA) (Bose, 185–92).

40. Records of Trial, Record Group 118, U.S. vs. Bopp, Ram Chandra et al. (NARA) (Bose, 185).

41. Ibid. (Bose, 186).

42. They were Harcharan Das, Mangu Ram, Gambhir Singh, and Harnam Chand.

43. Records of Trial, Record Group 118, U.S. vs. Bopp, Ram Chandra et al. (NARA) (Bose, 190).

44. Ibid. (Bose, 189). One has to wonder why Hari Singh would have trusted Star-Hunt enough to confide in him to this extent; and also why Star-Hunt was convinced they were *not* bound for India.

45. Bose, 191–92. The document contains the following observation: "Note: S. H. states that after Kurrachee and the hyphen there was a name of another place which he does not remember, but thought at the time to be the name of the province. It was a pretty long name and when Baluchistan and Afghanistan were mentioned to him he remarked that he thought the name sounded something like that." So it sounds as though there was even a possible connection contemplated between the northwestern and ocean prongs, in addition to the overlap between the northeastern and ocean prongs.

46. Bose, 191–92.

47. Ker, 248–50; Isemonger and Slattery, 157. Of the two in Singapore, Isemonger and Slattery say that one was interned and harmless, while the other turned approver. Yet Mangu Ram stayed in Manila for at least six more years, working with the Ghadar group there, before returning to India: see Mark Juergensmeyer, *Religion as Social Vision: The Movement against Untouchability in 20th Century Punjab* (Berkeley: University of California Press, 1982), 283–89. Hari Singh later married in Indonesia and remained there until 1937. Malwinderjit Singh, ed., *Diary of Baba Hari Singh Usman: Life and Writings* (Amritsar: Ravi Prakashan, 1991); cited in Tatla, 77.

48. Letter from Helfferich to A. C. Bose (Bose, 154–58).

49. As it turned out, he had fled across the Pacific to the United States. He stayed briefly in California with Dhan Gopal Mukerji, brother of his old comrade Jadu Gopal Mukherjee, discovered Socialist internationalism, made his way to New York, then had to flee again to Mexico, where he embarked on his career as a Communist luminary.

50. Sedition Committee Report, 124–25.

51. W. Bengal Paper #83 (Bose, 137); (Secret) Deposit, November 1916 #44, Statement of Abani Nath Mukherji under arrest in Singapore and Supplementary Statement of Abani Mukherji sent by Brigadier General Rideout (Bose, 240–56, 265–66). Mukherji was in Japan training in textiles in 1910, visited Germany in 1911, then returned home in 1912, still quite apolitical at this point. In 1915 he was again in Tokyo, looking for work, during which time he visited Dr. Sun a few times and talked about politics with him. Then from nowhere he got a letter from Bhagwan Singh. A friend warned him not to get involved, but he allowed himself to be recruited to pass messages and such. At Bhagwan Singh's recommendation he met with "Thakur" (aka Rash Behari Bose) in Tokyo, and then evidently took on a more active role in the arms shipping scheme. He later played a role in the expatriate Communist movement of the 1920s, first as an associate of Roy's and then as part of the Berlin circle.

52. Ker, 261; Note in Foreign Office, 27.8.1915, D, October 1915–43: "German Intrigues" (Bose, 147–53). This was "the German plot" in the Andamans and Rangoon, according to German Secret Service agent "A" (Boehm), who also claimed that eight thousand rifles were laid up in Burma with German officers waiting in Batavia, in preparation for the anticipated revolt.

53. Home Department, Political, 262/11, 1923.

54. G.E. Law, 12 March 1915, "State of Affairs in Siam" (Bose, 116–17).

55. Spring-Rice to U.S. Secretary of State, 15 February 1915. Home Department, Political, Deposit, January 1915 #43 (Sareen, 65).

56. Spring-Rice to U.S. Secretary of State, 15 February 1915 (Sareen, 63–64). See also Ker, 263–66.

57. B, August 1915 #414–439, "Dissemination of Ghadar Literature in Southeast Asia, Siam," (Secret) Letter from Minister at Bangkok to Secretary of GOI, Foreign and Political Department, Simla, 2 August 1915 (Bose, 257).

58. Ibid.

59. "Memorandum on Evidence of Sukumar Chatterjee," Deposit, 16 May 1916; "German-American Conspiracy in America" (Bose, 217–18).

60. Bose, 154 (undated letter from Helfferich to Bose). See also Ker, 260; Popplewell, 263–64.

61. Note in Foreign Office, 27.8.1915, D, October 1915–43 (Bose, 150).

62. Ker, 260. He was described as a Punjabi who arrived in Bangkok in summer 1915 and was then deported to Singapore.

63. Ker, 261.

64. Ibid., 262–63. Boehm also had on him the names of Hassan Zade, Jo [sic] Singh, Sukumar Chatterji, and Chenchiah.

65. Unless otherwise noted, the following narrative comes from the Statement of Jodh Singh, 23 January 1917, File #9.10.3, Record Group 60, Reel 3, Department of Justice 8445, part 3 (Bose, 192–206); Records of California Trial, Record Group 118, U.S. vs. Bopp, Ram Chandra et al. (SANA Box 10:4).

66. Letter from British ambassador in Bangkok to Secretary, Foreign and Political Department, GOI 12.8.1915, Sept 1915 (Bose, 221–22).

67. This was the alias Ajit Singh himself used in Persia: DCI 19.9.1911, B, October 1911 #46–69 (Bose, 118).

68. Ker, 266; Tatla, 83.

69. Ker, 267–68.

70. Ibid., 265.

71. For example, Jodh Singh was aware that there was another simultaneous arms shipment scheme under way at the German consulate, in addition to the Siam mission, and that they were scheduled to arrive at their destination (Batavia to Bengal) first. But the participants were unaware of one another's identities until later, and the consul himself seemed none too clear on which Indians were participating in which scheme.

72. Ker, 260.

73. Isemonger and Slattery, 157.

74. Ker, 262.

75. Chatterjee was arrested in Siam in August 1915; he became the first prosecution witness in the San Francisco case. W. Bengal Paper #83, "Bengali Revolutionaries Abroad, 1900–1920" (Bose, 133–41).

76. Home Department, Political, A, *Proceedings*, September 1916 #403–410. Mandalay Conspiracy Case (Bose, 272).

77. As reported by the Sedition Committee Report, 171. In another incident related in Confidential #42, 1915 #254–57: "Arrest of Indian Seditionists in Siam" (Bose, 268), the English consul in Siam, W. A. R. Wood, wrote to the British envoy extraordinary and minister plenipotentiary at Bangkok from Chiengmai on 22 September 1915 regarding something he had heard from informant Ishar Singh. While spending the night on a railway platform, Ishar Singh had encountered two Indians at 3:00 a.m. When they asked

who he was and he told his name, the questioner, who was in European dress and fluent in English, replied: "I know about you, Ishar Singh of Chiengmai. You have refused to help us. Do you call yourself an Indian? You should be ashamed to do so. If you think it wise to side with the English, side with them and die with them, for they will all be killed soon. I am not afraid of dying. If we all die, it does not matter, for our sons will carry out our work." Major Trolle and Wood both thought this man might be Sohan Lal Pathak; but that even if he wasn't, he still sounded like someone "who might with great advantage be taken into custody."

78. Telegram, 25 October 1915, to Secretary to the GOI, Foreign and Political Department, Simla (Bose, 269).

79. Home Department, Political, A, *Proceedings,* September 1916 #403–410A (Bose, 270); on verdicts from Burma and Mandalay Conspiracy cases, see also Isemonger and Slattery, 155–56 and appendix N; Ker, 266–67; Tatla, 145–46.

80. C. R. Cleveland, introduction to Ker, xi–xii.

81. Sareen, 12.

82. Sedition Committee Report, 155.

83. Home Department, Political, A, Files #318–23.

84. On the deployment of the British Indian army overseas, see Thomas Metcalf, *Imperial Connections: India in the Indian Ocean Arena, 1860–1920* (Berkeley: University of California Press, 2007); Laura Tabili, *We Ask for British Justice: Workers and Racial Difference in Late Imperial Britain* (Ithaca, NY: Cornell University Press, 1994); Michael Adas, "Contested Hegemony: The Great War and the Afro-Asian Assault on the Civilizing Mission Ideology," *Journal of World History* 15.1 (March 2004); Priya Satia, "Developing Iraq," *Past & Present* 197 (2007), 3. Vizram, *Asians in Britian.*

85. Brown, 152, quoting Bishan Singh's history of the party in *Independent Hindustan,* May 1921.

86. Record Group 60, Section 1, Files #1923–1924, Reel 2, Department of Justice, "Indian Nationalist Party Case of Violation of Espionage Act" (Bose, 173–84).

·87. "Memorandum on Evidence of Sukmar Chatterji and Jodh Singh," Deposit, 16 May 1916 (Bose, 217). Bose's note (209) says he eventually settled in Mexico and remained there until his death in 1948. I do not know if he lived there under the name of Gomez!

88. Mathur, 99.

89. Record Group 85, "Memoranda on Movements of Bhagwan Singh aka Pritam Singh aka Jakh Singh in Panama circa 1916–17" (NARA); "Memorandum on Sedition among Indians in Central America and the West Indies," Deposit, November 1916 #30 (Bose, 169–71); "Information from the India Office regarding the Activities of Bhagwan Singh and Other Seditious Indians in America and the West Indies," Deposit, March 1917 #35 (Bose, 172–73).

90. Deposit, November 1916 #30 (Bose, 169).

91. Puri, 117.

92. Jensen, 82.

93. *U.S. v. Ram Chandra et al.,* 254 *Federal Reporter* 635–37 (District Court [S.D.] California, First Division, August 4, 1917, #6133) (SANA Box 4:2).

94. Jensen, 215.

95. Record Group 118, Reel 4, U.S. Attorney, CA, N. Dist., on "The Organization of the Hindu-German Conspiracy" (Bose, 161–69).

96. Bose, 163–65.

97. Puri states that the only BIC project to incorporate significant Ghadar Party participation was the Siam-Burma scheme, whereas "in the rest of the German projects, in which some Indians participated, Ghadar share was practically nil" (119).

98. This conspiracy clause has been invoked time and time again by the British Indian courts, such a prominent component of South Asian historiography, to produce convictions based on association—that is, if one can be linked to a group, whether a criminal caste or tribe, a ring of alleged dacoits, and then from the early twentieth century onward seditionists and/or foreign bodies such as the AA or the CI, then one may be considered effectually guilty for any illegal act perpetrated by any member as part of the group's stated program.

99. Summary: *U.S. v. Ram Chandra et al.*, 254 *Federal Reporter* 635–37 (District Court [S.D.] California, First Division, August 4, 1917, #6133) (SANA Box 4:2).

100. Ibid.

101. Senate Fact-Finding Committee, *Seventh Report on Un-American Activities in California,* 1953, 214.

102. Record Group 118, U.S. vs. Bopp, Ram Chandra et al., Summary of Court Cases, Box 15 (NARA). For lists of sentences, see also Isemonger and Slattery, appendix R; Khushwant Singh, appendix; Tatla, 160. Their prison terms were as follows: Gopal Singh, one year and one day; Bhagwan Singh, eighteen months; Taraknath Das, twenty-two months; Gobind Behari Lal, ten months; Bishan Bihari Hindi, nine months; Santokh Singh, twenty-one months; Godha Ram, eleven months; Niranjan Das, six months; Mahadev Adaj, Nandekar, and Sundar Singh, three months; Munshi Ram, sixty days; Nidhan Singh, Imam Din, and Dharindra Sarkar, four months; Chandra Kanta Chakravarty, thirty days and a $5000 fine.

103. Puri, 118, quoting from the *San Francisco Call.* The Calcutta High Court ruled that the San Francisco defendants could still be tried under the Indian Penal Code after their return. The legal opinion was that the U.S. case was distinct and irrelevant, given that it was about U.S. laws violated, and thus that the U.S. court was "incompetent" to rule on Indian Penal Code Article 121 (waging war against the king-emperor). See Home Department, Political, A, Files #24–25, 1919.

104. Report of 27 August 1921, from State Hospital for the Insane at Talmage, CA. File 9.10.3.817. Record Group 118, Work Papers and Evidential Materials, U.S. vs. Bopp, Ram Chandra et al.

105. Sardar Singh to Friends of Freedom for India office, 11 May 1920 (Bud Dhillon, private papers).

106. Report of 27 August 1921, from State Hospital for the Insane at Talmage, CA. File 9.10.3.817. Record Group 118, Work Papers and Evidential Materials, U.S. vs. Bopp, Ram Chandra et al.

4. THE REPUBLICAN GHADAR

1. DCI 21.9.1907, B, October 1907 #40–49 (Bose, 17). The Indians were Parameshwar Lal and a Mr. Ghosh; the Irish were unidentified representatives of the National Party, and the Egyptian was Mr. Hafiz Awad Effendi.

2. A. C. Bose, *Indian Revolutionaries Abroad, 1905–1922, in the Background of International Developments* (Patna: Bharati Bhawan, 1971), 94.

3. DCI 10.5.1920, Deposit, June 1920 #78 (Bose, 333).

4. Barooah, 118. Chatto and Acharya had shifted operations to Stockholm from Berlin circa 1917–18.

5. See C. A. Bayly, "Representing Copts and Muhammedans: Empire, Nation, and Community in Egypt and India, 1880–1914," in *Modernity and Culture from the Mediterranean to the Indian Ocean*, ed. C. A. Bayly and Leila Fawaz (New York: Columbia University Press, 2002). On the distinctions among the competing Ottoman/Islamic, Egyptian regional, and wider Arab identifications that typified the development of Egyptian nationalism in the first decades of the twentieth century, see Anshuman Mondal, *Nationalism and Post-Colonial Identity: Culture and Ideology in India and Egypt* (New York: RoutledgeCurzon, 2003); Albert Hourani, *Arabic Thought in the Liberal Age, 1798–1939* (New York: Cambridge University Press, 1983); P. J. Vatikiotis, *The History of Egypt* (London: Weidenfeld & Nicolson, 1969); Israel Gershoni and James Jankowski, *Egypt, Islam, and the Arabs: The Search for Egyptian Nationhood, 1900–1930* (New York: Oxford University Press, 1987); John Obert Voll, *Islam, Continuity, and Change in the Modern World* (Syracuse, NY: Syracuse University Press, 1994).

6. That is, a political federation of (anti-British) cultural brethren, united in diversity, as Afghani had formulated it after his experiences in both Egypt and India, as well as in other parts of the Ottoman world. He was considered the founder of the political Pan-Islamism that produced the Indian Khilafat movement.

7. Note that even among those parts of this solidarity that were sympathetic to or identified with the Islamic world, they seem to overlook the fact that the homeland of *liberté, egalité,* and *fraternité* also had subject peoples.

8. In the United States this alliance also raises the issues of racialization, assimilation, and the possibility of attaining the grail of white status. At the time of entry, some educated Indians seemed to feel they had a claim on this status despite having dark skin, while many Irish were essentially excluded from it despite having light skin. See Nicholas Ignatiev, *How the Irish Became White* (New York: Routledge, 1995).

9. Cited in Puri, 83. Incidentally the article also suggested one could learn much from recent and current Russian and Mexican conflicts.

10. (Secret) DCI 23.1.1909, B, February 1909 #2–11 (Bose, 19–27). O'Donnell had just returned from the United States and had written a letter to the editor of the *Indian Sociologist* in which he justified the Mutiny of 1857 and made suggestions for the Indians to further their cause of "reform and freedom" through better publicity in America, and through internal unification (Bud Dhillon, private papers). See also Pauline Collombier-Lakeman, "Ireland and the Empire: The Ambivalence of Irish Constitutional Nationalism," *Radical History Review* 104 (Spring 2009), special issue on the Irish Question.

11. Barooah, 32; Indulal Kanailal Yajnik, *Shyamaji Krishnavarma: Life and Times of an Indian Revolutionary* (Bombay: Lakshmi Publications, 1950), 281–85, 310. The DCI's report of 5 May 1914 (Bose, 94) reported the interception of a packet of objectionable materials sent from Madame Cama in Paris to V. V. S. Aiyar in Pondicherry that included copies of the *Hindustanee Student* (published in San Francisco and associated with an organization linked to M. P. T. Acharya, Har Dayal, Taraknath Das, and Sarangadhar Das), *Ghadar*, Cama's own *Bande Mataram*, and *La Patrie Égyptienne*.

12. On these variations, see, for example, Ayesha Jalal, *Self and Sovereignty: Individual and Community in South Asian Islam since 1850* (New York: Routledge, 2000). Ghadarites used both *qaum* and *vatan* as well as the Sanskritic *desh* in their writings.

13. (Secret) DCI 23.1.1909, B, February 1909 #2–11 (Bose, 19–27).

14. Bose, 23–24.

15. Caxton Hall meetings on 18, 19, and 21 December 1908. Home Department, Political, Secret #3 of 1909, March 1909 #148–150 (Bose, 28–30).

16. This was still, however, less pronounced than among the secular-liberal regional Egyptianists associated with Lutfi al-Saiyyid, a tendency that became most prominent in the years following the war. Both of course shared a vehement opposition to the British presence in Egypt, though they still debated over the nature and closeness of their connection to the Sublime Porte. Kamil's followers did not object to being associated with it but simply wanted better Egyptian representation in Istanbul, whereas Abduh and Lutfi's Hizb-al-Umma, or People's Party, wanted full autonomy, free of Ottoman as well as British influence.

17. Home Department, Political, Secret #3 of 1909, March 1909 #148–150 (Bose, 28–30).

18. Ibid.

19. Ibid.

20. Barooah, 33 n. 75; Yajnik, 310.

21. Prog. #34, DCI 9.10.1909, B, November 1909 #32–41 (Bose, 40). The report also mentioned Har Dayal hoping to go to Geneva for the second meeting of the Egyptian Congress in September 1909.

22. Prog. #116, DCI 25.9.1909, B, October 1909 #11–117 (Bose, 23).

23. (Secret) DCI, Calcutta, 23.1.1909, B, February 1909 #2–11 (Bose, 26).

24. Bose, 32.

25. Barooah, 27, 32 n. 72; Yajnik, 310.

26. Barooah, 32 n. 71; Yajnik, 310. See also excerpt in Sareen, *Unsung Heroes*, 235–37.

27. DCI 13.9.1910, B, October 1910 #1–8 (Bose, 41–42); DCI 5.10.1910, B, November 1910 #17–24 (Bose, 44). The organizers of the Indian meeting decided to postpone the event from August to the third week of September, which would place it in calculated proximity to the Egyptian Congress.

28. *Kirti*, November 1927, quoted in Sohan Singh Josh, *Hindustan Gadar Party: A Short History* (New Delhi: People's Publishing House, 1977–1978), 179–80.

29. Deposit, April 1911 #7 (Bose, 48).

30. DCI 25.10.1910, B, November 1910 #317–24 (Bose, 45). Hamid el Alaily had hosted Kashi Prasad Jayaswal at Damietta on the latter's way to India.

31. DCI 5.10.1910, B, November 1910 (Bose, 44).

32. Deposit, April 1911 #7 (Bose, 48).

33. DCI 25.10.1910, B, November 1910, #317–24 (Bose, 45). Barooah (28) claims Chatto actually wrote it, along with a manuscript titled "Some Unpublished Facts on the Egyptian National Movement," in which he asserts a link between Dhingra and Wardani.

34. The tie was solid enough that when Har Dayal returned to Europe in 1914 he roomed with Rifaat in Geneva.

35. DCI 29.11.1910, B, December 1910 #7–10. Cama was helping with this, though she was also much occupied with the Savarkar case.

36. Home Department, Political, Secret #3 of 1909, March 1909 #148–150 (Bose, 29–30).

37. Prog. #102, DCI 14.3.1911, B, April 1911 #101–104 (Bose, 51).

38. DCI 29.11.1910, B, November 1910 #7–10 (Bose, 48, 122). Har Dayal reportedly left for Djibouti in September, after quarreling with Aiyar and Cama, "probably with the intention of getting into touch with the Hajis" before proceeding to Algiers and Martinique. Acharya went to Rotterdam to learn engraving, then accompanied Aiyar to Berlin to "spread their propaganda amongst the few Indian youths there."

39. Mathur, 79.

40. Popplewell, 223–42 n. 44. Previous rumors that Egyptians and Indians were united to kill Kitchener circa 1911 had not come to pass. Gobind Behari Lal had come to London in March 1915 in connection with this idea but couldn't find a volunteer.

41. Ker, 247; Popplewell, 223–26; Barooah, 57. The plot was revealed in the DCI weekly report of 29 June 1915. The Swiss government sentenced Chatto in absentia for his involvement, fining him 1,000 francs, 2.5 years in prison, and forbidding him ever to enter the country.

42. Popplewell, 223–24.

43. Spring-Rice to U.S. Secretary of State, 15 Feb. 1915, citing Home Department, Political, Deposit, January 1915 #43 (Sareen, 74). See also Foreign Office No. 371, 1916, cited in Sareem, *Unsung Heroes*, 181–96.

44. *Independent Hindustan* 1:4, December 1920, p. 93. Nehru Memorial Museum and Library (NMML).

45. Spring-Rice to U.S. Secretary of State. Home Department, Political, Deposit, January 1915 #43 (Sareen, 71).

46. *Independent Hindustan*, February 1921, p. 130 (NMML).

47. History Sheet on Aiyar, Deposit, November 1909 #32 (Bose, 52–53). Aiyar was sometimes known as Savarkar's right-hand man; he had corrected the proofs of Savarkar's writings on the mutiny. He attended subsequent meetings of the Indo-Egyptian Nationalist Association in February, then helped to organize the mutiny commemoration celebration in May, where he was one of the main speakers.

48. See Howard Brasted, "Indian Nationalist Development and the Influence of Irish Home Rule, 1870–1886," *Modern Asian Studies* 14.1 (1980). Billington (182) further suggests that Irish nationalism periodically alternated between the two "Italianate" forms of Mazzinian romantic nationalism (Young Ireland) and the "rival Carbonari model of republican conspiracy" (IRB), which Billington further associates through a rather blurry equation with "a typical alternation between national and social revolution." To reiterate,

I would argue that in colonized regions the separation between the two was never as clear-cut as it may have appeared in nineteenth-century Europe, the focus of Billington's study.

49. In exploring the particular incidences of comparison from each of these angles, I think it is important to second Brasted's note that from the perspectives of both insurgency and counterinsurgency, it was not a matter of modular importation or direct tutelage, but of observation, comparison, and conclusions drawn by learning from and applying aspects of the two situations. The Indo-Irish anticolonial relationship has gained attention through several books reviewed in a special issue of *Radical History Review* 104 (Spring 2009): Tadhg Foley and Maureen O'Connor, eds., *Ireland and India: Colonies, Culture, and Empire* (Dublin: Irish Academic Press, 2006); Julia Wright, *Ireland, India, and Nationalism in Nineteenth-Century Literature* (Cambridge: Cambridge University Press, 2007); Kaori Nagai, *Empire of Analogies: Kipling, India, and Ireland* (Cork: Cork University Press, 2006); Kate O'Malley, *Ireland, India, and Empire: Indo-Irish Radical Connections, 1919–1964* (Manchester: Manchester University Press, 2008).

50. Then, to read the later memoirs of interwar-period militants in both countries— for example, Dan Breen's *My Fight for Irish Freedom* (1924) and Manmathnath Gupta's *They Lived Dangerously* (published in 1969 but focused on the activities of the early 1920s and the following years of jail)—is to be struck by the similarity of the revolutionary programs of raids on police posts for arms, holding up trains, attempting to free arrested comrades, assassinating egregious officials, etc. It sounds as if the main difference was simply that the militant faction, and its level of popular support, were proportionally much larger in Ireland than in India.

51. Home Department, Political, A, July 1908 #137–139.

52. Brown, 62. On the alliance of Indian anticolonialists with various oppositional causes and marginal subcultures relative to the imperial mainstream, see Leela Gandhi, *Affective Communities: Anticolonial Thought, Fin-De-Siècle Radicalism, and the Politics of Friendship* (Durham, NC: Duke University Press, 2006).

53. *Independent Hindustan*, February 1921, p. 130.

54. Sareen, 5.

55. Jensen, 163. For the U.S. government, an internal security network for watching borders began in 1906 with the purpose of monitoring Mexican revolutionaries, then compounded by the fear of domestic socialism.

56. Popplewell, 36, 147.

57. Jensen, 198–99.

58. See Arvind Ganachari, *Nationalism and Social Reform in the Colonial Situation* (Delhi: Kalpaz Publications, 2005).

59. Sareen, 4.

60. Foreign Department, Secret Internal, February 1910 #56–59 (Sareen, 4).

61. Ganachari, 138.

62. B, October 1910 #17. History Sheet on Myron H. Phelps (Bose, 77–78). Phelps's other correspondents included Krishnavarma, Naoroji, the staff of Acharya's *Hindu*, and S. K. C. Ratnam in Ceylon, whose own contacts included Madame Cama and John Devoy.

63. (Secret) Prog. #78, DCI 20.6.1908, B, July 1908 #72–91 (Bose, 18).

64. Prog. #78, DCI 20.6.1908, B, July 1908 #72–78 (Bose, 74).

65. Spring-Rice to U.S. Secretary of State. Home Department, Political, Deposit, January 1915 #43, (Sareen, 72).

66. Ker, 238–39.

67. Ker, 274–75.

68. Devoy suggests in his memoir that much of the reason for the failure of the mutiny attempted in 1866—planned in ways reminiscent of the Ghadarite mutiny a half century later—was a split in the U.S. branch corresponding with a rift between the American and Irish branches, in which the Irish were horrified by the American branch's decision to raid Canada instead of coming to fight in Ireland itself.

69. But, remarks Plowman (89), "whether Casement was following the Indian example, or the Indians were following Casement's lead, is difficult to say." Given the close relations of the leaders of the two communities it seems plausible for them to have come up with it simultaneously. The same question even applied to one of their favorite catchphrases; Ker (238) notes: "For many years Indian revolutionaries have held the view, copied perhaps from their Irish supporters in New York, that England's difficulty would be India's opportunity."

70. The Irish, though, were more adamant about not accepting funding, but only purely military aid, to avoid any suggestion of obligation; was this perhaps because they had a longer history of such provisional relationships with the powerful enemies of England?

71. U.S. vs. Bopp, Ram Chandra et al., *Ghadar* extracts (NARA).

72. Ibid.

73. Accessed through James Connolly Internet Archive, http://marx.org/archive/connolly/index.htm (my italics). By "exceptional opportunities" I wonder if he means he talked to Cama—the Socialist Congress delegate—in Stuttgart, or if he had some regular contact with Indians in New York.

74. Cited in Plowman, 85.

75. Matthew Plowman, "Irish Republicans and the Indo-German Conspiracy of World War I," *New Hibernia Review* 7.3 (Autumn 2003): 80–105.

76. Plowman, 89–90; 91–92: "Meyer did meet with John Devoy at a Clan-na-Gael meeting . . . in New York, where he identified the Irish cause with that of Egyptian nationalism; so it would not be a stretch to infer his support of Indo- Irish Republicans and the Indo-German Conspiracy of World War I."

77. Padmavati Chandra, interview by Mark Juergensmeyer and Vidya Rasmussen, 18 November 1972, transcript, SANA Box 4:1.

78. Plowman, 86.

79. Bose, 348; Plowman, 95.

80. DCI, Simla, 27.9.1920, Deposit, September 1920 #71 (Bose, 348).

81. Plowman, 96.

82. According to Plowman (99), de Valera's visit to New York "predate[d] the split of the New York Clan-na-Gael into the John Devoy and Eamon de Valéra factions with respect to the proposed Free State Treaty. . . . Former Indo-German conspirators De Lacey and McGarrity sided with De Valéra. . . . However, the position of the Indian nationalists

and of such conspirators as Karr and Das seems less clear. . . . The Indian publications clearly supported De Valéra's staunch position on Irish independence. However, few Indians would have known of Devoy's quiet support of the Free State Treaty and would likely have continued supporting both factions. Yet, De Valéra was clearly the champion of the Indian cause after his 1920 New York speech."

83. Puri, 238; Janice MacKinnon and Steven MacKinnon, *Agnes Smedley: The Life and Times of an American Radical* (Berkeley: University of California Press, 1988), 59, 67.

84. Josh, *Hindustan Gadar Party*, 181–82. This sentiment was echoed in a resolution passed by an Irish Self-Determination club (in Omaha, Nebraska) in October 1919.

85. Josh, *Hindustan Gadar Party*, 182–83. A Punjabi translation of de Valera's February 1920 speech, "India atte Airlaind," refers to Ireland's version of "Panchayati Raj" (SANA Box 2:5).

86. Agnes Smedley to Ed Gammons, 18 March 1920 (Bud Dhillon, private papers). See also descriptions of the parade in MacKinnon and MacKinnon's and Price's biographies of Smedley.

87. Plowman, 100.

88. *Independent Hindustan* 1:4, December 1920, p. 93.

89. *Independent Hindustan*, February 1921 (NMML).

90. Home Department, Political, 1926, F, #8 (NAI).

91. Breen, 161. A commitment for which, somewhat ironically, Breen's most approximate Indian counterparts bitterly condemned the Mahatma, accusing him of derailing the Indian revolution into compromise, ineffectuality, and consignment of dedicated patriots to the gallows; and for the leftists, abandonment of class struggle to pander to bourgeois and feudal national elites—not to mention his spiritualistic tone, which they regarded as reactionary, opening the door to the fatal poison of communalism.

92. Breen, 162.

93. *Balance Sheet of British Rule* (SANA Box 1:24).

94. "India and Ireland: An Address by Hon. Sean T. O'Ceallaigh" (New York: Friends of Freedom for India, 1924).

95. Josh, *Hindustan Gadar Party*, 184.

96. Quoted in Josh, *Hindustan Gadar Party*, 188.

97. Quoted in Josh, *Hindustan Gadar Party*, 188–89 (emphasis in original).

98. The *Independent Hindustan* of January 1921 printed the text of the speech given to the Friends of Freedom for India.

99. See Thomas Bartlett, "The Irish Soldier in India, 1750–1947," in *Ireland and India*, ed. Denis Holmes and Michael Holmes (Dublin: Folens, 1997).

100. Home Department, Political, 1926, F, #8.

101. DCI, 25 October 1920.

102. Josh, *Hindustan Gadar Party*, 185.

103. *Independent Hindustan*, February 1921; "Hindustanees in California Sympathize with Irish and Indian Patriots in India," reported the Notes and News item.

104. Plowman, 101.

105. Josh, *Hindustan Gadar Party*, 87.

106. *Independent Hindustan* 1:3, November 1920.

107. Cemil Aydin, *The Politics of Anti-Westernism in Asia: Visions of World Order in Pan-Islamic and Pan-Asian Thought* (New York: Columbia University Press, 2007). Aydin (123) points out that even as Turkish and Iranian constitutionalists were studying Japan's system for possible application, Japanese politicians were studying Western techniques for colonial administration. He offers the telling example that top politician Okuma Shigenobu had just introduced the Japanese translation of Lord Cromer's book on the British administration of Egypt and suggested applying that very model to Korea.

108. Valentine Chirol, *Indian Unrest* (London: Macmillan and Co., 1910), 148.

109. On this, see in particular chapters 5 and 6. "The book was conveniently silent," notes Aydin, "about [Japan's] nationalism in Korea and China." It also conveniently overlooked certain key distinctions between Aurobindo Ghose and Gandhi, enabling Okawa to portray them both as representatives of a resurging Indian spirit equivalent to the Young Turks and Mustafa Kemal Pasha as representatives of a resurging Turkish spirit. While Ghose and Gandhi may have shared Okawa's antipathy to Western modernism, these particular Turks most certainly did not. Aydin, 148–53.

110. "Memorandum on Indian Revolutionaries Abroad," Home Department, Political, A, August 1915 #216 (Sareen, 61), based on a series of reports from December 1913 to April 1914. The Gaekwad's local point man was an Indian merchant named Torabally, based at Kobe, while the leader on the Japanese side was a politically influential "notorious intriguer" named Nakano Tsunetaro, who was also in regular communication with Barakatullah.

111. "Memorandum on Indian Revolutionaries Abroad," Home Department, Political, A, August 1915 #216 (Sareen, 61). (It is not stated whether anyone bothered to test it.)

112. Chenchiah, "History of the Freedom Movement in India: The Ghadar Movement, 1913–1918," 35.

113. "The Far East," DCI, Simla, 21.9.1918, B, September 1918 #191–194 (Bose, 226–27).

114. Ibid.

115. DCI 20.7.1918, B, July 1918 #413–416 (Bose, 223–25).

116. "The Far East," DCI, Simla, 21.9.1918, B, September 1918 #191–94 (Bose, 226–27).

117. Mathur, 85.

118. Chopra, 51.

119. Mathur, 84, 97.

120. Aydin, 148. While it drew an interested response and much discussion among Japanese Pan-Asianists, Aydin reports that "a pro-British daily, *The Far Eastern Review*, denounced Taraknath Das, together with Sun Yat-sen, as promoters of Japanese colonial rule in Asia under the name of Pan-Asianism and the Asia Monroe Doctrine," after which British authorities banned it and attempted to curtail its distribution.

121. Let me note, looking ahead, that these views indicate a divergence in Das's thinking from the "Ghadar core principles"; cf. Usmani's conversation with Acharya in the next chapter, differentiating the right-wingers, including Das, from the Roy and Chatto/Barakatullah factions in postwar Moscow and Berlin. The latter had the closer Ghadar affinities.

122. "Japanese Affairs," DCI 20.7.1918, B, July 1918 #413–416 (Bose, 225).

123. Das to Recht from Leavenworth, 5 September 1918, Record Group 118 (NARA).

124. Incidentally, regarding vocabulary, the Ghadar writings use the terms *mulk* (implying political unit—as in *azad* or *ghulam mulk*, "free" or "slave") and *qaum* variously, but especially to differentiate national from religious matters (*qaumi* vs. *mazhabi*); but displaying the eclecticism of their use of Hindustani language, they also use *desh* and *deshsewak*, as well as *vatan* and *vatanparast*, to indicate active patriots.

125. D, 32 November 1909, History Sheet of B. C. Pal (*vide* Appendix C.I. Circular #7 of 1909) (Bose, 57) (my italics).

126. For example, those criticisms leveled by sympathizers such as Paul Richard, or indeed by German romantics and Russian Slavophiles—with both of whom Indian nationalists abroad had certain affinities or interactions. For example, Aydin quotes this passage from Richard's *The Idea of the East*: "The sad problems of Western society turn us to seek a higher solution in Indian religion and Chinese ethics. The very trend of Europe itself, in German philosophy and Russian spirituality, in its latest developments, towards the East, assists us in the recovery of these nations themselves nearer to the stars in the night of their material oblivion." See also Vasant Kaiwar and Sucheta Mazumdar, eds., *Antinomies of Modernity: Essays on Race, Orient, Nation* (Durham, NC: Duke University Press, 2003).

127. There was a minority element of "Easternists" in the 1920s who participated in the League against Imperialism and Pan-Asian venues. See Gershoni and Jankowski; Aydin.

128. Home Department, Political, 262/11, 1923: Appendix I: Note on Santokh Singh.

5. THE COMMUNIST GHADAR

1. This must be seen in the context of the debacle in China, the Guomindang attack on the CCP, for which Roy was held partially responsible. This "Far Left" line lasted until 1935, when it was superseded by the United Front policy. Between 1920 and 1928, however, as the application of the national-colonial theses was still being tested, things were less clear-cut. Here it was a double strategy of working with the leftist factions of the national movement to revolutionize it from within in partnership with legal Worker Peasant parties, while simultaneously building an autonomous, illegal Communist Party alongside it. See also Sanjay Seth, *Marxist Theory and Nationalist Politics: The Case of Colonial India* (New Delhi: Sage Publications, 1995).

2. Eugene Overstreet and Marshall Windmiller, *Communism in India* (Berkeley: University of California Press, 1959), 30.

3. See M. N. Roy, *Memoirs* (Bombay and New York: Allied Publishers, 1964); John Haithcox, *Communism and Nationalism in India: M. N. Roy and Comintern Policy, 1920–1939* (Princeton, NJ: Princeton University Press, 1971). Roy, of course, had been pursuing his own separate relationship with the Bolsheviks ever since he had abandoned his role in he Bengali arms trans-shipment scheme during the war, sojourning in the company of activists affiliated with the HGP and/or FFI in the United States, where he was converted to Communism, and then fleeing south of the border, where he catalyzed the formation of the Communist Party of Mexico in 1917 under the tutelage of Michael Borodin. Interestingly, Pandurang Khankhoje formed even closer and more lasting associations with the Mexican Left when he arrived there in the mid-1920s.

4. See Bhagwan Josh, *Communist Movement in Punjab, 1926–47* (Delhi: Anupama Publications, 1979); Gurharpal Singh, *Communism in Punjab: A Study of the Movement up to 1967* (Delhi: Ajanta Publications, 1994); also Gail Omvedt, "Armed Struggle in India: The Ghadar Party I–III," *Frontier* 7:29 (November 9, 1974), 7:30 (November 19, 1974), 7:31 (November 23, 1974) (SANA Box 4:9). Rattan Singh comments on this too in his "Brief History of the Hindustan Gadar Party," submitted to the LAI in 1927 (SANA Box 4:12).

5. See Tilak Raj Chadha on "Red and White communism" in "Punjab Communists: An Analysis—II," *Thought* 4.31 (25 August 1952) (SANA 4:29); on the Lal Communist Party, see Singh, *Communism in Punjab*; Shalini Sharma, "Developing a Communist Identity: The Case of the Naujavan Bharat Sabha," *Journal of Punjab Studies* 14.2 (Fall 2007).

6. Josh, *Communist Movement in Punjab*, 108–9. In addition to the Comintern, Kirti also maintained communications with the Red Peasants International (Krestintern) and League against Imperialism (Petrie, *Communism in India*, 83–87; Bhagwan Josh, *Communist Movement in Punjab*, 64).

7. Muzaffar Ahmed, *Myself and the Communist Party of India*, 2–3. On the development of Indian communism, see Overstreet and Windmiller; Muzaffar Ahmed, *The Communist Party of India and Its Formation Abroad* (Calcutta: National Book Agency, 1962); G. Adhikari, ed., *Documents of the History of the Communist Party of India* (New Delhi: People's Publishing House, 1971–1982); and on Punjabi communism in particular, Singh, *Communism in Punjab*; Josh, *Communist Movement in Punjab*.

8. Rattan Singh, 3.

9. Home Department, Political, December 1919, A, Files #1–7: report on the Near East; and K.W. Eastern Section to *Soviet Land*, 1920: "All Moscow organisations at present working in opposition to British rule should be given every possible assistance in the war of arms, literature and money. This side of the question must however, be kept strictly secret."

10. Sohan Singh Josh, *Hindustan Gadar Party: A Short History* (New Delhi: People's Publishing House, 1977–1978), 205.

11. Josh, *Hindustan Gadar Party*, 205, quoting Chinmohan Sehanavis, *Lenin and India* (Calcutta: Manisha, 1969).

12. Jon Jacobson, *When the Soviet Union Entered World Politics* (Berkeley: University of California Press, 1994), 8–9.

13. DCI 5.4.1920, Deposit, April 1920 #103 (Bose, 330).

14. Prog. #495, DCI 12.5.1919, B, June 1919 #494–97 (Bose, 322).

15. DCI 26.1.1920 (Bose, 328).

16. Indeed, throughout his revolutionary career he was never entirely trusted by those connected with Ghadar and Kirti. Throughout the mid-1920s he traveled in the Baltic states, lecturing and showing anti-British "picture shows" on "India and her present life." According to the DIB he traveled on an Afghan passport and lived by journalism. He was in contact with both Kirtis and Akalis in Punjab, from whom he requested propaganda materials. He also visited the United States in 1925–26, offering his services to the Ghadar Party as their representative in Moscow. They refused and disavowed him in 1929. In the next decade he traveled frequently as a "business agent for manufacturers" of electrical

appliances, textile machinery, gas masks, armaments, and explosives, taking orders from firms in the United States and Germany for arms that he wanted to sell in the Middle East. By 1939 he was said to be living in Germany, having developed extensive connections there, with a German wife and an adopted seventeen-year-old Indian son, and on good terms with the Nazis. His German son joined the Indian Legion of the German army, and his Indian son was linked to a UP terrorist group seeking to import arms. IOR/L/PJ/12/65.

17. Cecil Kaye, *Communism in India, 1919-1924* (1924; repr., Calcutta: Editions Indian, 1971). In addition to Liebknecht, he counted Radek as an "intimate friend," and was also alleged to be an "intimate" of such key figures as Har Dayal, Barakatullah, M. P. T. Acharya, and Mahendra Pratap. IOR/L/PJ/12/65.

18. DCI 27.9.1920, Deposit, September 1920 #71 (Bose, 344-60). This time he received funding from German general Hoffman and deposed Ottoman minister Talat Pasha.

19. "Indian Communists—Reports on Individuals," DCI 21.6.1920, Deposit, July 1920 #13.

20. Bose, xxxix-xl. Regarding this more meaningful link, in fact, one of Smedley's biographers even suggests that when Chatto was seeking recognition from Moscow for the Indian independence movement abroad, it was his implied association with Ghadar and the American Friends of Freedom for India that give him credibility. Ruth Price, *The Lives of Agnes Smedley* (New York: Oxford University Press, 2005), 90-98.

21. Joan Jensen, *Passage from India: Asian Indian Immigrants in North America* (New Haven, CT: Yale University Press, 1988), 256-65; Harold Gould, *Sikhs, Swamis, Students, and Spies: The India Lobby in the United States, 1900-1946* (New Delhi: Sage Publications, 2006), 266-73. Senator Royal S. Copeland's proposed 1926 bill, S 4505, regarding who should count as "White" included Mexicans, Arabs, Indians, Jews, Gypsies, Eastern Europeans, Slavs, and Mediterraneans. The bill was defeated in 1927. Copeland, "Hindus Are White: A Plea for Fair Play to Americans" (New York: Hindu Citizenship Committee, 1927) (SANA Box 4:4).

22. Jensen, 224.

23. Appendix to DCI weekly report for 14 July 1919.

24. Home Department, Political, October 1919 File #28.

25. Home Department, Political, B, February 1919. Progs. #181-184. DCI weekly report, February 1919.

26. Jensen, 236.

27. See Janice MacKinnon and Stephen MacKinnon, *Agnes Smedley: The Life and Times of an American Radical* (Berkeley: University of California Press, 1988); Ruth Price, *The Lives of Agnes Smedley* (New York: Oxford University Press, 2005); Agnes Smedley, *Daughter of Earth* (New York: Coward-McCann, 1929).

28. Record Group 60, Section I, Files #1923-1924, Department of Justice, Reel 2, Indian Nationalist Party, Case Violation of Espionage Act (NARA).

29. *Novi Mir* was a Russian-language Socialist organ founded in 1911 in the United States. Originally Menshevik-identified, it was taken over by a Bolshevik faction in 1917. Until it was forcibly shut down in 1920, it expressed support for the Soviet government and also had connections to the American CP.

30. DCI weekly report. Home Department, Political, B, April 1919. Progs #148–152 (ACH, 1919:14); weekly report, 31 March 1919, CID Simla (Bose, 322).

31. Tapan Mukherjee, *Taraknath Das: Life and Letters of a Revolutionary in Exile* (Calcutta: National Council of Education, 1998), 134.

32. According to Gould (242), the government's only response to the letter was a grand-jury indictment of all the above-named officers.

33. Record Group 60, Section I, Files #1923–1924, Department of Justice, Reel 2, Indian Nationalist Party, Case Violation of Espionage Act (NARA).

34. The evidence was indirect: not the letter itself, but a *mention* of such a letter in correspondence from Wotherspoon to his father-in-law.

35. Jensen, 233–35. Wotherspoon was threatened with disbarment for his support of Das, and for harboring said false representatives in violation of said act, despite a letter from Wotherspoon to President Wilson arguing that citizens should have the right to freely address the president on the welfare of the country (Das had been granted citizenship in 1914). "We recognize that, in wartime, Free Speech has its dangers," Wotherspoon acknowledged. "But suppression of speech is at all times dangerous."

36. W. Bengal Paper #83 (Bose, 323).

37. Jensen, 235.

38. T. R. Sareen, *Select Documents on the Ghadr Party* (New Delhi: Mounto Publishing House, 1994), 181.

39. DCI 23.6.1919, B, June 1919 #701–704 (Bose, 319); and Prog. #158, DCI 9.11.1918, B, December 1918 #158–159 (Bose, 316–19). See also Savitri Sahwney, *I Shall Never Ask for Pardon: A Memoir of Pandurang Khankhoje* (New Delhi: Penguin Books, 2008), for details of his life, career, and leftist political engagement in Mexico from the 1920s to the 1950s.

40. Jensen, 228–29. Jensen mentions that the Labor Department received "insinuating reports" from the head of military intelligence after the war, regarding sexual relations between Indian men and American women and suggesting hopefully that publicizing such things among the Indians might "interfere with their anti-British propaganda." This might have referred not only to Agnes Smedley but to Evelyn Roy, Frieda Hauswirth, and Mary Keatinge Morse, to name the most prominent. See also Kumari Jayawardena, *The White Woman's Other Burden* (New York: Routledge, 1995), 229–44.

41. Jensen, 228–29.

42. Appeal addressed to "The Friends of India" against the deportation of Gopal Singh in 1919, for which the warrant went out on the day of his release from a year-and-a-day prison term following the San Francisco case (SANA Box 3:9).

43. Josh, *Hindustan Gadar Party*, 201. Kar had been accused in the San Francisco Conspiracy Case but exempted from appearing in court because of his tuberculosis.

44. Kar to Gopal Singh, 31 March 1920 (Bud Dhillon, private papers).

45. Puri, 238.

46. Indicated in a letter from Ghose, quoted in DCI 26.1.1920 (Bose, 328–29).

47. Smedley to Gammons and Gopal Singh, 31 October 1919.

48. Puri, 225.

49. Correspondence between the Friends of Freedom for India and the Hindustan Gadar Party, 1919–1921 (SANA Box 4).

50. Jensen, 238.

51. Appeal, "To the Friends of India," Correspondence of FFI/HGP, 1919–1921 (SANA Box 3:9; and Bud Dhillon, private papers).

52. Ed Gammons, "India Is in Revolt," HGP, San Francisco, 1919 (SANA Box 2:15).

53. Smedley to Gammons and Gopal Singh, 11 November 1919 (Bud Dhillon, private papers).

54. Smedley to Gammons and Gopal Singh, 31 October 1919 (Bud Dhillon, private papers).

55. Letter to Labor Unions from FFI, signed Agnes Smedley and Robert Morss Lovett, date unclear.

56. Letter to Labor Unions from FFI, signed Agnes Smedley and Robert Morss Lovett, date unclear (Bud Dhillon, private papers).

57. Josh, *Hindustan Gadar Party*, 173–74. Other speakers discussed education, the effects of economic exploitation, the Hindu-Muslim question, the current independence struggle, international conditions, and America's duty to the Indian struggle.

58. Amir Haider Khan, *Chains to Lose: Life and Struggles of a Revolutionary* (New Delhi: Patriot Publishers, 1989), 236–38.

59. MacKinnon and MacKinnon, 65–68.

60. Khan, 238.

61. Khan, 173.

62. Jensen, 242, 245.

63. Smedley to Bishan Singh, 5 August 1920.

64. Smedley to Bishen Singh, Santokh Singh, and Kar, 10 September 1920 (Bud Dhillon, private papers).

65. Isemonger and Slattery, 152–54. See also Home Department, Political, File #262/11, 1923: Appendix I: Note on Santokh Singh.

66. Other officers included Harjap Singh as president, Bishan Singh, and Niranjan Singh Dhillon.

67. Josh, *Hindustan Gadar Party*, 202.

68. Home Department, Political, File #262/11, 1923.

69. Puri, 238–39.

70. Josh, *Hindustan Gadar Party*, 202.

71. *Independent Hindustan* 1:5, January 1921; and 1:7, March 1921.

72. Das to his "dear brothers" of Ghadar, 23 September 1920 (Bud Dhillon, private papers).

73. Puri, 239; Josh, *Hindustan Gadar Party*, 202.

74. Quoted in Josh, *Hindustan Gadar Party*, 243.

75. Josh, *Hindustan Gadar Party*, 245 (emphasis in original). This was a precise parallel to the stated goal of the Hindustan Republican Association, which became the Hindustan Socialist Republican Association in 1928, as the *United States of India* was ceasing operations.

76. Josh, *Hindustan Gadar Party*, 249–50. The preceding examples are from the June, July, and October 1924 issues.

77. Josh, *Hindustan Gadar Party*, 248–49.

78. Ibid., 250–53.
79. Ibid., 208.
80. *Independent Hindustan* 1:5, January 1921.
81. Home Department, Political, File #262/11, 1923.
82. Josh, *Hindustan Gadar Party*, 200.
83. Ibid., 211; Puri, 246. Home Department, Political, File #262/11, 1923—August 1921. Reports noted that "mutual quarrels and the non-receipt of funds from India resulted in strained relations between Santokh Singh and other Sikhs." Meetings were held at Brawley in December 1921 and Stockton in January 1922 at which they "indulged in wild talk about introducing arms into India and of 'deadly preparations.'. . . 'We need a million volunteers.'"
84. Josh, *Hindustan Gadar Party*, 214. Home Department, Political, File #262/11, 1923.
85. DCI, Simla, 27.9.1920, Deposit, September 1920 #71 (Bose, 349).
86. Ibid.
87. Josh, *Hindustan Gadar Party*, 291. The CP of Germany also helped out at disembarkation points, as the Americans did at embarkation points.
88. Sareen, 94 (editor's annotation). See Senate Fact-Finding Committee, *Seventh Report on Un-American Activities in California, 1953*, 213–46.
89. Senate Fact-Finding Committee, *Seventh Report*, 221.
90. Ibid.
91. Ibid.
92. Home Department, 1926, Political, *Proceedings*, File #236/II/26 (Bose, 418).
93. DCI 12.1.1920, D, February 1920 #52, "Indian Revolutionaries Abroad" (Bose, 327–28).
94. Bose, 405. Compare Josh's Appendix 10 in *Hindustan Gadar Party*, 330–32, listing Ghadar students in Moscow. One of the black students must have been Harry Haywood.
95. Home Department, Political, File #193, in Josh, *Communist Movement in Punjab*, 109; Puri, 252.
96. Josh, *Communist Movement in Punjab*, 110.
97. Quoted in Kaye.
98. Josh, *Hindustan Gadar Party*, 275–76.
99. Ibid., 289.
100. Ibid., 277–78.
101. Ibid., 291–92.
102. Ibid., 218. See also Shaukat Usmani, *Historic Trips of a Revolutionary: Sojourn in the Soviet Union* (New Delhi: Sterling Publishers, 1977); Muzaffar Ahmed, *Myself and the Communist Party of India, 1920–1929* (Calcutta: National Book Agency, 1970).
103. Josh, *Hindustan Gadar Party*, 293, quoting Rattan Singh Gholia.
104. Josh, *Hindustan Gadar Party*, 294–95, quoting Jawala Singh and Raja Singh.
105. Josh, *Communist Movement in Punjab*, 109 (Home Department, Political, File #193).
106. Josh, *Hindustan Gadar Party*, 294.
107. Senate Fact-Finding Committee, *Seventh Report*, 241.
108. Ernestine Evans had written from England and Germany during the war, later became the Balkan correspondent for the *London Daily News*, and was repeatedly

suspected but not proved to be involved with Communist front organizations in the United States.

109. Ernestine Evans, "Looking East from Moscow," *Asia* 22 (December 1922) 972–76.

110. Political and Secret Department, File #1040/1922. After 1925 there were instructors fluent in Punjabi, Farsi, and Urdu.

111. M. N. Roy's American wife, Evelyn Roy, is often credited with substantially guiding his ideological transition to socialism.

112. Evans's further investigations revealed that thirty boys in the dormitory room got two meals a day, and some had additional food from their sponsoring societies or brought with them from home (975). The Armenians were from peasant families who grew wheat, barley, and raisin-grapes in Russia. After finishing school, these boys worked in a tobacco factory near their parents' farms and then joined a Communist Youth society started by a Persian youth in their town. Evans.

113. Evans, 975.

114. Foreign & Political Ex. Progs. #556-X 1935 (Secret). Chelmsford to DIB, 21-7-34.

115. Bose, xxxix–xl.

116. Puri, 240–41.

117. DCI, Simla, 27.9.1920, Deposit, September 1920 #71 (Bose, 349).

118. Home Department, Political, File #4/1926 (Bose, 415).

119. Home Department, 1926, Political, *Proceedings,* File #236/II/26, "Secret Intelligence Requirements in America with Special Reference to the Ghadar Movement" (Bose, 418).

120. "Strictly Secret," Home Department, Political, 8 File #235/11/26, 1926, "Supplementary Note on Sikh Conspiracy" (Bose, 402). An intelligence note of January 1926 reported that Sikhs in Amritsar and Kabul were in covert touch with Moscow and Istanbul, as well as with the Ghadar Party in the United States. Home Department, 1926, Political, *Proceedings,* File #236/11/26 (Bose, 417–18).

121. "Strictly Secret," Home Department, Political, 8 File #235/11/26, 1926, "Supplementary Note on Sikh Conspiracy" (Bose, 410).

122. Foreign & Political, Near-East Progs. #565-N, 1931, and #225-F, 1931, regarding the smuggling of arms from San Francisco to India picking up in 1930.

123. Fowle to GOI Foreign Secretary on 11 July 1931, Foreign & Political, Near-East Progs. #565-N, 1931, and #225-F, 1931.

124. Omvedt (see note 4 above).

125. A, April 1915 #216–218, "Alleged Revolutionary Movement in Hankow," by F. Isemonger, 10 August 1914 (Bose, 115). The total Indian population in China was unknown as of April 1915, but a tally three years prior had found 1,228 Indians in Shanghai alone. Isemonger and Slattery, 52. Another note to the DCI from the Superintendent for Sikhs, Shanghai Municipal Police, said there were 1,100 Indians in Shanghai, of whom about 900 were Sikhs, of whom 500 were ex-sepoys, plus 50 additional Punjabi Muslims and Pathans employed as police, and the remainder as watchmen. There were 2,000 Indians in Hong Kong, "many" in the Straits Settlements, who were mostly "downcountry coolies," but there were also many Sikhs in Singapore, Penang, Kelantan, and Kuala Lumpur.

126. Josh, *Hindustan Gadar Party,* 258.

127. Ibid., 239.

128. Josh, *Communist Movement in Punjab*, 63.

129. "Supplementary Note on Sikh Conspiracy" (Bose, 408).

130. Josh, *Hindustan Gadar Party*, 240–41; drawing on a 1973 interview with Bud Dhillon, aka Shamsher Singh, one of the Ghadarite trainees. The mission included Dasaundha Singh, age 26, who left the University of British Columbia to join the mission; Shamsher Singh, age 23, son of the secretary of the Stockton Khalsa Diwan; and Inder Singh, age 36, "uneducated but said to be an important member of the Ghadar party."

131. "Supplementary Note on Sikh Conspiracy" (Bose, 408).

132. Ibid. (Bose, 411).

133. Omvedt, 9, referring to Petrie report on the eighty Sikh watchmen who formed a GMD military unit in Hankow.

134. Josh, *Hindustan Gadar Party*, 265–66.

135. Ibid., 267.

136. Ibid., 263.

137. Omvedt, 10 (SANA).

138. See *Ghadar Dhandhora*, Nanking, 1930–1. Eastern People's Association (by India section with Hindustan Gadar Party sponsorship) (SANA Box 7:19).

139. Josh, *Hindustan Gadar Party*, 266–67. Quoting Petrie's report in translation.

140. Josh, *Hindustan Gadar Party*, 269–70.

141. Rattan Singh, 7.

142. Josh, *Hindustan Gadar Party*, 260. The men then offered their services to the Chinese governor of Canton instead.

143. "Supplementary Note on Sikh Conspiracy": Personal and Confidential Letter from Special Immigration Agent in Vancouver to Mr. Cory, August 1925 (Bose, 411–15).

144. Josh, *Hindustan Gadar Party*, 284. These places included Hong Kong, Singapore, Shanghai, Malaya, New Zealand, Nairobi, Oregon, California, Washington, Canada, Mexico, Panama, and Argentina.

145. Puri, 257.

146. Home Department, 1926, Political, *Proceedings*, File #236/II/26 (Bose, 418).

147. Bose's note (418) on the preceding document.

148. Josh, *Hindustan Gadar Party*, 289. Josh gives this example of a translated verse entitled "Aims and Means":

Our aim is complete independence—not to remain under the yoke of any foreigner and suffer disgrace. Its content is workers' freedom, don't attach any other meaning to it. This has to be seized after spilling blood—after fighting the enemies and suffering all eventualities. The Gadar Party's sacred ordainment is: Wrestle we must, whether we win or lose.

149. Josh, *Communist Movement in Punjab*, 63.

150. "Strictly Secret," Home Department, Political, 8 File #235/11/26, 1926, "Supplementary Note on Sikh Conspiracy" (Bose, 402). This conflicts with Foreign & Political, Frontier Progs. #20, 1932 (or is this another Ishar Singh?).

151. "Supplementary Note on Sikh Conspiracy" (Bose, 406); Foreign & Political, Frontier Progs. #20, 1932.

152. Senate Fact-Finding Committee, *Seventh Report*, 221–22.

153. Josh, *Communist Movement in Punjab,* 108.

154. DCI, Simla, 1.9.1919, B, September 1919 #454–457 (Bose's annotation of the documentation of the project comments: "This appears highly impossible.")

155. Sareen, 100–101. Note that there was, to my knowledge, no Ghadar propaganda in Tamil or other southern languages, and relatively little mobilization of the indentured population in Trinidad, Guiana, or environs.

156. Bhagat Singh Bilga, interview by Teena Baruah in *Harmony Magazine,* April 2005, http://www.harmonyindia.org., "Talking about a Revolution"; Jaspal Singh and Jagdip Mann, interview, 30 June 1997, published with Jaspal Singh, "A History of the Ghadar Movement," http://www.panjab.org.uk/english/histGPty.html. See also Home Department, Political 29/88/38, 1938. The Punjab CID made note of a man called Bhagat Singh who was "believed to be a supporter of the Ghadar Party in Argentina"; 3–1–39 (23–12–08).

157. Josh, *Hindustan Gadar Party,* 288.

158. Ibid.

159. Ibid., 284–86, 289–90, drawing upon statements made to him by eleven of the Moscow trainees.

160. Josh, *Hindustan Gadar Party,* 290.

161. Ibid.

162. Senate Fact-Finding Committee, *Seventh Report,* 223.

163. Ibid.

164. Puri, 267.

165. Josh, *Hindustan Gadar Party,* 222 (J. Crear, an official, to the viceroy's private secretary, 5 November 1923).

166. Home Department, Political, File #41/1926. British Consul General in San Francisco to British Consul General in Mexico City (Bose, 414–16); also see Petrie, *Developments in Sikh Politics, 1900–1911: A Report* (Amritsar: Chief Khalsa Diwan, 1972).

167. Petrie in Home Department, Political, Files #262/11, 1923, and #7, 1924. A series of letters revealed some agitation about what to do with this "undoubtedly . . . very dangerous man, to whom the giving of security under the Criminal Procedural Code means nothing at all." The decision could set a precedent for other "Indians involved in Bolshevik or other analogous activities abroad." Crear responded that despite copious information on the detainee, they had no evidence of his doings in Russia; there was evidence from the U.S. case, but it could not be used afresh. Still, there could not be "any reasonable doubt that he return[ed] to India after his experience in Russia . . . with a definite mission, and with a definite intention, to foment trouble among the Sikhs." Thus his release would be most "unwise" given the "present state of excitement" among the Sikhs following the Akali Conspiracy trials; best to keep him restrained. Home Department, Political, File #262/11, 1923; letter from Mr. Townsend of the Punjab Civil Secretariat, Lahore, 25–10–23, to J. Crear, Secretary to GOI, Home Department, Delhi: regarding a decision not to proceed under Re. III of 1818 against Santokh Singh.

168. Josh, *Hindustan Gadar Party,* 286, from Home Department, Political, File #235/11/26, 1926. His letters, written from Mexico and Berlin, alluded to money to be sent to Kabul from the United States and Canada; Russian assistance for agricultural work in Tashkent, which the Home Department supposed was actually something ominous to do

with weapons; and his own intentions to travel to Cuba, Paris, and Constantinople. Home Department, Political, File #41/1926, Public, P&J (S) 474. J.E. Ferard, Secretary, Public and Judicial Department, to India Officer, 8 April 1926 (Bose, 399–400). He also planned to rendezvous in Italy with the first batch of Moscow-bound trainees from California, although, as it turned out, they took a different route. He finally arrived in Punjab in time to meet with Bhupendranath Dutta before returning to Kabul.

169. Josh, *Hindustan Gadar Party,* 287, from Home Department, Political, File #235/11/26, 1926.

170. Josh, *Hindustan Gadar Party,* 106–8.

171. "Strictly Secret," Home Department, Political, 8 File #235/11/26, 1926, "Supplementary Note on Sikh Conspiracy: Note on Emissaries" (Bose, 403).

172. Josh, *Hindustan Gadar Party,* 218–19; Josh, *Communist Movement in Punjab,* 65 (quoting from Home Department, Political, File #262/11, 1923). The Akali movement already encompassed a "radical bloc" and a more communalist, reactionary section; the émigré revolutionaries were the backbone of the radical wing.

173. Santokh Singh received 10,000 rupees from Kabul to purchase the press, plus 3,200 more from America.

174. Petrie, as cited in "Supplementary Note on Sikh Conspiracy" (Bose, 402). Home Department, Political, File #122, 1938: Notes on *Kirti,* January 1926, Amritsar (NAI).

175. Sohan Singh Josh, *My Tryst with Secularism: An Autobiography* (New Delhi: Patriot Publishers, 1991), 105–6.

176. Ibid.

177. Josh, *Hindustan Gadar Party,* 225.

178. Josh, *My Tryst with Secularism,* 110. The idea is credited to Harjan Singh.

179. Josh, *Hindustan Gadar Party,* 227.

180. Home Department, Political, File #122, 1938: Notes on *Kirti,* January 1926, Amritsar.

181. "Supplementary Note on Sikh Conspiracy" (Bose, 402).

182. Josh, *My Tryst with Secularism,* 116–17.

183. Ibid., 120.

184. Josh, *Hindustan Gadar Party,* 226.

185. Ibid.

186. Ibid.

187. *Kirti,* October 1924 issue.

188. Josh, *Hindustan Gadar Party,* 225.

189. Josh, *My Tryst with Secularism,* 104–5.

190. Ibid., 114. Is this the same Gurmukh Singh? The cognomen of "the traveler" would fit.

191. Josh, 115. Yet again, this criticism of the *Ghadar/Kirti* is perhaps unintentionally revealing.

192. Josh, *My Tryst with Secularism,* 101.

193. Ibid., 104.

194. Ibid., 106–8.

195. Ibid., 102.

196. Does he mean the University of the Toilers of the East?

197. Josh, *My Tryst with Secularism*, 110–11.

198. See Tanika Sarkar for analysis of different portrayals; also Neeti Nair, "Bhagat Singh as Satyagrahi: The Limits to Non-Violence in Colonial India," *Modern Asian Studies* 43.3 (2009).

199. See, for example, Ajoy Ghosh, *Bhagat Singh and His Comrades* (New Delhi: People's Publishing House, 1979); Gopal Thakur, *Bhagat Singh: The Man and His Ideas* (New Delhi: People's Publishing House, 1962); L. P. Mathur and Gurdev Singh Deol, *Shaheed-e-Azam Sardar Bhagat Singh: The Man and His Ideology* (Nabha: Deep Prakashan, 1978); S. R. Bakshi, *Bhagat Singh and His Ideology* (New Delhi: Capital Publishers, 1981); Sohan Singh Josh, *My Meetings with Bhagat Singh and on Other Early Revolutionaries* (New Delhi: Communist Party of India, 1976). His writings have also been collected and commented on in multiple editions: see collections of his writings and LCC documents by Shiv Varma, ed., *Selected Writings of Shaheed Bhagat Singh* (New Delhi: National Book Centre, 1986); Malwinderjit Singh Waraich and Gurdev Singh Sidhu, eds., *The Hanging of Bhagat Singh: Complete Judgment and Other Documents* (Chandigarh: Unistar Books, 2005); S. Irfan Habib, ed., *To Make the Deaf Hear* (Gurgaon: Three Essays Collective, 2007). Note that in the following section, wherever I have cited page numbers from one author, such as Deol or Thakur, for example, the quotations or information in question can usually be found in multiple sources. Nevertheless, I must briefly rehearse the basic story here, if only to emphasize the multiple points that link him to the revolutionary movement abroad.

200. See Sumit Sarkar, *Modern India, 1885–1947* (Delhi: Macmillan India, 1983), 127–29; Petrie, *Developments in Sikh Politics*. Besides in Europe and Persia, Ajit Singh was particularly active in Argentina and Brazil, which were to become Teja Singh Swantantra's chief recruiting grounds for batches of Moscow students in the 1920s. Bhagat Singh Bilga also recalls that Ajit Singh was the first person he encountered in Argentina. See interview in *Harmony Magazine* (note 156 above).

201. Deol, *Shaheed-e-Azam Sardar Bhagat Singh*, 12.

202. "Strictly Secret," Home Department, Political, 8 File #235/11/26, 1926, "Supplementary Note on Sikh Conspiracy" (Bose, 401).

203. Josh, *Communist Movement in Punjab*, 92–93, drawing from *Kirti*, May 1928, and the Meerut Conspiracy Case file. For another version of the Kirti/NBS reconstitution and merger, see Singh, *Communism in Punjab*.

204. Josh, *My Tryst with Secularism*, 118. Josh's first address as president of the All-India WPP conference in Calcutta in December 1928 emphasized these Kirti planks: that class consciousness was required for national liberation, and that to attain complete *swaraj* national independence must be accompanied by just redistribution of wealth (120).

205. See Deol, *Shaheed-e-Azam Sardar Bhagat Singh*, 25; Bakshi, 40; Josh, *Communist Movement in Punjab*, 90.

206. Verma, 160–61, 165.

207. Ibid., 122.

208. Josh, *My Tryst with Secularism*, 133.

209. And for that matter the Yugantar group circa 1908—whose name the HGP adopted for its San Francisco headquarters, as did Bhagwan Singh for the 1917 newspaper he put out as the "true" successor to Har Dayal's *Ghadar*.

210. Verma, 167–68. Cf. Isemonger and Slattery, 47, on the Ghadar plan of action for 1915.

211. Extensive documentation of these trials can be found in Malwinderjit Singh Waraich and Gurdev Singh Sidhu, eds. *The Hanging of Bhagat Singh: Complete Judgment and Other Documents* (Chandigarh: Unistar Books, 2005).

212. Deol, *Shaheed-e-Azam Sardar Bhagat Singh*, 31.

213. Verma, 133; cf. 143.

214. Of the other accused, seven got transportation for life, two got shorter periods of rigorous imprisonment, three were acquitted for lack of evidence, and five absconded. Bhagwati Charan Vohra was killed in an accidental explosion on the bank of the Ravi, May 1930, while testing a bomb for use in an attempt to free Bhagat Singh and B. K. Dutt. Chandrasekhar Azad was shot and killed in a police encounter in February 1931, an event tolling for many the death knell of the HSRA. The NBS had already been outlawed in 1930 under the Seditious Meetings Act.

215. Josh, *Hindustan Gadar Party*, 284–85, drawing upon statements made to him by eleven of the Moscow trainees.

216. SANA, Box 2:20; see also Tatla, 31, 33–34.

217. Harold Laski wrote comparing the Meerut trial's significance to that of the Mooney and Sacco-Vanzetti trials in the United States, the Dreyfus trial in France, and the Reichstag Fire trial in Germany.

218. Puri, 248.

219. T. R. Chadha, "Punjab Communists: An Analysis—I," *Thought* 4.29 (19 July 1952) (SANA Box 4:29).

220. Josh's trajectory had led from the radical wing of the Akali Dal to the Naujavan Bharat Sabha in 1926 and the Kirti in 1927 to the CPI in 1928. He was jailed in the Meerut case 1929 and later emerged as "the most important CPI organiser in the Punjab." Swatantra too began in the Akali Dal but came to Kirti by way of Ghadar's wide-ranging international circles and was in the mid- to late 1920s "the leading communist peasant organiser in Punjab." So while Omvedt attaches the epithet "most important" to both, one might compare the subtle difference between the most important *CPI* organizer and the most important *peasant communist* organizer. Omvedt, "Armed Struggle in India: The Ghadar Party, I–III," *Frontier* 7:29 (November 9, 1974): 3–6; 7:30 (November 19, 1974): 4–6; 7:31 (November 23, 1974): 9–11.

221. Josh, *Communist Movement in Punjab*, 95–96.

222. Ibid., 96. Might the contradiction between such a call for control by the cultivators themselves under the management of elected *panchayat* councils, and the call expressed elsewhere for nationalizing all means of production, be explained by the presence of multiple author-contributors to the journal?

223. Bakshi, 42.

224. Verma, introduction to *Selected Writings of Shaheed Bhagat Singh*. See also Bakshi, 27, 181. Verma was one of the co-accused in the Second Lahore Conspiracy Case and

later editor and commentator on a volume of Bhagat Singh's writings. His critique has to do with the relative emphasis given to political and military aspects of the struggle and of the organization; in the 1920s, attention to the political aspect was increasing in theory even while in practice the HSRA members were still involved in armed action outside political institutions. Still, Verma also cautions us to judge "national revolutionaries, anarchists, nationalists," and others by ideological content and not just by superficial tactical similarity.

225. This was true in the literal sense: Har Dayal's "Marx: A Modern Rishi" appeared in 1912 in Calcutta's *Modern Times;* Bhagwati Charan Vohra still quoted Mazzini in the NBS manifesto in 1926. To name one example noted by the DCI, the High Court Vakil of Madras, M. C. Rajagopalachari, was known as an "ardent pro-Bolshevist" who wanted to attain his desired revolution by fomenting labor unrest. In this project he was aided by a young barrister named Sukhini Narayan Iyer, recently returned from Ireland, where he was associated with Sinn Feiners. CI and CPI Abroad: Home Department, Political, April 1920 #35, weekly report #6 for week ending 20 March 1920.

6. THE KHILAFATIST GHADAR

1. John Riddell, ed., *To See the Dawn: Baku, 1920, First Congress of the Peoples of the East* (New York: Pathfinder Press, 1993), 159 (words of Matushev).

2. Riddell, 143 (words of Pavlovich).

3. Riddell, 142.

4. On the Khilafat movement, see Azmi Ozcan, *Pan-Islamism: Indian Muslims, the Ottomans, and Britain, 1877–1924* (New York: Brill, 1997); Gail Minault, *The Khilafat Movement: Religious Symbolism and Political Mobilization in India* (New York: Columbia University Press, 1982); Mushirul Hasan, *Regionalizing Pan-Islamism: Documents on the Khilafat Movement* (New Delhi: Manohar, 2005); Nikki Keddie, *An Islamic Response to Imperialism: Political and Religious Writings of Sayyid Jamal ad-Din "al-Afghani"* (Berkeley: University of California Press, 1968).

5. Edmund Burke, III, "Pan-Islam and Moroccan Resistance to French Colonial Penetration, 1900–1912," *The Journal of African History* 13.1 (1972); Burke, "Moroccan Resistance, Pan-Islam, and German War Strategy, 1914–1918," *Francia* (Munich) 3 (1976). This tactical program is virtually identical with the outline the Germans developed with the Indians during the war.

6. Journalist, scholar, and future Khilafatist leader Abul Kalam Azad was one of the most prominent Muslim champions of a united India in the face of separatist Pakistani nationalism.

7. P. N. Chopra, ed., *Indian Freedom Fighters Abroad: Secret British Intelligence Report* (New Delhi: Criterion Publications, 1988), 138. Khan later took up the study of law and was called to the bar in 1910.

8. Chopra, 138.

9. Prog. #17, DCI 6.12.1910, B, January 1911 #17–19 (Bose, 45). The meeting was on 2 November 1910. Note that Chatto and Cama apparently did not discriminate between Persian and Turk, or between Shi'ite, Sunni, and secular-progressive; they seem to have

counted on a blanket solidarity among all the world's Muslim peoples to stimulate the Indian members of that family. Since then, the DCI reported, Chatto "continue[d] to cultivate the friendship of the Persians," pursuing the link from various locations.

10. Bose notes (117) that Amba Parishad was accorded the title Sufi "because of his saintly way of life and deep knowledge of Sufism." B, January 1911 #85, letter from Shiraz correspondent in *Najaf,* edited by Shaik Hussain of Tehran.

11. *Najaf,* February 1911 (Bose, 117–18).

12. Chopra, 165. History Sheet on Das/Hussain. Prior to this he had also been in Japan, visiting with "seditious Indians resident there" between 1905 and 1907.

13. DCI 19.9.1911, B, October 1911 #46–49 (Bose, 118–19).

14. DCI 11.1.1912, B, February 1912 #65–68 (Bose, 120–21).

15. Ibid.

16. DCI 21.11.1911, B, January 1912 #121–123 (Bose, 119–20).

17. DCI 11.1.1912, B, February 1912 #65–68 (Bose, 120–21).

18. Ibid.

19. Prog. #112, DCI 11.9.1909, B, October 1909 #110–117 (Bose, 21).

20. Sukh Sagar Dutt to A.C. Bose, 30 March 1958 (Bose, 38–39).

21. Prog. #116, DCI 25.9.1909, B, October 1909 #111–117 (Bose, 22–23); and Prog. #32, DCI, Simla, 4.4.1909, B, November 1909 #32–40 (Bose, 38–39). The November report continued that V.V.S. Aiyar had then wired Acharya ten pounds for passage to Buenos Aires and instructions to go to Lisbon.

22. Incidentally, Irish militant Dan Breen (on whom see chapter 3) also shared something with Acharya and Dutt, in that he too had considered joining up with the Rif rebellion in Morocco, though more than a decade after the Indians' attempt. Breen says that an "emissary of Abdul el Krim, leader of the Riffs" (whom he knew as "Patton") had offered him a significant sum of money to come and help in the rebellion against Spain. But upon hearing that some of his old adversaries from the Irish Auxiliaries had already joined up, Breen declined. Dan Breen, *My Fight for Irish Freedom* (Dublin: Anvil Press, 1964), 162.

23. On Acharya, see K.H. Ansari, "Pan-Islam and the Making of the Early Indian Muslim Socialists," *Modern Asian Studies* 20.3 (1986); Shaukat Usmani, *Peshawar to Moscow: Leaves from an Indian Muhajireen's Diary* (Benares: Swarajya Publishing House, 1927); M.N. Roy, *Memoirs* (New York: Allied Publishers, 1964). See Rattan Singh et al. for "Moscow as Mecca."

24. This conflict was an important catalyst for the growth of the Khilafat movement, as Austria-Hungary was trying to detach the Balkan provinces from the Ottoman grip; Khilafatists framed this as an attack by Christendom on the domain of Islam.

25. See also the biographical sketches of Nawab Khan and Chagan Lal/Husain Rahim in Chopra, 11–12. According to the Sedition Committee Report, Nawab Khan later became an approver.

26. Isemonger and Slattery, 10.

27. Ibid., 22–23.

28. Sareen, 59.

29. Home Department, Political, #671–84, Part A, 1915 (see Banta Singh and Achchar Singh statements). Both bombs were later retrieved and examined by a government

chemical examiner who detected chlorate of potash, red sulphide of arsenic, and leaden rifle bullets.

30. G. Graham, Esq., to Lieutenant Colonel S.G. Knox, special officer at Resident's office in absence of Resident, 17 March 1915. *Ghadar* in Isfahan: including the issues of 13 December 1914 and 21 July 1914.

31. N.K. Barooah, *Chatto: The Life and Times of an Indian Anti-Imperialist in Europe* (New Delhi: Oxford University Press, 2004), 37. These are two of the three currents often identified in cold war–era third-world decolonization contexts; the third, Communism, was not yet in the picture.

32. A.C. Bose, *Indian Revolutionaries Abroad, 1905–1922, in the Background of International Developments* (Patna: Bharati Bhawan, 1971), 99.

33. Barooah (37), quoting Kaiser Wilhelm, 30 July 1914. Again, note the disregard for potential differences among this bouquet of assorted Muslim anti-British elements.

34. Bose, 99–100.

35. Barooah, 45, and 58 n. 67; quoting letter of Har Dayal to German Consul General in Geneva, 2 September 1914. Barooah notes here that Har Dayal also sent a telegram to New York requesting that German-Ghadar liaison Chakravarti send the "largest possible number of Hindu boys from California for work in Constantinople." He also encouraged the opening up of communications via cable or courier to "Hindus in China, the USA, and East Africa."

36. Barooah, 65–74; see also Brown, 179–85.

37. Barooah, 69–70.

38. DCI 13.7.1918, B, July 1918 #413–416 (Bose, 294).

39. Ibid.

40. Sedition Committee Report, 169.

41. DCI 28.7.1914, B, August 1914 #259–262 (Bose, 121).

42. Barooah, 69 n. 28 (Dayal to BIC, 16 April 1915).

43. Sedition Committee Report, 169.

44. Barooah, 68.

45. On Har Dayal's public change of heart, seen as apostasy and betrayal by his comrades, see Brown; Har Dayal, *Forty-Four Months in Germany and Turkey, February 1915 to October 1918: A Record of Personal Impressions* (London: P.S. King & Son, Ltd., 1920).

46. Barooah, 51–52.

47. Ibid., 65–66. See also Priya Satia, *Spies in Arabia* (New York: Oxford University Press, 2008); Tabili.

48. B, January 1911 #85 (Bose, 116).

49. See Keddie on these two main themes of Afghani's.

50. DCI 4.1.1919, B, January 1919 #160–163 (Bose, 294–95).

51. Barooah, 66.

52. Bose, 102.

53. Ibid.

54. Barooah names him Ismail Husni (66).

55. Bose, 116.

56. Ibid., 115.

57. Barooah, 52.

58. Birendranath Dasgupta statement, quoted in Bose, 117 n. 88.

59. Bose, 119 n. 89. Das then proceeded to Japan, wrote on geopolitics and Pan-Asianism, and then in 1917 went to the United States, where he was imprisoned in the San Francisco Conspiracy Case.

60. Bose, 199 n. 89; and from Dasgupta statement.

61. *Independent Hindustan* 1:4, December 1920, 89 (report from October 21).

62. T. R. Sareen, *Select Documents on the Ghadr Party* (New Delhi: Mounto Publishing House, 1994), #7.

63. Sareen, 175–76.

64. Sareen, 169–70. Sareen's gloss notes that this was distributed widely by the Ghadar Party; text appears here as recorded in Punjab Police Abstract of Intelligence, January 1915.

65. Sareen, 169–70.

66. Note here the suggestion of intermingled blood. Bhagwan Singh elaborates on this theme of an Indianizing through fusion of ethnic stocks from multiple sources in his piece in the form of a Q&A between "Baghi" (a rebel) and "Ferenghi" (in this case, a Western professor) in the *Yugantar* of August or September 1917 (SANA Box 10:7–8). Only religion divides Indians, he suggests, not race, blood, or nation; and religion should be irrelevant to national administration and social harmony.

67. See Barooah, 70–74, for further detail, including the roles of Chatto, Acharya, and Pillai.

68. Khankhoje and Agarche made the trip from New York to Turkey in September 1914; Dutt had arrived the previous March (Bose, 101). See also Sawhney; Christopher Sykes, *Wassmuss, the German Lawrence* (London: Longman, Green & Co., 1936).

69. Sareen, 66. As for the level of existing radical Indian presence in the area: although Ajit Singh was by this time traveling in Europe and South America, Amba Parishad was still active in Persia in 1915.

70. Sawhney, 199.

71. Bose, 105. The sources he draws on for this information are letters from Pandurang Khankhoje and Bhupendranath Datta. Datta's was written to Freeman in March 1915; Khankhoje is quoted in Datta's account.

72. It was rumored that Amba Parishad actually committed suicide the day before his scheduled execution. Bose, 106 n. 39. See also Mathur, 80; M. Naeem Qureshi, *Pan-Islam in British Indian Politics: A Study of the Khilafat Movement, 1918–1924* (Boston: Brill Academic Publishers, 1999).

73. Sawhney, 174–225.

74. Bose, 107–8. Kazim Bey was added to the mission as requisite Turkish member.

75. Jodh Singh said in his account: "A few days previous to my meeting the Jhind Prince, Chattopadhyay took me over to the government press. . . . He gave me to understand that the superfine paper was intended for printing a circular letter (twenty-four in number) to be addressed to the Indian princes." The German government would write a draft that the Indian Revolutionary Society would then translate into "various vernaculars." Jodh Singh glimpsed the Persian version but "did not know its contents." (Bose, 197).

76. Text of "Fetwa of the Jehad, Memed-Reshad" [sic], 29 October 1914, SANA Box 6:11. See also Box 6:12: Bismila, "Kalifat India," 1939.

77. Political & Secret—Memoranda re: Afghanistan, NWFP, Baluchistan, Gilgit, and the Persian Gulf (NMML Institutional Papers, microfilm), Viceroy to Foreign Dept., 23 May 1919, "Memorandum on the Arrival of Party of Germans, etc., in Afghanistan," in August 1915. Regarding indications of Bolshevik/Afghan contact and friendliness: memorandum, 30 December 1915. See also Home Department, Political, A, 22, and Deposit, 22, 1916.

78. For more on the other officeholders, see below. They were Defense Minister Muhammed Bashir/Abdur Rahim, who had previously served the North-West Frontier tribal militants as "representative for foreign affairs" (Josh, *Hindustan Gadar Party*, 235); Foreign Minister M. Pillai; Ghadarite Mathra Singh and *muhajirin* Khuda Bhaksh and Muhammed Ali (Sipassi) as ministers plenipotentiary; Ghadarites Harnam Singh Kahuta and Kala Singh/Gujar Singh plus *muhajirin* Zafar Hassan, Allah Nawaz, Abdul Aziz, and Abdul Bari as secretaries. See Khushwant Singh and Satindra Singh, appendix, 94. Perhaps the fact that so many of these members were not only Muslim but had been politically active as such prompted the atheist Josh's observation that the list of officers, "if one reads between the lines, smacks of communalism" (235). To me this rechanneling or reframing of religiously defined political activity is precisely what is of interest.

79. Isemonger and Slattery, 87. The authors noted that to their knowledge no weapons actually came from this source.

80. Isemonger and Slattery, 87.

81. Another emissary, Kala Singh, went to Nepal in summer 1917 (Bose, 293). The king, like the Afghan amir, was to be promised a large piece of Indian territory. If he was unwilling to help, they asked him to stay neutral at least; they were confident they could convince the Sikhs, but the king's Gurkhas were too loyal (Bose, 338–39).

82. Sedition Committee Report, 173–79. See also A, Prog. #3241–430, "Summary of the Silk Letters Case by C. E. W. Sands" (Bose, 298–99).

83. See Rajat Ray, "Revolutionaries, Pan-Islamists, and Bolsheviks: Maulana Abul Kalam Azad and the Political Underworld in Calcutta, 1905–1925," in *Communal and Pan-Islamic Trends in Colonial India*, ed. Mushirul Hasan (New Delhi: Manohar, 1981).

84. Home Department, Political, B, File #408, 1922 (Bose, 336–42). Statement from Teja Singh, a POW in Austria who later escaped detention in Russian Turkestan, was in Kabul with Pratap, and then left to represent the PGI on a mission to Nepal. Teja Singh told the king of Nepal that most of the frontier tribesmen had the policy of rooting out any friendly disposition to the British evident among them, "and thus having removed or overcome opposing sections from amongst themselves, [went] against the British. In the trans-frontier districts and in the Afghan border there are several long-standing colonies where disaffected Indian Mohammedans find asylum and whose fighting strength varies from 200 to 2000 fighting-men ready to take up arms at any time required." Or as he says elsewhere, even up to a lakh of armed men with two hundred rounds of ammunition apiece: "They receive pecuniary help from their co-religionists in India. These and the tribesmen are never in want of good rifles and ammunition which they can and do manufacture at various places. Even a child among them knows how to handle or to put together

the parts of a rifle" (337). Teja Singh said that they had surrendered perhaps a thousand rifles, which they had previously looted from the British, but that he did not think they would ever part with their own, "which are dearer to the men than their own children" (337). He predicted they would open the campaign to weaken the British, after which the amir would bring his army in to occupy the country as far as Attock. The local residents would offer no resistance, since "the political views of Hindus and Mohammedans have become the same and they are trying for a free and independent India" (338).

85. Bose, 110.

86. A, Prog. #241–430, Foreign & Political, 1918, "Summary of the Silk Letters Case" (Bose, 298–303); Sedition Committee Report, 174–76.

87. Bose, 112–13; Isemonger and Slattery, 159.

88. See K. H. Ansari, *The Emergence of the Muslim Socialists in North India, 1917–1947* (Boston Spa, UK: British Library Document Supply Centre, 1985); Muzaffar Ahmed, *The Communist Party of India and Its Formation Abroad* (Calcutta: National Book Agency, 1962), 153–55.

89. Ahmed, 155. He lists their names as Khushi Muhammed (Muhammed Ali Sipassi), Abdul Hamid, Zafar Hasan, Allah Nawaz, Abdul Bari, Muhammed Abdullah, Abdur Rahman, Abdur Rashid, Rahmat Ali, Abdul Majid (Kohat), plus more unnamed.

90. Josh, *Hindustan Gadar Party,* 301.

91. Foreign Department, Political, 1918, A, Prog. #241–430, Confidential (A), 7 December 1916 (Bose, 297).

92. Ibid. (Bose, 296–303).

93. Ibid. (Bose, 281). Hasan's main contact inside India, Hamidullah, in the words of the Sands report, "kept himself in touch with the Muslim revolutionaries working separately in such widely separated countries as Arabia, India and the NWFP." He also remitted money for the subsistence of the families of political exiles, and for the use of activists. Sands report (Bose, 284).

94. Sedition Committee Report, 173–79.

95. Incidentally, a previous emissary had carried copies of the Ghalibnama from Mecca to Bombay concealed in a mirror frame (Sands report; Bose, 284); by contrast, Pratap's letter to the czar was inscribed on a gold plate (Bose, 280).

96. This translation was included as Appendix G (L/P & S/10/633) to the Sands report (Bose, 286).

97. Appendix G to Sands report (Bose, 289).

98. Ibid. (Bose, 289–92). Letter, Obeidullah to "Hazrat Maulana Sahib" [i.e., Hasan?], Medina, 9 July 1916.

99. See Aziz Ahmed, discussed below. Obeidullah's concept of the form and function of the *jamaat* was analogous to the Marxist-Leninist revolutionary party as utilized by the Bolsheviks.

100. Appendix G to Sands report (Bose, 289).

101. Ibid.

102. Ibid. (Bose, 292).

103. Foreign Department, Political, 1918, A, Prog. #241–430 (Bose, 303).

104. Appendix G to Sands report (Bose, 289).

105. Ibid. (my italics).

106. Dr. W. O. von Hentig of the AA, and Kazim Bey of the Ottoman War Office.

107. Appendix G to Sands report (Bose, 293).

108. Ibid. (Bose, 282).

109. Ibid.

110. Sedition Committee Report, 225.

111. DCI 26.5.1919, B, January 1919 #494–497, Proclamation of the PGI (Bose, 295–96).

112. T. R. Sareen, *Secret Documents on Singapore Mutiny, 1915* (New Delhi: Mounto Publishing House, 1995), 63.

113. Ibid. Note that some of the names mentioned in this report as "principle malcontents" in the colony were also on Hatano's and Barakatullah's contact list in Tokyo, notably the Marican family. Bose notes that this South Indian Muslim family ran one of the oldest Indian business houses in Thailand. G. E. Law letter; Bose, 116–17.

114. Sho Kuwajima, 28. (Is this the same Veer Singh mentioned in the newspaper report?)

115. Sho Kuwajima, 28.

116. Mathur, 83.

117. James Campbell Ker, *Political Trouble in India, 1907–1917* (Calcutta: Superintendent Government Printing, 1917; repr., Calcutta: Editions Indian, 1972), 266.

118. Sedition Committee Report, 171; Ker, 266–67; Isemonger and Slattery, 155. The latter said he was "armed to the teeth" with twenty packets of dynamite (for railway bridges and tracks), fuses, detonators, fourteen pistols stocked with "expanding bullets so as to cause the greatest injury," two hacksaws, wirecutters, chemicals for making explosives, poison intended for use by officers' servants on the officers, and Turkish-issued fatwas exhorting "the duty of Muhammedans in regard to the war."

119. Sedition Committee Report, 169.

120. Ibid., 170.

121. Ibid; see also Singh and Singh, appendix, 92; Isemonger and Slattery, appendix. The courts-martial yielded 41 death sentences and 125 assorted prison sentences.

122. Sareen, 769.

123. Sedition Committee Report, 170. There also seemed to be German involvement, though a German under suspicion in Bangkok wrote to a newspaper, in the interest of clearing his name, that "an educated Indian, a leader of a revolutionary movement and well supplied with gold . . . told [me] he was going to Singapore to cause a rising there" and that he had equally well-funded comrades at work elsewhere. Isemonger and Slattery, 153; Ker, 264.

124. Sedition Committee Report, 170. Mul Chand's letter was intercepted April 1915. Sho also allots influence to Nur Alam Shah, a *pir* based at a mosque in Singapore. Men of the Fifth Light Infantry would visit him as he "held court and preached sedition against the Government, and incited sipahis to rise against the British." There was some evidence that he was affiliated with a "Revolutionary Party," which Sho thinks (though he cannot prove) could have been Ghadar (46, 140). After all, it's not as if there were other obvious candidates in the area that matched such a description.

125. Kasim Mansur's letter was intercepted on 28 December 1914. Sho, 35–36; Sareen, 766–67. Kasim Ismail Mansur was executed for treason in connection with the mutiny on 31 May 1915. Mathur credited him along with Jagat Ram with instigating mutiny. Sho thought it impossible to know how big his influence was. Mathur (82–83) credits Kasim Mansur and Jagat Singh with instigating the revolt.

126. Sedition Committee Report, 171–72.

127. Sareen, 770–71, as reported in the *New York Times*, 2 May 1915.

128. Sareen, 149.

129. Sareen, 13–16. Japanese troops landed and retook the Alexandra barracks, though the British later denied or downplayed their role. See the extract from Koji Tsukuda's book on the event, translated by the Foreign Office (Foreign Department, External B, Confidential B of 1918 #41–60—NAI), plus comments annexed by general staff at the military headquarters in Singapore, 23 September 1917. The British also downplayed the influence of Ghadar propaganda and underreported the British casualties in the wrap-up announcement that appeared in London papers on 24 February. A four-hundred-page report on the uprising was published in Simla in May 1915 but never made public. Sareen, 16–19.

130. Account of Lt. Malcolm Bond Shelley of the Volunteer Rifles, recorded in 1927, in Sareen, 798–817.

131. Sareen, 776.

132. Mathur, 82. According to Sareen the total was twelve British officers and fifteen civilians dead, and many wounded, although there are more names than this listed in the *Straits Times*, 20 February 1915 (818–19). Subadar Dunde Khan and Jemadar Chisti Khan (thought to be ringleaders—see Sho, 56) were shot publicly to make an example on 21 April, and more were executed later, until 17 May.

133. Sareen, 783; this according to Robert C. D. Bradley, British adviser in Johore State, in a letter to Major F. I. Lugard, 28 September 1933. Gandhi had left the region by then, but the memory of his mobilizations among the Indians in South Africa would still have been fresh, and there was a Ghadar center in what later became Kenya; see Zarina Patel, *Unquiet: The Life and Times of Makhan Singh* (Nairobi: Zand Graphics, 2006).

134. *New York Times*, 24 February 1915; Sareen, 765.

135. Statement, 2 March 1915; Sareen, 769.

136. *New York Times*, 2 May 1915; Sareen, 770.

137. Sho, 28.

138. Ibid., 35.

139. Ibid., 26–27, 59.

7. GHADAR AND THE BOLSHEVIK *MUHAJIRIN*

1. John Riddell, ed., *To See the Dawn: Baku, 1920, First Congress of the Peoples of the East* (New York: Pathfinder Press, 1993), 251–52.

2. Foreign and Political Department (Secret), F, February 1920 #77–171.

3. Political (Secret), File #1229, Part 1, Appendix C.

4. Political (Secret), File #1229, Part 1, Appendix C, 1919, "Report on the Bolshevik Menace to India."

5. In his analysis of the geopolitical situation presented at the second session of the Baku conference, Radek summed up the British and czarist empires' primary desires in controlling this region this way: the czar wanted a warm-water port on the Black Sea, and Britain wanted an open land route to India, plus a railway link (across Arabia and Mesopotamia) between what Radek called the two pillars of its global power: namely, the mineral and agricultural resources of Africa and Egypt, and its bottomless treasure-house, India. Riddell, 81–83.

6. Chief of General Staff Malleson in Simla to Director of Military Intelligence, 30 May 1919; Viceroy to Army Department, 14 June 1919: Political & Secret—Memoranda re: Afghanistan, NWFP, Baluchistan, Gilgit, and the Persian Gulf (NMML Institutional Papers).

7. Ibid.

8. M.N. Roy, Memoirs (New York: Allied Publishers, 1964), 420.

9. Political (Secret), File #1229, Part 1, Appendix C.

10. CI and CPI Abroad: Home Department, Political, April 1920 #35, weekly report #6 for week ending 20 March 1920.

11. Political (Secret), File #1229, Part 1 of 1920, Appendix C, D, "Note on Bolshevism in India."

12. CI and CPI Abroad: Home Department, Political, April 1920 #35, weekly report #6 for week ending 20 March 1920.

13. Quoted in K.H. Ansari, "Pan-Islam and the Making of the Early Indian Muslim Socialists," Modern Asian Studies 20.3 (1986): 519.

14. On their ideological trajectory, see Majid Hayat Siddiqi, "Bluff, Doubt, and Fear: The Kheiri Brothers and the Colonial State, 1904–45," Indian Economic & Social History Review 24 (1987): 233.

15. Ansari, "Pan-Islam," 518. See also DCI, Simla, 27.9.920, Deposit, September 1920 #71; Foreign and Political Department (Secret), F, February 1920 #77–171, transmission of a radio telegram from People's Commissars, Moscow to Tashkent, January 1919; and DCI 11.1.1919, B, January 1919 #160–163, summarizing the above in a report from Bolshevik wireless stations in December 1918.

16. DCI 27.7.1919, B, August 1919, "Memorandum to Bolsheviks" (Bose, 354–55).

17. Foreign and Political Department (Secret), F, February 1920 #77–171.

18. CI and CPI Abroad: Home Department, Political, April 1920 #35, weekly report #6 for week ending 20 March 1920.

19. DCI 2.8.1920, Deposit, August 1920 #110 (Bose, 343).

20. Secret A 184, Issue 3, Brought up to 31 October 1919, re: "Central Asia, Persia, and Afghanistan" and "Bolshevik and Pan-Islamic Movements and Connected Information."

21. Josh, Hindustan Gadar Party, 204.

22. Riddell, 251.

23. Ibid., 252.

24. Political (Secret), File #1229, Part 1, Appendix C.

25. Ibid.

26. Riddell, 251–52.

27. Ibid., 231–32.

28. The main source on which this section is based is Rafiq Ahmad's account, put to paper (in English) in 1966, headed "CI and CPI Abroad: Journey to Tashkent and Back—1920; By Rafiq Ahmad's Statement (Typed and Corrected by Author)," and narrating events of nearly half a century before. The introduction explains that it was first recounted in 1960 to Muzaffar Ahmed—one of Roy's first organizers inside India and a founding member of the CPI, who had himself been active in the Khilafat movement previously—and printed in the Bengali paper *Parichai* under the title "An Unforgettable Journey." It was later translated and printed in a number of magazines and newspapers in various Indian languages—but not Urdu, Rafiq Ahmad's own native tongue, in which he had first told the story. So the editor of this document—Muzaffar Ahmed?—now stated his intention to translate it back into Urdu from Bengali. But to guard against changes and distortions from the multiple translations, he says, he returned to "Rafique Bhai," who told it all again. The narrative is supplemented by Shaukat Usmani's two accounts, which parallel and largely corroborate Rafiq Ahmad's: *Historic Trips of a Revolutionary* (New Delhi: Sterling Publishers, 1977) is a more polished and reflective elaboration on Usmani's earlier account, *From Peshawar to Moscow: Leaves from a Muhajireen's Diary* (Benares: Swarajya Publishing House, 1927).

29. For details of this geographical and political odyssey see Usmani, *From Peshawar to Moscow*; Ansari, *Emergence of the Muslim Socialists*; and Ansari, "Pan-Islam." Josh remarked in his address as president of the All-India Worker Peasant Party in December 1928 that if the Khilafat agitation had accomplished "one good thing" it was in sending "some Hijratis to Afghanistan from where some of them went to the Soviet Union, and on their return to India brought with them communist ideas" (*My Tryst with Secularism*, 140).

30. They included Shaukat Usmani, Muhammad Shafiq, and Abdullah Safdar.

31. Ansari, "Pan-Islam," 509.

32. His employer was Obeidullah Khan, although the ruling nawab of Bhopal at this time was a woman, Begum Jahan, who was sympathetic to Turkey but still contributed money and troops to the British war effort on the condition that her men not fight in the Ottoman sphere. Her son and successor, an Aligarh student, was an ardent Khilafat supporter.

33. Shaukat Ali and Mohammed Ali, quoted in Ozcan, 195, 196.

34. Ansari, "Pan-Islam," 523–24. Other accounts report as many as thirty-six or thirty-eight thousand. From *Independent Hindustan* 1:1, September 1920, "News & Notes: Afghanistan Offers Free Land to Politically Oppressed Indians."

35. Ozcan, 196.

36. For example, we learn from Rafiq's statement at his arrest that his father, Nur Ahmad Sayed, received a state pension of twenty rupees for his services as a teacher. Rafiq himself was identified in the report as "a Vernacular scholar, having read up to Munshi Fazal." Statements of "Indian Revolutionaries intercepted en route from Russia to India," given at Peshawar, 3 December 1922.

37. Rafiq Ahmad, "An Unforgettable Journey" [henceforth RA]. All details in the following account, unless otherwise specified, are taken from this source.

38. RA, 3.

39. RA, 7; Usmani, *Peshawar to Moscow,* 9.

40. Usmani, *Peshawar to Moscow,* 9. Usmani also asserts (10) that the amir's reasons for sending Indian arrivals there was to influence their mentality and "mould it pro-Afghan," and also to sniff out any Indian Intelligence Branch agents who might be among them. (There were some.)

41. Usmani, *Peshawar to Moscow,* 10–12.

42. Ibid., 11. The secretary of state for India in London telegrammed the viceroy on 10 December 1917: "It is considered by Indian Committee in Berlin that no rising would be successful in India unless supported by an attack from Afghanistan." Home Department, Political, B, File #185, February 1919.

43. RA, 10.

44. Muzaffar Ahmed, *Myself and the Communist Party of India, 1920–1929* (Calcutta: National Book Agency, 1970), 51.

45. Ansari, "Pan-Islam," 520; Sareen, *The Russian Revolution and India* (New Delhi: Sterling Publishers, 1977), 59.

46. Ansari, "Pan-Islam," 533.

47. Sareen (60) said the difference was that Suritz, Rub, and Acharya were in favor of joining forces with the Bolsheviks, while Barakatullah, Obeidullah, and Pratap (i.e., the PGI officers) still favored "the old way" of revolutionary nationalism.

48. Home Department, Political, File #263, 1925; D. Petri, 10.6.1923. See Ansari, "Pan-Islam," 520–21, for further details on this split and move. The group also fed into the CPI, declared among the *muhajir* trainees in Tashkent a few months later, though the Revolutionary Association remained in existence at least until 1924.

49. RA, 10. Usmani described the flag of the *muhajirin* as black with a red crescent and star.

50. Usmani, *Peshawar to Moscow,* 20, 27.

51. Usmani, *Peshawar to Moscow,* 12–13. He adds: "At one stage we came across huge boulders with Buddhist inscriptions. We could not understand these ancient writings but we realised that some Buddhist teachers must have reached even such remote places in Asia." Was this Bamian?

52. Usmani, *Peshawar to Moscow,* 19; RA, 13–15.

53. This corresponds roughly to the territory of present-day Turkmenistan, Uzbekistan, Tajikistan, and Kirghizistan.

54. Usmani, *Historic Trips of a Revolutionary,* 47–48.

55. Ibid., 40. It would be interesting to find an account by a member of this Islamist faction, to hear what they thought of the left-leaning.

56. Usmani, *Peshawar to Moscow,* 22. He and those who shared his sympathies observed other social changes noted here as well—in education, access to food and medical treatment, status of women, and labor standards, for example—and said that although they had not yet plumbed the theory behind what they saw, they saw the results.

57. Usmani, *Historic Trips of a Revolutionary,* 53–54.

58. Literally modernists, i.e., the progressive faction in power in the new Bokharan Soviet Republic.

59. Usmani, *Historic Trips of a Revolutionary*, 64. RA (22) mentions several incriminating clues: the brown Russian bread in their bags, and Akbar Shah's fair skin and blue eyes(!).

60. RA, 23.

61. Usmani, *Historic Trips of a Revolutionary*, 69–70. (Note here that India's cause takes precedence—not the Khilafat's or the *millat's*.)

62. RA, 25.

63. Usmani, *Historic Trips of a Revolutionary*, 37.

64. Ibid., 90.

65. Nevertheless, Usmani, *Historic Trips of a Revolutionary*, remarked—revealing some internalized Orientalism—that its "completely Persian" appearance as "a mystic city with eastern mysticism as its culture".remained unchanged (92). Elsewhere he described Bokhara as a "town of large mosques and gold-domed cathedrals, full of parks and theatres" (42); "the wonderful sun-drenched city of the East" (43); "the city of lofty madressahs resembling India's Jama Masjid" (43). Rafiq favorably compared the relatively intact postseizure condition of Bokhara to the utter devastation he witnessed in Jalalabad following the British attack (32).

66. Sareen (67) said that the coordinators of the Indian Revolutionary Association in Tashkent "while giving lectures on communism . . . had not neglected religion," and students were always reminded of other "ancient heritage of heroic glory, self-sacrifice and knowledge." Roy and the IRA then differed on which must come first and enable the other: political or social transformation.

67. Political and Secret Department, 1040/1922. In his Chitral testimony he specifies that this was reserved for the "men of better physique and qualifications." Sultan Majid names Ferozuddin Mansur, Abdul Majid, Fida Ali, Gauhar Rehman, and Akbar Shah as also being in the aviation program.

68. Political and Secret Department, 1040/1922, Statement of Habib Ahmed, 3 December 1922.

69. Rafiq recounted his own such attempt one chilly morning when a teacher came to rouse them. Reluctant to leave his warm bed, Rafiq begged sickness. But instead of being left alone, he was showered with the unwanted ministrations of a doctor, and an ambulance was sent to take him to the hospital for two or three days' observation. He protested that he felt fine and wanted to leave, but the doctor diagnosed that he was suffering due to bad food, and prescribed chicken soup, milk, and eggs. Although this would seem to be a drastic improvement over the usual fare of—surely enough to make anyone sick—a meager ration of black bread that Roy (460) suspected contained as much grit and earth as flour; a daily "pilaf" of rice and rancid mutton fat from suspiciously preserved meat; and apple tea, for which Roy gave the recipe of "boiling water poured over apple shavings until blood red, and drunk with a side of raisins in the absence of milk or sugar." Rafiq made his escape wearing only a hospital gown; his normal clothes were later returned to the school. RA, 34–35.

70. Roy, 460.

71. Usmani, *Peshawar to Moscow*, 17–19.

72. Roy, 472.

73. See Ansari, "Pan-Islam and the Making of the Early Indian Muslim Socialists"; M. Ahmed, *The Communist Party of India and Its Formation Abroad* (Calcutta: National Book Agency, 1962).

74. Usmani, *Historic Trips of a Revolutionary,* 113.

75. Political and Secret Department, 1040/1922.

76. Ibid.

77. Ibid.

78. RA, 43–44. Although at some point they were separated into smaller groups to be less conspicuous, the total group now included Rafiq Ahmad, Habib Ahmad, Abdul Majid, Ferozuddin Mansoor, Fida Ali Zahid, Sultan Mohammed, Abdul Qadir Sehrai, Sayid, Abdul Hamid, and Nizamuddin. Fazl Elahi and Abdullah Safdar were also supposed to go but at the last minute decided to stay in Moscow. That only sixteen of the original fifty Tashkent students took this return trip Usmani blamed on Abdur Rab's factional machinations.

79. RA, 45.

80. Ibid., 47.

81. Ibid., 48.

82. Ibid., 49–50.

83. Ibid., 52.

84. Ibid., 53.

85. Home Department, Political, File #103, 1923, Part 1, Peshawar Conspiracy Case Judgment.

86. Appendix 2 on Agents and Emissaries in Home Department, Political, File #261, 1924, & K. W. (Bose, 393). The first four were arrested while crossing into the country; the latter three surrendered at the Chitral Border Office. Abdul Hamid was left behind in the Pamirs.

87. Political and Secret Department, 1040/1922. Chief Commissioner of NWFP Peshawar to GOI Foreign Secretary, Foreign and Political Dept., Delhi, 26 December 1922.

88. Usmani to A.C. Bose (Bose, 363). Usmani was not, although he says he corresponded with Azad and met him much later in jail during the Meerut case.

89. RA, 57.

90. Political and Secret Department, 1040/1922. Chief Commissioner of NWFP Peshawar to GOI Foreign Secretary, Foreign and Political Dept., Delhi, 26 December 1922.

91. Ibid. All statements, including Rafiq's, recorded on 3 December 1922 at the Intelligence Bureau in Peshawar by Superintendent J.M. Ewert.

92. For full details of Peshawar Conspiracy cases, see Gangadhar Adhikari, ed., *Documents of the History of the Communist Party of India* (New Delhi: People's Publishing House, 1971–1982), 2: 26–50. Akbar Khan Qureishi, as a ringleader, received a total of ten years' rigorous imprisonment in the first two cases. The third judgment, handed down in May 1923, sentenced Rafiq Ahmad, Ferozuddin, Abdul Majid, and Habib Ahmad to one year's rigorous imprisonment. Two others got two years, although Abdul Qader was acquitted, and Fida Ali and one another went on record as approvers. The fourth case a year later gave Mohammed Shafiq three years. Fazl Ilahi Qurban got three years, reduced from five, in the fifth and last Peshawar case in 1927.

93. Nikki Keddie, *An Islamic Response to Imperialism: Political and Religious Writings of Sayyid Jamal ad-Din "al-Afghani"* (Berkeley: University of California Press, 1968).

94. Telegram, Consul-General in Meshed to GOI Foreign Secretary, Foreign and Political Department, Delhi, 27 April 1922.

95. Ibid.

96. Muhammed Ali, aka Khushi Muhammed, was one of the original Lahore students who had come to Kabul in 1915. He later became Roy's CPI anchor abroad, based in Paris.

97. Political and Secret Department, 1040/1922, Statement of Abdul Qader. As to the nature of the "conspiracy," Abdul Qader claimed at some length in a later jail interview that all the batches sent from the Moscow university had been "directed to establish themselves at Industrial Centers and work for organisation and development of Labour Unions under the leadership of Shafiq, Peshawari and Gupta, Bengali, who were to maintain connection through Mohammed Ali in Kabul and devise a sea route too—the Unions all to remain affiliated to the Moscow International where they were to send delegates at meetings and to provide more candidates for fresh classes at the University. Women workers were also to be engaged for the Unions—particular work wherein was to do propaganda by regular lecturing, writing, etc, special secret committees to be formed of inner workers, propaganda also to be done in the Army by enlistment or otherwise."

98. Introduction to RA.

99. Josh, *My Tryst with Secularism*, 82–85. See also Gurharpal Singh, *Communism in Punjab: A Study of the Movement up to 1967* (Delhi: Ajanta Publications, 1994).

100. Josh, *Communist Movement in Punjab*, 52.

101. Ibid., 92.

102. See Home Department, Political, File #202/25, "Memorandum on British Indian Revolutionaries in Moscow" (dated 24.4.1925), "Notes to Kanpur Conspiracy Case" (Bose, 395–96). Aviators or aviation trainees included Nazir, Abdul Karim, Siddiqi, and Sultan Majid.

103. Home Department, Political, File #202/25, "Memorandum on British Indian Revolutionaries in Moscow" (dated 24.4.1925), "Notes to Kanpur Conspiracy Case" (Bose, 395–96). Abdul Qayoum translated a speech of Stalin's into Urdu at Comintern behest. "Three million copies" (?) were being prepared to send into India. The Comintern issued an Urdu booklet called *Zulm-e-Sermayadar* (The Oppression of Capitalism) (Bose, 396). Wafar wrote an Urdu play, translated into Russian, "which describes the horrors of British rule in India. Nazir was asked to translated it into Pushtu, but refused" (Bose, 395).

104. Home Department, Political, File #202/25, "Memorandum on British Indian Revolutionaries in Moscow" (dated 24.4.1925), "Notes to Kanpur Conspiracy Case" (Bose, 395–96). Wafar, Nazir, Malik (Fazl Elahi), and Abdulla Jan were "employed in going about among Russian factories and making propaganda speeches to the effect that Indians at home are slaves and are brutalized by the British."

105. "Supplementary Note on Sikh Conspiracy" (Bose, 411). A "well-known political suspect," Zafar Hassan was close to Obeidullah and had served as an officer in the PGI, to which he was passing money from the Comintern, and in the Army of God.

106. Josh, *Communist Movement in Punjab*, 52; cf. Singh, *Communism in Punjab.*

107. Senate Fact-Finding Committee, *Seventh Report on Un-American Activities in California* (1953), 242.

108. Not to be confused with the postpartition Communist Party of Pakistan, founded in 1948.

109. Usmani, 19-20. Nevertheless, he does refer to the journey multiple times as a "pilgrimage."

110. Note that Shaukat Usmani did not like or trust Obeidullah when he encountered him in Kabul, calling him a reactionary "nightmare." However, Usmani sounds like one of the more unequivocally opposed to any sort of religious language, which he would have equated automatically with reaction.

111. Ansari, "Pan-Islam," 513.

112. Aziz Ahmad, *Islamic Modernism in India and Pakistan, 1857-1964* (London: Oxford University Press, 1967), 195. See also W. C. Smith, *Modern Islam in India* (New Delhi: Usha Publications, 1979); Moin Shakir, *Khilafat to Partition: A Survey of Major Political Trends among Indian Muslims during 1919-1947* (Delhi: Ajanta Publications, 1983); Barbara Metcalf, *Islamic Revival in British India: Deoband, 1860-1900* (Princeton, NJ: Princeton University Press, 1982).

113. Sands report on the Silk Letters Conspiracy (Bose, 283).

114. Ansari, "Pan-Islam," 516-17.

115. Political and Secret Department, 1040/1922, Statement of Fida Ali. Fida Ali also said that he had met one of the Russian aviation instructors at Tashkent in 1921, who was en route to Kabul with two planes, although one of them crashed in a practice flight. He said Shafiq went to Lahore but feared arrest, and so he too had retreated to Kabul.

116. Political and Secret Department, 1040/1922.

117. Josh, *Hindustan Gadar Party*, 332.

118. "Strictly Secret," Home Department, Political, 8 File #235/11/26, 1926, "Supplementary Note on Sikh Conspiracy."

119. Home Department, Political, File # 41/1926, Public, P & J (s) 474.

120. "Supplementary Note on Sikh Conspiracy: "Ghadar Party in America" (Bose, 410-11).

121. "Supplementary Note on Sikh Conspiracy" (Bose, 405). Funds received "through the secretary of the Russian Consulate and Zafar Hassan in Constantinople."

122. Ahmad, *Islamic Modernism*, 196.

123. Ibid. Ahmad suggests that Obeidullah's status as a convert may have contributed to his ability to see culture and religion syncretistically.

124. Ahmad, *Islamic Modernism*, 196.

125. Obeidullah's *Khutbat*, 20-21, quoted in Ahmad, *Islamic Modernism*, 198.

126. Ahmad, *Islamic Modernism*, 199.

127. Ibid., 198. It should be noted that Ahmad himself does not endorse these analogies.

128. On Barakatullah's life and career, see P. N. Chopra, ed., *Indian Freedom Fighters Abroad: Secret British Intelligence Report* (New Delhi: Criterion Publications, 1988), 15-16; Muhammed Irfan, *Barkatullah Bhupali: Ek Jhan Gasht-i Inqalabi* (Bhopal: Irfan Publications, 1969; London: British Library Document Supply Centre, 1985); Sohan Singh Josh,

My Meetings with Bhagat Singh and on Other Early Revolutionaries (New Delhi: Communist Party of India, 1976); IOR/L/P&J/12/213.

129. D, October 1915 #43. Note of Foreign Office, 27.8.1915.

130. Letter, von Hentig to A. C. Bose, 7 April 1956 (Bose, 305).

131. Chopra, *Indian Freedom Fighters*, 15–16.

132. Ibid., 15–16.

133. DCI 10.4.1909, B, June 1909 #108–114. The report notes in particular that "Freeman had been taking a great interest in the appointment."

134. D, October 1915 #43. Note of Foreign Office, 27.8.1915 (Bose, 112–13).

135. Chopra, 16. It is perhaps easy to see from this why, in looking for anti-British colleagues, he would have favored the Yugantar branch that led toward Ghadar, as opposed to the Anusilan Samiti branch that later led far rightward. It was in any case the former who were more likely to pursue international activity.

136. "Memorandum on Indian Revolutionaries Abroad," Home Department, Political, A, August 1915 #216 (Sareen, 60). This might be said to be the basis for all future Islamic studies in Japan, as they developed thanks to Okawa in the 1920s; see Aydin, *Politics of Civilizational Identities*, 173–218. Home Department, Political, A, *Proceedings*, August 1914, #7–16, identifies Hatano as Hasan U. Hatano, editor of "proscribed El Islam," 14-7-14.

137. DCI 10.4.1909, B, June 1909 #108–114.

138. DCI 11.1.1912, B, February 1912 #65–68. Also cf. Smith, 30: Yusuf Ali, writing in 1933, referenced Barakatullah positively as an example of a modern writer who doesn't recognize the caliph's temporal authority. (Remember his compromised relationship with the British government vis-à-vis the anticolonial movement.)

139. Bose, *Indian Revolutionaries Abroad*, 69. In May 1912, "An-Nazir al-Uryan," and in early 1913, "Akher al-Helal Saif," both in Urdu; as well as "Proclamation of Liberty" in English.

140. In a letter dated 9 May 1914, the British ambassador at Tokyo, Greene, says Hatano claimed to have paid the "murderer designate" 1,000 yen to leave the country; British intelligence agreed to pay him 252 for the information but refused his request of reimbursement for the 1,000 yen.

141. Bose, *Indian Revolutionaries Abroad*, 69–70; Home Department, Political, A, *Proceedings*, #143–151, 7 April 1914, telegram 6-3-14, noting that Barakatullah, the "notorious seditionist," was to be replaced as Urdu teacher in Tokyo. DCI Cleveland reported: "I think it is pretty certain that the Japanese authorities will expect us to send a man who will combine the duties of Urdu teacher and Government spy, and that he will be very closely watched." Therefore they should be sure to ensure there were no connections there with any "spy business on his part."

142. Josh, *Hindustan Gadar Party*, 35.

143. Home Department, Political, A, *Proceedings*, August 1914, #7–16. A telegram from Secretary of State to DCI, 22 July 1914, contains details of a poisoning plot revealed by Hatano, supposedly coordinated by K. C. Kohli and Bhagwan Singh, identified as the deportee from Canada. Another telegram, sent on 11 May 1914, from the ambassador at Tokyo to the DCI, tracked Bhagwan Singh's movements from Shanghai to Hong Kong to Singapore to Yokohama, and from there to San Francisco with Barakatullah.

144. Foreign & Political Wars, Progs. #32–34, February 1916 (Secret), Part B 1916; two letters from Har Dayal to Barakatullah sent by T.W. Haig, GOI consul general in Khurasan, from Meshed, 17 December 1914, to Foreign Secretary of GOI in Delhi: the first from Geneva to Zurich, 5 January 1915; the second from Hamburg to Berlin, 9 March 1915.

145.. See Adhikari, vol. 1; Irfan, 214–25. Also along were M.P.T. Acharya, Abdur Rab, Dalip Singh Gill, and Barakatullah's personal assistant Ibrahim.

146. Josh, *Hindustan Gadar Party*, 279; Irfan, 263.

147. Josh, *Hindustan Gadar Party*, 280; Irfan, 265.

148. Josh, *Hindustan Gadar Party*, 282–83; Irfan, 270.

149. Political & Secret—Memoranda re: Afghanistan, NWFP, Baluchistan, Gilgit, and the Persian Gulf (NMML Institutional Papers), regarding indications of Bolshevik/ Afghan contact and friendliness: Viceroy to Foreign Dept., 23 May 1919.

150. It may also be worth noting here the words of Hasrat Mohani, who presided at the first CPI conference inside India in 1925; Mohani stated that they were Indian Communists but not Bolsheviks; Bolshevism was only one particular form of Communism, whereas they, the Indians, had no need to subject themselves to (or be accused of subjecting themselves to) any foreign doctrine. They asserted the right to express their own version of Communism, appropriate for Indian cultural and social conditions. For the text of Mohani's speech, see Adhikari, 2: 640–42.

151. Several versions of Barakatullah's interview are extant: Foreign and Political Department (Secret), F, February 1920 #77–171 (appearing in *Izvestia*, 6 May 1919); same file, captioned "Bolshevik designs of Afghanistan and India (Interview with Professor Barakatullah)" (Bose, 355–56); Josh, *Soviet Land* 21, November 1971, "Indian Freedom Fighter in Kazan," by L. Mitrokhin. Variations in translation are minimal yet intriguing and perhaps significant; for example, the Foreign and Political Department version (published in *Izvestia*) translates "natural allies," while Josh *(Soviet Land)* has "genuine allies."

152. This segment appears in *Izvestia* (Foreign and Political Department; see previous note). Note that although anti-imperialism is presented as primary, Barakatullah still makes capitalism and not English rule the fundamental issue.

153. Secret A 184, Issue 3, Brought up to 31st October 1919, re: "Central Asia, Persia and Afghanistan" and "Bolshevik and Pan-Islamic Movements and Connected Information" (NMML Institutional Papers).

154. Josh, *Hindustan Gadar Party*, 280.

155. Ibid., 281 (my italics); Ansari, "Pan-Islam," 519–20. Foreign and Political Department (Secret), F, February 1920 #77–171, for partial translation of "Bolshevism and the Islamic Body-Politics," Tashkent, 5 March 1919. This is the book Shaukat Usmani said he had read; Usmani said Barakatullah wrote another book called *Islam and Socialism*, read widely in Persian and Turkish versions.

156. IOR/L/PJ/12/213.

157. Josh, *Hindustan Gadar Party*, 281–82.

158. Ibid., 282.

159. For "Muslim national communism," see Alexandre Bennigsen and Stephen Wimbush, *Muslim National Communism in the Soviet Union: A Revolutionary Strategy*

for the Colonial World (Chicago: University of Chicago Press, 1979). Sultan-Galiev was a Tatar Communist leader, part of the Central Executive Committee of the Tatar Republic, and the highest-ranking Muslim in the central CP hierarchy as member of the Narkomnats (and editor of its official organ), the central Muslim commissariat, as well as other posts. He also took part in the All-Russian Muslim Congress in 1917. He was later purged for "nationalist deviation," and sentenced to ten years of hard labor in 1928. He disappeared from the record in 1939.

160. The *muhajirin* thus attended during the peak of this Sultan-Galievist period, while the American Ghadarites did not arrive until 1924 and after, when presumably they were taught a more orthodox Leninism.

161. Letter, Shaukat Usmani to A. C. Bose, date unspecified (Bose, 362). Usmani said that he did not meet Barakatullah in Moscow, though he did read the latter's book *Islam and Socialism*, which was widely circulated at the time in Persian and Turkish.

162. IOR/L/PJ/12/213, March 1923. At the end of 1922, Barakatullah was also one of the members of a "Supreme Oriental Council" started by the ex-khedive in order to affiliate "various revolutionary societies in India, Arabia and Egypt."

163. In correspondence with Chicherin some of his plans were detailed: he proposed that (via the Russian ambassador to Afghanistan, Raskolnikov) Iqbal Shaidai, Ghulam Muhammad Aziz, and Fazl Ilahi form an organization in Chamarkand by which they could establish centers among all the "Independence Tribes" along the Frontier, from Chitral to Baluchistan, who would then rise unified and in alliance with India, Afghanistan, and Soviet Russia. Primary schools were to be established at the headquarters of each tribe, as well a Hindustani newspaper. Monthly progress reports would be sent to the IIP in Berlin via the Soviet legation in Kabul. Apparently no longer did tactical utility trump ideology: in Rome circa 1924 Barakatullah made an abortive attempt to form an Indo-Italian Commercial Syndicate with ties to Mussolini's brother Arnaldo and the Fascist Party, along with other old members of the Berlin India committee, but "the scheme did not materialize . . . owing to differences among the founders." IOR/L/PJ/12/213.

164. Home Department, Political, #135/V, 1926. Proscription of monthly *El Islam*, published by Barakatullah in Berlin.

165. See Bose, *Indian Revolutionaries Abroad*, 69–70; Sareen, 182. Home Department, Political, A, *Proceedings*, August 1914, #7–16, telegram from British ambassador at Tokyo to DCI, 9 May 1914: a list of publications Barakatullah edited or was believed to be connected with include *Islamic Fraternity, El Islam, An Nazir-al-Ulyan, Proclamation of Liberty*, and *The Sword Is the Last Resort*. He denied the last three.

166. Sareen, 182.

167. Ibid.

168. Sareen, 183–84.

169. Not that he sees the founding of the Indian National Congress as much of an accomplishment: "From the constitutional history of England the Hindu learned a scheme of making noise in chorus annually in the [hope] of reaching the ears of the benign sovereign! From 1885–1905 he regularly kept up his annual shouting, of course, within the constitutional limits." Sareen, 184. Here note that he is using "Hindu" in the specific sense, not in its generic sense of "East Indian."

170. Sareen, 184.
171. Ibid., 185.
172. Ibid., 185–86.
173. Ibid., 186.
174. Ibid.
175. Ibid.

EPILOGUE

1. Josh, *Communist Movement in Punjab*, 107.

2. Mark Juergensmeyer, *Religion as Social Vision: The Movement against Untouchability in Twentieth-Century Punjab* (Berkeley: University of California Press, 1982), 42–44, 283–89. The book focuses on the transpositions of a religious idiom into social movements.

3. Juergensmeyer, *Religion as Social Vision*, 43, 284.

4. Ibid., 43.

5. Ibid., 286–87.

6. DCI weekly reports, September 1920, April 1920.

7. Juergensmeyer, *Religion as Social Vision*, 43–44.

8. Ibid., 288. Although this seems to have been the extent of active Ghadar involvement in the Untouchable "uplift" movement, Juergensmeyer says that to his knowledge Mangu Ram had not bothered to avail himself of ample opportunities to draw upon his old Ghadar connections in Punjab, though he did maintain ties with his *Maverick* shipmate Hari Singh, and with the editor of a newspaper founded by Ghadarites in Ludhiana, who had given him a tip-off about a government plan for subdividing scheduled castes that served as a catalyst for the establishment of Ad Dharm.

9. Juergensmeyer, *Religion as Social Vision*, 288–89, from an interview with Mangu Ram, 1973.

10. IOR/L/P&J/12/500; Police File MEPO 3/1743.

11. Ibid.

12. Ibid.

13. IOR/L/PJ/12/500. Incidentally, the pro-Congress *Lahore Tribune* expressed the opinion on 16 March 1940 that Azad had intended to emulate the IRA; the court had also discreetly referred to a recent IRA trial as precedent for restricting access to the courtroom to avoid spectacle.

14. Rosina Vizram, *Asians in Britain* (London: Pluto Press, 2002), 269–73. Similarly, something that bears much more attention than it has yet received is the important role of South Asian immigrants, specifically Ghadar-influenced Sikhs, in the Nairobi-based East African labor and anticolonial movements of the 1940s–1960s. See Zarina Patel, *Unquiet: The Life and Times of Makhan Singh* (Nairobi: Zand Graphics, 2006); Tom Odhiambo, "Biography of a Trade Unionist and the Resurrection of the 'Indian Question' in Twenty-First Century Kenya," *Social Dynamics* 33.2 (2007); Amarjit Chandan, *Gopal Singh Chandan: A Short Biography and Memoirs*, Punjabi Diaspora Series 4 (Jalandhar: Punjab Centre for Migration Studies, 2004).

15. See Hindustan Gadar Party, Organization of Indian Marxist-Leninists Abroad (HGP-OIMLA), *Documents of the First Congress of the HGP-OIMLA, 1968–77* (Toronto: Norman Bethune Institute, 1978), 15–17; *Chingari: Organ of the Hindustani Ghadar Party (Marxist-Leninist)* 5.3 (June 1, 1973) (SANA Box 13:10).

16. Since "Baba Bilga's" passing the details of his life narrative are readily available online: see, for example, http://uddari.wordpress.com/2009/05/22/talking-about-a-revolution-bhagat-singh-bilga/; www.harmonyindia.org/hportal/VirtualPrintView.jsp?page; http://johntyrrell.co.uk/2009/06/tribute-to-baba-bhagat-singh-bilga-in-bi/; obituary in the *Tribune*, Jalandhar, May 23, 2009, viewable at http://bilga.com/edoc/BBSBtribune.jpg; and Chaman Lal, "Tribute: Baba Bhagat Singh Bilga and Vimla Dang—Pride of Punjab," *Mainstream* 48.35, 15 August 2009 (Independence Day special issue).

17. Rattan Singh, "A Brief History of the Hindustan Gadar Party" (San Francisco, 1927), 1 (SANA Box 4:12) (originally submitted to the League against Imperialism).

18. Shiv Verma, introduction to *Selected Writings of Shaheed Bhagat Singh* (New Delhi: National Book Centre, 1986).

19. This famous poem of martyrdom is attributed to Ram Prasad Bismil; it appears in the 1920 Ghadar publication *Lal Jhanda aur Inqilab-e-Hind* (SANA Box 2:28).

20. Bose, 10. Moreover, diasporic circuits are just as likely to produce radical internationalisms as to produce nationalist conciousness, as Benedict Anderson himself has begun to explore; see his *Under Three Flags* (New York: Verso, 2006); also Leela Gandhi, *Affective Communities* (Durham, NC: Duke University Press, 2006); Mrinalini Sinha, *Specters of Mother India* (Durham, NC: Duke University Press, 2006); Anthony Parel, introduction to *Hind Swaraj and Other Writings*, by M.K. Gandhi, ed. Anthony Parel (Cambridge: Cambridge University Press, 1997).

BIBLIOGRAPHY

ARCHIVAL SOURCES

Archives on Contemporary History, Jawaharlal Nehru University, Delhi.
Desh Bhagat Yadgar, Jalandhar, India.
Hoover Library and Archives, Stanford University, Palo Alto, CA.
India Office Records, British Library, London. [IOR]
National Archives of India, Delhi. [NAI]
Nehru Memorial Museum and Library, Delhi. [NMML]
South Asians in North America Collection, Bancroft Library, University of California, Berkeley. [SANA]
United States National Archives and Records Administration, College Park, MD; San Bruno, CA. [NARA]
Van Pelt Rare Documents Collection, University of Pennsylvania, Philadelphia, PA.

PUBLISHED DOCUMENTS

Adhikari, Gangadhar, ed. *Documents of the History of the Communist Party of India.* Vols. 1–3. New Delhi: People's Publishing House, 1971–1982.

Bose, A. C. *Indian Revolutionaries Abroad, 1905–1927: Select Documents.* New Delhi: Northern Book Centre, 2002.

Chopra, P. N., ed. *Indian Freedom Fighters Abroad: Secret British Intelligence Report.* New Delhi: Criterion Publications, 1988.

Isemonger, F. C., and James Slattery. *An Account of the Ghadr Conspiracy, 1913–1915.* Lahore: Superintendent Government Printing, 1919. Reprint, Berkeley: Folklore Institute, 1998.

Kaye, Cecil. *Communism in India, 1919–1924.* 1924. Reprint, Calcutta: Editions Indian, 1971.

Ker, James Campbell. *Political Trouble in India, 1907–1917.* Calcutta: Superintendent Government Printing, 1917. Reprint, Calcutta: Editions Indian, 1973.

Petrie, David. *Communism in India, 1924–1927.* 1927. Calcutta: Editions Indian, 1972.

———. *Developments in Sikh Politics, 1900–1911: A Report.* Amritsar: Chief Khalsa Diwan, 1972 [1991].

Riddell, John, ed. *To See the Dawn: Baku, 1920, First Congress of the Peoples of the East.* New York: Pathfinder Press, 1993.

Sareen, T. R. *Secret Documents on Singapore Mutiny, 1915.* New Delhi: Mounto Publishing House, 1995.

———. *Select Documents on the Ghadr Party.* New Delhi: Mounto Publishing House, 1994.

———. *Unsung Heroes: Select Documents on Neglected Parts of India's Freedom Struggle.* New Delhi: Life Span Publishers, 2009.

Sedition Committee (S. A. T. Rowlatt, President). *Report.* Calcutta: Superintendent Government Printing, 1918.

Senate Fact-Finding Committee. *Seventh Report on Un-American Activities in California.* Sacramento: California Senate Printing Office, 1953.

Waraich, Malwinderjit Singh, and Gurdev Singh Sidhu, eds. *The Hanging of Bhagat Singh: Complete Judgment and Other Documents.* Chandigarh: Unistar Books, 2005.

———. *Komagata Maru: A Challenge to Colonialism; Key Documents.* Chandigarh: Unistar Books, 2005.

Waraich, Malwinderjit Singh, and Harinder Singh. *Ghadar Movement: Original Documents.* Chandigarh: Unistar Books, 2008.

OTHER SOURCES

Acharya, M. P. T., and Bishember Dayal Yadav. *M. P. T. Acharya: Reminiscences of an Indian Revolutionary.* New Delhi: Anmol Publications, 1991.

Agarwal, S. N. *The Heroes of Cellular Jail.* Patiala: Publication Bureau, Punjabi University, 1995.

Ahmad, Aziz. *Islamic Modernism in India and Pakistan, 1857–1964.* London: Oxford University Press, 1967.

Ahmed, Muzaffar. *The Communist Party of India and Its Formation Abroad.* Calcutta: National Book Agency, 1962.

———. *Myself and the Communist Party of India, 1920–1929.* Calcutta: National Book Agency, 1970.

Anderson, W. K. *James Connolly and the Irish Left.* Dublin: Irish Academic Press, 1994.

Ansari, K. H. *The Emergence of the Muslim Socialists in North India, 1917–1947.* Boston Spa, UK: British Library Document Supply Centre, 1985.

———. "Pan-Islam and the Making of the Early Indian Muslim Socialists." *Modern Asian Studies* 20.3 (1986).

Anschel, Eugene. *Homer Lea, Sun Yat-sen, and the Chinese Revolution.* New York: Praeger, 1984.

Avrich, Paul. *The Russian Anarchists*. Princeton, NJ: Princeton University Press, 1971.

Aydin, Cemil. *The Politics of Anti-Westernism in Asia: Visions of World Order in Pan-Islamic and Pan-Asian Thought*. New York: Columbia University Press, 2007.

———. "The Politics of Civilizational Identities: Asia, West, and Islam in the Pan-Asianist Thought of Ôkawa Shûmei." PhD diss., Harvard University, 2002.

Azad, Chaman Lal. *Bhagat Singh aur Dutt ki Amar Kahani*. New Delhi: Satya Prakashan, 1966.

Bakshi, S. R. *Bhagat Singh and His Ideology*. New Delhi: Capital Publishers, 1981.

Ballantyne, Tony. *Between Colonialism and Diaspora: Sikh Cultural Formations in an Imperial World*. Durham, NC: Duke University Press, 2006.

Barooah, Nirode. *Chatto: The Life and Times of an Indian Anti-Imperialist in Europe*. New Delhi: Oxford University Press, 2004.

Barrier, Gerald. *Banned: Controversial Literature and Political Control in British India, 1907–1947*. New Delhi: Manohar, 1974.

Barrier, Gerald, and Verne Dusenbery, eds. *The Sikh Diaspora: Migration and the Experience beyond Punjab*. Delhi: Chanakya Publications, 1989.

Bayly, Christopher, and Leila Fawaz, eds. *Modernity and Culture from the Mediterranean to the Indian Ocean*. New York: Columbia University Press, 2002.

Bennigsen, Alexandre, and Stephen Wimbush. *Muslim National Communism in the Soviet Union: A Revolutionary Strategy for the Colonial World*. Chicago: University of Chicago Press, 1979.

Billington, James. *Fire in the Minds of Men: Origins of the Revolutionary Faith*. New York: Basic Books, 1980.

Bose, A. C. *Indian Revolutionaries Abroad, 1905–1922, in the Background of International Developments*. Patna: Bharati Bhawan, 1971.

Brasted, Howard. "Indian Nationalist Development and the Influence of Irish Home Rule, 1870–1886." *Modern Asian Studies* 14.1 (1980).

Breen, Dan. *My Fight for Irish Freedom*. Dublin: Talbot Press, 1924. Reprint, Dublin and Tralee: Anvil Press, 1964.

Brooks, Van Wyck. *An Autobiography*. New York: E. P. Dutton, 1965.

Brown, Emily. *Har Dayal: Hindu Revolutionary and Rationalist*. Tucson: University of Arizona Press, 1975.

Buchignani, Norman, and Doreen Indra. *Continuous Journey: A Social History of South Asians in Canada*. Toronto: McClelland & Stewart, 1985.

Bufe, Charles, and Mitch Verter. *Dreams of Freedom: A Ricardo Flores Magon Reader*. Oakland, CA: AK Press, 2006.

Buhle, Paul, and Dan Georgakas, eds. *The Immigrant Left in the United States*. Albany: SUNY Press, 1996.

Burke, Edmund, III. "Moroccan Resistance, Pan-Islam, and German War Strategy, 1914–1918." *Francia* (Munich) 3 (1976).

———. "Pan-Islam and Moroccan Resistance to French Colonial Penetration, 1900–1912." *The Journal of African History* 13.1 (1972).

Caldwell, John Taylor. *Come Dungeons Dark*. Edinburgh: Luath Press, 1988.

Chandrasekhar, S., ed. *From India to America: A Brief History of Immigration; Problems of Discrimination, Admission, and Assimilation*. La Jolla, CA: Population Review Publications, 1982.

Cheng, Lucie, and Edna Bonacich. *Labor Immigration under Capitalism: Asian Workers in the United States before World War II*. Berkeley: University of California Press, 1984.

Chirol, Valentine. *Indian Unrest*. London: Macmillan and Co., 1910.

Coury, Ralph. *The Making of an Egyptian Arab Nationalist: The Early Years of Azzam Pasha, 1893–1936*. Reading: Ithaca Press, 1998.

Davis, Richard. "India in Irish Revolutionary Movement, 1905–1922." *Journal of Asiatic Society* 22.1 (April 1977).

Deol, Gurdev Singh. *The Role of the Ghadar Party in the National Movement*. New Delhi: Sterling Publishers, 1969.

———. *Shaheed-e-Azam Sardar Bhagat Singh: The Man and His Ideology*. Nabha: Deep Prakashan, 1978.

Devoy, John. *Recollections of an Irish Rebel: The Fenian Movement; Its Origin and Progress . . . A Personal Narrative*. New York: Charles Young Company, 1929.

Dharmavira. *Lala Har Dayal and Revolutionary Movements of His Times*. New Delhi: India Book Company, 1970.

———, ed. *Letters of Lala Har Dayal*. Ambala Cantt.: Indian Book Agency, 1970.

Dignan, Don. *The Indian Revolutionary Problem in British Diplomacy, 1914–1919*. New Delhi: Allied Publishers, 1983.

Dubofsky, Melvyn. *We Shall Be All: A History of the Industrial Workers of the World*. Urbana: University of Illinois Press, 2000.

Fischer-Tine, Harald. "Indian Nationalism and the 'World Forces': Transnational and Diasporic Dimensions of the Indian Freedom Movement on the Eve of the First World War." *Journal of Global History* 2 (2007).

Foley, Tadhg, and Maureen O'Connor, eds., *Ireland and India: Colonies, Culture, and Empire*. Dublin: Irish Academic Press, 2006.

Ganachari, Arvind. *Nationalism and Social Reform in the Colonial Situation*. Delhi: Kalpaz Publications, 2005.

Ganguly, A.B. *Ghadar Revolution in America*. New Delhi: Metropolitan Book Company, 1980.

Gershoni, Israel, and James Jankowski. *Egypt, Islam, and the Arabs: The Search for Egyptian Nationhood, 1900–1930*. New York: Oxford University Press, 1987.

Ghosh, Ajoy. *Bhagat Singh and His Comrades*. New Delhi: People's Publishing House, 1979.

Gordon, Leonard. *Bengal: The Nationalist Movement, 1876–1940*. New York: Columbia University Press, 1974.

Goswami, Manu. "Autonomy and Comparability: Notes on the Anticolonial and the Postcolonial." *boundary 2* 32.2 (2005).

Gould, Harold. *Sikhs, Swamis, Students, and Spies: The India Lobby in the United States, 1900–1946*. New Delhi: Sage Publications, 2006.

Gupta, Manmathnath. *They Lived Dangerously*. New Delhi: People's Publishing House, 1969.

Habib, Irfan. *To Make the Deaf Hear: Ideology and Programme of Bhagat Singh and His Comrades*. Gurgaon: Three Essays Collective, 2007.

Haithcox, John. *Communism and Nationalism in India: M. N. Roy and Comintern Policy, 1920–1939.* Princeton, NJ: Princeton University Press, 1971.

———. "Nationalism, Communism, and Twentieth-Century Jacobinism: Royist Tactics in India, 1927–1940." PhD diss., University of California, Berkeley, 1965.

Har Dayal, Lala. *Forty-four Months in Germany and Turkey, February 1915 to October 1918: A Record of Personal Impressions.* London: P. S. King & Son, Ltd., 1920.

———. *Marx Comes to India: Earliest Indian Biographies of Karl Marx.* Delhi: Manohar Book Service, 1975.

———. *Writings of Lala Hardayal.* Benares: Swaraj Publishing House, [1923?].

Harper, R. W. E., and Larry Miller. *Singapore Mutiny.* New York: Oxford University Press, 1984.

Hasan, Mushirul, ed. *Communal and Pan-Islamic Trends in Colonial India.* New Delhi: Manohar, 1981.

———. *Regionalizing Pan-Islamism: Documents on the Khilafat Movement.* New Delhi: Manohar, 2005.

Heehs, Peter. *The Bomb in Bengal: The Rise of Revolutionary Terrorism in India, 1900–1910.* New York: Oxford University Press, 2004.

———. *Nationalism, Terrorism, Communalism: Essays in Modern Indian History.* New York: Oxford University Press, 1998.

Horowitz, Irving. *Radicalism and the Revolt against Reason: The Social Theories of Georges Sorel.* New York: Humanities Press, 1961.

Hourani, Albert. *Arabic Thought in the Liberal Age, 1798–1939.* New York: Oxford University Press, 1970.

Irfan Khan, Muhammed. *Barkatullah Bhupali: Ek Jhan Gasht-i Inqalabi.* Bhopal: Irfan Publications, 1969. Reprint, London: British Library Document Supply Centre, 1985.

Jacobson, Jon. *When the Soviet Union Entered World Politics.* Berkeley: University of California Press, 1994.

Jensen, Joan. *Passage from India: Asian Indian Immigrants in North America.* New Haven, CT: Yale University Press, 1988.

Johnstone, Hugh. *The Voyage of the Komagata Maru: The Sikh Challenge to Canada's Colour Bar.* Delhi: Oxford University Press, 1979.

Josh, Bhagwan. *Communist Movement in Punjab, 1926–47.* Delhi: Anupama Publications, 1979.

Josh, Sohan Singh. *Baba Sohan Singh Bhakna: Life of the Founder of the Ghadar Party.* New Delhi: People's Publishing House, 1970.

———. *Hindustan Gadar Party: A Short History.* New Delhi: People's Publishing House, 1977–1978.

———. *My Meetings with Bhagat Singh and on Other Early Revolutionaries.* New Delhi: Communist Party of India, 1976.

———. *My Tryst with Secularism: An Autobiography.* New Delhi: Patriot Publishers, 1991.

Juergensmeyer, Mark. "The Gadar Syndrome: Ethnic Anger and Nationalist Pride." *Population Review* 25.1–2 (1981).

———. *The Ghadar Syndrome: Nationalism in an Immigrant Community.* Amritsar: Guru Nanak Dev University, 1977.

————. *Religion as Social Vision: The Movement against Untouchability in Twentieth-Century Punjab*. Berkeley: University of California Press, 1982.

Juergensmeyer, Mark, and Gerald Barrier, eds. *Sikh Studies: Comparative Perspectives on a Changing Tradition*. Berkeley: Graduate Theological Union, 1979.

Kapur, Harish. *Soviet Russia and Asia, 1917–1927*. London: Pinter Publications, 1989.

Keddie, Nikki. *An Islamic Response to Imperialism: Political and Religious Writings of Sayyid Jamal ad-Din "al-Afghani."* Berkeley: University of California Press, 1968.

Khan, Amir Haider. *Chains to Lose: Life and Struggles of a Revolutionary*. New Delhi: Patriot Publishers, 1989.

Khuri-Makdisi, Ilham. "Levantine Trajectories: The Formulation and Dissemination of Radical Ideas in and between Beirut, Cairo, and Alexandria, 1860–1914." PhD diss., Harvard University, 2004.

Knowles, Robert. "Anarchist Notions of Nationalism and Patriotism." R.A. Forum. http://raforum.info/article.php3?id_article = 2221.

Kornbluh, Joyce, ed. *Rebel Voices: An IWW Anthology*. Ann Arbor: University of Michigan Press, 1968.

LaBrack, Bruce. *The Sikhs of Northern California, 1904–1975*. New York: AMS Press, 1988.

Lal, Chaman. *Bhagat Singh: The Jail Notebook and Other Writings*. New Delhi: LeftWord Books, 2007.

————. "Gandhi, Bhagat Singh, and What the Historians Say." *Economic and Political Weekly* 44.25 (2009).

Leonard, Karen. *Making Ethnic Choices: California's Punjabi Mexican Americans*. Philadelphia: Temple University Press, 1992.

Lynch, David. *Radical Politics in Modern Ireland: The Irish Socialist Republican Party, 1896–1904*. Dublin: Irish Academic Press, 2005.

MacKinnon, Janice, and Stephen MacKinnon. *Agnes Smedley: The Life and Times of an American Radical*. Berkeley: University of California Press, 1988.

Manjapra, Kris. "The Illusions of Encounter: Muslim and Hindu Revolutionaries in First World War Germany and After." *Journal of Global History* 1.3 (2006).

Marks, Steven G. *How Russia Shaped the Modern World*. Princeton, NJ: Princeton University Press, 2003.

Mathur, L.P. *Indian Revolutionary Movement in the United States of America*. Delhi: S. Chand, 1970.

Melendy, H. Bret. *Asians in America*. Boston: Twayne Publishers, 1977.

Metcalf, Thomas. *Imperial Connections: India in the Indian Ocean Arena, 1860–1920*. Berkeley: University of California Press, 2007.

Miller, Sally. *The Radical Immigrant*. New York: Twayne Publishers, 1974.

Minault, Gail. *The Khilafat Movement: Religious Symbolism and Political Mobilization in India*. New York: Columbia University Press, 1982.

Mitchell, Barbara. *The Practical Revolutionaries: A New Interpretation of the French Anarchosyndicalists*. Westport, CT: Greenwood Press, 1987.

Mondal, Anshuman. *Nationalism and Post-Colonial Identity: Culture and Ideology in India and Egypt*. New York: RoutledgeCurzon, 2003.

Moss, Bernard. *The Origins of the French Labor Movement, 1830–1914: The Socialism of Skilled Workers.* Berkeley: University of California Press, 1976.

Mukerji, Dhan Gopal. *Caste and Outcast.* Edited by Gordon Chang, Purnima Mankekar, and Akhil Gupta. New York: E. P. Dutton, 1923. Reprint, Stanford, CA: Stanford University Press, 2002.

Mukherjee, Tapan K. *Taraknath Das: Life and Letters of a Revolutionary in Exile.* Calcutta: National Council of Education, 1998.

Musa, Salama. *The Education of Salama Musa.* Translated by L. O. Schuman. Leiden: Brill, 1961.

Nair, Neeti. "Bhagat Singh as Satyagrahi: The Limits of Non-Violence in Late Colonial India." *Modern Asian Studies* 43.3 (2009).

O'Dwyer, Michael. *India as I Knew It, 1885–1925.* London: Constable & Co., 1925.

O'Malley, Kate. *Ireland, India, and Empire: Indo-Irish Radical Connections, 1919–1964.* Manchester: Manchester University Press, 2008.

Overstreet, Gene, and Marshall Windmiller. *Communism in India.* Berkeley: University of California Press, 1959.

Ozcan, Azmi. *Pan-Islamism: Indian Muslims, the Ottomans, and Britain, 1877–1924.* New York: Brill, 1997.

Panikkar, K. N., ed. *National and Left Movements in India.* New Delhi: Vikas, 1980.

Patel, Zarina. *Unquiet: The Life and Times of Makhan Singh.* Nairobi: Zand Graphics, 2006.

Persits, M. *Revolutionaries of India in Soviet Russia.* Moscow: Progress Publishers, 1983.

Plowman, Matthew. "Irish Republicans and the Indo-German Conspiracy of World War I." *New Hibernia Review* 7.3 (Autumn 2003).

Popplewell, Richard. *Intelligence and Imperial Defence: British Intelligence and the Defence of the Indian Empire, 1904–1924.* London: Frank Cass, 1995.

Price, Ruth. *The Lives of Agnes Smedley.* New York: Oxford University Press, 2005.

Puri, Harish K. *Ghadar Movement: Ideology, Organisation, and Strategy.* Amritsar: Guru Nanak Dev University, 1993.

Qureshi, M. Naeem. *Pan-Islam in British Indian Politics: A Study of the Khilafat Movement, 1918–1924.* Boston: Brill, 1999.

Reetz, Dietrich. *Hijrat: The Flight of the Faithful; A British File on the Exodus of Muslim Peasants from India to Afghanistan in 1920.* Berlin: Verlag Das Arabische Buch, 1995.

Rodinson, Maxime. *Marxism and the Muslim World.* New York: Monthly Review Press, 1981.

Roth, Jack. *The Cult of Violence: Sorel and the Sorelians.* Berkeley: University of California Press, 1980.

Roy, M. N. *Memoirs.* Bombay and New York: Allied Publishers, 1964.

Ryan, Desmond. *The Rising: The Complete Story of Easter Week.* Dublin: Golden Eagle Books, Ltd., 1949.

Salerno, Salvatore. *Red November, Black November: Culture and Community in the Industrial Workers of the World.* Albany: SUNY Press, 1989.

Sareen, T. R. *Indian Revolutionary Movement Abroad.* New Delhi: Sterling, 1979.

———. "Secret Documents on Singapore Mutiny, 1915." *Journal of Southeast Asia Studies* 28.2 (1997).

Sarkar, Sumit. *Modern India, 1885–1947.* Delhi: Macmillan, 1983.

———. *The Swadeshi Movement in Bengal, 1903–1908.* New Delhi: People's Publishing House, 1973.

Satia, Priya. *Spies in Arabia.* New York: Oxford University Press, 2008.

Sawhney, Savitri. *I Shall Never Ask for Pardon: A Memoir of Pandurang Khankhoje.* New Delhi: Oxford India, 2008.

Seth, Sanjay. *Marxist Theory and Nationalist Politics: The Case of Colonial India.* New Delhi: Sage Publications, 1995.

Shakir, Moin. *Khilafat to Partition: A Survey of Major Political Trends among Indian Muslims during 1919–1947.* Delhi: Ajanta Publications, 1983.

Sharma, Shalini. "Developing a Communist Identity: The Case of the Naujavan Bharat Sabha." *Journal of Punjab Studies* 14.2 (Fall 2007).

Sho, Kuwajima. *Mutiny in Singapore: War, Anti-War, and the War for India's Independence.* New Delhi: Rainbow Publishers, 2006.

Singh, Gurharpal. *Communism in Punjab: A Study of the Movement up to 1967.* Delhi: Ajanta Publications, 1994.

Singh, Jane, et al., eds. *South Asians in North America: An Annotated and Selected Bibliography.* Berkeley: Center for South and Southeast Asia Studies, 1988.

Singh, Khushwant, and Satindra Singh. *Ghadar 1915: India's First Armed Revolution.* Delhi: R & K Publishing House, 1966.

Smedley, Agnes. *Daughter of Earth.* New York: Coward-McCann, 1929.

Smith, W. C. *Modern Islam in India.* New Delhi: Usha Publications, 1979.

Sood, Malini. "Expatriate Nationalism and Ethnic Radicalism: The Ghadar Party in North America, 1910–1920." PhD diss., SUNY, Stony Brook, 1995.

Spratt, Philip. *Blowing up India: Reminiscences and Reflections of a Former Comintern Emissary.* Calcutta: Prachi Prakashan, 1955.

Subramanyam, C. S. *M. P. T. Acharya, His Life and Times: Revolutionary Trends in the Early Anti-Imperialist Movements in South India and Abroad.* Madras: Institute of South Indian Studies, 1995.

Sykes, Christopher. *Wassmuss, the German Lawrence.* London: Longman, Green & Co., 1936.

Tabili, Laura. *"We Ask for British Justice": Workers and Racial Difference in Late Imperial Britain.* Ithaca, NY: Cornell University Press, 1994.

Tatla, Darshan Singh. *A Guide to Sources: Ghadar Movement.* Amritsar: Guru Nanak Dev University, 2003.

Thakur, Gopal. *Bhagat Singh: The Man and His Ideas.* New Delhi: People's Publishing House, 1962.

Thorpe, Wayne, and Marcel van der Linden. *Revolutionary Syndicalism: An International Perspective.* Aldershot, Eng.: Scolar Press, 1990.

Usmani, Shaukat. *Historic Trips of a Revolutionary: Sojourn in the Soviet Union.* New Delhi: Sterling Publishers, 1977.

———. *Peshawar to Moscow: Leaves from an Indian Muhajireen's Diary.* Benares: Swarajya Publishing House, 1927.

Van der Veer, Peter. *Nation and Migration: The Politics of Space in the South Asian Diaspora.* Philadelphia: University of Pennsylvania Press, 1995.

Vatikiotis, P. *The History of Egypt.* London: Weidenfeld & Nicolson, 1969.

Vatuk, Ved Prakash. *Thieves in My House: Four Studies of Indian Folklore of Protest and Change.* Varanasi: Vishwavidyalaya Prakashan, 1969.

Verma, Shiv, ed. *Selected Writings of Shaheed Bhagat Singh.* New Delhi: National Book Centre, 1986.

Voll, John Obert. *Islam: Continuity and Change in the Modern World.* Boulder, CO: Westview Press, 1982.

Ward, Alan J. *The Easter Rising: Revolution and Irish Nationalism.* Arlington Heights, IL: AHM Publishing Corporation, 1980.

Worley, Matthew, ed. *In Search of Revolution: International Communist Parties in the Third Period.* London: I. B. Tauris, 2004.

Yajnik, Indulal Kanailal. *Shyamaji Krishnavarma: Life and Times of an Indian Revolutionary.* Bombay: Lakshmi Publications, 1950.

INDEX

Abdulla, Hafiz, 51
Abhinava Bharat (London), 36
Aboj, Mahadev, 254n155
Achar Singh (Cheema), 151
Acharya, M. P. T.: and Berlin India Committee, 73; and Egyptian nationalism, 265n38; and German-Ottoman Pan-Islamist initiatives, 178; and Gill, 272n17; and Indian Committee in Stockholm, 263n4; and Irish independence movement, 104; and *muhajirin*, 172, 204–5; and Pan-Islamism, 170, 171, 172, 202, 283n21
ACLU (American Civil Liberties Union), 67–68
Ad Dharm, 234, 235
Adaj, Mahadev, 262n102
Afghani, 222, 263n6
Afghanistan: and Communist Ghadar, 145, 276n120; and Hijrat movement, 202; and Pan-Islamist Ghadar, 185–86; Silk Letters plot, 185–89, 286–87nn84,93,95. *See also* Provisional Government of India
Agarche, 183, 285n68
Ahmad, Abdul, 185
Ahmad, Aziz, 296nn122,126
Ahmad, Kabir, 202
Ahmad, Muzaffar, 186
Ahmad, Rafiq, 202, 203, 214, 216–17, 228, 291nn27,31,35, 294n91. *See also muhajirin*
Ahmed, Habib, 209, 210, 212–13, 214, 294n91

Ahmed, Mansur, 74, 178, 182
Ahmed, Muzaffar, 125, 216–17, 217, 291n27
Ailan-i-Jang (Bhagwan Singh), 159, 253n123
Aiyar, V. V. S., 264n11; and Egyptian nationalism, 99, 265n38; on Italy, 102; and Pan-Islamism, 170, 172, 283n21; and Savarkar, 265n47
Ajit Singh: and Berlin India Committee, 73; and Bhagat Singh, 158; and British colonial policies, 18; and early North American activists, 25; and German-Ottoman Pan-Islamist initiatives, 285n69; *Ghadar-di-Gunj* on, 43; and Ghadar movement pre-World War I activism, 39; and Jodh Singh, 84; and Pacific Coast Hindi Association, 32; and Pan-Islamism, 170–71, 172; and South America, 150, 280n200
Akali Dal, 44, 45, 153, 253n135, 271n16, 279n172
Akhwat, 176
el-Alaily, Hamid, 100
El Alam, 99
Albayan, 197
Aldred, Guy, 67
Ali, Muhammed, 185, 216, 295n96
Ali, Yusuf, 297n137
Alien Bill (1920) (United States), 135
Alien Land Law (1913) (California), 24–25
Alien Land Laws (1920) (United States), 127
Alienation of Land Act (1901) (India), 18

ment of India, 74–75, 125, 146; Siam-Burma
scheme, 81–88, 260nn62,64,71,75,77, 262n97.
See also German-Ottoman Pan-Islamist
initiatives; Hindu-German Conspiracy
Trial
Bernhardi, Friedrich von, 72
Bernstorf, Johan von, 78
Bertoni, Luigi, 101
Bertrand, Charles, 256n185
Beshhamba, Ali Bey, 182
Bey, Farid, 100, 101
Bey, Kadri, 183
Bey, Muhammad Abd al-Halim, 178
Bey, Niazi, 190
Bey, Tewfik, 190
Bhag Singh "Canadian," 153, 156
Bhagat Singh, 7, 11, 157–58, 159, 160–62, 235,
240n6, 254n135
Bhagwan Singh: and Barakatullah, 225; and
Batavia-Calcutta arms importation scheme,
77, 259n51; and Berlin India Committee, 73;
and Communism, 144; and Dayal's arrest,
47; deportation of, 40, 43, 131, 249n41; and
East Asian initiatives, 75, 77, 258n32; on
ethnic fusion, 285n66; and *Ghadar-di-Gunj,*
249n46; and Hindu-German Conspiracy
Trial, 262n102; and *Komagata Maru*
incident, 48–49; and Pan-Asianism, 116;
and post-Ghadar Mutiny regrouping, 60,
61, 62, 281n209; and Smedley, 129; and
South America, 150; and World War I
uprising, 251n79
Bhai Bhag Singh, 245n41
Bhaksh, Khuda, 286n78
Bharat Mata Society, 18
Bhattacharji, Narendranath. *See* Roy, M.n
BIC. *See* Berlin India Committee
Bilga, Bhagat Singh, 150, 237, 280n200
Billington, James, 69, 265–66n48
Bishan Singh (Hindi), 114, 254n155
Bishen Singh, 128
Bismil, Ram Prasad, 301n19
Biswas, Basanta Kumar, 252n110
Boas, Franz, 132
Boehm, George Paul, 82, 88, 260n64
Bokhara, 208, 293n64
Bolshevik appeals to Pan-Islamism, 194–201;
Baku Congress, 195, 199, 200–201; British
fears of, 198–99; and geopolitics, 195, 290n5;
and Kemal, 196; Kheiri brothers on, 197–98;
and Khilafat movement, 196, 197, 199–200

Bolshevism. *See* Bolshevik appeals to Pan-
Islamism; Russian revolutionary movements
Bolshevism and the Islamic Body Politik
(Barakatullah), 227–28, 298n154
Bopp, Franz, 91
Borodin, Michael, 270n3
Bose, A. C., 5, 127, 237, 283n10, 288n113
Bose, Rash Behari: and Batavia-Calcutta arms
importation scheme, 77, 80, 81, 259n51; and
China mission, 146; and Pan-Asianism, 116,
117–18; and World War I uprising, 53–54, 56,
59, 252n101
Bose, Subhash Chandra, 233
Brasted, Howard, 266n49
Breen, Dan, 111, 266n50, 283n22
Brincken, William von, 108
British colonial forces, 161, 245n41; and China
mission, 147, 148; East Asian postings, 75,
257n23; and German-Ottoman Pan-Islamist
initiatives, 177–82; and Irish independence
movement, 112–15; and *Komagata Maru*
incident, 48; and Sikh Sabha, 243n7;
Singapore and Rangoon Mutinies, 121, 189–93,
288nn113,118,121,124, 289nn125,129,132,133;
and syndicalism, 63; veteran emigration, 17,
18–19; and World War I participation, 90;
and World War I uprising, 55–59
British colonial policies: and Ghadar
publications content, 40; and Hindu-
German Conspiracy Trial, 94, 262n103; and
Indian emigration, 18; and World War I,
89–90. *See also specific laws*
"British Rule in India" (Bryan), 40
Brown, Emily, 30, 46, 90, 173, 252n108
Bryan, William Jennings, 40
Bujha Singh, 236
Burjor, Dady, 18
Burma, 190. *See also* Siam-Burma scheme

C (informer). *See* Chand, Sagar
California dynamite conspiracy case (1916), 66
California Ghadar movement: and Afghanistan, 145; criminal activity suspicions,
148–49; and Pan-Islamism, 172–73;
post-Ghadar Mutiny regrouping, 60–62,
254n155; postwar reincarnation of, 136; and
Singapore and Rangoon Mutinies, 189. *See
also* Ghadar movement birth; Ghadar
movement pre-World War I activism;
Ghadar publications; World War I uprising;
specific people

range of, 14, 44, 75, 248n27; later influence
of, 233–37, 300n8
Ghadar movement birth: and British/Canadian
hostility toward immigrants, 18–19, 28; and
class differences, 23, 36, 244n25; early
activists, 25–33, 245nn35,40,41; and extent of
Indian immigration, 17, 242–43nn3,4;
Ghadar term, 35, 247n6; and immigrant
rights vs. anticolonialism, 25, 31; and Indian
Independence League, 30–31, 246n61; and
labor movement, 23–24, 244n26; Pacific
Coast Hindi Association, 32–33, 35–36, 173,
246nn65,68, 247n70; and Punjabi laborers,
17–20, 25–26, 243n10, 244n18; and racism,
18–19, 22, 244n25; and Sikh religious
organizations, 18, 19–20, 243n7; and student
immigration, 20–23, 243n13; and student vs.
laborer roles, 22–23, 244n23; and U.S.
anti-immigrant policies, 24–25, 27, 244n26,
245n32; and U.S. imperialism, 24. *See also*
Ghadar movement pre-World War I
activism
Ghadar movement connections with other
radical movements, 2–3, 4–5; and French
colonialism, 263n7; and Ghadar movement
pre-World War I activism, 39, 46–47; and
Ghadar publications content, 39; and
post-Ghadar Mutiny regrouping, 60–61,
255n161; syndicalism, 62–69, 255n167. *See
also* Egyptian nationalist-Ghadar
connections; Irish-Ghadar connections;
Pan-Asianism
Ghadar movement pre-World War I activism:
action committee, 45–47; *Ghadar* founding,
35, 37, 247nn6,14; Ghadar Press, 40–45,
249nn41,45,46; Ghadar publications
content, 38–40, 248nn27,29,37; *Komagata
Maru* incident, 3–4, 47–49; propaganda
tours, 34–35; and South Africa, 248n27;
Yugantar Ashram, 36–38
Ghadar Mutiny of 1915. *See* World War I
uprising
Ghadar publications, 40–45, 249nn41,45,46;
and China mission, 148; content of, 38–40,
248nn27,29,37; distribution in India, 44–45,
77, 249n58; founding of, 35, 37, 247nn6,14;
Ghadar-di-Gunj, 41–43, 67, 79, 181, 249n46,
253n123; global reach of, 44, 77, 81, 173, 175;
and Irish-Ghadar connections, 107; and
Jodh Singh, 84; languages in, 247n14,
248n25; and post-Ghadar Mutiny

regrouping, 60–61, 62, 255n161; postwar,
136–38, 274n75; and Siam-Burma scheme,
81, 86; and Singapore and Rangoon
Mutinies, 190, 191; and syndicalism, 67
Ghadar Sandesa, 253n123
Ghali, Butrus, 99
Ghalib Pasha, 186–87
Ghalibnama. See Silk Letters plot
El Ghayati, 99
Ghose, Aurobindo, 269n109
Ghose, Sailendranath, 108, 118, 119, 128, 129–31
Gill, Dalip Singh, 126–27, 271–72nn16–18
GMD (Guomindang), 147, 270n1
Gopal Singh, 109, 128, 131, 132–33, 262n102
Gopal Singh (Sohi), 254n155
Goswami, Narendra Nath, 240n9
Goumah, Loutfi, 100
Gujar Singh, 253n116
Gujar Singh (Kala Singh), 286n78
Guomindang (GMD), 147, 270n1
Gupta, Heramba Lal, 61, 82, 91, 105, 116, 118,
261n87
Gupta, Manmathnath, 266n50
Gurdit Singh, 3, 47–48, 49, 250n76
gurdwaras, 19–20
Gurharpal Singh, 162
Gurmukh Singh, 145, 279n190; and Akali Dal,
153; and Communist Ghadar, 163; and
Hindustan Republican Association, 158;
and *Kirti*, 157; and Rattan Singh India
mission (1923), 152; and Swatantra, 149
Guru Gobind Singh scholarships, 20–21
Gyani Gurmukh Singh (Musafir), 156, 279n190

Hafiz, Abdul, 101, 182
Hamid, Abdul, 294n85
Hardit Singh, 153
Hari Singh, 79, 80, 258n44, 259n47
Hari Singh (Fakir), 254n155
Hari Singh (Usman), 38
Harjap Singh, 132, 140
Harnam Singh, 37, 56, 58, 170, 191
Harnam Singh (Chima), 22
Harnam Singh (Kahuta), 185, 286n78
Harnam Singh (Sahri), 27, 28, 86
Harnam Singh (Tundilat), 35, 36, 45, 55, 249n46
The Harp, 107
Hasan, Mahmud, 186–87
Hasan, Zafar, 189, 217, 286n78, 295n104
Hatano, Hasan U., 116, 223, 224–25,
297nn139,142

Sikh role in Ghadar movement: and Communist Ghadar, 162; and Ghadar Press
publications, 42–43, 45; Ghadar transcendence of, 4; and *Komagata Maru* incident,
3–4, 48; and Pan-Islamism, 168
Sikh Sabha, 18, 20, 243n7
Sikhs: Akali Dal, 44, 45, 153, 253n135, 271n16,
279n172; immigration to Canada and the
United States, 17–20, 25–26, 243nn7,10,
244n18; religion-based political consciousness, 18, 20, 243n7, 253–54n135. *See also* Sikh
role in Ghadar movement; *specific people*
Silk Letters plot, 185–89, 286–87nn84,93,95
Sinclair, Upton, 132
Singapore and Rangoon Mutinies (1915), 121,
189–93, 288nn113,118,121,124,
289nn125,129,132,133
Sinn Fein, 103, 114
Sipassi, Muhammed Ali, 221, 286n78
Slattery, James, 27, 32, 44, 47, 59, 251n79,
252n101, 253n114, 254n147, 259n47
Smedley, Agnes, 119, 129; and China mission,
147; and Friends of Freedom for India, 128,
131, 132, 134, 135–36; and Indian-white sexual
relations, 273n40; and Irish independence
movement, 100, 108; and Nidhan Singh,
151
"Social Conquest of the Hindu Race," 41
socialism, 6; and anticolonialism, 9–10; and
Ghadar Press, 41; and *Komagata Maru*
incident, 48; and syndicalism, 64, 68; and
U.S. internal security, 266n55; and World
War I uprising, 60. *See also* Communist
Ghadar
Society for the Advancement of India, 104
Sohan Singh (Bhakna), 30, 32, 34, 49, 240n6,
245n40, 246n61
Sohan Singh (Josh). *See* Josh, Sohan Singh
Sondhi, Kedernath, 183
South Africa, 248n27
South America, 150, 278n155
Soviet Union. *See* Comintern policies;
Communism; Communist Ghadar; Russian
revolutionary movements
Spencer, Herbert, 28–29
Spring-Rice, Cecil, 35, 65–66, 104
SS Korea, 50, 51
Stack von Goltzheim, Moritz, 108
Star-Hunt, John B., 78–80, 258n44
Stoppard, Tom, 242n26
Strickland, Walter, 256n5

student vs. laborer roles: and Communist
Ghadar, 125, 162–63; and Ghadar movement
birth, 22–23, 244n23; and Ghadar Press
publications, 41; and Pacific Coast Hindi
Association, 35, 36; and post-Ghadar
Mutiny regrouping, 61; and U.S. anti-
immigrant policies, 136; and World War I
uprising, 50
Sultan-Galiev, Mir-Said, 226–27, 228,
299nn158,159
Sun Yat-Sen, 46, 117–18, 269n120
Sundar Singh, 262n102
Sundar Singh (Ghali), 254n155
Swadesh Sevak, 27, 246n52
Swadesh Sevak Home, 27
Swadeshi movement, 69; and Egyptian
nationalist-Ghadar connections, 98; and
Hindustan Socialist Republican Associa-
tion, 160; and Indian immigration, 20; and
Irish-Ghadar connections, 103; and
Pan-Islamism, 170, 181; and World War I
uprising, 53
Swatantra, Teja Singh, 149–51, 152, 163, 217, 218,
221, 277n148, 281n220
Swayne, E. J., 19
syndicalism, 6, 62–69; and American Civil
Liberties Union, 67–68; and Dayal, 64–65,
66, 68–69; European, 68; and Irish-Ghadar
connections, 104; lifespan of, 64, 255n167;
and Mexican Revolution, 63, 66–67, 69; and
nationalism, 63, 69, 256n185; and World
War I, 66, 67, 69, 256n185

tactics, 6, 240n14; and Afghanistan base,
204–5, 292n46; and Communist Ghadar,
149, 159–60, 163; and early North American
activists, 29; Ghadar Press publications on,
43; and Irish-Ghadar connections, 266n50;
and pre-World War I activism, 46–47,
250n67; propaganda by the deed, 161, 164;
and Rattan Singh India mission (1923), 152;
and syndicalism, 63; and World War I, 71;
World War I uprising, 52, 54; and Yugantar
Ashram, 36–37
Tagore, Rabindranath, 115
Talim-i-Quran (Obeidullah), 220
Teja Singh, 20, 286–87n84
Teja Singh (Swatantra), 149–51, 152, 163, 217, 218,
221, 277n148, 281n220
Tenyo Maru, 251n84
Tenzin, Okura, 115

TEXT 10/12.5 Minion Pro
DISPLAY Minion Pro
COMPOSITOR Westchester Book Group
INDEXER Do Mi Stauber
CARTOGRAPHER Bill Nelson
PRINTER AND BINDER Maple-Vail Book Manufacturing Group